D1682773

9780837101606

DECISIONS IN SYRACUSE

Metropolitan Action Studies / No. 1

DECISIONS IN SYRACUSE
Metropolitan Action Studies / No. 1

ROSCOE C. MARTIN
FRANK J. MUNGER
JESSE BURKHEAD
GUTHRIE S. BIRKHEAD
———
HAROLD HERMAN
HERBERT M. KAGI
LEWIS P. WELCH
CLYDE J. WINGFIELD

INDIANA UNIVERSITY PRESS
BLOOMINGTON

Copyright © 1961 by Indiana University Press
Manufactured in the United States of America
Library of Congress catalog card number: 61-16954

The Authors

GUTHRIE S. BIRKHEAD, Professor of Political Science,
Syracuse University

JESSE BURKHEAD, Professor of Economics, Syracuse University

HAROLD HERMAN, Assistant Professor, Institute of Local and State Government, University of Pennsylvania

HERBERT M. KAGI, Coordinator of Public Administration Programs,
Syracuse University

ROSCOE C. MARTIN, Professor of Political Science,
Syracuse University

FRANK J. MUNGER, Associate Professor of Political Science,
Syracuse University

LEWIS P. WELCH, Assistant Professor of Political Science,
Graduate School of Public Affairs, State University of New York

CLYDE J. WINGFIELD, Assistant Professor of Public Administration,
The Pennsylvania State University

Contents

Foreword   xi

Preface   xiii

PART 1: INTRODUCTION

I. Power Structure and Its Study   3
II. The Syracuse Metropolitan Area   20
III. The Post-War Report   47

PART 2: PUBLIC DECISIONS

Introduction   77
IV. The Metropolitan Sewage Treatment Plant   80
V. Water for the Suburbs   111
VI. Health and Welfare: Four Case Studies   131
VII. Education: The Special District Solution   157
VIII. Reorganizing County Government:
       Proposals for Reform, 1934–1943   175
IX. Reorganizing County Government:
       The County Director Proposal   197
X. Cooperation, Contract, or Consolidation?   214

PART 3: PUBLIC-PRIVATE DECISIONS

Introduction   235
XI. Real Estate Development: Five Case Studies   240
XII. Syracuse Industrial Park   262
XIII. Private Economic Development and the
       Metropolitan Problem   283

PART 4: CONCLUSION

XIV. Community Power and Metropolitan Decision-Making 305

Appendix: Principal Participants in the Decision-Making Process in the Syracuse Metropolitan Area 335

Notes 343

Index 360

Tables, Maps, Figure

TABLES

1. A Model of Decision-Making 7
2. Changes in Population: Syracuse and Onondaga County, 1850–1960 23
3. Full Value of Real Property: Syracuse and Onondaga County, 1945–1959 29

MAPS

1. Major Local Governments of Onondaga County 31
2. Some Suburban Service Districts in the Syracuse Metropolitan Area 78
3. Some Real Estate Developments in the Syracuse Metropolitan Area 238

FIGURE

1. Metropolitan Decision-Making: A Schematic Representation 322

Foreword

ORIGINALLY, most Americans were rural; over the decades more and more of them moved to the cities, until it was proper to classify a majority of the American people as urban. An important variation on this gradual movement has been occurring within the last generation: while more and more people are leaving the rural areas to adopt an urban way of life, increasingly large numbers of these people do not live within the limits of any city, or, if they do, it is likely to be a satellite, suburban city without the full range of urban activities. For millions of American people, it is now difficult to find any clear distinguishing line between city and country.

Governmental patterns have changed along with patterns of living, although usually in halting, lagging fashion. Our traditional local government institutions were developed to fit, on the one hand, extensive, scattered rural settlement patterns with limited needs for governmental services and, on the other hand, the tightly clustered corporate communities living in cities. The most difficult governmental adjustments (short, perhaps, of those involved in adapting to international tensions) for this generation and probably the next one are involved in trying to adapt our ways of governing to the new metropolitan populations which are not adequately served by the historical institutions of either rural or urban character.

The United States Census Bureau defines 212 metropolitan areas in the United States; in 1960 sixty-three percent of the national population lived in these areas. Each of them includes a central city or cities and a suburban area which is nearly always growing more rapidly than the central city. In every one, there have been problems and controversies concerning the alternatives of public policy and governmental machinery involved in trying to provide appropriate services both for the central cities and for the rapidly urbanizing areas around them. Always these problems and controversies have involved the handling of specific governmental functions; frequently they have also involved some kind of deliberate effort to face up to the general problem of governmental institutions for the metropolitan area. Confronted with problems and needs which are not met by the existing public institutions, civic leaders of metropolitan areas will inevitably continue these discussions and self-appraisals.

In the hope that something useful can be learned through careful inspection of the processes through which some particular communities have tried to adjust to some of their metropolitan governmental problems, the Ford Foundation made a series of grants to help support case studies of these processes in several different communities. These case studies are being made, ordinarily, by groups of social scientists at a university in or near the metropolitan community involved. A grant was also made to Indiana University to enable it to attempt some coordination of the individual case studies.

This volume is one of the first results of these studies. Syracuse, as this study indicates, is one of the older, more stable American cities, but it has been unable to avoid the problems associated with metropolitan growth and dispersal. A Syracuse University group composed of political scientists and economists, many of whom have had long experience in the study of public problems all over the country, has looked intensively into the way in which their own urban community has adapted itself to social and economic change over the last generation. Their report provides many insights into the ways in which this and other communities have, sometimes consciously and sometimes unconsciously, adopted or refused to adopt innovations designed to meet emerging or newly perceived problems.

In the volumes to follow this first one, approaches of a considerably different kind, in communities of substantially different character, will be reported. Perhaps, from this and the other volumes of the series, a better understanding of the processes of governmental adaptation to social change, and of community decision-making in general, will be promoted.

YORK WILLBERN

Professor of Government, Indiana University

Preface

THIS is a study of public decision-making in the Syracuse metropolitan area. It examines governmental experience concerning a number of issues called up for decision at the metropolitan level. It raises and attempts to answer such questions as these: What kinds of metropolitan problems are brought up for decision? On whose motion, or by whose instigation? By what private individuals, public officials, or agencies or organizations (public and private) are decisions made? By what process? By searching out the answers to these questions and others like them, the study seeks to make some contribution to the understanding of metropolitan politics. It seeks also to illuminate a fundamental aspect of the structure and exercise of community power in a metropolitan context, namely that which centers on action by government.[1]

The questions raised employ terms which it would seem advantageous to define early rather than late. It is not the purpose to engage in any extensive expedition into terminology, but only to define a few key phrases as they are used here.

By Census definition the Syracuse Metropolitan Statistical Area now embraces three counties (Onondaga, Oswego, Madison). Until 1960, however, the Census identified the Syracuse Metropolitan Area with Onondaga County. That remains the sense in which the term is understood and employed locally, and it is the definition employed in this study. The enlarged area was adopted to take account of factors relating to trade and commuting patterns which are not basic to Syracuse metropolitan thought or action. Moreover, 75 per cent of the population of the expanded metropolitan area resides in Onondaga County, which embraces the whole of the metropolitan complex centering on Syracuse. It is of major significance to the definition adopted here that Syracuse lies near the geographical center of Onondaga County, that its associated urban population resides in a series of suburban communities contiguous to the central city, and that the remainder of the county's population feathers out rapidly into rural areas characterized by small villages and by farm occupancy. Again, while metropolitan problems frequently find their way to the Onondaga County doorstep, none has yet commanded the attention of the surrounding counties. There are, it is true, several multi-county districts established by state departments which center on Syracuse, and there is a seven-county Central New York Regional Market Authority based on the city. None of these, however, is concerned with metropolitan problems, except perhaps in some wholly incidental way. Onondaga County is so concerned, not incidentally and intermittently but directly and continuously. In this study, the Syracuse metropolitan area is identified with Onondaga County.

The term "metropolitan problem" is employed here to refer to a problem which, though stemming from urban conditions, is beyond the competence or jurisdiction of any particular municipality. Most (though not all) such problems arise in, or from conditions inseparable from, the City of Syracuse. The city resolves many such issues before they become publicly recognized—by furnishing water to a suburban industry, for example. Some, however, it is unwilling or unable to meliorate: its geographical jurisdiction may be deemed too narrow or its resources too limited, or the problem may be thought primarily suburban in its import, or the prospective beneficiaries may reside outside the city. Given a particular set of circumstances such a problem, which may indeed have drifted along for years under ineffective public action (or none at all), may come to command attention at the metropolitan level. "Metropolitan ac-

PREFACE

tion" occurs when two or more units of government combine to deal with a metropolitan problem, or when a unit of sufficient geographical spread to embrace the problem—almost always the county—accepts responsibility.

The method employed here for the analysis of metropolitan action is the case study. The case method (in the present context) is evaluated in Chapter I; it will therefore suffice at this point to indicate the kinds of cases chosen for analysis. In the first place, the issues selected include substantially all significant metropolitan action taken in Onondaga County in the last 25 years. Two or three decisions of some importance have been omitted by design; if there are others, they have not come to light. Second, the incidents chosen are suggestive of all the kinds of action that might have been taken in that they reflect all cognate governments, and a broad spectrum of private interests as well, at work in the mitigation of metropolitan tensions. Third, they pay especial attention to the role of real estate in suburban development, and so emphasize the highly significant part played by this segment of the economy in metropolitan decision-making. In sum, the cases were chosen to reveal the issues, the actors, the methods employed, and the results obtained in the metropolitan decisions taken in the Syracuse metropolitan area during the last quarter-century.

As explained elsewhere, this study is a part of a larger enterprise sponsored by the Ford Foundation. The authors wish to acknowledge the financial support extended by the Foundation and to express their thanks for it. They desire further to record their indebtedness to the scores of public officials who made available the records of their offices and who gave countless hours in interviews, and to the many private citizens, sometime participants in the developments recorded, who contributed materially to such understanding as was finally achieved. To voice thanks for cooperation is not, of course, to impute responsibility; that remains, as always, with the authors. Eileen W. James made the maps, and the authors wish to express their appreciation of her service.

In his capacity as director of the parent project, Professor York Willbern undertook certain responsibilities with regard to the present study. One role played was that of counsel, another that of reader and critic of the manuscript. The debt which the authors owe to Professor Willbern for his generous assistance is great. Others who read the manuscript and offered suggestions for its improvement include Edwin A. Bock, Staff Director of the Inter-University Case Program; Webb S. Fiser, Associate Professor of Political Science at Syracuse University; Harvey C. Mansfield, Professor of Political Science at Ohio State University; George A. McCulloch, Director of Urban Renewal, City of Syracuse; and Peter H. Rossi, Director of the National Opinion Research Center, University of Chicago. None of these would wish to be taxed with responsibility for the book as it stands, but all contributed substantially to whatever merit it may possess. The authors are profoundly grateful for the assistance rendered by these vigorous but friendly critics.

Part 1

INTRODUCTION

I

Power Structure and Its Study

THE attempt to identify an inner circle of individuals who control the making of decisions by government is as old as government itself. Every court has had its gossip over who has the ear of the king, just as every city hall has had its inside dope as to who really runs the town.

On the municipal level the systematic study of political influence might be dated from the writings of Lincoln Steffens. Today the language employed draws heavily on the work of Floyd Hunter, and the subject is often called by the title of his pioneer work, *Community Power Structure*.[1] Although often criticized as to both conclusions and methodology, Hunter's volume possesses an unusual distinction in the literature of the social sciences: in an area where many studies ask for replication and few receive it, his procedure for identifying community leadership has been imitated time and again. Indeed, it would hardly be saying too much to assert that Hunter's book stands as the center and source of a major subdivision of contemporary social science, the study of power relations within the local community.

This is not the place for an appraisal of Hunter's approach.[2] Nor is it the place for a historical review of the literature on community

---

Frank J. Munger prepared this chapter.

power structure.[3] Both types of analyses can be found elsewhere. It seems fair to assert, however, that as lines of research have converged, increasing consensus has appeared within the last few years on a model that purports to describe the decision-making process in the local community. At the risk of some distortion, that model is outlined as background for the succeeding studies of specific decisions.[4]

A Model of Community Decision-Making

The method of analysis employed here emphasizes decision-making as a focus for the study of government. Governmental action is viewed as a continuous process in which individuals make choices between alternatives. Some choices are minor, others major. Some are made by a single individual; others are made simultaneously by many individuals, as when an issue at referendum is determined by the whole electorate.[5]

From this vantage point, it is possible to view governmental decision-making as the product of a contest to control public action conducted by groups and individuals within the community. These contestants may be classified in various ways. Wallace Sayre and Herbert Kaufman in their study, *Governing New York City,* identify seven categories of contestants: the public officials of the city; the members of the city government's bureaucracies; the hierarchies of political party functionaries; the nongovernmental groups most commonly thought of as interest groups (business, labor, etc., including also such illicit interests as organized crime); the press (including other mass media of communication as well as the newspapers); the electorates; and the officials and bureaucrats of state, federal, and neighboring governments.[6]

These seven categories are distinguished by the functions they perform within the governmental process rather than by their composition, for obviously their memberships overlap. (The first through the fifth, for example, are all included in the electorates.) It must also be noted that the categories are not homogeneous; diverse and conflicting interests are included within each. To some the contest to control governmental decisions may be incidental to other more important concerns; a newspaper, for example, may regard its political activities as an incident of news-gathering and newspaper-selling.[7] To other individuals and groups, the political contest may be primary. They share, however, the characteristic that each is interested in making use of government to achieve certain goals which either are attainable in no other way or are attainable with greater economy of effort through government.

The goals or rewards sought can be described as what people get out of politics. Again Sayre and Kaufman provide a catalogue, based upon their studies of New York City. Describing these rewards as the "prizes of political action" and "the currency of politics," they group them in four classes: (1) public office or employment, (2) money, (3) service, and (4) intangible rewards—prestige, social recognition, companionship, the satisfaction of altruistic impulses, the sense of power for its own sake, etc. Most commonly, these authors suggest, the individual or group seeks some combination of these rewards.[8]

In their efforts to secure the rewards or prizes that attract them, the contestants employ numerous weapons and pursue various strategies. Robert Dahl, from his studies of decision-making in New Haven, Connecticut, has sought to classify the most important weapons or resources used in American urban communities to influence government officials. Formally defined, these "resources of influence" are "objects that in a given social system provide rewards or deprivations or otherwise affect cognitions."[9] Dahl's enumeration includes money and credit; control over jobs; control over the information of others; social standing; knowledge and experience; popularity, esteem, charisma; legality, constitutionality, officiality; ethnic solidarity; and the right to vote.[10]

The outstanding contribution of Dahl's analysis, however, is not his catalogue of resources of influence but his interpretation of the relationship between potential and actual influence. The potential influence of a group or individual depends upon possession of resources that might be converted into political influence. The actual influence the group or individual wields is dependent, however, first upon willingness to employ these resources for political purposes—what Dahl describes as the *rate* at which the resources are used; and second upon the *efficiency* with which these resources are employed. Potential influence, Dahl suggests, is "a forecast about A's future influence, *assuming* certain conditions as to the magnitude and variety of one's resources and the *rate* and *efficiency* with which they are used."[11]

At this point the studies of community power structure which, like Hunter's, have sought to identify key individuals through interviewing can be linked with those focused upon the making of decisions, such as Dahl's study of New Haven and the Sayre-Kaufman study of New York. The most realistic interpretation of the findings of Hunter and his followers would appear to be that they identify those individuals within the community with the reputation of possessing the most *potential* power. Indeed, the question asked by Hunter of his Regional City informants would seem to be designed to produce an estimate of potential power: "If a project were before the community that required decision by a group of leaders—leaders that nearly everyone would accept—which ten on the list of forty would you choose?"[12] Possession of such potential power is not equivalent to its exercise as actual power, as Dahl's analysis makes clear, since actual power is dependent upon the rate and efficiency of use as well as on potential resources. Consequently, the examination of actual decision-making processes may identify as powerful a different group from that possessing the most potential power[13] (or the reputation of possessing the most potential power, which may be its equivalent).[14]

In summary form, this model suggests that governmental decision-making can be viewed as a contest between groups and individuals seeking rewards attainable through favorable governmental action. The potential power structure of the community is determined by the distribution of the relevant resources of influence among the parties to the contest. For any particular decision, however, the actual power structure is dependent also upon the willingness of the contestants to use their resources for purposes of political influence and the effectiveness with which they employ them. This interpretation of community decision-making is expressed in tabular form in Table 1.

TABLE 1

A Model of Decision-Making

The Contestants in Governmental Decision-Making	Seek These Prizes by Means of Government Action	They Employ These Potential Resources	With Results Determined by
City public officials	Public office and employment	Money and credit	Possession of potential resources
City bureaucracies	Income and wealth	Control over jobs	Rate of use
Party functionaries	Government services	Control over information	Efficiency of use
Nongovernmental groups	Intangible rewards (prestige, power, etc.)	Social standing	
The press		Knowledge and experience	
The electorates		Popularity, esteem, charisma	
Public officials and bureaucrats of state, federal, and neighboring governments		Legality, constitutionality, officiality	
		Ethnic solidarity	
		The right to vote	

The Comparative Study of Community Decision-Making

The pattern of decision-making so far described is a general one; it is, presumably, equally descriptive of the power structure of Atlanta, Georgia, or Smolensk, U.S.S.R. Variations among community power structures depend not on the presence or absence of this pattern of decision-making, but on the relative weights given to its components. By using the language of the model presented above it would be possible to produce innumerable schemes for classifying structures of influence. Communities might be classified in terms of the contestants for power, the goals most avidly sought, the resources of critical influence and their distribution among how many and what kinds of people, the efficiencies and rates at which resources are used, or any combination of these. Sufficient community studies have been accumulated by now to permit the beginning of tentative classifications of such variations; indeed, several classificatory schemes have been advanced that seem to possess utility for understanding the most significant variations in community behavior.[15]

Tight vs. Slack Systems

One of these, developed by Dahl, distinguishes among community power structures primarily on the basis of the rate at which resources are employed for purposes of political influence by the contestants who possess them. In other words, this classification is based upon the extent to which potential power is realized in actuality.

At one extreme, Dahl suggests, stand "tight" systems in which all contestants employ close to their maximum resources for the purposes of political influence. The prototype of such a system is a community within a totalitarian society. In such a community, Dahl argues,

access to resources of influence is distributed in a highly unequal way; in addition the individuals with the greatest access, the leaders, employ their resources fully and efficiently virtually to the limit of present knowledge; and even though most people have only limited access to resources of influence, they exploit these resources to the full. Thus the whole system is one with few untapped reservoirs of available influence;

there is no slack in the system. And except for the effects of outside factors like war or death or long run structural changes that elude the control of the leaders, the system tends to settle on an "equilibrium" where one and only one distribution of influence is consistent with the distribution of access to resources. Significant short run changes in distribution of influence are thus extremely difficult.[16]

This is, of course, a description of a society in which the acts of government are of critical, day-to-day importance for every individual. The opposite is what might be called a "slack" or a "liberal" system in which most or all of the contestants are using only a small part of their available resources in the contest for control of governmental decision-making, either because they are not employing these resources at all or because they are using them primarily in more attractive nongovernmental activities. Dahl describes such a community in this way:

Very few people seem to exploit their resources to the limit in order to influence political officials; and even political officials often have resources available to them which they do not fully use. But precisely because of the existence of these slack resources, a great many significant, abrupt, short run changes in the distribution of influence can be brought about; for whenever some one in the community begins to exploit his available and hitherto unused resources more fully and efficiently than before, he gains markedly in influence.[17]

Dahl concludes that, except for very rare moments of crisis, the rate of use of political power resources in American urban life is relatively low for virtually all groups. As a result, those who use their resources at a high rate are likely to be few in number and highly influential. Consequently, almost anyone who uses the minimal personal resources at his disposal (e.g., time and energy) at a high rate in order to gain influence is likely to make himself felt. Since the principal illustrations of "tight" community power structures are found outside the United States, the remainder of this section will be concerned with sub-categories of "slack" systems.

Monolithic Systems

Probably the most significant distinction among the "slack" systems of power found in American cities concerns the question most frequently discussed in the literature of community power structure, the extent to which an inner circle exercises effective dominance over public affairs. Since a community dominated by a small number of individuals is frequently described as possessing a monolithic power structure, Rossi has suggested the term "polylithic" to describe its opposite, a community in which competition for leadership takes place and contests over questions of public policy occur.[18]

The classic description of a monolithic power structure is still that provided by Floyd Hunter for his Regional City. Although the accuracy of his reporting has been challenged, Hunter presents Regional City as a place where a limited number of individuals, drawn primarily from the business community, exercise predominant influence over community policy. With their approval, projects move ahead; without their consent, little or nothing can be done.[19]

Variations can undoubtedly be found within the type. Rossi draws a distinction between a pyramidal type of monolith, in which a single individual or a very small group of men stand at the head of affairs, and a caucus type of monolith in which a larger number share power and find it necessary at times to negotiate with their fellows to compromise conflicts. Similarly, pyramidal systems may be divided into those in which a member of the business community directs affairs personally through the power of his personal prestige, those in which the ruling business group governs through an agent in the form of a public official (e.g., a city manager), and those in which the controlling inner circle is concealed behind a party boss as deputy—the classic pattern described in earlier years by Lincoln Steffens.

The common feature in all the variations, however, lies in the fact that the controlling group is drawn from the business community. No study of community power, at least among those based upon urban communities within the United States, has failed to show active political participation by businessmen disproportionate to their numbers in the whole population. In consequence, the only distinction that can in fact be observed among community power structures is that between systems in which only the business community exercises significant power and systems in which the business community shares power with other social groups.

Polylithic and Anonymous Systems

A system in which power is shared among competitive social groups is characterized as polylithic. There are at least two distinctive ways in which power may be shared. To one the term "a polynucleated elite" has been applied to describe a situation in which a number of leadership cliques have staked out their own areas of rule within which they remain undisturbed by others. Often these subareas of control are identified by governmental functions, as education, zoning, police administration, etc., within each of which a different set of groups and individuals make decisions in the name of the whole community. These fiefdoms may also be geographic in character, as when certain individuals and groups exercise sovereignty over particular neighborhoods or sections of the city.

The alternative to such an arrangement is what has been called a system of countervailing elites. Its existence implies a regularized conflict over issues of community policy between groups—two groups are presumably the most frequent number—that settle their differences through bargaining, elections, or the courts.[20] As indicated above, one of these groups will ordinarily be the business community, although that group may itself be divided along special-interest lines.

Most commonly the other groups that have offered challenges to the dominance of the business community have been the leaders of the political parties, professional public officials (the two are not necessarily identical), and organized labor. One of the significant circumstances producing such a system of countervailing elites is political competition within the community.[21] Thus Rossi argues that the most important single factor distinguishing monolithic from polylithic systems is the existence of party competition within the latter. Without a competitive party structure, it is difficult for party leaders effectively to challenge the power of the business leaders. Moreover, the existence of a competitive party structure is generally a prerequisite to the exercise of community influence by organized labor, since labor's principal access to power is through its influence upon elective officials concerned with mass mobilization of numbers. Similarly, a mayor is more likely to be in a position of independence vis-à-vis the business community if he is the head of an effective vote-getting coalition.

The monolithic and polylithic systems are the principal types projected in the literature on community power structure. Rossi notes the necessity for the inclusion of a third and residual category to describe communities in which the exercise of power is anonymous, i.e., in which no identifiable group regularly controls or influences policy making over a period of time. Instances of such a pattern do occasionally appear in the literature; the only example he cites, however, is that of the Mexican city of Tia Juana.

Frequency of the Types

It would no doubt be possible to spin out the distinctions, to invent other definitions, and to multiply the number of types of community power systems defined. At the same time it may be noted that not all of those who have studied the subject would accept the definitional scheme here employed. It may serve, however, as a rough indicator of the kinds of power structure identified in the various community studies.

More controversial is the question of what communities fall into which category. Some students of power structure would argue that there are no communities so tightly controlled as to deserve the classification of monolithic under a rigorous definition of that term. Certainly the line of distinction between a "monolithic system of the caucus type" and a "polylithic system with a polynucleated elite" is fuzzy enough to permit classification of many communities in either category.

Fortunately, the controversy over categorization need not be resolved here. Further, it may be granted that some of these types of systems may have no contemporary illustrations. It is appropriate, however, particularly in view of the character of some of the case studies that follow, to note that one of the reasons for conflicting interpretations of the location of power lies in the distinction between "big" decisions and "little" decisions. Any community necessarily appears polylithic if lesser decisions over the details of public policy are considered, since the inner circle (if one exists) lacks time and interest for the consideration of every single choice between alternatives.[22]

The Relevance of Institutional Considerations

These and other generalizations that might be drawn from the research on community power structure so far conducted warrant the conclusion that we no longer lack sufficient data to discuss in general terms the decision-making process in American cities. More information is still needed, and in particular more information that would permit comparisons, but a substantial number of published and unpublished studies have by now been accumulated. There is, however, one very striking omission in this rich literature: there has been no serious effort to relate the patterns of influence within the community to the institutional structures of the community government. It is a commonplace of political science that institutional arrangements have something to do with who gets what, when, and how. Working with decision-making by small groups, the social psychologists have concluded that controlled experimental variations in the institutional structure prescribed profoundly affect the decisions reached; but with the exception of some mild attention to decision-making in the city manager city, the two strands of community research, power structure and institutional, have proceeded separately and at a discreet distance.[23]

An obvious illustration of the relevance of institutional factors to community power structure is found in the municipal budget system. So long as a single municipal budget is prepared, subject to the interaction of political interests, it would appear highly unlikely that a power structure could exist with *no* single point of focus. Those seeking increased expenditures will confront those opposing higher taxes. Those favoring the use of one revenue source, e.g. property, will oppose those preferring another, e.g. sales. Those seeking expenditures for one purpose within a limited total budget will oppose those seeking expenditures for an alternative use. From the collision of these forces a series of decisions must necessarily be reached as to what the budget figure will be, where the money will come from, and how it will be allocated. Whether a particular decision is reached by negotiated compromise or by the triumph of one of the contestants, this is major policy with a vengeance in Hunter's sense of the term; and it would seem inconceivable that any interest group playing a significant role in the destinies of the city could remain aloof from the conflict.

If all city governments prepared their budgets in this way, it would appear improbable that any could be subject to control by the feudal type of system termed above a polynucleated elite. But they do not. While the above description of budgetary policy-making may be realistic for some cities, in many others budgetary policy is not set in a single decision at a single time and in a single decision-making unit. For one thing, the distinction between the city's operating budget and its capital budget introduces a complicating note. Ordinarily, the operating budget is developed through replication of existing items of expenditure, with minor adjustments that represent lesser policy decisions (as yielding to the importunities of the city's policemen who are seeking higher pay), state-mandated increases, or compulsory increases forced by the necessity of maintaining parity with competitive municipalities or private employers. Accordingly, if the political conflict finds any single focus it will be upon the capital budget.

Even on the capital side, however, forces are at work that serve to fragment budgetary decision-making. If the school board possesses fiscal independence, its budgetary decisions will be partially separated from the pressures affecting other segments of the budget. If the state constitution limits the authority of the municipality to borrow and the city has already reached its legal limit, another alternative is foreclosed. If the state legislature has prohibited the use of certain taxes or forbidden expenditures above a certain level, the city's freedom of choice is again restricted. With each closed door another interest or cluster of interests finds its objective either attained or hopelessly blocked and withdraws from the budgetary contests. Indeed, in some cities the municipal government may find virtually no decisions left for it to make except those concerning which beggar's requests will be taken to the state legislature this year. Thus the budget will be made up in the almost complete absence either of political pressure or of choice.[24]

The lack of attention to institutional factors in the study of community power structure applies also to a striking feature of modern government, otherwise given heavy emphasis in modern social science research, the problem of the metropolitan area. It will be recalled that the term "metropolitan" is used here to describe an urban area which has sprawled beyond the bounds of a single city and so falls within the jurisdiction of two or more local governments. This institutional fact in particular—the existence of multiple governments within the urban complex—has been very largely ignored in the study of community power structure.

The one principal exception to this generalization would probably be the work of Floyd Hunter himself. In interviewing informants within the Regional City metropolitan area, Hunter asked only for identification of persons who were powerful, without specifying the governmental unit concerning which they were assumed to be influential. In seeking verification of the accuracy of his conclusions, however, he analyzed in some detail a decision actually taken regarding metropolitan reorganization in the area in which Regional City was the central city.

Herbert Kaufman and Victor Jones, in their review of Hunter's book, commented on the fact that it was concerned with the power structure of a community that "controls the policy decisions of a population that spills out of the central city into twenty-three suburban municipalities and the unincorporated areas of three counties" and complimented the author for having framed his study in such a fashion.[25] But Hunter's description of the manner in which a single power group operated with equal ease in each of the governmental units was so foreign to the experience of political scientists in the metropolitan field [26] that it was hardly surprising that the reviewers reported they could "not but feel dissatisfied with Hunter's tantalizing description" of how the Plan of Development came to be adopted. If the powerful are equally powerful throughout the governments of the metropolitan area then the whole "metropolitan problem" of integrating governments is an illusion.

Hunter's emulators have at times couched their conclusions in the language of the metropolitan community and its leadership, but without exercising Hunter's care to examine in detail the applicability of the leadership pattern to actions requiring cooperative effort by several governments. It is hardly surprising that studies of decision-making in specific areas, as Sayre and Kaufman's in New York and Dahl's in New Haven, time consuming as they are, have focused exclusively on decision-making in the central city. The result, however, is that virtually nothing is known of the relative effectiveness of "urban influentials" in securing action from the central city and from each of the several metropolitan area governments outside.

Partly in an effort to fill this gap, a series of studies has been projected of decisions taken in metropolitan communities on major proposals for metropolitan reorganization.[27] When completed, these will provide evidence as to the identity of the forces influencing action within the separate governmental units of a metropolitan area—or perhaps will reveal that such forces cannot be identified. Two limitations-in-prospect can be noted, however, as to the conclusions that may be drawn from these studies: first, since they will be concerned with decisions taken in separate metropolitan areas across the country, they will be comparable only in a general way; and second, since by definition they will treat of extraordinary decisions in the metropolitan area, they will provide an imperfect picture of the day-to-day forces of influence at work within the metropolis.

The present study, though it is a segment of the program described above, has a somewhat different purpose. Through a series of case studies of lesser decisions involving two or more governments within a single metropolitan area—that centering on Syracuse—an attempt will be made to identify the forces that encourage cooperative action to solve metropolitan problems and those that discourage it, to discern the links that join together separate governments in the pursuit of common programs, and to discover the extent to which those links can be equated with a community power structure capable of inducing common action among the several governmental units.

Cases and Case Studies

The goal of this study, therefore, is a better understanding of the nature and operation of community power within the metropolitan area; the method is case analysis. A description of the setting of the cases is reserved for the next chapter; a few comments are in order here on the technique employed.

As a scholarly device the case study has a long and honorable history. Employed first in the fields of law and business administration, the case study approach was introduced to political science by way of public administration.[28] Since that time numerous case studies have been prepared, some in the general field of public administration, others in such specialized fields as natural resources administration, military administration, etc. More recently the case method has been extended generally to political science for the study of such subjects as the legislative process, political party organization, and political campaigning.

One result of the current vogue of the case study approach has been to blur the meaning given to the term. The name "case study" has been applied to many different kinds of research and, to a considerable extent, has come to be used to refer to what are basically historical studies. In one sense, of course, any reconstruction of a past event may be considered a case study. The Board for the Inter-University Case Program, however, uses the term in a much more restrictive sense. To that body a case study consists of research focused upon a particular administrative decision or series of closely related decisions; its unique character lies in the fact that it attempts to illuminate the circumstances relevant to the decision and to explore the causes that had direct influence in determining the outcome. It is impossible in practice to arrive with full assurance at such a result, but this defines the goal aimed at.

The distinctive character of the case study might be suggested by an analogy to the field of voting motivation research. One possible approach to the study of why voters vote as they do would be to make a preliminary determination of the most probable motives for voting and from these to construct a series of questions concerned with socio-economic characteristics, attitudes on issues, psychological variables, and so on. This schedule of questions might then be administered to a sample of individual voters. Comparison of the answers to these questions with the individual's report of how he voted would permit the identification of some factors as related to the voting decision and the rejection of others as irrelevant. By contrast, the case study approach would begin with the decision itself and, by analysis of the personality of the individual making the decision, the environment in which he lives and operates, and the forces weighing upon him, would attempt an explanation of why he voted as he did.

Given this conceptual framework, the case study method of analysis emerges as a study of behavior—of voters' behavior in the example above, of the behavior of public officials in the cases to be examined in this study. The context is provided by the central decision, that is, by the solution agreed upon for the problem at hand. The immediate question is, *what did an individual do in a particular situation?* A secondary question is, from the evidence at hand, why did he do it? In seeking an explanation of official action or reaction in a given situation, the research worker may uncover influences and relationships and may identify motives not suspected when the inquiry began. Pursuing the evidence wherever it may lead without preconception as to result expected, he need recognize no limits save those of time, resources, and the availability of data. To be sure, these may be severe, even controlling, in a given situation, but they are in fact nothing more than normal hazards of research. The factor of subjectivity also answers this description. The case method *per se* would seem to present no overwhelming obstacles to meaningful research. On the contrary, it has been found very useful as a means of analysis of administrative behavior *in a particular decision-making context.*

The last phrase suggests a shortcoming which some have identified in the case method: that the cases, dealing as they do with individual decisions, lend themselves well to descriptive particularization but ill to conceptual generalization; they illuminate the issues and actors at a given point of decision, but provide a very insecure basis for general conclusions about administrative behavior. The point hinges on the disparate character of case analyses and the resulting lack of comparability in issues, participants, and timing, and so in findings and conclusions. Herbert Kaufman among others has urged that an effort be made to focus a series of case studies on a single problem area as a means of facilitating generalization.[29]

This study seeks in a modest way to meet the challenge of non-comparability of incidents analyzed and so to further the cause of generalization. First, the cases chosen are limited to Syracuse and its environs, and so are subject to the same general ecological factors. If Syracuse is Republican for one it is Republican for all, and the "business climate," benign or otherwise, affects all alike. Second, the emphasis is on decisions affecting the metropolitan area, and this provides a point of concentration not normally found. The cases here are not disparate but focused. The camera holds steady on the principal actors—the city, the county, the towns, the villages, the state, their officials and their citizens—as they go about the business of precipitating and solving (or sometimes evading) metropolitan problems. Third, the issues were chosen to illuminate public action on public problems, though often the action takes the form of reaction and sometimes the problem distinctly resembles a private project clothed in public habit.

The cases are not uniformly clear or sharp, and for some there is no identifiable "point of decision;" indeed, some are not cases at all under any rigorous definition of the term. But all relate to action incident to public decision-making, and in the aggregate they should provide a reasonably accurate reflection of the way decisions are made on metropolitan problems in the Syracuse metropolitan area. About that subject they would seem to afford a sound basis for generalization.

II

The Syracuse Metropolitan Area

SYRACUSE is a city of 216,038 people located at the center of what is generally referred to as "upstate" New York. It is almost equidistant from Buffalo and the state capital at Albany, almost equidistant from the Canadian border and the Pennsylvania state line. It is the center also of what is classified by the 1960 Census of Population as a three-county metropolitan area with a total population of 563,-781. The more common definition (employed here) confines the metropolitan area to Onondaga County, which in 1960 had 423,028 people. Syracuse is one of the many "middle-sized" metropolitan areas in the United States. Consideration of "the metropolitan problem" not unnaturally has tended to focus upon the great cities—New York, Chicago, Los Angeles, Philadelphia. Sometimes lost from view are the 70 metropolitan areas between one-quarter and three-quarters of a million population. Syracuse is one of these. Size may be suspected of being an important factor in determining the decision-making pattern of a city; hence an examination of Syracuse may serve as a point of departure for hypotheses concerning decision-making in other metropolitan areas of its population group.

It will prove advantageous to begin with a brief description of the social and economic characteristics of the Syracuse metropolitan area,

---

Frank J. Munger prepared this chapter.

both to provide a backdrop to the chapters that follow and to identify the features which may differentiate Syracuse's patterns of decision-making from those of other areas of similar size.[1]

The Rise of the City

As it happens, the two factors that played the greatest roles in encouraging the initial growth of the city of Syracuse have little impact on its life today. The first of these was the Erie Canal. More than from any other single cause, the city's growth resulted from the construction of the Erie Canal across upstate New York, together with the construction of the Oswego Canal extending to the north and intersecting with the Erie at Clinton Square, now in the heart of Syracuse. The Erie Canal was completed in 1826, the Oswego in 1828. The Village of Syracuse was incorporated in 1825. By 1830 it had risen from 500 to 2,500 persons. Railroad lines were carried through to Syracuse in 1838 and 1839 and by 1840 the village had a population of 11,074.[2]

It was natural enough that Syracuse should have emerged as a transportation center. The city lies at the point of intersection of two natural avenues of movement across upstate New York and was the crossing-point for two important Indian trails even before the coming of the white men. This was one of the principal reasons why the seat of government for the Iroquois nations was located at a site just to the south of the present city limits. The attractiveness of the route was enhanced by a geologic freak, the presence of a deep glacial cross-channel in the northeastern part of the present city which facilitated east-west transportation from the Hudson River to the Great Lakes. The routes of the Indian trails were followed first by the roads of the early settlers, then by the canals, and later by the railroads. Syracuse, located at the conjunction of these routes, soon surpassed in size the earlier-settled villages of Salina, Geddes, Lodi, and Onondaga Valley, ultimately absorbing them all.[3]

The second principal factor in the early growth of the city was the existence of salt deposits at the foot of Lake Onondaga, now the northwestern boundary of the city. The manufacture of salt provided the Syracuse area with its first major industry, an activity encouraged by the availability of good transportation facilities. The salt industry was originally located in the Village of Salina, a vigorous rival to the growing Village of Syracuse. In 1847, however, the two villages combined to create the City of Syracuse with a total population of close to 20,000 persons. Table 2 records the growth of population in Syracuse and in the surrounding areas of Onondaga County from 1850 to the present day.

As Table 2 indicates, the growth in the population of the metropolitan area, though rarely dramatic, has been consistent and continuous since the incorporation of the city in 1847. The steady increase in population slackened during the depression decade of the 1930's, but resumed during World War II. Two significant changes occurred, however, parallel with the resumption of population growth, only one of which is visible from the table.

Before 1930 the increase of population was confined largely to the City of Syracuse, principally because additional land was annexed to the city as its population threatened to spill over the city boundaries. The last major annexation, however, occurred in the 1920's when the Villages of Eastwood, North Eastwood, and Onondaga Valley were added to the city. Since that time population growth has come in the areas outside the central city, first slowly in the 1930's, then with a rush after 1945. The result has been to alter the ratio of city to non-city population within the metropolitan area.

Originally the city provided only a minor part of the total county population, and as late as 1880 its population was still less than half that of the county. By 1890, however, the city provided 60 per cent of the county's population, and by 1930 the city's share reached its peak at 72 per cent. Since then the proportion has been declining steadily, falling to 51 per cent in 1960.[4] In the Syracuse metropolitan area as elsewhere, city dwellers are moving to the suburbs.

The second major change in the character of population increase in the Syracuse metropolitan area concerns the source of the new residents. Before 1920 much of the growth reflected the influx of immigrants; with the curtailment of immigration through the national quota system, however, population increase has resulted from the movement of residents of other parts of the United States to Syracuse. Before 1950 this internal migration was almost entirely

TABLE 2

CHANGES IN POPULATION: SYRACUSE AND ONONDAGA COUNTY, 1850–1960

	Syracuse	Increase or Decrease	Percentage Change	Rest of County	Increase or Decrease	Percentage Change	Percentage of Total County Population in City
1850	22,271			63,619			26
1860	28,119	5,848	26	62,012	−1,607	−2	31
1870	43,051	14,932	53	61,132	−880	−1	41
1880	51,792	8,741	20	66,101	4,969	8	44
1890	88,143	36,351	70	58,104	−7,997	−12	60
1900	108,374	20,231	23	60,363	2,259	4	64
1910	137,249	28,875	27	63,049	2,686	4	69
1920	171,717	34,468	25	69,748	6,699	11	71
1930	209,326	37,609	22	82,280	12,532	18	72
1940	205,967	−3,359	−2	89,141	6,861	8	70
1950	220,583	14,616	7	121,136	31,995	36	65
1960	216,038	−4,545	−2	206,990	85,854	71	51

Source: United State Census of Population

white; in 1950 the Census of Population reported only 1.8 per cent of the Onondaga County population as non-white. Soon thereafter, however, the Negro population began to grow rapidly, with the result that, in terms of percentage of the total, it has about doubled in the last ten years. No reason exists to anticipate a reversal of the trend.

The Syracuse metropolitan area is still dominated numerically by people from the later immigration. Although the number of foreign born has declined steadily—one in every four in the city in 1880 and 1890, they were one in six in 1930 and one in seven and a half by 1940—the proportion of the population made up of children of immigrant parents remained constant at a little more than one-third throughout the period from 1880 to 1940. By 1960, the number of second-generation Americans had also begun to decline, but it remains true that the bulk of the population consists of persons whose ancestors came to this country after 1840.

Chief among these groups have been the Irish, the Germans, the Italians, and the Poles. Differential assimilation makes some nationality groups more visible than others today. Studying the population of the city in 1943, sociologist William C. Lehmann reported that the German group had been the largest in the city in 1890, when 9.5 per cent of the population consisted of German-born and an additional 9.5 per cent of those of German parentage. By 1930—the last year for which census information on second-generation Americans is available—the figures were down to 1.6 and 6.7 per cent.[5]

By 1940 the Italian-Americans had become the largest visible immigrant group. Although less than one-half of one per cent of the population in 1890, Italian-born persons made up 4 per cent of the total in 1930 while an additional 6.2 per cent were of Italian parentage. The number of Italian-born was declining by 1940 and has continued to decline since, and the Italian population like its predecessors among nationality groups has begun to lose some of its distinctiveness. The Irish were once a large immigrant group in Syracuse but, writing in 1943, Lehmann noted that the Irish were "now largely lost in the third and fourth generation." In part because of their more recent arrival, the Polish community, though far smaller in point of numbers than those of German or Irish descent, is more readily visible.

As in many other cities, the visibility of recent nationality groups is accentuated by their residence in distinctive, homogeneous neighborhoods. Actually Syracuse offers a fair approximation of the classic pattern of ethnic and economic neighborhoods described by the Chicago school of sociologists in the 1920's. And as in Chicago, from which the model was drawn, a pure concentric pattern is interrupted principally by a body of water which prevents the even development of the urban neighborhoods prescribed.

The original major intra-city manufacturing area was located at the foot of Lake Onondaga. Extending south from this manufacturing center is first a warehouse section and then the central business district. Surrounding this business-industrial area on all except the lakeshore sides and partially intermixed with it are the residential neighborhoods of the lowest-income residents. Farther out from the center of the city are middle-income residential areas, while two of the finest residential districts are located at the southwestern and eastern extremities of the city. The principal exceptions to the concentric pattern are the continued maintenance of a high-income residential area near the city core in the "Sedgwick Tract," traditional home of the city's elite, and the existence of a manufacturing corridor extending eastward across the city along what was formerly the route of the Erie Canal.

The principal nationality neighborhoods of the city have been formed by this pattern. Characteristically, each newly arrived immigrant group has located in the low-income residences in the central city district. As rising incomes have facilitated a move and as new immigrant groups have displaced the first comers from the poorest housing, the nationality neighborhood has moved outward from the core. In this fashion the Irish have been pushed steadily west and south by the establishment of a later Polish community to the west of the city center; the Jewish population has been moved out of its original ghetto on the Near East Side, which has become Negro, while the Jews have moved into newer and more attractive areas to the east; and the Germans who once dominated the city's North

Side have been replaced in their original neighborhood by Italians and have moved farther north.

The homogeneity and clear identity of these nationality neighborhoods have been somewhat dissipated by time, assimilation, and the barriers to new immigrants. Yet the areas persist and retain distinctive cultural characteristics. And although succeeding generations display less and less attachment to the original nationality traditions, the patterns of national migration within the city have had a substantial impact upon the characteristics of the suburban populations, with the western suburbs receiving disproportionate shares of Irish, the northern suburbs Germans and Italians, and the eastern suburbs original-stock Protestants.

The Economy of the Area

The Erie Canal, now a segment of the New York State Barge Canal, no longer has much significance in the economy of the city. In the early twentieth century, when the canal system was enlarged and renamed, the Erie was rerouted to the north of Syracuse; and although a connection with Lake Onondaga still provides access for barge traffic, its use is minimal. But the transportation advantages which originally were responsible for the route assigned to the canal today apply to new forms of transportation. The railroads still serve the city of Syracuse, which also lies at the intersection of two superhighways of the interstate system, the New York State Thruway running from east to west and the Empire Stateway (often referred to as the Penn-Can Highway) from north to south. Syracuse enjoys the distinction of being the only city in New York with as many as five interchanges on the Thruway. In addition, an adequate municipal airport affords scheduled air service by American, Eastern, and Mohawk Airlines.

The city's transportation advantages, together with its strategic location, have encouraged its development as a wholesale and retail center for central New York.[6] They have also attracted national industrial firms. The original Syracuse industry was based on the use of a locally available natural resource (salt). By 1960 the only major industries still in operation dependent on local resources were the

Solvay Process Company, using salt brine for chemical production, and the nationally famous chinaware industry, employing local deposits of clay. The bulk of the area's manufacturing industry was in the national market and depended on national sources of supply.

In general, the economy of the Syracuse metropolitan area may be summarized thus:

1. Despite more rapid increases in employment in other sectors, manufacturing continues to play a dominant role in the Syracuse economy. About one-third of Onondaga County's employment is in manufacturing. Manufacturing activity increased sharply during World War II and after, but the rate of increase has since rapidly declined. Although the working force in the metropolitan area grew steadily through the 1950's, the increases, as elsewhere in the country, occurred principally in the service trades.

2. An increasing share of the area's industry is represented by local plants of national corporations. This trend has asserted itself particularly since World War II; it has been accentuated by removal and dissolution of old firms, absorption of local companies into national corporations, and establishment of branch plants in the Syracuse area by the larger enterprises. The differences in policies and allegiances between industries locally owned and managed and those operated as units in a national corporation can be substantial.

3. Manufacturing enterprises in the Syracuse metropolitan area are highly diversified in character. One of the boasts of the Syracuse Post-War Report was that Onondaga County was one of only 33 counties in the United States with some representation in each of the 20 industrial groups employed by the Census of Manufacturing.[7] The 1954 Census of Manufacturing showed this claim to be no longer true, since no local firms were then reported in the rubber products field; but its spread of manufacturing activity through 19 areas is sufficiently unusual to make Onondaga one of only six counties in New York State so diversified.

4. The diversification of industrial employment has limited the influence of any single employer on the local economy. In his economic study of the Syracuse metropolitan area Ralph C. Limber concluded that, contrary to widespread opinion, the diversification of manufacturing activity had done little to protect the Syracuse econ-

omy from fluctuations in the business cycle. Since so large a share of employment was concentrated in producer goods, Syracuse actually showed fluctuations in manufacturing employment and other economic indices as great as (or even greater than) the national economy.[8]

The greatest impact of diversification, Limber concluded, was in limiting the economic power of any single employer. In 1940, for example, there were five manufacturing firms in the metropolitan area each employing 1,000 workers or more. Together these accounted for 21 per cent of total manufacturing employment in the county. Since 1940 this situation has substantially changed. By 1958 six manufacturing firms employed over 2,000 employees each, and together they accounted for one-half the area's manufacturing employment. In all, about four-fifths of all manufacturing employees were found in the 40 establishments which employed 200 persons or more. Despite the tendency toward concentration, however, the Syracuse metropolitan area is still not dominated by a single manufacturing firm, or even by a combination of two or three.[9]

An incidental consequence of this industrial diversification also affects leadership and power within the community. Because the major manufacturing firms are in different industrial areas, no single labor union dominates the local scene. Large units of the International Union of Electrical Workers, the United Automobile Workers, the United Steelworkers of America, and the United Mine Workers of America are found in the area, but the fragmentation of workers among several national unions has served to limit their influence and that of their leaders in community affairs.

5. The principal area of industrial activity has shifted from the central city to the suburbs. Originally, manufacturing firms congregated in the district immediately to the south of Onondaga Lake. The first shift of industrial activity, from this central area to the outskirts of the city, was confined within the city limits. Thus from 1913 to 1940 the proportion of workers employed in plants within one-half mile of the center of the city declined from 40 per cent to 18 per cent.[10]

At the outbreak of the war very few manufacturing enterprises of any consequence were located outside the city limits. This pattern was drastically changed by the war and post-war construction of space-consuming, one-story factories in the suburban areas surrounding the city. The effect upon property assessments is recorded in Table 3. A comparison of these figures with the percentage figures given above for the shares of the population within and outside the

TABLE 3

Full Value of Real Property: Syracuse and Onondaga County, 1945–1959 *

	Syracuse	Onondaga County	Per Cent in City
1945	$ 338,917,064	$ 441,583,635	77
1946	360,418,622	483,483,365	75
1947	372,800,845	503,992,407	74
1948	375,032,651	519,374,035	72
1949	379,596,339	535,125,801	71
1950	385,730,771	551,890,373	70
1951	393,755,600	571,820,923	69
1952	398,919,168	589,431,276	68
1953	404,648,929	608,109,476	66
1954	411,342,704	628,492,770	65
1955	974,481,100	1,569,233,990	62
1956	990,248,930	1,652,223,280	60
1957	1,058,523,221	1,828,472,823	58
1958	1,050,712,925	1,850,264,870	57
1959	1,061,913,874	1,952,208,448	54

Source: Reports of Commissioners of Equalization.
* These figures exclude a small amount of property exempted from taxation under special provisions applicable to veterans.

city produces interesting results. Although a slightly larger proportion of population than of taxable property is still found in the suburban area, for the last 15 years property has been moving outside the city limits at a faster rate than population.

The General Plan prepared for the city in 1959 reflected these changes by assuming "aggregate stability" in employment within the city with growth taking place in the suburban ring. This assumption rested on the experience of the years 1950–1958, during which employment in the non-city part of the county increased by 14,000 jobs. That it may have been too optimistic in its expectations for the city is suggested by the subsequent loss by the city of one manufacturing company (Smith Corona) and the movement of another (New Process Gear) from the city to a suburban site.

6. The economy of Syracuse is closely interrelated with that of the group of counties surrounding Onondaga. In 1959 it was estimated that 12,000 workers commuted from other counties to jobs in Onondaga County. The greater part of these—about 10,000—came from Oswego and Madison counties. This was one of the principal reasons for the 1960 redefinition of the Syracuse Standard Metropolitan area to include three counties instead of one. So far as trade and business are concerned, the phenomenon reflected by the change is not a new one; a document prepared for the Post-War Report in 1943 indicated that Syracuse was already the center of a retail trade area in specialty, apparel, and other shopping goods that was wider than Onondaga County.

The New York Department of Commerce recognizes an even larger area, labeling as the "Syracuse Economic Area" a five-county region made up of Oswego, Cayuga, Cortland, Madison, and Onondaga counties, while the planning report of the Onondaga County Regional Planning Board in 1960 concluded: "In many matters of future development, study will need to be made in terms of a five-county area to insure consideration of the interrelationship with adjacent communities." [11]

Government in the County

The 1957 Census of Governments reported some 107 governmental units for Onondaga County: the county itself, the City of Syracuse, 15 villages, 19 towns, 35 special districts, 35 school districts, and one other public school system. Not listed was the government of New York State, which of course overlies and in some sense overshadows all these. Omitted also were 417 special town improvement districts which do not qualify as units of government. The major local units—county, city, towns, villages—are shown on Map 1. It is proposed to describe briefly the governmental organization of these units, scan the principal substantive functions for which

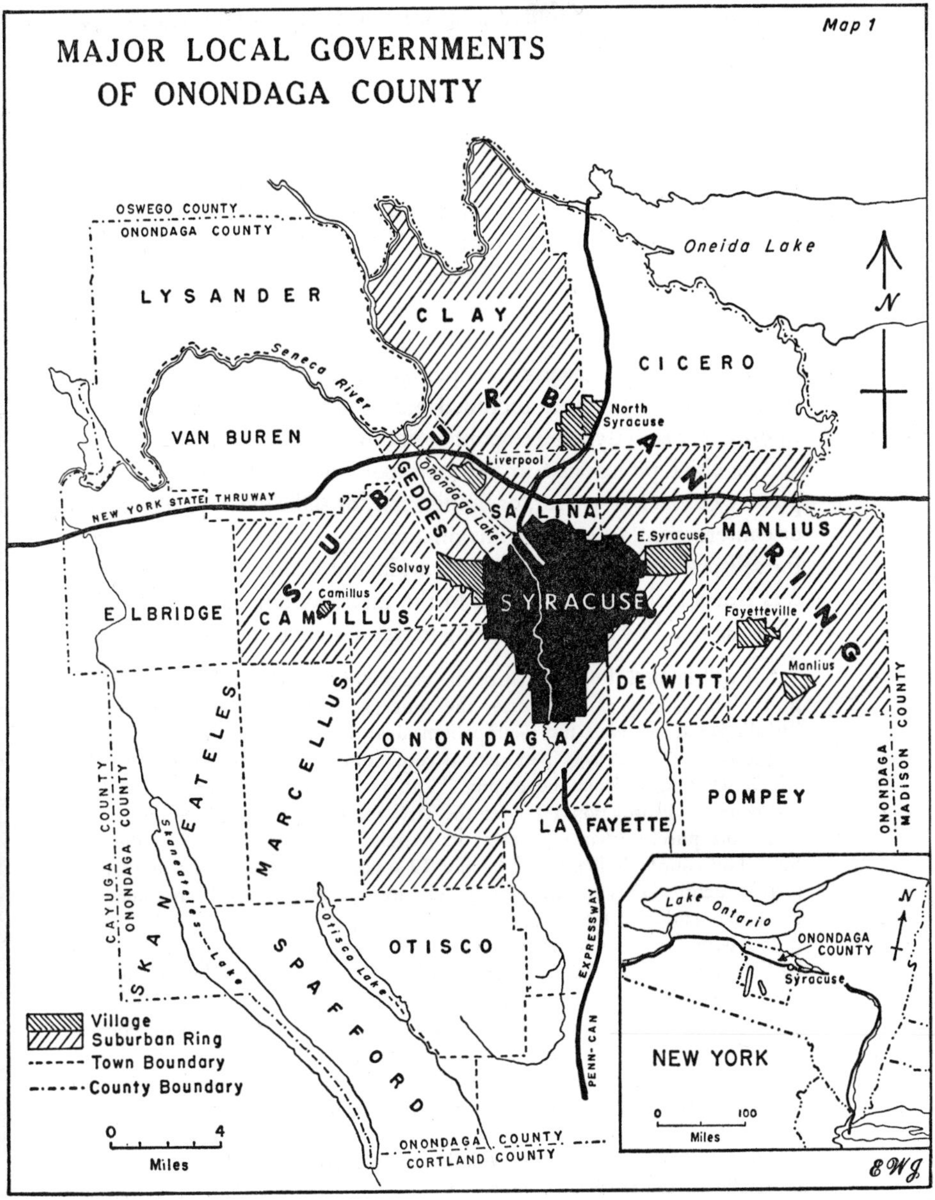

Map 1

MAJOR LOCAL GOVERNMENTS OF ONONDAGA COUNTY

they profess responsibility, and summarize the main features of their financial systems.*

Governmental Structure

Although New York State has not concerned itself with metropolitan problems as such, it has many agencies whose programs bring them into close touch with those problems. The state maintains a new and commodious office building in Syracuse, and it is filled with state employees who have regional and local responsibilities. The number of departments and programs represented is not important here; but it is interesting that, beginning with "Agriculture" and ending with "Workmen's Compensation," there are more than 80 state telephone listings. Included are agencies concerned with virtually every activity of metropolitan significance.

The chief protagonist in the metropolitan drama, the unit whose penury (or lack of power, or limited size, or selfishness, or perversity, or conservatism, or want of imagination, or contentedness, or instinct for self-preservation—the choice is wide and widely exercised) transfers issues from the municipal to the metropolitan stage is the City of Syracuse. The city has a strong-mayor system of government, with

---

* It will be useful to summarize the geographical relationships among these units. The county is, of course, the unit (and the only unit) of general jurisdiction throughout the metropolitan area. The city is reckoned as a part of the county, though as a municipal corporation it pursues certain activities which set it apart from the county. With respect to a number of functions the county's jurisdiction includes the city; with regard to others (generally of a more purely urban character) its exercise of authority ceases at the city line. The county is blanketed by the 19 towns, with the exception that no town structure exists within the city. The incorporated village bears somewhat the same relation to the town that the city bears to the county: geographically it lies within the town, which has general jurisdiction throughout its limit with respect to a number of functions (those historically rural in nature) but which yields to the village with regard to certain newer and less distinctly rural activities. County, city, town, and village are all units of general government. The special districts and school districts serve special government purposes; they lie within the towns, though frequently laid out without reference to town boundaries. Each has its own governing body. This is not true of the *special improvement district,* which, defined geographically in terms of the individual function to be performed, is administered by the town, and more especially by the town supervisor.

all executive departments except education responsible to the chief executive. The Syracuse educational system is supervised by an independently elected, seven-member Board of Education, but is fiscally dependent upon the city government in that the educational budget is subject to review by the Mayor through the Board of Estimate, which must approve it. Inasmuch as the Board of Estimate consists of the Mayor, the President of the Common Council, and the Director of Finance (who is appointed by the Mayor), it is apparent that decisions on the educational as well as the general-government budget can be controlled by the Mayor.

The principal limitation upon the potentialities of the Mayor's office has been a restriction on his term. Before the revision of the city charter in 1935 the Mayor was eligible to succeed himself, and Mayor Rolland Marvin employed reelection and successive terms to exercise great influence within the city. In that year, however, the Mayor's term was extended from two to four years and he was prohibited from succeeding himself. Not until 1960 did a further charter revision eliminate this restriction. What effect the recent modification will have cannot be foreseen, but conceivably it could lead to a re-Marvinization of the office of mayor.

The Common Council consists of a President and four members elected at large, along with five members elected by districts. The council enjoys the customary legislative powers, and the measures it passes are subject to veto by the Mayor. In any contest with the Mayor the Common Council is likely to come off second best, but party discipline ordinarily is such as to obviate a trial of strength. Syracuse's government is run, then, by a system of consensus in which the Mayor's is the controlling voice. Public decisions regarding metropolitan issues, like others, are subject to the standard procedure of initiation by the mayor and approval by the council.

The county has witnessed significant changes in the last several years, particularly in the direction of assumption of new functions. These changes have not affected in any significant way basic county organization, which remains substantially as it was half a century ago. (See below, Chapters VIII and IX.) Thus Onondaga County retains the system by which supervisors elected one from each town, or in the city from each ward, serve as a governing board for the county as a whole. The county board comprises 38 supervisors, 19 elected from the towns, an equal number from the city wards.

The county's administrative organization defies description in reasonable space, but it may be characterized briefly. First, a number of administrative and quasi-administrative officers are elected by popular vote. Second, although the Board of Supervisors has a chairman, that official is in fact little more than a presiding officer and the county is without an effective executive head. Third, the county government leans heavily on the traditions of an earlier day; the product of an agrarian past, it remains basically non-city in outlook and orientation. This habit of thought requires a word of explanation.

The towns in the inner ring surrounding the City of Syracuse are essentially bedroom communities in the typical suburban pattern. They vary in their degree of urbanization, of course; but only Otisco and Spafford towns, separated by a range of hills in the southwest corner of the county, remain preponderantly rural. Nevertheless a deep-running city-town schism divides the urbanized towns from the city and unites them with their more rural counterparts. The schism is symbolized by the almost universal usage of "city" to refer to Syracuse and "county" to refer to that part of the county outside the city; and the county's government, as personified in the Board of Supervisors, tends to represent the county in the popular sense. If this observation seems difficult to square with the fact that 19 of the 38 supervisors come from city wards, it finds explanation in the fact that the Republican Party in Onondaga County, which provides the amalgam necessary to political success, is fundamentally a town rather than a city organization. The election to the board of a few Democrats from city wards, by reducing Republican representation from the city, guarantees that the Republican Party caucus (which makes the important decisions) will be dominated by town supervisors. The upshot is that county government in Onondaga is essentially government by and for the towns. The relaxation in rustic attitudes which may be expected ultimately as a result of the growth in urban population is only now beginning to be manifest.

The towns, as active units of local government, bear a closer resemblance to the New England town than to the midwestern township. As noted above, the incorporated villages, though sometimes urbanized, ordinarily associate themselves with the towns as defenders of grass-roots democracy. Both towns and villages have elective governing boards, though the shadow of the supervisor falls heavy across local affairs. That official is regarded as the head of his town's government, which he normally runs without serious challenge. His powers with respect to the village are not so great, though often he is very influential there as well.

Governmental Functions

It is not necessary for present purposes to attempt an analysis, or indeed even a listing, of the programs of local government. We shall, however, list the principal functions that generate metropolitan issues, and the chief interests of the governments responsible for their administration.

To begin with the metropolitan interests of the three major governments, it may be observed that the state's concern stems from two main sources: its responsibility in a wide variety of functional fields, and its responsibility for the structure of local government and the conduct of local affairs. So far the first concern has given rise to a much more lively involvement than the second. Indeed, it may be said that New York State has manifested little significant interest in the solution of metropolitan problems as such, and that any part it may play in seeking metropolitan solutions may be expected to flow from programmatic considerations. Its interest in the resolution of metropolitan issues is therefore almost wholly pragmatic. The state's interest in metropolitan problems is explored with some care in Chapter X.

Much the same may be said of the City of Syracuse, which is shaken out of its municipal routine only when one or another of its traditional functions boils over into the suburbs. This may happen (a) when the city extends (or refuses to extend) an activity to the suburbs; (b) when a fringe development, residential or industrial, jockeys itself into a position where it can demand a municipal service of the city; or (c) when the city and the county (or other public unit or body) decide on their own initiative that a given function should be undertaken on a broader-than-city basis. Syracuse has responsibility for the full range of normal municipal functions, which it pursues within its legal boundaries except in the unusual—though increasingly frequent—circumstances described.

The story of Onondaga County is a quite different one; for if the city has undertaken many kinds of municipal activity, the county has pursued a much more cautious course. Originating as an administrative district for convenience in executing a limited number of state functions, the county only slowly and over the course of decades established its right to consideration as a unit of general government. That trend indeed is still in process, although it is now clear that the county will maintain and broaden its position as a basic unit of local government. The development which has been responsible above all others for the growth in vitality of the county is the growth in urban population, and more especially the increase in urban needs which the cities have not been able to gratify. More and more, functions previously reserved exclusively to the cities, and quite particularly those functions which frequently spilled over municipal boundaries or which the city did not wish or was not able to assume, have passed to the counties.[12] This is an accurate description of events in Onondaga County, which in the course of the last three decades has taken on new programmatic responsibilities that have launched it on the way to becoming what might be called a county-city. That it has assumed these new duties reluctantly in no wise vitiates the trend. Onondaga County has the geographical reach, as potentially it has both the powers and the resources, to become a key factor—*the* key factor is hardly too strong —in the resolution of metropolitan issues. It cannot avoid responsibility for an active role in metropolitan developments.

The functions selected for summary mention are those which have been involved, or which have threatened to become involved, in metropolitan action in the Syracuse area. Typically they have been administered traditionally by the city, though occasionally a state-administered function also demands special consideration. In either case, they represent activities for which existing administrative arrangements have proved unsatisfactory. They are, so to speak, urban services in search of more inclusive administrative areas.

A function that bears little relation to the historical units of local government is education. The state has created a series of special districts for school administration, 35 of them in Onondaga County, each directed by its own school board. Each district has responsibility for its own budget and its own program. It exists independently of any other unit, and need have no relationship to town boundary lines. Even where there is a superficial coincidence, closer examination normally will disclose that a substantial degree of autonomy resides in the school system. School district consolidation therefore is a matter for decision by the state and the districts involved, as becomes clear in Chapter VII below.

In the field of law enforcement there is an amplitude of machinery. Within Syracuse, the city police department has jurisdiction; outside, the county sheriff's department holds sway; and above, the state police department keeps a discreet eye on both. In addition, there are one town and 14 village police departments. This structure has provided opportunities for both cooperation and conflict. The growth of the suburbs, together with changing concepts arising from new needs, has resulted in a considerable expansion in law enforcement activities in the area. This has occurred principally in the sheriff's department, which for all its development of recent years nevertheless remains essentially a rural constabulary.

The City Department of Public Works has charge of the construction and maintenance of municipal streets. Outside the city there is, as in other functional areas, a network of activities and a maze of public agencies. The Thruway, interstate highways, arterial highways, and state highways are the responsibilities of the New York State Thruway Authority and the State Department of Public Works. Both agencies maintain district offices in Syracuse. County roads are the preserve of the County Highway Superintendent, who, appointed by the Board of Supervisors, is responsible to that body's Highway Committee. Each town has a highway superintendent who has charge of all town roads. Elected by popular vote, he works closely with the town board. The location and relocation, construction, classification, and maintenance of roads and highways frequently involves collaboration by a number of agencies representing all levels of government. The resulting problems can become fairly complicated, particularly in such a field as suburban industrial development (see below, Chapters XI and XII).

Health services in the metropolitan area are provided by state, city, and county health agencies, and by town and village health officers. The State Health Department maintains both regional and district offices in Syracuse. The most advanced county program is that concerned with mental health, about which there has recently been some controversy. As noted, the towns and villages have their own health officers. Relations among the several agencies are summarized below in Chapter VI, which describes the futile efforts to create an integrated county health department. City, county, state, and federal governments all operate hospitals within the county. Welfare activities, formerly splintered among a number of agencies as health services still are, were consolidated in 1938 in a successful move to establish a county welfare department. That story also is told in Chapter VI.

Water supply has long been the province of local governments, particularly municipalities, though for many years the state has taken a hand in dealing with water problems. The principal state agencies are the Division of Water Power and Control of the Conservation Department, which is concerned with sources of supply, and the Water Pollution Control Board (an affiliate of the Department of Health), whose interest is in the quality of water. Within the region several supply sources and distribution systems developed with growing needs over the years. The city water system was by far the largest, but there were also a number of town and village systems and in addition a network of special water districts. The major water problem was not distribution but supply; the former could be handled after a fashion piecemeal, but the latter required a concerted attack, especially after the more economical sources had been tapped. The efforts to focus interest and energies on this problem, which led to a temporary solution in the establishment of the Onondaga County Water Authority, are related in Chapter V below.

The state's concern for sewage disposal centers in the Department of Health, and more particularly in the Water Pollution Control Board. The city, while operating (not with uniform satisfaction) a disposal system for its own sewage, perforce has taken an active interest in sewage problems originating outside the city. There it has come into contact with the network of sanitary districts charged with the disposal of suburban wastes. The fact that Syracuse and the urbanized area surrounding it lie within a common drainage basin sped the creation many years ago of the County Public Works Commission, with responsibility for representing the county in sewage disposal ventures. The movement toward a metropolitan approach to waste disposal is traced below in Chapter IV.

It would appear that planning, above all things, must be undertaken on a broad basis if orderly development is to be introduced into the metropolitan area. The City of Syracuse in fact has a well developed and widely accepted Department of Planning, whose jurisdiction extends to approval of all new subdivisions within three miles of the city limits. Two-thirds of the 34 towns and villages have planning boards of varying scope and competence. In 1957 the Board of Supervisors created a Regional (County) Planning Board, on which, however, it bestowed only advisory powers. Nonetheless the board announced plans for a fairly ambitious program, and employed a professional planner and a full-time executive secretary. Recently the board requested appropriations to retain a consulting firm to conduct an intensive land-use study of the areas surrounding the 27 interstate and arterial highway interchanges built or to be built in the county. It is too early to say what will come of the Regional Planning Board, though its first years give promise of substantial achievement.

The list of programs singled out for mention here is not inclusive, but it is substantially representative of the issues that have been cast up for consideration in metropolitan terms. Moreover, the table of attendant agencies, while again not complete, will serve to illustrate the complexity involved in building a broad approach to area-wide problems. The recital reveals both a multitude of narrow programs and a host of administrators of limited horizons; it identifies none to serve as a spearhead for metropolitan action.

One government is conspicuous throughout for its absence. Three federal agencies administer programs which have direct consequences for metropolitan developments. The Federal Housing Administration and the Veterans Administration might bring potent lateral influence to bear through exercise of their review of subdivision plans. There is no evidence that they have concerned themselves substantially with anything save soundness of the properties for mortgage insurance. The Bureau of Public Roads has remade the urban countryside with its vast highway systems, but again there is little evidence of any interest save that of speeding traffic on its way. Notwithstanding rumblings in which some see promise of an awakening, the federal government remains largely oblivious of the broader significance of urbanism. This is not to say that the federal government has been without metropolitan impact; on the contrary, federal programs (notably those mentioned) condition both the contour of the metropolitan problem and local decision-making regarding it in significant ways. What is wanting is not influence but prior recognition of the fact of influence and planning for its direction and effect.

Public Finance

Both the City of Syracuse and Onondaga County have very greatly expanded the dollar volume of their governmental activity in the years since World War II. City expenditures, including schools, have almost doubled, moving from $15,500,000 in 1946 to about $30,000,000 in 1959. County expenditures have moved upward at a substantially greater rate—from $9,500,000 in 1946 to $30,000,000 in 1959, for a threefold increase. The more rapid rate of growth in county activities is likely to continue for the indefinite future as additional responsibilities are undertaken for water, sewerage, and recreation.

The largest single item of general revenue for the city remains the tax on real property, which in the post-war years has provided about half of its revenue. Revenue from the tax for city operating purposes, however, is limited by the constitution to 2 per cent of the equalized value of property (averaged over the previous five years).* The city also relies upon a tax on sales, whose introduction in the late 1940's precipitated a political storm and whose continued existence provides a standing argument for adoption of a county-wide

---

* In New York equalized values are an approximation of current market values; equalization ratios are determined for each taxing jurisdiction for purposes of converting assessed values to equalized values. The ratios used for determining tax and debt limits are established annually by the state.

sales tax. In 1959 the sales tax produced a little less than one-seventh of all city revenues. State aid, almost entirely for educational purposes, provides about one-fifth of general revenues.[13]

The principal financial resource drawn upon by the county in meeting its expanding functional responsibilities continues to be the property tax, supplemented by state aid funds. The location of a major share of taxable property within the city has often led to vocal city criticism of county revenue and expenditure policies. The grievances voiced have taken two forms. First, Syracuse has resented the equalization rates assigned to the towns by the Equalization Commissioner and the Board of Supervisors, alleging that these rates favor the towns in the distribution of county tax burdens. Moreover, in New York a State Board of Equalization and Assessment fixes its own ratios for state purposes, primarily the allocation of state aid for education; and the state agency is thought to favor the towns as against the city. Second, Syracuse has been critical of the distribution of expenditures between the city and non-city areas. Many of the county government's departments operate exclusively in the areas outside the city; highways, sheriff's patrol, and public health nursing are examples. Since all tax burdens are levied without discrimination on city and town property-owners, complaints are made that city taxpayers carry more than their share of the load. In turn, the towns have a grievance of their own. Since 1938, when the welfare program was integrated in a county department, town taxpayers have treasured the belief that they are paying unduly to support what they regard as essentially city welfare charges.

The incorporated villages are somewhat more hard-pressed financially than the unincorporated towns because the county assumes a smaller relative proportion of their program costs. In both towns and (to some extent) villages it is common practice to organize special districts for water supply, sewage disposal, street lighting, and fire protection, and to finance these services by special assessments on property.

With respect to municipal indebtedness, Syracuse has had a checkered history. In the two decades between the wars the city borrowed heavily, with the result that by 1937 its bonded debt (exclusive of water service bonds, otherwise accounted for) approached $37,000,000. A change in policy began the next year, after welfare activities—and costs—had been transferred to the county. Each successive year from 1938 to 1944 saw more bonds retired than issued, and at the end of the latter year Syracuse turned entirely to pay-as-you-go financing.

It will come as no surprise, therefore, that the differential expansion in activities experienced by the city and the county after the war was accompanied by quite different debt financing policies. Onondaga County debt has increased from about $8,000,000 to $25,000,000 in the years 1946–1959; while Syracuse has pursued a most conservative debt policy, cutting its total debt from $15,000,000 in 1946 to $8,000,000 in 1959, with long-term bonded indebtedness in the latter year reduced to about $4,500,000. The city's debt policy resulted in considerable deterioration in capital facilities, and there is now the possibility that in the near future substantial new municipal indebtedness will be incurred to finance urban renewal, schools, and airport facilities.

The Politics of the County

Brief descriptions have been provided of the population of the Syracuse metropolitan area, its economy, and its government. In all these respects, it may be suspected, Syracuse is not substantially unlike other metropolitan areas of the northeastern United States, nor indeed the middle-sized metropolitan areas of the nation as a whole. There is one particular, however, in which Syracuse appears to differ materially from the typical American metropolis: that is, in the role played by the political party in guiding governmental affairs.

The stereotype of an American metropolitan area pictures a Democratic central city surrounded by Republican suburbs, the city locked in constant battle with its neighbors. The image assumes also a state legislature always Republican by reason of an apportionment that overrepresents rural districts, exerting its influence on the side of the suburbs as against the Democrats of the city. It is unlikely that this stereotype actually describes many metropolitan areas outside the northeastern states. In the South the likelihood is high that both city and suburban governments will be dominated by Democrats; in the Western states the probability is that both sets of governments will be run either by nonpartisan officials or by individuals bearing party labels but maintaining only the loosest of ties to a party organization.

The distinctive character of the Syracuse metropolitan area is that (1) both the central city and the suburban governments are regularly controlled by municipal officials elected on the Republican ticket; and (2) these officials are held together by a relatively disciplined, cohesive, common party organization.

It is not difficult to demonstrate that these are the facts. Since the incorporation of the Eastwood and Valley areas into the City of Syracuse by annexation in the 1920's, only one Democratic mayor has been elected to office. During that period the Democratic party has never once controlled a majority of the members of the Common Council of the city or of the Board of Education. In only two of the five councilmanic districts, those on the North and West Sides, have Democrats ever been elected, and a majority of the councilmen from these districts have been Republican in recent years. Three additional pieces of evidence can be supplied. Syracuse Republicans boast that their city was the largest in the country to go for Alfred M. Landon in 1936. In the presidential election of 1956, President Eisenhower carried every election district (precinct) within the county. In the mayoralty election of 1957 the Democratic candidate ran third behind a Republican and an independent Republican candidate.

If the Democrats are weak within the city, they are weaker still outside. Democrats are elected to the County Board of Supervisors from some city wards; and occasional Democrats are elected supervisors from the towns outside the city, usually as a result of a local conflict over property assessments, a zoning change, or the like. Such rural victories so far have proved always to be temporary in character. And indeed the Democrats have never threatened to take control of the Board of Supervisors, which has remained permanently and staunchly Republican. The one governmental unit which has been durably Democratic in recent years has been the Village of Solvay; even so, the Town of Geddes within which it is located remains Republican.[14]

The reasons for this Republican predominance are difficult to identify with assurance. In terms of numbers of industrial workers, members of the most recent immigrant groups, and Catholics and Jews—groups ordinarily Democratic in affiliation—it might be expected that Syracuse would be substantially Democratic. The explanation for the departure from typical voter behavior appears to lie in the tension that exists in New York State politics between New York City and the middle-sized upstate metropolitan areas. Much of the content of New York State politics is explained by the struggle between these two groups. Since New York City is Democratic, the Democratic party has come to be identified with New York City control. Although it is probable that few voters consciously vote Republican to prevent New York City dominance, the heritage of a century of conflict with Tammany Hall produces an atypically Republican majority vote in the upstate urban areas.[15]

If the reasons for Republican strength in Onondaga County are difficult to discern, its consequences are clear enough. Three in particular can be identified. First, the dominant party contains as a major constituent element the business and industrial leaders of the metropolitan area; and those groups which are traditionally tied to the Democratic party—principally labor—are relatively ineffective in community decision-making because of their affiliation with a minority party. Second, party competition and conflict serve to unify the metropolitan area governments rather than divide them, for Republican officials in the city, the county, and the towns cooperate in the pursuit of common party goals. Democratic strength, which does not as yet constitute a real threat, is nevertheless sufficient to keep the Republican organization taut. Third, the state legislature, regularly Republican in New York, is dominated by interests and individuals sympathetic to the demands made by the Republican governmental leaders of the Syracuse area.

The first consequence flows from the character of the Republican vote within the city; Syracuse is more Republican than most other cities of its size, but the social composition of its vote parallels generally the party composition of the nation. The Democrats are strongest in the working-class wards and in the sections including the largest proportions of recent immigrants. Their difficulty arises from the fact that they are not as strong relatively in these areas as national averages would suggest as normal, and are even weaker in the wealthy areas than the national experience would lead one to expect. The result is to isolate such interest groups as labor within what is almost invariably the minority party.

The extent to which the Republican party tie produces a common front in metropolitan decision-making is most dramatically indicated by the voting patterns in the Board of Supervisors. Most matters that come before the board are approved unanimously, and virtually all other issues are decided by straight party votes. The latter are issues that the minority Democrats choose to raise for their effect upon community opinion and the electorate. Only a few matters are decided on divided votes other than along party lines, and most of these result from divisions among the minority Democrats. The only major divided decision taken in recent years on other than a straight party basis concerned the proposed county-wide sales tax. The measure was strongly supported by city merchants interested in cutting off the tax-free competition of suburban stores, and this pressure was sufficient to cause a few city Republican supervisors to support it. The towns, however, were resolutely opposed, and all town supervisors, both Republican and Democratic, voted against the tax.

As a result of the effective discipline imposed by the party organization, all significant decisions by the Board of Supervisors are taken in advance of the formal meeting by action of the party caucus. The same procedure is followed in the city's Common Council, where it produces either unanimity or party-line voting. The only disturbance to this equilibrium in recent years resulted from the presence on the council for four years of an independent-minded Republican from the North Side who followed his own counsel.[16] He was an unsuccessful independent candidate for mayor in 1957. Although partisanship is less significant in the local activities of the town governments, decisions there are taken within a general context of Republican predominance, and supervisors are at times subjected to discipline by the county party organization, which controls their opportunities for advancement.

Finally, the city's Republicanism has a statewide impact. Because both Syracuse and the state legislature are Republican, Syracuse legislators are in a position to work with rather than against the legislative majority. In actual fact Syracuse assemblymen and senators have played important roles within the coalition of legislators from upstate metropolitan areas and New York City suburbs that has usually dominated the state legislative process.[17] As a result, the metropolitan area has generally been able to secure whatever legislation it has sought, and in that respect shows a sharp contrast to the stereotype of a Democratic city at the mercy of a Republican legislative majority.

The demographic, economic, governmental, and political characteristics of the Syracuse metropolitan area all have important consequences for the local decision-making process. In comparing the pattern of decision-making which prevails here with that found in other middle-sized metropolitan areas, the chief point of contrast in most instances will be the effect of party organization. This is the most distinctive feature of the Syracuse area; its impact will be seen frequently in the case studies that follow.

III

The Post-War Report

FROM 1943 to 1945 Syracuse experienced such an outburst of civic planning activity as had not been known before nor has been since. The most tangible product of this frenetic interlude, the Post-War Report,[1] stands as a testament to the fear of a post-war recession and the conviction (or the hope) that a community might through positive action avert that fate or abate its consequences. The report provides a convenient platform from which to launch a study of the public problems of metropolitan Syracuse and of the area's methods of dealing with those problems. Chief among the questions to which contemplation of the report gives rise are these: What problems were identified as worthy of attention as the war drew to a close? What agencies and organizations (and individuals) were involved in the planning enterprise? In particular, what part was played by governmental units and their officials and employees? What processes and procedures were employed? What attention was paid to the larger problems of the metropolitan area, as distinguished from those of the city proper? What were the net results, what was the sedimentary deposit of the total planning effort? In sum, what problems did Syracuse consider crucial to its future, and how did it propose to deal with them?

Guthrie S. Birkhead prepared this chapter.

"The whole thing started with the housing business," said Sergei Grimm in 1960. He hastened to affirm, however, that the backdrop of World War II and the bright prospect of war's end crystallized the idea and brought to fruition the Report of the Syracuse-Onondaga Post-War Planning Council. In three years of study the people of Syracuse probably came intermittently as close to high excitement about planning as people in a locality can come. More than 300 citizens were directly involved in the study effort. Walter Blucher, then Executive Director of the American Society of Planning Officials, estimated midway that "half the people in Syracuse were talking, arguing, drawing sketches in pencil on the backs of old envelopes, scheming how Syracuse could be made over." In those three years Syracuse citizens read a great deal of newspaper copy, listened to numerous radio programs, saw experts of many different types visiting their city, witnessed or participated in countless arguments, and tangled with some of the fundamental problems of broad community planning. An accurate profit-and-loss statement for Syracuse's planning effort may never be written. This is simply the story of the Post-War Report.

Sergei Grimm was the protagonist of the post-war effort. It *did* all start with the housing business, in the sense that there he gained his own special excitement about the need for refurbishing American communities. Among Grimm's characteristics people long acquainted with him ordinarily mention first his ability to "dream"—"he's an idea man," "he's usually ahead of everyone else." Grimm's experience with the Syracuse Housing Authority in New Deal days produced in him the conviction that, as he stated it in 1960, housing should be seen "as a part of the broader community picture." By the early forties he was discussing housing and other elements of planning with a number of people in the New York City area. Similar talk was of course going on in the Federal Housing Authority and the Committee on Economic Development, and among those persons in whom interest in local planning had been aroused by the publications of the National Resources Planning Board. Sometime late in 1942 Guy Greer, a new member of the Board of Editors of *Fortune* magazine,[2] accosted Mr. Grimm at a luncheon in New York City and asked him if Syracuse might not be interested in becoming a testing ground for planning post-war development.

Fortune's editors had already decided to publicize the need for a nation-wide effort of this kind. A feature article in November 1942 said, "Our cities and towns are long overdue for a major operation. . . . Each urban community [might] proceed at once to work out for itself a long-range master plan." [3] The editors supported the idea of compensatory fiscal policy. A December 1942 supplement to *Fortune*, "The United States in a New World: III. The Domestic Economy," was labeled a:

work of penance rather than prediction. The sin to be absolved is America's ten heavy years of depression and unemployment which it took a war to end. . . . We seek a new role for the American businessman [not] his Coolidgean role. . . . There is nothing inevitable about extreme business fluctuations any more. . . . We are the masters of our economic fate.

The editors proposed "that the government guarantee reasonably full employment" through a "flexible program of public works." [4] At other places, they wrote of the need for pursuing other aspects of community planning. It nonetheless seems clear 18 years later that the editors of *Fortune* thought of the Syracuse project as an exercise in public works planning. They never quite got over the fact that Syracuse tried to do many other things.

The meeting between the Syracuse planning director and the *Fortune* editor struck the spark that lit the post-war planning effort in Syracuse. Mr. Greer came to Syracuse on December 9, 1942, for a luncheon arranged by Mr. Grimm. Twelve local people attended, including Mayor Thomas Kennedy and Vice-Chancellor Finla G. Crawford of Syracuse University. Afterward, Mayor Kennedy appointed a six-member working group which drew up the bare bones of the planning effort. They took their recommendations for an organization and its tasks to the Mayor, who on January 2, 1943, announced the establishment of a Post-War Planning Council in which city, county, and numerous civic groups would participate. Among the Mayor's advisers in launching the council were spokesmen of the Chamber of Commerce, Syracuse University, the City

Planning Commission, the Board of Education, the Council of Social Agencies, and the League of Women Voters.

Mayor Kennedy explained in a news release that the council was created to:

    a. Coordinate planning activities of agencies having the duty of preparation of various plans.

    b. Prepare a general post-war plan for fullest use of resources—manpower, business, industrial, cultural, social, and physical facilities of the community.

    c. Determine practical ways and means of developing such plan and its realization.

    d. Obtain complete use of community resources not essential for the immediate war effort, in connection with the development of the post-war plans.

    e. Provide fullest possible presentation of the plan to the public, with a view to its general understanding and support.

    f. Present recommendations as to the foregoing objectives.

One local paper, however, said tersely that the Mayor was "taking steps to cushion shocks by providing public works." [5]

What were *Fortune*'s expectations? It was agreed that Time, Inc., was to have "exclusive rights of national publication of the . . . processes" (sic), although local publication was reserved for local media. Greer wrote to Grimm on December 21:

I don't care particularly what the planner makes Syracuse look like (although, of course, I should protest vehemently if he made it into what seemed to me an aesthetic monstrosity), so long as he stays within the framework of what is required for the health and happiness as well as the economic well-being of all who live and work in the city and its environs.

Thus were Syracuse and its people launched upon a vigorous enterprise in "community thinking."

Organization

By the first meeting of the Syracuse-Onondaga Post-War Planning Council on January 20, 1943, most of its members were selected.

The chairman was Chancellor William P. Tolley of Syracuse University, a recent arrival in Syracuse. Chancellor Tolley's selection as chairman had been made by the Mayor and Mr. Grimm some time before December 15, and he was to remain in charge throughout the next three years. The chiefs of the three principal working groups of the council were Carlton Brown, President of the Chamber of Commerce and Vice-President of the L. C. Smith-Corona Typewriter Corporation, Chairman of the Ways and Means Group; Vice-Chancellor Finla G. Crawford of Syracuse University, Chairman of the Research and Planning Group; and F. Ware Clary, Advertising Manager of the Crouse-Hinds Company and President of the Board of Education, Chairman of the Public Participation Group. These men were (so far as one can tell today) important leaders of opinion, and their selection attested to the strength of the ferment then working in Syracuse.

The composition of the 77-member council further attested to the forces at work, for virtually every important business and community group was represented by its chief executive or another top official. Banks, principal manufacturers, real estate concerns, law firms, unions (to the extent that unions were well organized in Syracuse at that time), the University, the Catholic, Protestant, and Jewish clergy, women's clubs, League of Women Voters, private welfare organizations—all had some important officer sitting on the council itself or on one of its many different committees. The council roster reads today very like a blue-book plus list of "community leaders."

A great point was made that no political party representatives were selected. And in retrospect it appears at least two other sectors of the whole community were slighted: residents of the county outside the city and the elected officials of city and county. At the first council meeting, Chairman E. O. Yackel of the County Board of Supervisors stated that he "would like to see more representation from the towns." The objection was partly offset by the council's establishing an Agricultural Committee to examine rural problems of the county. (The committee was made up almost entirely of town residents.) Further, no one from the Board of Supervisors other than its Chairman [6] and no one from the Common Council was appointed to the council. The by-laws enacted at the first council meeting did make it clear that both supervisors and Common Councilmen could attend meetings of the council and its various committees, but this was hardly to be regarded as the equivalent of membership.

The impressive roll call of community leaders that was on hand at the first meeting of the council approved, almost precisely as Mr. Grimm and the staff recommended, a methodical organization and series of goals for the coming effort. Rather than organizing a large central staff to do the research, the leaders chose to adopt a decentralized plan of operations. Responsibility for 17 reports was parceled out to six existing community organizations: the Chamber of Commerce, Council of Social Agencies, City Planning Commission, County Regional Parks and Planning Board, County Public Works Commission, and Syracuse Housing Authority. At the first meeting, Grimm was made General Secretary and Executive Director, and thus he became officially the council's most important coordinating force. From the first Grimm exercised his leadership primarily through (1) his service as a loose coordinating agent for all the research and study performed in the participating organizations, and (2) his activities as Director of the City Planning Commission and the Syracuse Housing Authority.

The original time schedule called for completing the final report by August 1, 1943. As to finances, it was estimated in various staff memoranda that the cost of post-war planning would be perhaps $170,000, to be shared in an unspecified manner by city and county governments, other local organizations, and *Fortune*. By mid-April, this estimate had been slashed to $75,000, of which the greater part was to come from existing appropriations to pay for personnel costs to city and county agencies. It was generally agreed from the beginning that the Council of Social Agencies would see to financing its work and that many other costs would be picked up by *Fortune*.

Staff work was to be performed primarily by the City Planning Commission, with the assistance of a large array of temporary helpers. *Fortune* agreed to furnish two planning consultants for five to six days a month for about eight months and two additional consultants (for legal and municipal finance problems) for a few days somewhat later in the planning process. Three new positions were created in the City Planning Commission, and they were subsequently filled by highly-qualified planners from outside of Syracuse. By the end of February, Grimm had completed negotiations to bring nine members of the Syracuse University faculty part-time to the staff of the council. Most of these men were senior professors in the social sciences and in architecture. An architect from Cornell University also came on the council staff full-time during 1943.

The picture, then, is that of a startling number of high-quality experts engaged in the planning effort.* Most of them reported through Mr. Grimm to the Research and Planning Group headed by Vice-Chancellor Crawford. At the same time, they had as counterweights and as reviewers of their work some 16 different committees established by the council and the six community organizations that were sharing responsibility for the studies. For example, there were committees on agriculture, credit, education, electrification, land use, prices, safety, traffic facilities, and sanitation, among others. The precise relationships among these committees and between the committees and the council was never clearly articulated. Simply stated,

---

* Among the following experts who devoted more than casual effort to Syracuse's post-war plan will be recognized many persons who in 1943 or subsequently held nation-wide reputations for professional achievement: Professors E. T. Apfel, E. H. Faigle, L. C. Dillenback, W. C. Lehmann, and K. G. Bartlett, of Syracuse University; Professor T. W. Mackesey of Cornell University; R. R. Isaacs, in 1960 Chairman of the Department of City and Regional Planning, Harvard University; Walter H. Blucher, Executive Director, American Society of Planning Officials; Hugh R. Pomeroy, President, American Institute of Planners; G. D. Kennedy, Vice-President, and D. G. Mickle, Automotive Safety Foundation; Dwayne Orton, Director of Education, International Business Machine Corporation; Dr. Ernest Fisher, American Bankers Association; Jacob Crane and R. Van N. Black, city planners; Bradley Buell, Executive Editor, *The Survey Mid-Monthly;* Carl E. Buck, American Public Health Association; Roy Sorenson, Associate General Secretary, National YMCA; Howard Russell, Director, American Public Welfare Association; A. H. Heckman, Director, Family Service Association; John Herring, New York State Department of Education; and Charles S. Ascher, National Housing Agency.

So far as can be found today, only the professors and the employees of the City Planning Commission received any remuneration from the City of Syracuse or any other local organization.

they were all attempting to cooperate in a community-wide study that they felt was for the betterment of Syracuse and Onondaga County. There were about 134 members of the various committees of the council, 63 members of the committees of the six community organizations, and 77 members of the Post-War Planning Council proper; while more than 60 persons served part- or full-time as staff members during the course of the study. In addition to those directly and closely associated with the planning process, there were perhaps 20 visiting consultants of varying hues, at least 10 of whom did substantial work.

A Year of Activity

The original time schedule was unrealistic. Some of the work of the council itself did not get organized and under way until late summer of 1943. The Ways and Means Group finished establishing its subcommittees and recruiting its members as late as August. Although the Easy Washing Machine Company provided two of its public relations men to serve as staff members of the Public Participation Group, this work also required much ground-laying. Many pieces of original research had to be prepared by professional technicians, relationships among the working groups had to be established, and public participation in and understanding of the planning process had to be cultivated. One searches in vain for blueprints for achieving these ends; the leaders played most of the time by ear, and unfortunately for the historian they left few records.

Work on the basic studies was started rapidly by Syracuse faculty members and by others as they came on the job. Thus during 1943 work proceeded on general investigations of local geography, economics, land use, agriculture, education, population characteristics, community facilities, traffic, the central business district, and other topics. Nearly every study necessitated a large amount of data-gathering, and some required original research. Further, as a number of committees began their work, it became evident that they were going to need additional expert help. Thus were added time requirements not originally foreseen or allowed for. From the first, it was apparent that these studies would turn out to be of several very different types. One group, of which the reports on geography and economics are examples, was assigned to professionals exclusively and eventuated in straightforward, primarily factual reports. A second group was prepared by citizen members of subcommittees with little or no professional advice. Reports on the arts and education were of this variety. A third group was handled in the first instance by professionals but soon became the focus of hot arguments —land use, housing, and the central district, to illustrate.

There were many pieces, then, to be fitted together, and many viewpoints to be harmonized. By mid-summer the chairman and the executive director had begun to realize that the job of coordinating the various segments of the Post-War Report was a big one. The task had two important aspects. The first grew from the fact that two kinds of activities, one relating to administration, the other to research, were to be carried along together. One of the public participation staff members wrote to Chancellor Tolley that the task of administrative head of the council and that of coordinator of the research projects needed to be separated and only one of them left with Grimm. The second concerned the coordination of the experts. Grimm himself wrote the Chancellor in early August, "It has been, as you know, quite a job to maintain the consultants' thinking in a harmonious pattern." The significance of this observation came to light when friction reached the point where one of the *Fortune* consultants—a nationally known planner—was released from his work with the council. The problem turned not only on temperamental clashes (although there were enough of these), but also on differences in philosophical and professional outlook. At one point Walter Blucher remarked, "I believe that the Syracuse-Onondaga Post-War Planning Project is being done to death by experts."

For the first ten months meetings of the council, committees, and technical staff were generally held with members of the press but not the public in attendance. Four or five council meetings and many more technical staff meetings were held during this period. In September and October, this staff (made up of the chief full- and part-time researchers) met every week. By early November the basic studies were beginning to appear in draft form and it was deemed possible to schedule the meetings at which their contents would be divulged to the public.

The staff of the Public Participation Group had been working closely with newspapers and other media since summer. Reports of council progress had appeared frequently in the newspapers. They were not, however, front-page news. They appeared regularly in the latter pages of the dailies or in the Sunday supplement. The Post-War Report was never front-page news until the printed document finally appeared.

The first progress report meeting, held on November 18, was carefully planned. The findings on population, economics, and geography provided the subject for discussion. The meeting was hot, with attention centering on a sharp exchange of comments about federal aid for Syracuse projects. The Pastor of the First Presbyterian Church inquired whether federal money would be sought for post-war building, and was told that the council would "be most conservative in accepting any outside funds." The role of government generally was played down. The speakers agreed that "encouraging industry to the area was one of their most important functions." The 350 persons present on this first occasion heard Mr. Greer of *Fortune* say that his magazine "has its fingers crossed, hoping something big and important comes out of [the Post-War Report effort]." [7]

The meeting produced a sharp sense of disappointment—to members of the staff and council, at least. The chairman wrote to Grimm: "There was a seriously unfavorable reaction to our first public meeting and we shall have to work hard to win back public confidence and support." The Dean of Journalism at the University wrote to the Chancellor that the meeting was "somewhat of a flop;" he complained that "no information [was] given the audience." From the meager record one may guess that the audience was disappointed because it heard only general, background, basic data. No startling, shiny new ideas were wheeled out to dazzle the public. The meeting served a useful purpose by raising publicly the question, "Where does the money come from?" This question was to remain in the forefront throughout the post-war planning years.

There is no record that any plans for public reporting were changed as a result of the disappointing first meeting. The Public Participation Group had spent about $1,500 per month for staff costs and publicity during the fall, and it continued to do so until the next March or April. The schools at this moment were beginning their part in the planning campaign by holding special sessions through the high school English departments, wherein the students could help to plan new facilities for youth. A series of 17 radio programs was being planned for the spring as a means of releasing results to a broader public. This series of Sunday afternoon programs, "Syracuse On Trial," featured one by one particular aspects of the basic studies—traffic, the central district plan, agriculture, unemployment, and so on. In fact, newspaper publicity during the first four months of 1944, when the public participation campaign was at its height, was restricted almost entirely to reporting "Syracuse On Trial." The Fifteenth Institute for Education by Radio on May 12, 1944, gave the series first prize as an "outstanding forum program;" and two years later the series was specially cited by the George F. Peabody Memorial Competition as a significant "'regional' broadcast in the public service." An average of 30,000 listeners were tuned to Station WFBL for these broadcasts, it was reported. Whatever crescendo there was toward the climax of the final report came during January to April, 1944, when this radio series was being broadcast.

So far as can be learned, only two public report meetings were held; but via radio programs and news reports of many council meetings, the work of a year was placed on display. The build-up to the presentation of the total series of basic studies was proceeding with irresistible inertia. Many persons, perhaps most of all *Fortune's* editors, thought post-war planning had already taken too long. Grimm wrote Greer in December of 1943, "we have experienced considerable delay while working out a new planning method based upon public participation. . . . It is the progress of the public participation that controls the progress of our entire project." Mr. Grimm might also have mentioned the problem of gaining acceptance of staff work by the committee and then by the council.

Troubled Waters

One by one the basic studies were reviewed. Two caused by all odds the most trouble when they were brought to the council for final clearance. These were the housing report and the central district plan. The work on the housing report was done by the small staff of the Syracuse Housing Authority under Mr. Grimm's direction, with assistance from two representatives of the National Housing Agency's New York Office (where Grimm's long-time acquaintance, Charles S. Ascher, was in charge). One man from the New York State Division of Housing also came in to aid, and about eight other authorities from across the country were consulted in the course of drafting. But the process of drafting was not publicized. Grimm reported to Tolley in late September, 1943, that he felt it was mandatory to keep the housing plans *sub rosa* in order to avoid the perennial controversies that surround the housing issue.

Presentation of the draft housing study to the Council on February 17 evoked immediate opposition. The Secretary of the Chamber of Commerce, who argued that the draft gave government too much prominence, won appointment of a committee of "businessmen and property owners" to suggest changes in it. Subsequently, housing questions were the subject of hot debate in at least seven meetings of the council. The special committee (for a time, the same one that examined the central district plan), which represented the Realty Board, architects, Better Builders of Onondaga County, and building supply dealers, was strongly supported by the Mayor. It took a position flatly opposed to public housing in any form, although its main objection was to references in the draft to federal assistance and funds for Syracuse housing. The committee stated in an April 28 council meeting that "private enterprise could do the job and there was no necessity for mentioning public housing in the report." Mayor Kennedy asserted, "As long as I am mayor there will be no public housing projects in Syracuse."

There is no record that any major compromise came out of this committee's work. At the June 1, 1944, council meeting, the representatives of architects and the building and real estate people were still attempting to get the housing draft amended, but the

THE POST-WAR REPORT   59

council voted to accept the Housing Authority's report as it had been amended by the authority up to that time. This, of course, was well after the date announced for finishing the draft of the entire report. In the report as finally published in 1946, however, there is only one rather vague mention of public monies for housing purposes. Whatever was won in the 1944 debate seems to have been "drafted out" before 1946.

The story of the opposition to the central district plan is not well documented today, but several obvious points may be mentioned in connection with it. First, it is significant that the Chamber of Commerce in the original allocation of duties for reports was assigned only "general plans for business and industrial activities." The City Planning Commission was given the job of master planning the "principal business district and civic center" and "traffic and transportation facilities." Work on the plans for development of the central business district proceeded through the summer and fall of 1943 with little reference to business interests or to the Chamber of Commerce and with few comments about it in council meetings.

It was primarily in connection with the central district that two representatives of the Automotive Safety Foundation were brought into the research and planning activities in the late summer of 1943. These two representatives broached the idea of an elevated traffic artery or "loop" encircling the central business district. Doubtless there were many discussions and arguments about this and other aspects of central district planning through the fall and winter of 1943–44. When on February 16 the long-awaited draft of the central district plan was brought before the council, representatives of the Chamber of Commerce objected to several of its features, including the "loop," location of a new state office building, a plan for a joint public-private authority to buy and reserve land in the central district, and other features.

A subcommittee of downtown merchants appointed by the Secretary of the Chamber of Commerce was asked to review this report. The subcommittee later was augmented by representatives of the public and the city government. Through the following weeks this group revised the central district recommendations; and its new draft was accepted by the council April 21, although some discussion of the plan carried over into the summer. In a sense, however, the chamber's victory was Pyrrhic. In the Post-War Report as finally printed every one of the ideas contained in the original central district plan appears. The effect of the debate turned out to be simply that the ideas are briefly presented as general concepts, with no specific and immediate means of implementation spelled out.

It was after the April 21 meeting, and primarily in connection with the housing report and the central district plan, that Mayor Kennedy "blew his stack." The Mayor told reporters that several basic studies still contained "some impractical and fantastic ideas" which must be eliminated before adoption. He proposed to turn all council reports over to the heads of city departments for their review before anything was done about them. Almost simultaneously, the Mayor reported to the press that two of the visiting consultants (Walter Blucher and Hugh Pomeroy) had told him that "Syracuse has made the best basic outline for postwar planning of any city in America."

The Mayor's irritation stemmed mainly from the arguments over the housing and central district problems. The general situation was one in which many different groups, committees, and experts were submitting frequent reports to the council, so that no one person or body was in a position to be blamed or praised. Mayor Kennedy was a man with a conservative economic philosophy, serving a community where conservative economic philosophies were dominant.[8] He doubtless felt some frustration at having sponsored a planning effort in which economic ideas with which he did not agree were being pushed. What the people of Syracuse thought is not known. One may speculate, however, on the April 3, 1944, "Syracuse on Trial" program, where the jury voted 6–0 that problems of the central shopping district "are a matter of public concern."

Climax and Denouement

On May 1, 1944, the final "Syracuse on Trial" program was given, with a review of all the recommendations the council had adopted to that point. Participants in the program were the presidents of Carrier, Smith-Corona, two radio stations, the Syracuse

Federation of Labor, the Chamber of Commerce, and the League of Women Voters; the Chancellor and Vice-Chancellor of Syracuse University; and the county chairmen of both the Democratic and Republican parties. Three days later some of the principal participants in the planning process took the Syracuse story to the annual meeting of the American Society of Planning Officials in Chicago. There Mayor Kennedy and Messrs. Grimm, Greer, and B. L. Finn (a Public Participation Group staff member) told of the past 15 months' experience. Whatever else the post-war planning process may have been, it was unquestionably the source of much favorable publicity for Syracuse throughout the nation.

Although all this was the climax to which the public participation build-up had led, there was little sense of fulfillment for individual council workers. A number of things were finished by the first of June, 1944, but some were still hanging fire. Virtually all of the basic studies originally projected were in draft form as reports of the committees and subcommittees of the council. The nine Syracuse and Cornell faculty members returned to their campuses during the spring. The Public Participation Group had brought its efforts to a high pitch, and the climax of post-war planning in Syracuse had been reached. The denouement, however, was to be long and rocky.

Whatever pitch of citizen interest was attained in the spring of 1944 seemed to slacken almost immediately. The Public Participation Group rapidly tapered off its activities after June 1, and newspaper publicity appeared in much smaller quantities than during the spring. The Normandy invasion, shortly after the peak of the post-war planning effort, contributed to the submersion of interest in planning in the general excitement about the war. Attendance at council meetings gradually fell off in the "dog days" of 1944, although meetings of both the council and some subordinate groups continued at intervals during the summer. These sessions were concerned primarily with finishing up the assigned task of the council as to reports, and this work dragged on throughout the summer. It deserves emphasis that there was no firm commitment as to the date at which recommendations would be passed along to the action agencies for implementation. Indeed, there seemed to be no great desire on the part of the leaders of the planning effort to finish their work. They continued to speak of the need for getting things ready to go as soon as the war was over.

The burden of shepherding the drafts along into final form fell to Sergei Grimm and the staff of the City Planning Commission, under the supervision of General Chairman Tolley and Research Chairman Crawford. The redrafting and polishing of individual reports, in line with council suggestions, proceeded slowly, for the planning commission was short on skilled editorial staff. Grimm's main reliance for this chore came to be Miss Barbara Terrett, Assistant to Walter Blucher. At long range Miss Terrett, whose office was in Chicago, read and edited the whole set of basic studies during the late summer of 1944. In November the drafts were handed for review to a new committee headed by Vice-Chancellor Crawford. As yet, be it noted, there was no general report, but simply a collection of special reports. The question of whether a general report should be prepared by the council was discussed all through the winter and into the summer of 1945. The distinction in the protracted council debate was that between a unified document carrying council approval and a series of reports submitted by the individual study groups.

Conservatism Conquers

At this point in the story, we may turn back briefly to pick up the strains of some of the background music for the report. The hue and cry against local use of federal funds, raised at the first public report meeting, was but one sign of a strong tide of economic conservatism that ran locally throughout the post-war planning years. To persons familiar with central New York, this state of mind will not be surprising. Readers may wonder why *Fortune's* editors chose an upstate New York city as the laboratory for testing ideas which were bound to depend for realization upon new or improved taxes or on government borrowing. "Economy" had long been a battle cry here, and federal expenditures in World War II did not calm the fears of men who blanched at Washington's "wild" spending in depression years.

Still, so far as can be determined today, public opinion was not united against public spending during the planning drive. About the only assessments of public attitudes from 1943 to 1945 are the utterances of elective public and semi-public officials, as recorded at the time. And public opinion surely is not always what leaders say it is; their assessments are, at best, intelligent guesses. A few Syracusans on and off the council had visions of a bigger role for government after the war. There is no way to find how "most people felt." But any analysis will disclose that the long-standing conservative economic policies of local governments survived the attack by post-war planners.

Some council leaders were inspired by the idea of producing a post-war plan that would set the pace for the entire United States. At an early meeting of the Public Participation Group, this proposition, thoroughly aired, survived unscathed in the minutes: "In all our publicity strive to present this thing in such a way that it presents a very wide vision, so that the people will form a very broad view, let it be about the nation, not just Syracuse [sic]."

The two polls taken by the council in 1943 indicated that the people who replied were ready to invest money in post-war work. For example, 80 per cent of the respondents to the questionnaire clipped from the daily papers said that they approved the use of a city sales tax to finance a post-war building program, and other results of the survey seemed to indicate an equally liberal attitude. Of course the survey in no sense can be said to reflect public opinion accurately, for it depended purely upon voluntary answers. The "Syracuse on Trial" program of January 2, 1944, ended with its jury of six voting 5-1 "that private industry can't take care of the unemployment problem," and 4-2 "that public works must be planned now." Cloud Wampler of the Carrier Corporation stated on that program that less than 12 Syracuse companies were doing a "thorough job of post-war planning."

Throughout 1943 and 1944 local officials were pushing hard for the United States Corps of Engineers to build a flood control dam on Onondaga Creek. The consultant in charge of the studies presented by the Council of Social Agencies to the Post-War Planning Council reported in August, 1944, that 70 per cent of Syracuse families used public health, welfare, and recreation agencies in 1942.

These are bits and pieces of evidence that indicate some approval in the Syracuse body politic for positive government. They could be used to argue that in the local populace there were groups favorable to the expenditure of public funds for more social services, and, if necessary, the imposition of higher taxes. But these pieces of evidence must be balanced off against countervailing forces. In the balance, the support for more active government was too weak.

What the Mayor, some members of the Common Council and the Board of Supervisors, and a few other public officials said carried the day against opinion favoring more active government, on and off the Post-War Planning Council. The attitudes of these officials reflected three basic concerns: their fear of city debt, their fear of state and federal intervention in local affairs (to the disadvantage of the business community), and their resentment at being passed by in the post-war planning movement.

Mayor Kennedy was the principal spokesman against incurring further municipal debt. In March 1943 he set the *leitmotif* that was to haunt the council throughout its life: ". . . all postwar improvements as suggested by the Syracuse-Onondaga Post-War Planning Commission will be done on a 'pay-as-we-go' basis. . . . My job is to reduce the city's debt and I don't propose to add to it. We will have improvements . . . but not until we can afford them." In July the *Herald-Journal* joined in the fray in these words: "Syracuse taxpayers are not being committed to heavy Public Works expenditures. . . . [The city must] receive the post-war plan . . . then adopt the suggestions that meet with public approval, providing they can be put into effect without the creation of unwieldy debt." During 1943 both the city and the county government presented to the Temporary State Commission for Post-War Public Works Planning long lists of possible public works projects for construction at the end of the war. The Mayor, however, carefully pointed out that the lists were aimed at taking advantage of the state's offer to share architecture and engineering costs. Said Kennedy again, "There will be no new bond issues as long as I am in office."

The Mayor might well have been two men. In these days he was sitting with the Post-War Planning Council and hearing of ways to spend money. To be sure, the council did have lengthy discussions of potential sources of revenue for the city. A local supplement to the state gasoline tax or a percentage return from that tax were discussed on many occasions, despite the fact that in 1943 and 1944 the legislature refused to pass a bill incorporating such a proposal. In its pages, *Fortune* discussed a number of different sources of revenue that might be employed after the war. Stewart Hancock on one "Syracuse on Trial" program called for a sales tax to be state-collected but returned 100 per cent to localities. This was another proposal that the legislature refused to adopt during its 1944 session.[9] Other "Trial" programs strongly suggested that participants wished the city to increase its budget. On one memorable occasion the city Assessment Commissioner was so bold as to suggest a city payroll tax!

Business leaders saw the problem from the business viewpoint. The Chamber of Commerce President wrote to his members in December, 1942: "Most of the responsibility of post-war readjustments will fall upon business. . . . Doubtless some governmental spending will be required, but it is the responsibility of every Chamber of Commerce to exercise every effort to keep the amount at an absolute minimum." And in February, 1944, the President of the Onondaga County Savings Bank told "Syracuse on Trial" that his post-war formula was to preserve real estate values, reduce the city's budget, reduce real estate taxes, and make property in the city more desirable.

Seventeen years later one finds in the files of the City Planning Commission a copy of a letter written in September, 1943, by a New York City investment firm to Mr. Greer of *Fortune:*[10] "It is our opinion that the financing of the post-war program for the City of Syracuse can definitely be accomplished without difficulty . . . with the huge reservoir of capital available there will be no difficulty in financing sound projects." There can be little doubt that this was an accurate portrayal of the city's financial status.[11] There is no record, however, that this letter was even brought to the attention of the Syracuse public. Nor do the minutes of the council and its subcommittees show that the problems of incurring debt or of finding new sources of revenue ever became the subject of a full-fledged debate. But there is ample evidence of the Mayor's economy-mindedness.

Related to the fear of debt was a second: the fear of governmental encroachment on the private sector of the economy—broadly, in fact, a fear of federal, state, or even city assumption of more powers. Such distrust of government underlay the catastrophic question about federal aid that was asked at the first public report meeting, and it spurred the attack on the draft of the housing and central district plans that were so vigorously debated before the council. The *Post-Standard* had this to say after the hottest meeting, that of April 24, 1944:

While the post-war planning job has been a great civic endeavor, with countless hours of voluntary help tirelessly donated, all has not been well with the report's progress in recent weeks as the final days neared.

Businessmen, property owners and realtors cut the vitals out of the preliminary central [downtown] district plan; a type of public housing recommendation was attacked by builders and the city administration, and a sheaf of costly public works projects was attacked as far too lavish.

It was known, too, that one major battleground has been on the fundamental issue of whether the plan, as it affects private, nongovernmental interests, shall be a guide to what the best minds of the community think is the road to betterment or whether it shall dictate to investors, real estate owners and the like.

From some champions [of] the former of these philosophies have come charges of 'dictatorship' and 'socialism' against advocates of the latter; one somewhat restrained example of this was when the Chamber of Commerce's sub-committee hurled the cry of 'super-government' at the professional planners' suggestion for a downtown district authority [commission] to tell property owners how their investments should be used.[12]

The mayor remarked, "We have no intention of telling business people how they must run their business in the future. I think they can be trusted to make their own decisions." Some prominent people were worried at the thought of any public works at all. Dr. Willis Carrier of the Carrier Corporation argued in 1945 that city leaders needed to be very careful since "Public Works . . . send wealth out of the city." Syracuse must not "allow Public Works to deprive expanding industry of labor."

Finally, many public officials felt considerable resentment at being left out of the post-war planning effort. City councilmen and county supervisors seldom attended meetings of the planning council or its committees. In his address of welcome to the 1944 Syracuse Common Council, President Carl A. Young said that the Post-War Planning Council was "not as cognizant of the legislators as it should be, despite the fact that the [common] councilmen have the greatest direct contact with the people." He went on to point out that it would be the Common Council which would vote for the jobs to be done after the war. Little, however, was done to integrate these elective officials in the work of the council. Note was made earlier of the short shrift given the county in the council's organization. In November, 1944, Mr. Grimm commented in a note to the Chancellor about the "entirely negative attitude" of county officials toward the post-war plans: "They regard it as a strictly city proposition." He urged that the report not be presented until this "matter of the county attitude is properly taken care of."

Even had a satisfactory draft of the final report been available in late 1944, it seems clear that the chairman and the executive secretary of the council would not have chosen to put it out. Not only did they view with alarm the "negative attitude" of county officials, but they also took very seriously the general worry about money. Grimm wrote to the Chancellor in November, 1944, that "job No. 1" is "to dispel the *fear* which has set in many people's minds . . . 'where is the money coming from?'" On the strength of these doubts, the two decided that "It might be advisable to continue the Syracuse-Onondaga Post-War Planning Commission until the end of June, 1945. Perhaps by that time the political feeling will have died down." Fortunately most council members seemed to feel there was no rush to produce a printed report until the war ended.

Despite all the critical discussion of the role of the federal and state governments *vis-à-vis* the city, and despite what seems to have been a general wish to avoid accepting outside financial help, the official report on this problem rendered by the Ways and Means

Group turned out to be a fairly realistic document. The first draft, dated June 24, 1944, examined the problems of public finance in a federal system, pointing out the need for sharing program responsibility and costs among all levels of government. Scarcely one function was mentioned for which the group was willing to assign sole responsibility to the locality. The "Ways and Means Report" was printed in the final Post-War Report.

The Final Report

In January, 1945, the special committee on the final report was still worrying with the preliminary draft. This preliminary draft was in reality nothing more than a collection of reports by separate agencies and committees to the council. The special committee had its hands full of hot potatoes—it clearly was undecided on its course. Should the reports be published as the responsibility of the separate committees or should they be integrated into a document that the whole council could sponsor? A mimeographed news sheet circulated among the staff, "Off the Record," said: "It required a great deal of care not to make the council a planning agency but a co-ordinating body, replacing the thoughts of the responsible groups with the ideas of the council as such." Grimm's idea at this time was that the *"general phase"* would end when the special committee reported. Then "a second phase of more specific planning and arrangement to assure the proper use of the general plans" would begin. By early March, 1945, the special committee had relinquished the draft once again to the Planning Commission staff.

As in the case of the committee drafts, there was a shortage in staff working on the general draft. The University provided an English professor in the early months of 1945 to try a rewrite, but he was able to work only a few hours a week. By March 5 the pages he was laboring with were termed a "fourth draft." In addition the single artist, provided by the Crouse-Hinds Company, needed help. Grimm bombarded the University and the Chancellor with requests for help. The University had for two years generously aided the community effort, but by 1945 was experiencing the first small wave of returning veterans and the bulge of military training programs that characterized many campuses; and it was most difficult to find a spare professor. Grimm and the Planning Commission staff, though short-handed, therefore continued to work on the report draft all through the summer of 1945. Of course many other activities also claimed the attention of the Planning Commission. Grimm himself rephrased and redrafted in his extra hours and evenings through 1945. He pieced the final draft together, bit by bit, with little assistance except from the reduced Planning Commission staff.

The council, meanwhile, continued to meet about once a month, although attendance dwindled after the reports of April, 1944. At the June 25, 1945, meeting it was finally decided that the council itself would be responsible for the final report. This decision marked the end of a long argument. It was also made clear then that the city would be able to finance printing the major report itself and a short popularly-written report.

Redrafting continued into the fall, and by the end of the year the task had been completed. On December 31, 1945, the Post-War Report was presented to the Mayor and the Chairman of the Board of Supervisors before the Common Council, the Board of Supervisors, and 200 of the people who had served on the planning council and its committees.[13] Newspapers termed the meeting a "milestone in history." In his speech of presentation, Chancellor Tolley stressed that the report emphasized coordination of community activities. In the "grass roots movements of thousands," the Chancellor explained, there had been "not a shadow of political or party interference." He praised the Mayor highly for his leadership of the movement, and he termed the report a monument to Vice-Chancellor Crawford who had headed the Research and Planning Group. Mayor Kennedy said that "public participation [had] been the keynote" of the Post-War Report. The newspapers that carried the story of this meeting also conveyed Chancellor Tolley's New Year's wish that the report not be allowed to "gather dust."

Mayor Costello, successor to Mayor Kennedy, took office the next day, January 1. One of his first acts was to endorse "pay-as-you-go" for city financing. He announced that he was taking steps to get in touch with the state government and the Public Housing Administration to try to get 1,000 demountable homes to handle the inrush of returning veterans! Mayor Costello also appointed retiring Mayor Kennedy to the City Planning Commission.

In effect the Post-War Report, organized in terms of the committees that had participated in the study, was a compendium of hundreds of suggestions as to things Syracuse might do after the war. Ideas for government reorganization or reform were notable for their omission. The report may not in truth be said to have presented a plan, nor yet a series of plans, for the city. Most of the ideas advanced were rather general. Indeed, the council did not pretend to have an action program. So varied and wide-ranging were the suggestions that it is little wonder no steps were recommended to relate the ideas to action. The council gave some little attention to the problem of implementation in its waning days, but in the end was satisfied to recommend that "A Successor Organization to the Post-War Planning Council should be established before the Council goes out of existence, to assure continuity of action." That and nothing more.

Appraisal

It is appropriate to appraise the Syracuse-Onondaga Post-War Planning Council and its work in terms of the interests and expectations of its two principal sponsors. Among the motives for which *Fortune* had joined the Syracuse enterprise, good copy must have been prominent. *Fortune* ran a series of six planning articles during 1943–1944, but only the first, that of May, 1943, dealt in concrete terms and at length with Syracuse. From that point forward it appears that the editors' estimate of the Syracuse experience steadily lowered, for the remaining articles either ignored or dealt summarily with Syracuse. The fact doubtless indicates the reactions of *Fortune*'s people to the course of Syracuse events. The first known open disagreement was that over the discharged planning expert in the fall of 1943. From that time on council leaders appeared to be on less than cordial terms with the *Fortune* people. *Fortune* lived up to its agreement to provide experts, and its representatives were present during the spring, 1944, climax; but its editors did not find much that they deemed newsworthy in the events of that period.

The editors made known their dissatisfaction, but one expert provided by *Fortune* sided with Syracuse and advised Grimm in December, 1943: "I think it has come to the point where the Syracuse people should have the say and not the *Fortune* group. The plan is for the people of Syracuse and Onondaga County." *Fortune* officials continued to come to Syracuse from time to time, although both their numbers and their visits gradually dwindled. Back in New York they complained. A consultant *Fortune* had furnished wrote to Grimm: "I understand that [one of the editors] is freely criticizing the Syracuse Post-War Planning Project. . . . Cease your worrying. You didn't make the headline project that he wants." Another cause for disenchantment grew from the fact that the project, originally scheduled for completion in seven months, required something like three years instead. All in all, then, *Fortune* contemplated its excursion into post-war planning in Syracuse with something less than unrestrained enthusiasm.

The stakes of the other sponsor were, of course, infinitely greater. From the point of view of the community the post-war planning project may be appraised first in terms of the process employed, second in terms of the concrete results achieved. As to process, literally dozens of citizens had had the experience of three years of intimate participation in a long, careful look at their community and its future. One may suppose that their perspectives from 1946 on were appreciably broadened. They had observed and talked with some of America's outstanding experts, outsiders who had come to take part in the planning process. A number of academicians from the University had given substantial time to the study of local problems, and the staffs of many city agencies had devoted more time to long-range thinking than busy officials ordinarily can afford to spend. Exactly how wide or deep participation was of course cannot be determined with accuracy, though its more tangible aspects are plain. First, the newspapers for three years were full of news stories, interviews, and editorials. One news letter to the number of 4,000 copies was mailed to the public. Two polls to measure participation on a voluntary basis indicated wide public interest. There was a campaign in the high schools to encourage discussion of the plan by students. A handful of public report meetings and a series of radio programs were perhaps the most successful contacts with the public. Observers reported many discussions among ordinary people on the street corners and in their homes. Finally, a good deal of national publicity was garnered for Syracuse and its planning project. Such evidence cannot be measured, but in the aggregate it suggests that the work of the post-war council was not without significant impact on the community as a demonstration in democratic planning. The high fever of excitement, however, could not be sustained for three years.

The concrete results of the post-war planning effort are equally difficult to measure. A local reporter in the spring of 1946 assessed the report's efficacy and found that a number of its recommendations had been carried into effect by one means or another. All the developments he identified had been recommended in the report, but that they resulted from it is disputable at best. There is no evidence that the planning council did anything more than provide encouragement, for most of the ideas which led to the achievements identified had been in existence before the council came along. It does appear today that some new ground was broken in the fields of housing and planning of arterials. What can be said definitely is that the council sponsored much discussion about such developments, and that its report may well have clarified thinking about many of them. But it is almost as easy to claim that the council had no relationship to subsequent events as it is to maintain that it was their prime inspiration.

In September, 1948, a Civic Development Committee was organized as the "successor" to the planning council, although it was without direct connection with city or county government. For more than three years the CDC discussed and publicized Syracuse and Onondaga County development. At a dinner in May, 1952, the results of a survey were unveiled in a document which commented in reference to the Post-War Report: "The reconversion period brought only a brief dislocation of employment. Syracuse was soon back at wartime levels. . . . If the expected post-war recession had materialized, however, it would have found Syracuse much better prepared than in the past."

This is perhaps the crucial point concerning the Post-War Planning Council and its work: the whole enterprise was conceived and executed in contemplation of a post-war recession which did not materialize. The fire engine was serviced and polished and ready to go, but there was no fire.

In another direction, one particularly important in the present context, the planning council missed its mark almost entirely. It was billed as the Syracuse-Onondaga Post-War Planning Council, but the emphasis from the beginning was on the city and its problems. The Chairman of the Board of Supervisors, who complained initially at the exclusion of county representation from the council, made his peace; he continued to take a passive part in the proceedings, but there is no evidence of any expression of real interest on his part. One genuflection to rural interests, the appointment of a committee on agriculture, did little or nothing to counteract county listlessness; another, an invitation to the (county) Regional Parks and Planning Board to contribute a report, was ignored. Sergei Grimm correctly appraised the rural attitude when he characterized it in a letter to Chairman Tolley as indifferent and even unfriendly toward the planning effort.

In this atmosphere one would scarcely expect to find any significant consideration given to "the metropolitan problem." It is true that in 1945 the metropolitan trend and its consequent dilemmas had not reached their later proportions and therefore commanded nothing like the attention bestowed upon them in 1960. It is also true, however, that the metropolitan complex centering on Syracuse had long since overrun that city's corporate boundaries, that the suburban areas were crying for services which the city was not equipped (or minded) to give, and that the county had been identified as a promising receptacle in which to deposit metropolitan problems. By 1945, indeed, more than one traditionally municipal service had been entrusted to the county. In the circumstances, the interest and energies of the county might have been enlisted to make the post-war report a joint product in fact as well as in name. Failing that, those responsible for the organization and agenda of the planning council could have identified more clearly the extra-city character of many of the problems they examined. In fact the county and the metropolitan area were given scant attention, with the consequence that the post-war report turned out to be in some part an exercise in municipal myopia. It is very useful for its material on the City of Syracuse, but for an appreciation of metropolitan problems we are forced to search elsewhere. In this sense the report is historical rather than prophetic.

Part 2

PUBLIC DECISIONS

Introduction

THE chapters of Part II examine the principal decisions taken on metropolitan problems by the governments of Onondaga County in the last quarter-century. "Public decisions" is not used as an exclusive term, for significant elements of private decision-making entered into the events examined; but public action was paramount. Some of the issues commanding attention go back almost three decades; some were laid to rest only toward the end of the fifties; and some, having failed of resolution, remain under consideration currently or enjoy an uneasy quiet in limbo. In a larger sense, metropolitan problems are seldom settled finally; hence the problems dispatched were not solved at all, but only alleviated. It will prove worthwhile nevertheless to examine the solutions worked out, for the forces at play in the decision-making process may be supposed to be significant whether their product prove permanent or only temporary. In those instances where geographical location was a factor, reference to Map 2 will prove helpful.

In the cases to come two features deserve special attention. First, the issues called up for decision have almost never been identified, discussed, or resolved in a metropolitan context. This was particularly true of the earlier cases, for only in recent years have the decision-makers accustomed themselves to think in metropolitan

Map 2

SOME SUBURBAN SERVICE DISTRICTS
IN THE
SYRACUSE METROPOLITAN AREA

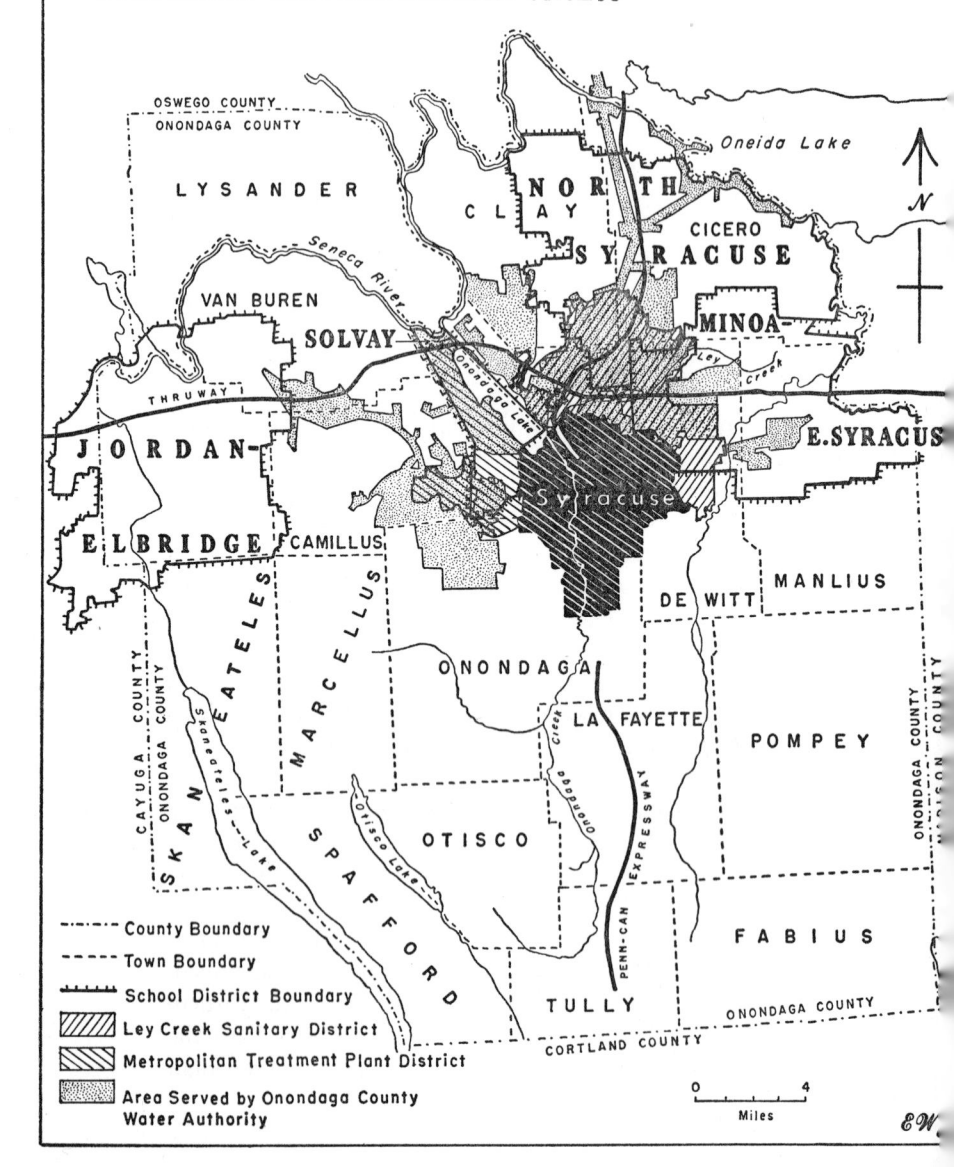

- ·-·-· County Boundary
- - - - Town Boundary
- ┼┼┼┼┼ School District Boundary
- ▨ Ley Creek Sanitary District
- ▩ Metropolitan Treatment Plant District
- ▓ Area Served by Onondaga County Water Authority

0   4
Miles

terms. Each problem has been approached on an *ad hoc* basis, as though no similar issue had been addressed before or would be again. In some part this was perhaps unavoidable, considering the variety of the problems treated and the complexity and anonymity of the parties involved in the decisions. Be that as it may, the failure to recognize the metropolitan character of the actions taken has militated against the emergence of a body of procedures or principles to guide the decision-makers, and has minimized the advantages that one might have expected them to draw from experience.

Second, notwithstanding the *ab initio* approach employed, Onondaga County repeatedly has come to the fore as the only unit capable of assuming major new extra-city responsibilities in the Syracuse metropolitan area. This is the more interesting because the county resists the encroachments of urbanism upon its traditional manner of government. It has neither stomach for metropolitan problems nor an organization capable of meeting them effectively; nor has there been manifest among county leaders any real desire to strengthen the county's government in response to the demands increasingly laid upon it. Nevertheless the county finds itself moving inexorably to the center of the metropolitan stage, because it offers the most practical solution to the puzzle of matching governmental resources to metropolitan needs.

The cases which follow therefore mark the course by which functions scarcely recognized as metropolitan are thrust upon—or thrust at—a government which protests its innocence of interest in or design on metropolitan affairs. It will be useful to observe the processes of decision-making which result in this odd state of affairs.

IV

The Metropolitan Sewage Treatment Plant

THE Post-War Report ranged over many topics. It reflected little effort to pass judgment on the comparative urgency of the problems identified, or even to separate the important from the relatively unimportant. Nevertheless it listed the issues either thought to be pressing or expected to become pressing in the years ahead, and in that sense at least provided an agenda of the city's post-war problems. Of all the problems called up for attention by the Post-War Planning Council, the one most insistently requiring action proved to be that of sewage disposal. As the many aspects of waste disposal came into focus, they settled upon two major issues: first, the system of sewerage as such; second, and in the context not less important, the pollution of Onondaga Lake. The solution ultimately arrived at called for a sewage treatment plant to be constructed and operated under metropolitan auspices.

The Metropolitan Treatment Plant is the most costly single capital project ever undertaken by Onondaga County. Its significance,

---

Harold Herman prepared this chapter.

however, goes beyond considerations of financial outlay. Its completion will signalize the successful culmination of efforts to eliminate a serious pollution problem through consolidation of the sewage disposal practices of a number of communities and industries. The plant thus represents cooperative governmental action to solve a long-standing metropolitan problem, one to which the individual governments had proved themselves unequal.

The plant was conceived as a means of rehabilitating Onondaga Lake and saving it from further pollution. The lake is approximately four miles long and one mile wide. Its southeastern half extends into the City of Syracuse. It is the center of a drainage basin comprising 12 communities that contain 80 per cent of the county's population and most of its heavy industry. These include the City of Syracuse, seven towns (Camillus, Cicero, Clay, Dewitt, Geddes, Onondaga, and Salina), and four villages (East Syracuse, Liverpool, North Syracuse, and Solvay). (See Map 1.) At the end of the second World War, residents of all these communities were contributing to the pollution of the lake, either directly or through discharge into the lake's feeder streams.

Few citizens can date the beginning of pollution in Onondaga Lake. Toward the end of the last century the first dead fish were sighted floating on its waters. By 1901 conditions had become so bad as to lead the State to prohibit the cutting of ice from the lake. Today its uses are extremely limited. In time it may be reclaimed as a recreational asset, but for many years it has served chiefly as a convenient and economical receptacle for sanitary and industrial wastes.[1]

Early Pollution and Its Treatment

With the exception of portions of the Towns of Dewitt and Salina and the Village of East Syracuse, which, along with a section of the city, were served by the Ley Creek Sanitary District and Treatment Plant, collection and treatment facilities outside the city were very poor in 1945. Liverpool was the only other jurisdiction with sewer and treatment facilities, although its plant was hardly more than a large septic tank in bad condition. The Village of Solvay was sewered. Its sewage flowed through the Solvay Process plant and discharged into Onondaga Lake after chlorination. The rest of the area was unsewered.

Although 34 municipalities and industries in the neighborhood were eventually cited by the State for unsatisfactory discharge practices, both in fact and in public image the major polluters of Onondaga Lake were the Solvay Process Company, now a Division of the Allied Chemical Corporation, and the City of Syracuse. The Solvay Process Company employs a process developed by the Solvay brothers of Belgium for the manufacture of alkalis. The company utilizes Onondaga Lake water for several purposes, but its largest use is for industrial cooling. This water, the company pointedly notes, is chlorinated and returned to the lake in better condition than when withdrawn. The lake also serves as an outlet for the company's sanitary sewers. Critics maintain that these sewers have been used for industrial waste discharges as well.

The issue that has resulted in the company's unfavorable public image concerns its disposal of the slurry or waste incidentally produced by the Solvay process. In the company's early years, great quantities of slurry were discharged directly into the lake. Later the company acquired land bordering the lake for slurry disposal. Liquid slurry was pumped to these waste beds, and chemically neutral though colored water was allowed to drain or was pumped out of the beds into the lake. The residue, when dry, formed a supporting but non-fertile sandy substance, and gray plateaus of dry Solvay waste hover over the western edge of the lake today.

The original beds have all been filled and the company has moved its disposal operations inland. But while they were used, the lake beds were a constant source of community discontent. On a number of occasions, the retaining walls gave way, allowing the slurry to pour into the lake. On Thanksgiving Day of 1943, a break on the land side permitted a wall of gray sludge seven feet high to flow across State Fair Boulevard, killing trees in its path, damaging several State Fair buildings, and inundating 11 homes in the community of Lakeland. Walter Pope, a filling station operator in Lakeland, paddled a canoe down the boulevard that day, helping to remove stranded families from their homes. The Thanksgiving Day catastrophe signaled the beginning of organized anti-Solvay action.

Until well after the beginning of this century, the bulk of the sewage produced by the City of Syracuse was discharged directly into Onondaga Creek and Harbor Brook, both of which emptied into Onondaga Lake. In 1907 the state legislature created the Syracuse Intercepting Board, which proceeded to construct two trunk sewers paralleling those streams. In 1924 the board built a primary treatment plant on Hiawatha Boulevard to serve the two trunks, which carry 90 per cent of the city's sewage. The plant followed simple sedimentation principles. Sewage was screened for larger solids and then allowed to settle. During the settling, the remaining solids formed a heavy sludge and the lighter water (effluent) was discharged into the lake. The lake's proximity and storage capacity were looked upon as physical and financial assets in municipal housekeeping economy.

Proximity to the Solvay plant also proved a financial asset. An arrangement was concluded with the company which led to a disposal operation said to be the only one of its kind in the world. In return for the use of city land for waste beds, the company allowed Syracuse to pump its liquid undigested sludge onto the beds to be mixed with the company's slurry. Resulting chemical action neutralized both wastes, to the mutual advantage of company and city. Moreover, the arrangement also relieved the city of the expense of installing and operating sludge digesters and dryers.

But the city was growing, and after only four years of operation the treatment plant proved inadequate to its task. At best, primary treatment affords only a minimum degree of purification. As the settling period was necessarily reduced to accommodate the increased sewage flows into the plant, the quality of the effluent discharged into the lake became correspondingly lower. It was clear that a supplementary or substitute treatment facility was required.

Ley Creek, which empties into Onondaga Lake, drains about 30 square miles lying in part within the city and in part within the Towns of Dewitt and Salina. By the late 1920's the Syracuse Intercepting Board had recognized the pollution of Ley Creek as one of its more pressing problems. None of the jurisdictions involved would assume responsibility for the area, however, and it proved very difficult to work out an agreement among them. The depression and the works projects funds made available by the federal government provided the needed stimulus to inter-local action. In 1933, upon request by the county and with the formation of a sanitary district in mind, the state legislature created the Onondaga County Sanitary Sewer and Public Works Commission, later renamed the Public Works Commission.[2]

It has been suggested by persons familiar with the complexities of New York State politics that the breadth of the powers granted the commission was due to inexperience and to the newness of this type of activity for county government; no law of this scope, it is said, would or could be passed today. The commission was in fact granted sweeping authority to plan and construct sewage and treatment facilities, subject only to the approval of the County Board of Supervisors. For almost 20 years, however, the commission restricted its activity to the construction of the Ley Creek Treatment Plant and the extension of trunk facilities. Lateral sewers were viewed as the responsibility of local government.

The Ley Creek plant was completed and put into operation in 1940. (See Map 2.) It was designed as a secondary treatment plant to afford up to 90 per cent purification through use of the standard rate activated sludge process. In addition to its high degree of treatment, this process provided a satisfactory method of sludge disposal. After effluent was discharged into Ley Creek, liquid sludge was digested and allowed to dry on beds within plant grounds for eventual disposal as fertilizer or land fill.

Expansion of industrial activity in the Ley Creek area during the war led to the plant's early becoming overloaded. After the war, movement into the area by the Bristol Laboratories, whose production of penicillin resulted in waste having a high bacteria content, provided the proverbial last straw. In 1950 and 1951, the plant was expanded to provide secondary treatment capacity of 9,000,000 gallons daily (m.g.d.), with an additional primary treatment capacity of 11 m.g.d. Still the plant did not operate at maximum efficiency. Although the flow of sewage was well within its capacity, the heavy concentration of industrial waste continued to interfere with the treatment given to the effluent. Like the city's Hiawatha Boulevard plant, the Ley Creek plant provided only a partial and temporary solution to the problem of sewage disposal.

Post-War Agitation

The Post-War Planning Council devoted considerable attention to the problem of sanitary waste disposal throughout the county, and more particularly to the pollution of Onondaga Lake. Staff work on sewage, water supply, and flood control was done for the council by the County Public Works Commission through its consulting engineer, Glenn Holmes. Holmes had been chairman of the Syracuse Intercepting Board and with Earl O'Brien, later his partner, had designed the Syracuse and Ley Creek plants.

The commission's report, or more accurately Holmes' report, emphasized the increasing pollution of Onondaga Lake and recommended a metropolitan course of action. It noted that the growing suburban areas to the west of the city would soon need sewage collection and treatment facilities, and suggested that the City of Syracuse not enlarge its treatment facilities independently of the county since the problem of pollution extended beyond the city's boundaries.[3] This suggestion met with some resistance in the council; hence it did not find its way into the Post-War Report. Instead, the council recommended four independent courses of action for reclaiming the lake: (1) elimination of pollution from industrial waste discharges, (2) negotiation with Solvay Process for the relocation of waste beds, (3) improvement of the Syracuse and Liverpool treatment plants, and (4) formation of a Geddes Brook sanitary district to include the suburban areas to the west of the city. Interestingly, neither Holmes nor the council apparently gave any consideration to a possible role for the Public Works Commission as an agency of sanitary control. This was in keeping with the commission's own limited view of its scope.

In 1945 a meeting to consider the problem of Onondaga Lake was called by the Liverpool Chamber of Commerce. The meeting was attended by more than 200 persons. Impressed by this evidence of interest in the problem, Crandall Melvin, William Maloney, and Walter Welch proceeded to form the Onondaga Lake Reclamation

Association. At its height the association represented only 200 sustaining members, but this number does not adequately reflect the intensity of its activities. Crandall Melvin had been the director of the work relief project which had built the parkway and park on the east shore of Onondaga Lake during the depression period. Although not always in tune with party leadership, as president of a local bank and head of a law firm which represented a number of towns in the northern part of the county, Melvin had been an important figure in the Republican Party. Throughout its existence, the reclamation association took the position that reclamation of the lake and legal action against Solvay Process were but different aspects of the same problem.

The association's leaders early decided to approach the lake problem through the avenue of state action. In 1945 and 1946, state legislative and executive leaders were bombarded with requests from the association to take corrective action in Onondaga County. The strategy appeared near success when, during the gubernatorial campaign of 1946, Governor Dewey toured the Onondaga Lake area and expressed disappointment in the despoilment of that community asset. In what was apparently a direct reference to Solvay Process, he stated his belief that no private company had the right to deprive a community of such a natural resource. If the association was encouraged by the Governor's view, it was nevertheless to be disappointed when, in 1947, word came from the Attorney General's office that prosecution of Solvay Process was being held up in the Governor's office.

Mounting pressures from local sources led to studies of the lake by the New York State Departments of Health and Conservation, which sent a summary report of their findings to the municipalities concerned on December 24, 1947. Admitting some incompleteness in their data, the departments nevertheless noted that the lake was visibly polluted and recommended that further studies be conducted looking toward corrective action. The report emphasized the area-wide nature of the problem. It estimated that elimination of all sources of pollution other than the city would still not result in sufficient upgrading of the lake's condition. Further, if the city undertook corrective action alone, the continued contamination of the lake's tributaries would still leave it in poor condition. The departments suggested that the several communities cooperate to make further studies, and gave them one year in which to submit plans individually or collectively. Except for a report prepared by Syracuse's city engineer, however, the one-year requirement was generally ignored. Nor did the Departments of Health and Conservation press the issue. In part their reluctance to proceed was due to the impending enactment of the Water Pollution Control Act and its prospective consolidation of state anti-pollution control activities.

While the state studies were being coordinated a committee of the Syracuse Junior Chamber of Commerce was also investigating the "appearance and pollution of Onondaga Lake." On May 1, 1947, it recommended that the Junior Chamber take action to encourage the communities to accept joint responsibility for the poor conditions it had found. The following year Robert Soule, President of the Chamber of Commerce, called for the creation of one area-wide agency to clean up the lake. In a more formal communication to the Mayor and the Chairman of the Board of Supervisors, the Board of Directors of the chamber called for the appointment of a body to study the pollution problem. To the several nongovernmental organizations interested in pollution abatement, Soule offered the services of the chamber as coordinator. Anti-pollution campaigns had already been begun by several American Legion posts, the County Federation of Sportsmen's Clubs, the Lakeland Improvement Association, and the Reclamation Association; and prospects for achievement of a united front appeared bright. Personal differences developed among the leaders, however, and in the end the promise of cooperative action failed to materialize.

The county's response to the extended publicity being given to Onondaga Lake was the appointment of a three-man commission to investigate pollution throughout the county. The task was much too big for a lay group with no resources. Its report, made to the Board of Supervisors in July of 1948, suggested the lack of cooperation that could be anticipated in any attempt at pollution abatement. The commission's hearings had been largely unattended. In the Onondaga Lake Basin hearing local officials who did attend refused to admit their jurisdiction's share in pollution, placing all the responsibility on the City of Syracuse.[4]

The one reply to the state's directive for further study was the report prepared by City Engineer Nelson Pitts and submitted to Mayor Costello on January 24, 1948.[5] In his report the city engineer called attention to two aspects of the city's problem: the need for rehabilitation of its trunk sewers and the need for new treatment facilities. He estimated that close to a million dollars would be needed to repair sewer lines to prevent leaking and overflowing into Onondaga Creek and Harbor Brook. Because the trunks had originally been designed to carry both sanitary and storm drainage, he surmised that there would always be some degree of leakage into the streams and therefore recommended that a treatment plant be designed for a maximum degree of purification. He estimated that for $9,000,000 the city could build a secondary plant similar to the Ley Creek plant with digestion and drying facilities that would not only yield a relatively pure effluent but also relieve the city of its dependence on the Solvay Process Company for sludge disposal. Referring to the state report and noting that pollution is a community problem, Pitts suggested that the city invite neighboring communities to contract with it for use of the proposed plant. With or without their participation, however, he urged that the city had a moral responsibility for the immediate construction of a plant, a position he supported at later hearings and in articles written for the *Herald-Journal*.

Perhaps the most important product of the agitation of the postwar years lay in the attention which it focused on the Public Works Commission. That agency since 1945 had been viewed increasingly as one which, reorganized and broadened in scope, might serve to control pollution in the county. One who held this view was former Mayor Thomas Kennedy (1942–1946), who saw in the Public Works Commission not only a potentially effective body for pollution control but also a means of shifting financial responsibility from the city to the county and thus preserving the city's pay-as-you-go fiscal policy. Mayor Kennedy was joined in this position by John A. Williams, an executive of the Niagara Mohawk Power Corporation, who was an equally staunch advocate of "pay-as-you-go." Turning to Earl O'Brien for technical counsel, Kennedy and Williams found their financial predilection buttressed by engineering judgment; for O'Brien favored the consolidation of pollution control activities under the direction of the Public Works Commission. It was his conviction that nothing less than an integrated sewer plan for the whole of Onondaga County would prove effective.

In 1948 the Governmental Research Bureau was established by the Chamber of Commerce, with the primary purpose of serving as a watchdog over municipal finances.[6] Its director, Richard Atkins, early undertook a study of the sewer problem. After due investigation, Atkins reported that conditions did not seem favorable toward metropolitan action. He saw little hope for any plan that would require cooperation between the Village of Solvay and the Town of Geddes, which had long been battling over alleged inequalities in assessments. Even if the communities could be brought together, Atkins did not feel that they would be inclined to participate in a large program. In fact, growing discontent with rising taxes throughout the county seemed to point to the likelihood of no action at all. Kennedy and Williams were content to wait. A multi-million dollar program was not likely to be undertaken hurriedly by the city. With no further pressure from the state, the Pitts report shelved, and a mayoralty election in the offing, interest in the lake subsided.

Crisis and Temporary Accord

But not for long. In June of 1950, employees at the Solvay Process Company went on strike. The shutdown of company operations deprived the city of its means of sludge disposal. Operations at the city's plant were discontinued, and while machinery was cleaned and repaired raw sewage from the city's trunks flowed directly into Onondaga Lake. Presently work resumed at Solvay, but under circumstances which made impossible the resumption of sewage treatment there by the city. The company at the time was preparing to redirect its waste discharges to new inland beds in the Towns of Geddes and Camillus. While the beds were being made ready, the towns passed ordinances prohibiting the discharge of Syracuse sludge within their limits. Despite passage of the ordinances, the city proceeded to lay a pipeline (at a cost of $80,000) to the new beds in Geddes. Upon completion of the line, the city requested permission of Solvay Process to use a pumphouse necessary for transmitting sludge. Faced with the conflicting requirements of their contract with Syracuse and the town ordinance, company officials sided with Geddes and refused permission to the city. Meanwhile untreated sewage continued to flow into the lake.

The waste bed controversy rekindled interest in the Pitts proposal, and Mayor Corcoran (who had been elected in 1949 as a Democrat) and City Public Works Commissioner Harmon prepared a request to the federal government for a planning loan for a treatment plant along the lines previously suggested by City Engineer Pitts. The Republican Common Council, which supported Pitts, was irritated to find Harmon's signature along with the Mayor's on the application for federal funds, and substituted the city engineer's name for that of the Commissioner of Public Works. The council's action helped to intensify the already strained relations between the city engineer and the Corcoran administration.

With interest in construction of a city plant revived, Kennedy and Williams felt the time had come to promote their plan actively. Assisted by Earl O'Brien, they recruited officials of two of the county's largest water-using and waste-discharging industries (Carleton Bates, Director of Operations of Solvay Process, and Edgar White, Plant Engineer of Crouse-Hinds and Chairman of the Manufacturers Association Public Works Committee) to work with them in promoting metropolitan action among their industrial colleagues and city and county officials. The group quickly learned that maintenance of "pay-as-you-go" would not be sufficient motivation for metropolitan action. Although Mayor Corcoran considered avoidance of further city debt a factor in the plan's favor, he feared any proposal that would switch program control from the city to the county; while County Attorney Major, Chairman of the Board of Supervisors Traister, and Republican County Chairman McNett were not at all sympathetic to a proposal that seemed to be inspired by a desire to shift what they regarded as a city debt to a county agency. Assurances that the interests of both the city and the county would be protected in any future program persuaded them nevertheless to go along with the metropolitan group, to the extent at least of appointing a commission to analyze the feasibility of a joint undertaking.

The instigation of the city-county study resulted from a recommendation of the Citizens' Non-Partisan Tax Commission. Early in his administration, Mayor Corcoran had appointed a Citizens' Advisory Committee whose five members included Thomas Kennedy and John A. Williams. The committee had warned the Mayor in his preparation of the 1951 budget that he could expect growing public resentment of anticipated higher governmental costs and taxes. In September of 1950 the Mayor and the Common Council appointed the five members of the committee to a ten-man Non-Partisan Tax Commission to work with the Governmental Research Bureau in reviewing the city's financial condition and the efficiency of its government. In effect, the commission, in the nomenclature of the day, constituted a Little Hoover Commission. Its major emphasis, however, was the study of revenue sources.

As members of the commission's public works committee, Kennedy and Williams were appointed a subcommittee on sewage treatment. While conducting their negotiations with city and county officials and with industrial leaders, they prepared a statement for the commission which was accepted and issued as its first recommendation. On May 5, 1951, the Citizens' Non-Partisan Tax Commission recommended that the city and county appoint a study commission to investigate the advisability of joint action in the construction of sewage treatment facilities. Two days later, the Common Council and the Board of Supervisors unanimously authorized the Mayor, the Chairman of the Board of Supervisors, and the Majority Leader of the Common Council to appoint three members each to serve as the Onondaga Lake Purification Commission.

The Purification Commission was organized on June 1, 1951, with its sole Democrat, retired Judge James Barrett, as chairman. As his three appointees, Mayor Corcoran had appointed the Judge and two Republicans, Thomas Kennedy and John Haley, Vice-President of Niagara Mohawk. (John Williams had asked to be excused from service because of business obligations.) The press and the **Democratic Party** had urged the Mayor to appoint Nelson Pitts or other city officials to the Commission, but he had declined to do so in the interest, he explained, of objectivity. The Chairman of the Board of Supervisors felt no similar obligation and appointed among his three members one member of the Public Works Commission.

The commission immediately asked for funds to contract for engineering studies. The Common Council and the Board of Supervisors both dodged the request. Neither wanted to bear the cost, but the council had additional motivations. Those who advocated construction of a plant by the city feared that money voted for the commission would be used to hire the engineering firm of O'Brien and Gere, whose position in favor of broader action was already known. The *Syracuse Herald-Journal* and some members of the council were dissatisfied with the exclusion of Pitts from the commission and felt that, in the absence of funds, the commission would have to turn to the city engineer for advice. In fact, the council directed the city engineer to place his department at the commission's disposal. If the denial of resources to the Purification Commission was intended to lessen the influence of O'Brien and make it dependent upon Nelson Pitts, the plan backfired. The commission requested only one technical study from Pitts. For general engineering service, it turned to O'Brien and Gere, Solvay Process, Crouse-Hinds, and Carrier, all of which made engineers available to it.

The commission was concerned primarily with one question: would it be less costly to build one large plant to serve both the city and the west side district (for which a separate treatment plant had been proposed earlier), or two plants, one for the city and one for the suburban area? On December 1, 1951, the Purification Commission recommended that the Public Works Commission be authorized to plan and construct joint facilities for the city and the west side.[7]

The coming holiday season caused postponement of immediate official action, although the recommendation occasioned a considerable amount of public discussion. The imminent announcement by the state of a preliminary classification of the water of the lake lent added timeliness to the issue. A memorandum from O'Brien to the County

Attorney of January 24, 1952, connected the Purification Commission's recommendation with the prospective announcement. Referring to a conversation with A. F. Dappert, Executive Secretary of the Water Pollution Control Board, O'Brien wrote:

Another important factor in considering the action of the (Public Works) Commission in taking over the sewage treatment problem is the matter of dealing with the Water Pollution Control Board. I believe I can say with assurance that local interests can deal with the Water Pollution Control Board with more satisfaction if one body can speak for all local interests. I have discussed the matter with representatives of the Water Pollution Control Board and I have been advised that the Board would accept a much more reasonable program of construction from one agency such as the Commission than is likely to be acceptable if the Water Pollution Control Board has to deal with two local agencies both of whom are involved in discharging pollution in one body of water such as Onondaga Lake.

Such a factor of course cannot be assigned any definite dollar value and also cannot be readily publicized in newspapers. . . . However I have been given pretty definite assurance privately that such would be the case and I believe you or other competent officials could get the same assurance privately.

On January 25, 1952, a decisive meeting was held in the Mayor's office. In attendance were the Mayor, members of the Public Works Commission, members of the Purification Commission, several supervisors and councilmen, and the county and city attorneys. After discussing the Purification Commission's report, the officials present unanimously approved the following resolution proposed by Alfred Haight, President of the Common Council:

Resolved that the report of the Onondaga Lake Purification Commission should be approved and that the governmental units affected should authorize the Onondaga County Public Works Commission to make the necessary engineering and financial studies and to proceed with the design, construction and operation of sewage treatment and disposal works to meet the requirements of the entire metropolitan area.

On January 28, the Common Council in special meeting approved and adopted the resolution and, in behalf of the city, authorized the Public Works Commission to proceed.

Deliberation and Delay

Subsequent events of the year 1952 indicated that, notwithstanding the widespread support commanded by the resolution at the time of adoption, considerable misgiving persisted as to the soundness of the course chosen. Mayor Corcoran himself apparently entertained some doubts. With the Intercollegiate Rowing Regatta scheduled to hold its first meet on Onondaga Lake in June, and perhaps to locate there indefinitely, discontinuation of the discharge of raw sewage in the lake had become imperative. There appeared to be no option to resumption of negotiations with the Town of Geddes for the reactivation of the waste bed disposal operation. Corporation counsel George Richardson enlisted the aid of Republican lawyer Lyle Hornbeck in this enterprise, and the two brought their joint talents to bear.[8] Their efforts, however, were to no avail, for the Town Board was determined not to permit the city to mix its sludge with the Solvay waste. To the argument that the disposal operations would end on completion of the proposed metropolitan plant, the answer was made that temporary disposal of sludge could be undertaken on city land. The majority leader of the Common Council went so far as to propose this solution, but was forced to retreat in the face of violent opposition within the city. Negotiations continued through May but the outlook for municipal use of Solvay's waste beds failed to improve. The city's defeat not only served to convince the Mayor (and others as well) of the futility of attempting to cooperate with the towns; it also consolidated opposition to any plan for disposal of sludge near the city plant. Indeed, the Polish Citizens Club, the North Side Businessmen's Association, the Industrial Council of the CIO, and the Democratic Party were to carry over the resistance conceived here to later plans for the metropolitan plant.

What appeared to some to be recalcitrance in the outlying units cropped out in yet another direction. Because of the importance of the west side district in the proposed project, Atkins and O'Brien had been urging the Public Works Commission to organize it without delay. The commission, however, was faced with the continued resistance of the Village of Solvay and the Town of Geddes; for both village and town officials, Democratic and Republican alike, feared that their jurisdictions would be charged with a disproportionate share of the cost of the new district. The alternative to district membership was posed by the commission, by A. F. Dappert, and by Solvay Process: either join the district or build a local plant at a cost far exceeding that of participation in a metropolitan project.

Meanwhile those who favored independent action by the city continued active and vocal. In his 1952 annual report City Engineer Nelson Pitts devoted a section to sewage treatment, ignoring the Public Works Commission completely and urging construction of a secondary plant by the city. Shortly thereafter, William Maloney introduced a taxpayer suit to force the city to begin construction of a plant. On the political front, the Democratic County Chairman announced that the proposed metropolitan plan would be a campaign issue in the 1953 local elections.

At least some of the unfriendly sentiment—Mayor Corcoran's restiveness in particular—stemmed from the uncertainties inherent in the situation, and these the Public Works Commission undoubtedly could have mitigated had it felt itself in a position to take bold action. Instead the commission's course was one of extreme caution, as is indicated by the fact that there was no significant public report of progress, or indeed of any action taken, in the four months following its acceptance of responsibility for metropolitan action. On June 1 the Mayor expressed his disappointment in a letter to Clarence Alberts, chairman of the commission; when may we expect action? he inquired. Both newspapers seconded the Mayor's complaint. In his reply, Alberts cited some of the difficulties encountered and stated that it would be another four months before the commission would have definite plans to present. The promised eight months of silence were broken when, on June 17, the announcement came that the commission had retained O'Brien and Gere as consulting engineers, with the Chicago firm of Greeley and Hansen also retained to review the findings and recommendations of the local engineers. Here at last was a prospect of action.

The prospect did not develop to the satisfaction of Mayor Corcoran, who in the early fall recommended that the Common Council rescind its resolution authorizing the commission to proceed. The

Mayor had been disappointed over the failure of negotiations for use of the Solvay Process waste beds; moreover, the reluctance of Geddes and Solvay to join the west side district was further evidence to him that metropolitan action was not a live prospect. Further still, no other community had passed an authorizing resolution, and the Mayor looked upon this as a sign of bad faith. Finally and in sum, the Mayor and a number of city councilmen and county supervisors from the city were experiencing growing doubt as to the wisdom of the metropolitan-area agreement. What had promised to be a cooperative undertaking appeared increasingly to be a county project in which the city's participation would consist chiefly in footing most of the bill. The city's elected representatives were encouraged in their growing disenchantment by the intensified "go-it-alone" campaign of Nelson Pitts, the *Herald-Journal,* and the Democratic Party.

The Common Council decided nevertheless to withhold action on the Mayor's request until the commission could be heard. Chairman Alberts promised a complete report by the end of November. When it became clear that that target date would not be made, Alberts invited the Mayor, the Common Council, and the supervisors of Geddes, Camillus, and Onondaga to a "clear the air" meeting on November 25. At the meeting, Earl O'Brien outlined a plan for providing primary treatment for city and west side sewage at a plant to be located on the present city site, the effluent to be pumped around the lake and into the Seneca River.

Whether or not the meeting served a useful purpose is open to question. On the one hand, its premature revelation of commission plans provided a rallying point—the defense of the Seneca River—around which opposition began to cluster. But on the other, it gave evidence of substantial progress in the thinking of the Public Works Commission, and lent authority to that body's promise that a report would be forthcoming at an early date. Its effect on Mayor Corcoran received conflicting appraisals by the Syracuse papers: one described him as satisfied with the progress reported; the other believed him to be simply treading water, displeased at the lack of cooperation shown by the towns and villages and waiting for a break. The attitudes of the newspapers themselves are revealed by their editorials of November 27. The *Herald-Journal* wrote:

> Although the people of the city of Syracuse are going to pay more than 90 percent of the cost of the proposed metropolitan area system, the work will be done by a county commission. . . . The city government which represents the taxpayers of this city won't have anything to say about it. Moreover, costs will be assessed by the Board of Supervisors. An extraordinary picture indeed.

But to the *Post-Standard*, "The news now being developed by engineers makes the program for restoring Onondaga Lake look more and more attractive."

A Metropolitan Plan

The long-awaited report was submitted to the Public Works Commission by its engineers during the last week in December, 1952. Actually there were two reports, one by the firm of O'Brien and Gere, another by Greeley and Hansen. For summary purposes the fourteen separate proposals offered by the two groups were reduced to three alternative plans. They were:

Plan 1: separate secondary treatment plants for the proposed west side district and the city, effluent discharging into Onondaga Lake.

Plan 2: one secondary treatment plant serving the city and the west side district, effluent discharging into Onondaga Lake.

Plan 3: one primary treatment plant, effluent bypassing the lake through a force main to a point of discharge in the Seneca River; the Ley Creek Plant to be converted to primary treatment, its effluent discharging into the proposed force main; the Public Works Commission to assume responsibility for operation.

Each plan had its virtues, but at the same time each posed certain problems. Plan 1, recognizing the resistance to cooperative effort, called for individual action by the city and its western suburbs. Presumably it could be effectuated with a minimum of negotiation and delay, for the steps it recommended were the least drastic of all. Yet it suffered from three fundamental defects. First, it would be by all odds the most expensive of the three alternatives. Second, the individual action which it contemplated was after all a relative thing; for it would still be necessary for the Village of Solvay and the Town of Geddes to join in support of the proposed west side district. Many felt that this battle, inevitable in any event, might be fought in a better cause. Third, while Plan 1 would result in a considerable upgrading in the quality of the lake's water, it would still fall short of the degree of purification which many believed desirable. Plan 1 was not destined to arouse any great enthusiasm.

Plan 2 represented a more novel approach to the problem, for it called for collaboration between Syracuse and the suburbs in utilizing one secondary treatment plant. Its principal advantage lay in the fact that it would be less expensive to effectuate than Plan 1; otherwise it was subject to the same criticisms as the first alternative. There remained the problem of effective cooperation among the units involved, which could be expected to be even more difficult under Plan 2 than under Plan 1. There remained, too, the issue of pollution of the lake, though the two plans were identical on this point. Like the first proposal, Plan 2 failed to command wide support when the time came for decision.

The third plan consciously assumed a major burden-of-proof in that it contemplated a greater degree of intergovernmental cooperation than either of the others; it was frankly an *area* rather than a governmental unit plan. In other respects its advantages over the alternative proposals appeared substantial. First, Plan 3 would eliminate all effluent from the lake, thereby making possible in time its complete rehabilitation. Second, it would be the most economical of the three alternatives. Third, it offered two pegs—economy in construction and maintenance and efficiency in operation—on which to hang the campaign for adoption. Here Syracuse and its neighbors to the west might find ground for common action. Fourth, Plan 3 represented a broad attack on a metropolitan problem, with the (County) Public Works Commission assuming primary responsibility; and if this seemed a weakness to some it emerged as a point of strength to others. Favored by the engineers and favorably presented in their report, Plan 3 immediately moved to the center of the stage. In the protracted discussions which followed, it became the symbol of metropolitan action.

Opposition and Support

The sewage treatment issue consumed the whole of 1953 and half of 1954, for it was to be a long year and a half before final action would be taken on Plan 3. The interval was punctuated by numerous proposals for modifications of varying degrees of seriousness, fitful discussion characterized by long periods of surface quiet broken by vigorous attack and counterattack, a number of public hearings, endless negotiation at the political level, and a municipal election. Sides had been pretty well chosen by the beginning of the year, though subsequent events made some converts while confirming most of the protagonists in their earlier roles.

Chief among the opponents were certain elements of the city government. Spokesmen for the Department of Public Works were loath to consider giving up an important municipal function to a county agency; and while their opposition was not consistently vigorous, it was always a background factor to be reckoned with. City Engineer Nelson Pitts was openly critical of the plan. In what was to be his final official pronouncement on the subject, he made public a letter of January 8, 1953, to the Mayor commenting on the O'Brien and Gere report. There he criticized the engineers' methods and recommendations on technical grounds and repeated his original proposal that the city construct a secondary plant and offer its facilities on a contract basis to other communities. He concluded by urging the Mayor not to involve the city in any "entangling alliances." Several months thereafter, Pitts was dismissed as a result of a school construction controversy; but he continued to oppose the plan to the end, bringing to bear such influence as he could as a private citizen. Mayor Corcoran, though at first favorably disposed, entertained increasing doubts that support of the proposed course of action represented a sound decision for the city. Moreover, he was never fully convinced that the obstacles could be overcome. Fortunately for the success of the plan his active support was not crucial, for he was a lonely Democratic Mayor in a staunchly Republican city. In sum, City Hall did not uniformly oppose the progress of Plan 3, but it was far from unrestrained in its endorsement.

Something of the same thing may be said of the Democratic Party. In the beginning leading Democratic spokesmen were openly hostile, viewing the proposal for metropolitan action as an attempt at a "power grab" by the Republican county machine. From outright opposition the party retreated gradually to what some considered simple obstructionism—a demand that the plan be spelled out more precisely, a request for more detailed cost figures, a recommendation that a county engineer be appointed to supervise the program. Democratic leaders early threatened to make an issue of the problem of sewage disposal in the fall's city election; but the party's candidate for mayor, Alfred Haight, refused to make the threat effective. By the end of the year, then, Democratic party opposition had lost a good deal of its sting, though it was still visible and vocal where criticism promised to be rewarding.

The Reclamation Association, speaking principally through William Maloney, remained consistent in its opposition to the plan. It chose now to emphasize the Seneca River bypass, on the ground that it would deprive the lake of the inflow necessary to dilute the polluted waters of the streams emptying into it. Seneca River, North Shore, and Lakeland residents opposed the bypass proposal for quite a different reason: they feared pollution of the river. The *Herald-Journal* conceded these dissidents a point, questioning the disposal of sewage "in a neighbor's yard" on ethical grounds. Doubts about the Seneca River aspect of the plan spread to the city, and influential voices there joined the residents of the suburbs in opposition.

On the positive side the concept of concerted action, and Plan 3 in particular, got off to a running start by reason of favorable presentation in the engineers' report. Earl O'Brien, who was credited with prime authorship of the basic report, at once became its chief spokesman as well. He lost no time in indicating his preference among the three alternatives: it was for Plan 3, which he championed vigorously at public hearings and in other public statements throughout the period the proposal was under discussion. Perhaps the feature which appealed to him most was the metropolitan approach implicit in Plan 3. O'Brien has been credited with having done more than any other individual to hold the plan on course during the 18 months necessary to bring it to the point of approval.

The cause of metropolitan action was strengthened by the support it received from the (state) Water Pollution Control Board, principally through its Executive Secretary, A. F. Dappert. As has been noted, the board was engaged during this period in a study of the problem of the pollution of Onondaga Lake, with a view to the classification of its water in terms of quality. Dappert was in Syracuse frequently in connection with this work, and so was able to maintain close touch with sewage disposal developments. He was therefore familiar with the report of the Public Works Commission's consulting engineers, with which he expressed general satisfaction. Dappert deemed it inappropriate as a state official publicly to express preference for one plan over another, more especially because he found all three acceptable as pollution control measures; but privately he voiced his preference for Plan 3. A concerted attack on the problem, he felt, held greater promise of success than separate action by the individual governments.

On technical grounds, then, Plan 3 seemed to be in good shape, with the recommendations of the two engineering firms fortified by the informal endorsement of the Water Pollution Control Board. Organized business support began to crystallize soon after release of the O'Brien and Gere report with the appointment by the Governmental Research Bureau of a committee to prepare a report on the sewage problem. The committee of five included, in Thomas Kennedy, John Williams, and John L. Haley, three members long known as advocates of metropolitan action. Directed to make a comprehensive and objective study of the various proposals under consideration, the committee came out strongly for Plan 3 in a report titled "Joint Sewage Treatment for the Metropolitan Area." The report was approved by the Governmental Research Bureau and endorsed by the Chamber of Commerce and the Manufacturers Association. The interlocking membership of the three organizations provided a ready forum for discussion both before and after completion of the report. Given wide distribution in the business community, the report commanded general and favorable attention.

The sources of support thus far noted could avail nothing of themselves, for the decision for or against Plan 3 would be based in the end on political considerations. Chief among these, of course, was the basic issue whether the city would embrace common action or elect to "go it alone." Inextricably bound up with this decision was the problem of accommodating the city's special interests, which entailed basically negotiating an understanding between the city and the county. Other units were involved, but agreement between these two was fundamental. The means for the required reconciliation were at hand in the Republican organization, which was in firm control of both city and county. There was, to be sure, a minor cause for embarrassment in that both Mayor and Common Council President were Democrats, but everybody understood that this aberration from normal practice would be rectified in the municipal election of the fall. Republican leadership therefore assumed that theirs was the decision and proceeded accordingly. Fortunately for Plan 3, the party early took a stand in favor of the proposed course of action, and its managers went systematically about the business of identifying and removing or mitigating the obstacles to its success. Without firm Republican support, the engineers' report would have been quietly laid aside.

The city's two daily newspapers helped the drive for adoption. The *Post-Standard* had been favorably inclined from the beginning and went down the line for the O'Brien and Gere report. The *Herald-Journal* first supported the position advanced and defended by City Engineer Pitts: that the city should act independently and maintain its individual responsibility; but with the passing of time, and more especially perhaps with the passing of Pitts from public office, the paper modified its stand in favor of support of Plan 3. The press therefore cooperated in helping to create a climate favorable to metropolitan action.

The Major Issues

It has been suggested that the basic issues to be resolved were political in nature, and that among these the first concerned the attitude to be adopted by the city toward the whole sewage disposal problem. A few weeks after the release of the O'Brien and Gere report, Republican members of the Common Council met in caucus with their adviser (Lyle Hornbeck), the County Chairman, and the Chairman of the County Board of Supervisors. The occasion for the caucus was a vote to be demanded by the council's lone Democrat on Mayor Corcoran's previous proposal to rescind the authorizing resolution. The Mayor himself had not pressed for the vote, but Democratic Councilman Eichenlaub chose to do so as a means of symbolizing his party's opposition to Plan 3. The Republican councilmen and the sixteen Republican county supervisors from the city were concerned over criticisms made by the *Herald-Journal* and municipal departments that under the proposed plan the city would have no voice in the management of the sewage program. Although independent of the city government, the county supervisors elected from the city thought of their role as that of protecting the city's interests in county board action. Indeed, they were hesitant to participate in a county decision without prior approval by their Republican counterparts in the Common Council. The purpose of the caucus was to establish a course for the guidance of the Republican members of both Common Council and Board of Supervisors.

The decision reached in the caucus was to place the problem of sewage disposal in the hands of the Public Works Commission. The vote represented a clear victory for the advocates of metropolitan action, and an equally clear rejection of the notion of separate city action. At the same time, certain concessions would be made to the city in recognition of its special interests. No program would be initiated by the commission without the approval of the Common Council. An earlier proposal to give equal representation to the city on the Public Works Commission would be renewed, and in addition the Public Works Act would be thoroughly reviewed and revised in preparation for the new undertaking. The only dissent was registered by Councilman Grosso. This energetic physician (who later ran for mayor under an Independent label) announced to the press: "I do not represent any 'metropolitan area' encompassing the towns outside of the City of Syracuse but the City of Syracuse. This problem should be solved by Syracuse for Syracuse." [9] The consensus in the caucus was, of course, not official; it was nevertheless highly significant, for it portrayed clearly the shape of events to come.

A proposed revision of the Public Works Act in line with the above agreements was worked out by an informal drafting committee at a series of meetings held during the last two weeks in January. Members of the committee were the City Attorney, the County Attorney, and the adviser to the majority members of the Common Council. The draft revision called for increasing membership on the commission to eight, four from the city and four from the county; requiring Common Council approval for initiation of all projects involving the city; requiring Common Council approval for acquisition of city property by the commission; permitting the transfer of sewage plant personnel from the city to the commission; and authorizing the commission to institute a system of user charges or sewer rentals for financing its projects.

The Republican members of the Common Council and Board of Supervisors reacted favorably to the recommendations of the drafting committee, thus presaging subsequent formal approval. The board was reluctant to grant power of veto to the city; but it was assured that the authority of the Common Council would not extend to operations and budgets, only to initial approval of projects. With the Public Works Commission retaining substantial freedom of decision, the Board of Supervisors accepted the proposed revision. Since the Public Works Act was a local law and since the Onondaga County legislative delegation recommended approval of its revision, the legislature found no reason not to act favorably on the proposal. In due course, therefore, it passed a revised Public Works Act incorporating the changes set forth above. Thus were the city's principal special interests recognized, and thus was removed a major obstacle to metropolitan action.

Plan 3 in effect called for two kinds of structure. The first, a metropolitan treatment plant, would be built and operated by the Public Works Commission. The second, a network of lines to convey sewage to the plant, would be constructed by a series of sewer districts. The plan contemplated the extension of one existing district and the creation of two new districts. Under the Public Works Act (as revised) the Public Works Commission was to map out a district and prepare a general plan for discussion at a public hearing. Following the hearing, the commission would recommend the plan to the Board of Supervisors, which in turn would conduct a public hearing and take appropriate action. Any plan approved by the board which involved the city would then go to the Common Council for consideration and decision. This was a complicated and, as events proved, time-consuming procedure.

The decision to adopt Plan 3 in principle was made early, as has been noted; but specific steps to implement that decision were slow to come. The Public Works Commission held a public hearing on the proposed west side district as early as January, 1953, but concluded that its action had been premature in view of the still incomplete plans for the metropolitan treatment plant, and in view further of the revision of the Public Works Act then under way. It was summer before the commission felt that conditions were such that it could move ahead. It directed its engineers to prepare maps and cost estimates for the proposed metropolitan treatment plant district for consideration at a public hearing set for July 22. The hearing, held as scheduled, was marked by bitter exchanges between opponents (led by William Maloney and Nelson Pitts) and supporters (headed by Earl O'Brien) of the proposal. The following day the commission sent to the Board of Supervisors recommendations for establishment of the west side and the metropolitan treatment plant districts.

The board moved promptly, scheduling a public hearing for August 31. Again a stormy scene ensued, with both antagonists of the first hearing, and particularly the opponents of the proposed action, strongly reinforced. In addition to the opposition which the hearing crystallized, there was the unrelieved animosity of Solvay and Geddes.[10] The Board of Supervisors, mindful both of the spirited resistance and of the municipal campaign then in full swing, discreetly suspended action.

On November 23, with the election past and the Republicans, as expected, victorious, the Board of Supervisors met for further consideration of the sewage disposal problem. Four resolutions were laid before the board. Two concerned extensions of the Ley Creek District; the third proposed to create a metropolitan treatment plant district, the fourth a west side district. The board approved three resolutions; the fourth (Solvay and Geddes again!) was laid aside for further study. The three resolutions which had received approval went before the Common Council for action that very evening; but that body, noting that in the circumstances any action it might take would be inconclusive, tabled all resolutions for further study.

At a meeting held on December 7 the Board of Supervisors, returning to consideration of the issue, passed the resolution creating the west side district. The Common Council, with all four resolutions now before it in due and proper order, passed the ordinances necessary to signify council approval the evening of December 7. Only Republican member Grosso and Democratic member Eichenlaub voted no. There had been speculation all along concerning the course Mayor Corcoran would take. He had not participated in the deliberations which preceded council action, and indeed was out of town when the vote was taken. Many believed he would veto the proposed ordinances. This in fact he did on December 23, declining, as he said, to "tie the hands of the new administration" that was to take office the following week. There was considerable talk of an attempt to override the veto, but nothing came of it. The decision therefore passed to the administration of Mayor Donald Mead, which assumed office January 1, 1954.

Decision at Last

As may readily be imagined, the patience of its supporters had worn thin in the more than a year since Plan 3 made its appearance. There had been a good deal of grumbling about what appeared to many to be unnecessary delays during the summer and fall, and those who favored action looked to the new Mayor for leadership. They were disposed not to press for immediate action, but when after three months no tangible progress had been reported, they grew restless. A petition by the Village of Liverpool requesting the Governor to declare Onondaga Lake a public menace emphasized the need for movement. In late March A. F. Dappert wrote Mayor Mead to the effect that the Water Pollution Control Board was disappointed at the city's lack of decision; the board, he stated, would be forced to take steps to compel action if nothing had been done by June 1. On April 19, representatives of the Governmental Research Bureau, the Chamber of Commerce, and the Manufacturers Association met to consider the problem. The discussion centered on a proposal to announce the position of the organizations once more and to call publicly on the Mayor for immediate action. Those attending were persuaded that such a pronouncement was not necessary, but they insisted on naming a committee to call on the Mayor and inform him of their feeling. The committee consisted of Thomas Kennedy and John Williams.

To these complaints Mayor Mead replied reassuringly, promising a final decision soon. Meanwhile, he announced progress in plans to reactivate the city's Hiawatha Boulevard treatment plant; and in late spring, with the annual rowing regatta just around the corner, he did in fact succeed in reopening the plant on a temporary basis after almost four years of idleness. He also announced that his departments were studying the proposal and that he had hired an outside consultant to advise him on the whole problem.

The Mayor's position did not appear to be a difficult one, for the major policy decisions had been taken. The Common Council and the Board of Supervisors had indicated their agreement on Plan 3, the Public Works Act had been amended to take care of the special concerns of the city, the measures to create the necessary sanitary districts had been pushed through (requiring only formal repassage by the Common Council and signature by the Mayor), the Republican organization had fallen into line, and Democratic strength had been tested in opposition and found wanting. For all this agreement in principle, however, there remained some thorny issues to be resolved. First among these was the method of sludge disposal, which continued to be highly controversial and which could have wrecked Plan 3 even at that late date. It was to these issues that Mayor Mead and his advisers devoted their energies.

On May 29, two days before the deadline set by the Water Pollution Control Board, the Mayor made public the results of his studies. Confirming the judgment that metropolitan action would be more advantageous to the city than separate action, he embraced Plan 3. At the same time he proposed several modifications, most of them technical in nature. Chief among them may be noted the following:

1. That final decision on the method of sludge disposal be withheld pending further study of the recommendation that disposal be by incineration, and that the sum of $1,000,000 be authorized for construction of an incineration plant if that method should be decided upon.

2. That a decision on location of the treatment plant be postponed to allow consideration of the proposal (made by the Mayor's consultant) that the plant be located at the point of discharge into the Seneca River.

3. That the Public Works Commission retain experts in the field to study methods of financing the construction and operation of sewage disposal works, and that the City Commissioner of Finance be consulted and be kept advised of progress on this front.

4. That protection be given the city's sewage treatment personnel to assure their transfer to the county agency without loss of status or wages.

5. That a city reservoir be excluded from the proposed west side sanitary district.

The Mayor's proposed modifications came before the Public Works Commission June 1. The commission found them acceptable in every particular and sent them along to the Board of Supervisors with its recommendation for approval. The board acted favorably, incorporating the first and second points in its formal action and giving the Mayor personal assurance that his remaining requests would be honored. On July 6, 1954, the Common Council added its approval (Republican member Grosso and a newly elected Democratic member dissenting) and Mayor Mead indicated his endorsement, thus concluding the action necessary to formal adoption of Plan 3. From submission of the engineers' report recommending metropolitan action to final acceptance by the city, somewhat more than 18 months had elapsed.

Conclusion

This lengthy conflict over the solution to the twin problems of sewage disposal and lake pollution illustrates the process of metropolitan decision-making in its classic form. A problem existed whose solution was beyond the resources of any one agency, public or private. The situation rocked along for years, growing gradually worse until at length something clearly had to be done. The something chosen in the beginning was a series of half-way measures designed to bring and keep the problem just within the limits of tolerance. Meanwhile public protests, at first tentative and muted, became more vocal under the goading of such initiators of action as the state Departments of Health and Conservation, the Syracuse Chamber of Commerce, the Manufacturers Association, the Liverpool Chamber of Commerce, the Governmental Research Bureau, and the Onondaga Lake Reclamation Association. Demand for action increased with public awareness until presently the issue could no longer be ignored. A strike at Solvay Process, which withdrew from use the city's means of sludge disposal and so precipitated a crisis, provided the clincher.

Recognition of the need for a sewage treatment plant was of course basic, but it was also preliminary; for there remained a score of decisions, each taken in turn, each growing from and leading to another, and all forming a chain of cause and consequence leading slowly and hesitantly toward resolution of the issue. What kind of plant would be required? Where should it be located? What agency of what unit should be responsible for construction? For maintenance and operation? How should costs be met? How should sewage be transported to the plant? This last involved the problem of construction and operation of sewer lines, and raised in turn a number of questions not greatly different in kind or complexity from those posed above.

The central problem, of course, turned on the fact that effective action required agreement among a number of governments. Any plan seriously pursued must be satisfactory to state, county, city, and a number of towns and villages. Among the public agencies with authority to scrutinize (and with varying powers of veto) were the state Departments of Health and Conservation; the Common Council, Mayor, and City Engineer of the City of Syracuse; the county Board of Supervisors and Public Works Commission; and various town and village boards. It is this multiplicity of interests which sets a metropolitan problem apart. Not all metropolitan action requires unanimity among the public units and agencies involved, but all action benefits from a reasonable consensus on proposed solutions. The building of consensus therefore lies at the center of metropolitan decision-making, for the alternative to agreement is either fiat action or stalemate. The sewage treatment plant is the first in a series of cases designed to reveal how metropolitan issues are selected for consideration, how the forces concerned employ their strengths to serve their interests, and how finally a negotiated decision emerges, if not to solve, then at least to mitigate, a problem.

V

Water for the Suburbs

WATER supply was another problem marked by the Post-War Report for early attention. This is the story of the search for water for the Syracuse metropolitan area. Since the city itself has been well served for many years by its Skaneateles Lake supply, the problem has been essentially that of finding water for the neighboring areas. This endeavor has been marked by three separate phases. The first saw the outlying districts dependent either upon their own sources, augmented by a private water company, or, increasingly over the years, on the city system. The second, hastened by the dwindling surplus in the city's fixed source, witnessed the take-over of the private company by a public agency, the Onondaga County Water Authority, and expansion in service by that agency to the limit of its available supply. The third, occasioned by the ceiling on the amount of water available to the two major existing systems and by continuously increasing demands, is characterized by an effort to make the development of a new source of supply a county-wide responsibility. For as it had before and will again, the county emerged from two decades of discussion as the unit most likely to succeed in the search for water for metropolitan Syracuse.

Roscoe C. Martin prepared this chapter.

City and Suburbs to 1950

The New York State legislature in 1888 authorized the Mayor of Syracuse to appoint a Board of Water Commissioners whose duty it was to investigate alternative sources for a municipal water supply. At that time a private water company, drawing from creeks and wells, supplied most residential and commercial needs. This system was augmented by privately owned wells and, for industrial uses, by the Erie Canal. The board of commissioners recommended that Skaneateles Lake be tapped as a source of municipal supply, and proposed a three million dollar bond issue in order to purchase the private company and begin construction.[1] After an initial defeat by the voters, the bond issue was approved by a narrow margin. It was expected that this action would ensure an ample supply of high quality water to the city for decades to come.

The first conduit (a 30-inch one) was opened in 1894, to the accompaniment of a great community celebration. A second conduit was added in 1910 and a third in 1927 to meet actual and anticipated water needs. In 1931 the state Water Power and Control Commission granted the city the right to divert up to 58 million gallons of water per day (m.g.d.) from Skaneateles Lake.[2] This figure represented the maximum withdrawal considered to have no harmful effects on either the level of the lake or the flow of the outlet stream. By 1950 the city's average daily consumption was 41 m.g.d., with peak days running as high as 50 m.g.d. Notwithstanding the substantial spread between the amount taken and that legally authorized, lake property owners and the Village of Skaneateles launched a defensive move against the city following World War II to make certain that the water system would have no damaging effects. The city thus was put on notice that any effort to increase the withdrawal maximum set in 1931 would meet with vigorous resistance.

Until the first decade of the twentieth century, individual wells provided water for most non-city households and industries in the county. Some villages had established individual water systems, either drawing from the generous supplies of ground water or developing their own reservoirs. Notable among these were Baldwinsville, Fayetteville, Manlius, and East Syracuse. The last-named, for example, constructed a reservoir in the Butternut Creek watershed southeast of the city. This system provided water for the residents of the village, the New York Central freight yards, and some householders along the route of the transmission main through the town of Dewitt. Other villages developed small spring sources. All such systems in the aggregate were limited, however, both in amount of water supplied and in capacity for growth. They were adequate to the needs of rural life; more than that they could not claim.

In 1907 the Onondaga County Suburban Water Company was authorized to develop Otisco Lake [3] for the provision of water to certain franchised areas, either not served at all or inadequately served, generally to the east and north of the city. Two primary factors led to this step: first, the New York Central, with its expanding Dewitt yards, needed soft water for use in locomotives; and second, a cast iron pipe company, looking for an outlet for its product, was ready to organize and finance the water company. The new company quickly proved its utility, and was able to serve its area with reasonable satisfaction (with a number of system improvements) for two decades. By 1927 the demands upon it had become such as to necessitate a petition to the Water Power and Control Commission to increase its diversion of Otisco water from 5 to 11 m.g.d. In one favorable action the commission granted the petition and extended the company's francise area west of the city.

Following several corporate changes, the Otisco system was acquired in the spring of 1929 by the New York Water Service Corporation. This transfer began a period of ownership during which the company was run by a New York financial holding corporation.[4] The principal aim of the corporation seemed to be to maximize short run gains at the expense of reserving funds for capital improvements, a policy whose full impact would be felt when expansion should become necessary to supply its franchise area. Policy apart, privately owned water companies were having a difficult time attracting capital. But whatever its policy and its problems, the New York Water Service Corporation was the major supplier of suburban water needs, both industrial and domestic. In 1948 the corporation sought and obtained an increase in authorized withdrawal from 11 m.g.d. to 16 m.g.d. Its 1950 sales averaged approximately 12 m.g.d.

A definite pattern of relationships between the city water system and major non-city suppliers began to develop during the decade 1940–1950. The smaller independent systems were limited in supply and relatively fixed in their jurisdictional limits. The city was in the best position in terms both of location of mains and of available supply to provide water to some of the non-city residential and industrial developments. Location of mains was an especially important factor in dictating the sale of city water to the residential sections of the Town of Dewitt and areas to the west. Technically, most of these areas were within the private water company's jurisdiction: by 1950 the city was supplying 4 m.g.d. to non-city users, 3.5 m.g.d. of the total going to consumers in the company's franchise area.

The industrial demand for city water in non-city areas was highlighted by the experience of three major industries which ended up being supplied by city water: General Electric, Bristol Laboratories, and Brown-Lipe-Chapin. Following World War II, General Electric decided to locate large electronics assembling plants to the north of the city. Negotiations with the New York Water Service Corporation did not prove satisfactory. In the first place, G.E. refused to pay for the extension of water mains to the new plants, as proposed by the corporation. But in the second place, G.E. was dubious of the private company's ability to deliver its gallonage requirement with sufficient pressure to ensure minimum fire insurance rates. In the end, then, General Electric determined to negotiate for Syracuse water. Through the efforts of former Lieutenant-Governor Edward Schoeneck (of Bond, Schoeneck, and King, attorneys for General Electric on local matters), the city agreed to extend a main from the city line to the new tract without cost to G.E. That company subsequently refused to grant a letter of commitment for water purchase to the New York Water Service Corporation even after the city had tentatively agreed to transfer the new main to the private water company's system, preferring to continue with what it regarded as the more dependable city supply.

During the same period Bristol Laboratories decided to locate in the Village of East Syracuse, just over the city line. In view of the village's limited supply, the city petitioned for and received permission to sell Bristol Skaneateles water. Shortly thereafter the New York Water Service Corporation attempted to obtain permission to supply Bristol Laboratories, through whose property its main ran; but permission was refused by the Water Power and Control Commission on the ground of an insufficient supply.

In 1951 another large industry came to the city for water. The Brown-Lipe-Chapin Division of General Motors had been negotiating for construction of a new plant in the franchise area of the New York Water Service Corporation. The anticipated need was more than 2.5 m.g.d., which was deemed to be beyond the private company's ability to produce with regularity or sufficient pressure. Consequently the city agreed to supply General Motors, which in turn agreed to pay for an $80,000 main extension from the city line to the plant.

By 1951 the City of Syracuse was supplying in whole or in part these non-city industrial consumers: General Electric, Halcomb Steel, Solvay Process Company, Crouse-Hinds, Will and Baumer Candle Company, Lamson Corporation, Brown-Lipe-Chapin, and Bristol Laboratories. The city had expanded its outside service over the years without plan or premeditation, responding to expressed needs when it appeared they might not be met otherwise and when its mains were favorably located. From its vantage point in Albany, the Water Power and Control Commission kept an eye on the growing pattern of dependence on the Syracuse water supply. The Bristol Laboratories case indicated that agency's awareness of the private company's limited ability to satisfy the needs of its natural customers, much less those of industrial users outside its franchise area. At the same time, the city gradually but unmistakably approached the limit of its legal authorization: on some days in a dry year it was already withdrawing from Skaneateles the maximum gallonage allowed.

The potential shortage of water was not acknowledged locally until after World War II. Even the Post-War Report did not mention a possible deficiency, satisfying itself with a note on the need for administrative coordination of the many distributing districts. Yet the figures of suburban population growth contained an implicit warning. The area served by the New York Water Service Corporation, which increased only some 9 per cent in the decade 1930–1940, grew almost 41 per cent from 1940 to 1950. The growth for the years 1950–1957 was to be 55 per cent. Most who observed this trend thought it good, but from the point of view of water supply it was ominous.

The problems created by the growth in demand for water might have been alleviated if the private water company could have brought itself to invest in betterment of its system. It did make some improvements, but they were limited to such things as installation of booster pumps and strengthening of short stretches of line, moves designed mainly to permit utilizing the existing mains to their full potential. The completion of a second conduit was imperative if full advantage was to be taken of the Otisco source, but the company did not see fit to make a capital investment for such a purpose. Increasing demand led to a taxing of the main conduit and intakes that on occasion constituted a serious health and fire hazard.

Customer discontent came to the surface in a hearing held by the Public Service Commission on May 22, 1950, on a petition for a rate increase filed by the New York Water Service Corporation. The Towns of Geddes, Dewitt, and Clay, along with the Villages of Solvay and North Syracuse, all submitted letters in opposition to the increase, not only on economic grounds but on those of insufficient service as well. George Cregg of Melvin and Melvin and Earl O'Brien of O'Brien and Gere, as attorney and engineer respectively for some of the towns and villages, appeared in opposition. The hearing brought out the usual engineering and expense-income data. Cregg, however, was able to score effectively in cross examination of the company's engineer, drawing admissions of inadequate storage supply, dependence on the city for emergencies, and insufficient pressure in parts of the system resulting in fire hazards and poor fire insurance ratings. These admissions were supported by O'Brien's testimony. Although the rate increase was subsequently approved by the Public Service Commission, the hearing reflected the dissatisfaction with the company's service that was to grow presently into a positive demand for public action.

By mid-1950, then, the criticisms of the improvident water service corporation were beginning to crystallize. Residential expansion was continuing and, although the large industrial users were satisfied with their arrangements with the city, more and more people were becoming aware of the limitations on growth created by the inadequate water supply. Industrial Park was in the early stages of development and Floyd Stover (of Eagan Real Estate), with the assistance of Myron Melvin, circulated petitions among industrial leaders requesting public action in response to long-range water needs for property and industrial development.[5] The fact that the policy of the New York Water Service Corporation was dictated from New York City did nothing to dispel the resentment of the town officials, who had much to gain from expanded real estate activity and who bore the brunt of the complaints about water service.

The problem facing metropolitan Syracuse was quite simply one of arranging for an increased supply of water for suburban areas in order to reduce dependence on the dwindling city surplus. What courses of action were available? Efforts to persuade the private water company to expand and improve its system had proved unsuccessful. The independent village systems had few possibilities of growth. The tapping of a new source by public action would require large amounts of capital, not to mention an administrative arrangement not then in view. Action by the county seemed to offer a possibility, but there were legal limits on what the county government could do. The County Water District Law, permitting intergovernmental action, had not yet been passed. The County Public Works Commission might be utilized, but it was generally regarded as a "sewer agency" with neither the desire nor (it was then thought) the statutory authority to undertake responsibility for a water system. The alternatives did not appear promising.

Limited Metropolitan Action

But action was soon forthcoming. Urged on by Myron Melvin, Earl O'Brien, and Thomas H. Dyer,[6] the Board of Supervisors in December of 1950 created a committee to study the county's water problem. Appointed to the study committee were Dyer, as chairman, and supervisors from Dewitt, Cicero, Geddes, Marcellus, and

Pompey. The committee gladly accepted the technical assistance volunteered by O'Brien and Gere. As part of its deliberations it journeyed to Albany, where it discussed with Cushman McGee,[7] Deputy Comptroller for Municipal Affairs, its developing plans for a county water authority. The committee's report to the Board of Supervisors endorsed the authority concept and recommended a resolution requesting the state legislature to pass the necessary authorizing statute.[8] In presenting the report Dyer made a verbal attack on the New York Water Service Corporation, noting that town and village officials were complaining about inadequate service. "Furthermore," Dyer added in an appeal to a county sense of proprietorship, "there have been reports that the water company . . . may even [extend its service outside] the County. I can see no reason why we should allow our own water to go out of the County."[9] The resolution passed the Board of Supervisors by a unanimous vote, as did all further resolutions concerning the authority brought up for vote during 1951.

Public authorities in New York State range all the way from the gigantic Port of New York Authority (created by interstate compact) to municipal parking authorities operating a single parking lot. A state commission has described them as "devices for the solution of interjurisdictional problems, that is, as means of overcoming what sometimes appears to be artificial barriers to natural and coherent development."[10] The arguments used to support a water authority for Onondaga County were several. First, it was pointed out that an authority would require neither the laying nor the earmarking of taxes; instead its income would be derived from users. Second, employment of this device would not interfere with constitutional debt limits nor would it affect county credit. Third, its use would facilitate the transition of the water supply system from private to public operation. Fourth, there was the appeal, widely exploited, of the business rather than the outright governmental approach. Fifth, an authority would be one step removed from the political arena. Finally, there was precedent for a water authority in other counties. Aside from all this it appeared that, unlike some other metropolitan problems, the water problem could not be dealt with at the town level, even in the short run, for technical and financial reasons.[11] Some form of county action seemed necessary.

The water authority bill was introduced in the legislature by Senator John Hughes and Assemblyman Searles Shultz of Skaneateles. The only amendment to the draft bill (written in Syracuse) was advanced by Shultz. Skaneateles residents wanted an express limitation on the new water authority to prohibit taking water from the Skaneateles watershed. Shultz, responding to this wish and encountering no opposition, changed the bill accordingly. The Onondaga County Water Authority Act was approved by the Governor on April 10, 1951.

The district covered by the new authority was practically identical with the New York Water Service Corporation's franchise area (Map 2). The statute was patterned after the Erie County Water Authority law, with the major exception that the Public Service Commission was given control over any direct purchase of the water service corporation by the authority. Former Senator George Fearon, local attorney for the corporation, realized that the Public Service Commission's valuation of the company might be lower than the price that might be arrived at by local negotiators; and during the writing of the bill he attempted to eliminate the provision which would admit that body to the proceeding. Former Lieutenant-Governor Edward Schoeneck, who had long been interested in the water problem, made it known that he disapproved of removing the Public Service Commission's jurisdiction over direct purchase. The issue was not pushed by Fearon and the bill went to Albany with the controverted clause intact.

The new authority's board of directors included, among others, Dyer as chairman and, in a non-partisan bid, one Democrat. It is significant to note that, except for a brief news story dealing with the original recommendation to the Board of Supervisors by the study committee, practically no publicity attended the creation of the authority. The metropolitan sewage treatment plant was currently the big public issue, and the water authority proposal slipped by without dissent and virtually without public notice. The persons responsible for the creation of the authority were such that their influence in community affairs, regarding this issue, at least, permitted them access to the local legislative machinery without the necessity of an appeal to public support.

The involvement of Melvin and Melvin (through Myron Melvin and George Cregg) as town and village attorneys, and of O'Brien and Gere as municipal engineers for the areas most in need of water and improved services, had the effect of focusing the interests of these two firms on the water business. They were duly appointed to serve the new authority, as legal counsel and engineering arm respectively.

With the change in city administration from Republican to Democratic in 1950, Syracuse adopted a somewhat more liberal attitude toward selling water to out-of-city customers. Nelson Pitts continued on as City Engineer, but his opposition to the sale of city water to outside areas was overruled by Mayor Corcoran. Following the agreement (mentioned earlier) to provide Brown-Lipe-Chapin with city water, the Mayor felt the need to allay the distress of some in-city persons who were against out-of-city water sales. In a letter printed in the *Herald-Journal,* he argued,

> we must not lose sight of the fact that it is only natural that industrial expansion take place in the suburbs of Syracuse rather than within the City itself. . . . It does not seem sensible or logical to deny industries settling around Syracuse. While these factories are not in the City, they employ Syracuse residents, they bring trade and commerce to our community and they generally contribute to our economic well being.[12]

The Mayor might have added that out-of-city industrial water sales were highly profitable for the city. The following day, the editor of the *Herald-Journal* raised the question of why the entire burden of providing industry with water should fall on the people of Syracuse. He added that there must be increased recognition of the county's responsibility to develop a new source of water supply and called upon the newly created authority for action.

About four months later, O'Brien and Gere submitted their first formal engineering report to the Onondaga County Water Authority. Essentially, this report was a complete review of water systems in the county, along with a forecast of future water needs.

The report accused the New York Water Service Corporation of failing to meet the demands for growth in its service area, stating that at the time there was a deficiency in supply of 7 m.g.d. O'Brien took the position that Otisco Lake could yield an additional 12 m.g.d. if a major betterment and improvement program were launched.

Following receipt of a subsequent engineering report on Oneida Lake as a source of supply, the Onondaga County Water Authority solicited letters of commitment for water purchase from large industrial users. No commitments were obtained. On the surface it appeared that industries were fearful of jeopardizing their relationship with the water company by committing themselves to purchase from a potential competitor. In addition, a great many people were prejudiced against Oneida Lake as a source of supply. But considerations of quantity and quality apart, there was a very good reason for the Oneida study. Cost data on the development of Oneida Lake as a source were needed in order to support negotiations already under way for purchase of the New York Water Service Corporation by the Onondaga County Water Authority. The authority wanted to assume the posture of meaning business, and of having a live option. While the threat of an alternative source seemed advantageous to some on the authority side, the Oneida Lake report was not without benefit to the water service corporation. As might have been expected, the company's engineer, Colonel Thomas Wiggin of New York City, immediately protested that the authority engineer's cost estimate on tapping Oneida Lake was much too low. This difference in judgment strengthened the hand of Senator Fearon, who was already pushing for condemnation of his client's property.[13] A high cost figure for developing a new source of supply would help focus county attention on the Otisco system.

Senator Fearon was invited to give his views on the water problem before the Manufacturers Association of Syracuse (February 9, 1953). His remarks on that occasion were prophetic of things to come. After outlining the facility limitations of the New York Water Service Corporation to take and distribute more than 13 m.g.d. from Otisco, he stated that "additional water distributing facilities will not be provided by the New York Water Service Corporation because it knows that the Onondaga County Water Authority must eventually take over the private corporation." Continuing, he observed that he "had discussed the entire matter with Myron Melvin and had pointed out to him that, while the corporation's holdings were not for sale, it seemed inevitable that the Water Authority would obtain these holdings in condemnation proceedings eventually." His recommendation to the Manufacturers Association was to "insist that the Water Authority commence condemnation proceedings immediately on an amicable basis, to take over the New York Water Service Corporation." Fearon even went so far as to suggest a fair value price; his figure was $6,982,560.

The emerging pattern of negotiations and plans gradually became clear. With the passing of the days the authority grew more and more anxious to get into business. The water service corporation, refusing to invest any money to meet increases in water demand, invited "friendly condemnation" of its properties. Real estate interests were increasingly restive about the hold-up of development in Industrial Park because of the water situation. On top of this, the bond financing limitations of a self-sustaining public benefit corporation such as the water authority were obvious: without an operating plant or customers in hand to underwrite capital indebtedness, the bond purchase market would never accept authority bonds. The drift was unmistakably toward condemnation action.

On June 4, 1953, the Onondaga County Water Authority began a process that was to take well over two and a half years for its completion: it filed an application with the Water Power and Control Commission for permission to begin condemnation proceedings against the New York Water Service Corporation.[14] The WPCC approved the application on the ground that the course proposed was justified by public necessity, and condemnation was on its way.

The events of the next 31 months were interesting in the extreme, but they were not central to the decision to develop a suburban water system. They concerned rather the legal procedure by which a public agency takes over the properties of a private company, in this instance with the complete approval, even the active cooperation, of the company in question, but over the vigorous protest of a second public agency, the State Public Service Commission. Highlights of the period may be summarized thus:

1. An application by the water service corporation for an increase in its allowable withdrawal from Otisco Lake from 16 m.g.d. to 20 m.g.d.[15] The Water Power and Control Commission granted the increase requested.

2. A petition filed by the water authority with the Onondaga County Court on September 28, 1954, stating that the public benefit required condemnation of the properties of the New York Water Service Corporation. The petition recited that "your petitioner has . . . been unable to acquire property and rights [by purchase] . . . for the reason that the owner refuses to sell." The petition also named $8,500,000 as a fair and reasonable price for the properties sought.

3. A finding by the Public Service Commission that the value of those same properties was $3,950,000.

4. The appointment of three appraisal commissioners, who heard evidence in December of 1954. One engineering firm came up with an appraisal of over $12,000,000, another expert thought $8,650,000 equitable. The commissioners recommended to the County Court an award of somewhat more than $9,000,000, and the judge of that court confirmed the report of the commissioners.

5. A motion by the Public Service Commission for "abandonment and discontinuance." Both the water authority and the water service corporation opposed this motion, which was denied by the County Court.

6. An appeal by the Public Service Commission to the New York Supreme Court, which in a 4–1 judgment upheld the commission's claim to status as a party to the proceedings, found the method of evaluation employed by the appraisal commissioners faulty, and remitted the matter to the commissioners for a new appraisal.[16]

7. A temporary but violent protest on the part of several towns, which discovered belatedly that they would lose sizable tax values with the transfer of the private company's properties to the tax-exempt water authority. A proposal to seek legislation removing the tax-exempt status of the authority came to naught through failure to muster sufficient political support.

8. A rehearing before the same three appraisal commissioners, who found cause for a token reduction of $50,000 but placed a value on the properties in question still in excess of $9,000,000.

There the matter came to rest. The water authority again moved for confirmation of the appraisers' findings, and again the Public Service Commission filed a protest. The latter had exhausted its legal recourse, however, and the way was now open for final approval. This was duly given, and on December 31, 1955, the properties of the New York Water Service Corporation passed to the Onondaga County Water Authority.

The water authority finally was in business, and none too soon if the evidence at hand is to be accepted. Real estate developers were loud in their public complaints that suburban growth, residential as well as industrial, was being held up for want of water; and they were joined in their outcry by some public officials. Meantime the city issued a water policy statement calling for the "transfer [of] as many out-of-city customers as possible to the system of the Onondaga County Water Authority." It behooved the latter agency forehandedly to prepare itself for the assumption of heavy responsibilities once the issue of condemnation was settled. This it sought to do by issuing water revenue improvement bonds in the amount of $12,600,000 in contemplation of the successful culmination of the condemnation dispute. How effectively it would in fact meet the growing needs of the metropolitan area remained to be seen.

Broad Metropolitan Action?

With the Otisco Lake system under the control of the Onondaga County Water Authority, a betterment and improvement program began without delay. The completion of a second transmission conduit was the most important single improvement; it permitted the bringing of new water to the areas north of the city, thereby relieving for the moment a serious limitation on real estate development and industrial growth. Within two years after the authority took over, however, water was again singled out as a major community problem. In short, the county gradually drifted into the same position it had occupied in 1950, with one major difference: this time it was a public benefit corporation rather than a private water company that was proving inadequate.

The water authority was in truth on thin ice financially, saved from serious danger only by a substantial increase in water rates in 1957 and new money from bonds in 1958. The limitations inherent in the authority device became increasingly clear to those pondering long-range solutions to the metropolitan water problem. The authority had to depend on the market for capital financing, and expansion plans for revenue income based on a 20- or 30-year growth projection hardly afforded a basis for sound investment by Wall Street standards. Completion of its second conduit meant that within a short time the authority would be drawing its maximum allowable yield from Otisco Lake. The simple fact was that the water authority did not have access to enough water to service its potential future customers. And while it might consider developing a third source of supply, without access to the county tax base it could do little more than make studies and report findings.

For its part, the city could no longer be counted on to alleviate water shortages in suburban areas. On December 28, 1958, the Mayor of Syracuse publicly stated: "I wish to take this opportunity to ask that serious consideration be given to a big problem ahead— a problem which will affect future growth and prosperity of Syracuse and Onondaga County. That problem is the need for an expanding water supply for this city and county." [17] In the early months of 1959 the fixed ceiling on the city's supply was emphasized when nine applications for city water from developments in the Towns of Dewitt and Onondaga were denied by the Water Power and Control Commission. This action had the effect of serving notice that the city's modest cushion was no longer available to meet new non-city demands.

Yet the water needs in the suburban areas continued to grow, and with them agitation for a permanent solution to the problem of supply. In June of 1958 the Manufacturers Association, in its "Profile of Syracuse Business Climate," said pointedly of the water supply: "Needs considerable improvement." Later that year the *Herald-Journal* surveyed the districts to the north and east of the city and reported that $50,000,000 worth of construction was being held up for lack of water. It became increasingly clear that more water must be made available to the suburban areas. The problem was not as simple, however, as it had been ten years earlier. Then it was supposed that a faltering private supply system could be taken over by a public body and made to yield sufficient water; now it was evident that a new source of supply must be developed.

This conclusion did not of course come as a complete surprise. As early as 1954 the Water Power and Control Commission had stated (in its decision to permit the diversion of 20 m.g.d. from Otisco Lake) that investigations should be undertaken and plans prepared for acquiring an additional supply of water from another source. The new water authority itself was not unmindful of the problem. In March of 1959, O'Brien and Gere submitted to the authority a report on developing a fresh supply. Five possible sources were listed: Butternut Creek, Salmon River, Oneida Lake, Seneca River, and Lake Ontario. The report designated Butternut Creek as the "most readily attainable" if the authority should elect to undertake the development independently and solely by revenue bonds, but concluded that there could be successful development of a larger source of supply "only if some form of cooperative action with the City of Syracuse be effected." The critical date set for the need of additional water was "five or six" years from 1959. This report, complete with estimates of cost, revenue, population growth, and future water needs, helped to push water to the forefront again as a continuing community concern.

Two features of the emerging water supply problem suggested the desirability of joint city-county action. First, the development of a new source would require substantial capital outlays, and these might be more readily arranged if the two cooperated. Second, the metropolitan area faced a shortage in the foreseeable future. Recognizing the dual nature of the problem, the Mayor of Syracuse and the Chairman of the Board of Supervisors on August 15, 1959, appointed a Joint City-County Water Committee to examine and make recommendations regarding the whole problem. Alexander F. (Casey) Jones, editor of the *Herald-Journal*, was named chairman of the water committee, which was approved by both the Common Council and the Board of Supervisors. The committee was granted an appropriation of $25,000 to finance its study, the cost to be shared equally by the city and the county. O'Brien and Gere were hired to begin work immediately.

The Joint City-County Water Committee went about its task with vigor, visiting both city and water authority installations, hearing testimony by a number of invited experts, receiving and considering reports (principally but not alone from O'Brien and Gere), and in its turn making a number of interim reports to its principals. The committee early turned to the County Water Districts Law, which had been passed by the legislature in 1953 as Article 5-A of the County Law. This statute was designed to permit cooperative action among city, towns, and county for the provision of water in a metropolitan area. Such cooperation was to be achieved through the medium of a county water district, which was to enjoy the power to levy and collect ad valorem taxes. The plan appeared practicable and the prescribed procedure reasonable, hence the committee determined to avail itself of the device authorized by the act. The measure provided for the creation of a county water agency, which was empowered to make recommendations to the Board of Supervisors concerning the proposed county water district.[18] This stipulation was readily met through the simple transformation of the Joint City-County Water Committee into the Onondaga County Water Agency, a move accomplished by resolution of the Board of Supervisors June 7, 1960.

The early progress reports made by the County Water Agency to the Board of Supervisors suggested the direction of its thinking, although the agency was careful at all times to emphasize that, pending presentation of a final report, its conclusions were to be regarded as tentative. The more significant of its decisions, as they stood at midsummer, may be summarized thus:

1. "A new source of water for Onondaga County must be developed to supplement the Otisco and Skaneateles supplies. If the Syracuse metropolitan area is to continue to grow and prosper, an adequate supply of good water must be available at reasonable rates for industrial, commercial and residential expansion. This water cannot be obtained from the present sources." The best source in the long run, though not the least expensive in terms of early outlay, is Lake Ontario.

2. The most feasible way to develop the fresh source is through creation of a new entity, a county water district. Such a district,

to be coterminous with the county, would have access to the county's tax base through power to issue general obligation bonds.

3. The sole function of the county water district would be to make new water available to the metropolitan area. This it would do by selling water at wholesale rates to the city and the water authority.

4. While some economies might be effected through consolidation of the city and the water authority systems, the difficulties involved in such a move would far outweigh its advantages.

5. The city and the water authority must redefine and expand their water service areas to provide full metropolitan coverage. This is necessary to "facilitate the integration that is essential to sound metropolitan development." [19]

Two features of the County Water Agency and its work, as summarized above, are worthy of emphasis. First, the body identified the impending water shortage as a metropolitan problem, invoking the metropolitan area symbol more than once as it developed its case. Second, though created as a joint city-county instrumentality, it came quickly to the conclusion that the hope of solution of the water problem resided with the county and rested its case on that conviction. However sound this conclusion, the repeated emphasis on the county's stake in the matter raised the specter of urban dissidence, concerning which public muttering began to be heard.

The problems which lie between recommendation and consummation of a county water district are many, but two stand out. The first is economic; it concerns the manner of financing the district's capital installations. Note has been made that the water district would have the power to issue county general obligation bonds, but how should the bonds be supported? The law makes provision (Sec. 270) for a system of differentiated taxes based on benefits received. The County Water Agency is wrestling with this problem (and with the attendant issue of water rates), which it has found to be extremely complicated. Meanwhile a collateral issue, once buried (though perhaps buried alive), threatens to become active again. A city Republican supervisor raised it in these words: "I think the city helping the county to get the water it needs is a magnanimous act, but one magnanimous act deserves another. I want to know why we can't have a county sales tax." The Republican majority leader on the board quickly dismissed this comment by labeling the sales tax a separate issue. But it was not to be pushed aside so easily. The *Post-Standard* subsequently observed that "Creation of the new agency was approved despite a warning the new water project the body will probably undertake will require enactment of a county-wide sales tax."[20] It is altogether likely that the County Water Agency would prefer not to have the issues of metropolitan water supply and county sales tax "confused," but it may prove impossible to bring about consideration of the one without opening the door to reconsideration of the other.

The second major problem is political (as, indeed, is the problem of financing in an important sense); in minimum terms, it concerns the matter of mustering the support necessary to procure adoption of the county water district plan. Two principal considerations are relevant to this issue. First, mention has been made of the threat of urban dissidence. A not inconsiderable element argues that the city has enough water in surplus to supply its needs for decades, in view of its relatively stable population and in view further of its loss of industry to the non-city districts. To those of this persuasion the prospective water shortage is a county, or at any rate a non-city, problem. Second, large areas outside the city, including most of the more rural towns and a number of villages, do not feel the need for additional water and in some cases will not for many years to come. These can hardly be expected to be enthusiastic about a county water district, which seems to promise the areas in good supply little more than new taxes.

The legal procedures required set up an additional hurdle. The County Water Districts Law provides (in Sec. 257) for a public referendum on a county water district proposal on request of not less than 100 property owners; and this forces the Board of Supervisors to share responsibility for the final decision with the voters. For there can be little doubt that a request for a referendum will be forthcoming if the time comes for such action. Adoption by the Board of Supervisors and approval by the people could turn out to be two quite different things. Indeed the very threat of a popular vote might be expected to have a sobering effect on the board.

The provision of an adequate water supply is generally recognized as basic to the sound growth of a metropolitan community. Prior to 1950, the city acted with considerable success to alleviate the problem by a series of *ad hoc* extensions of service; but the time came when, because of the diminishing gap between growing need and fixed supply, continuation of this policy became risky. The Onondaga County Water Authority then took over prime responsibility for servicing new demands outside the city; but it, too, soon came to feel the pinch of a limited supply. The fundamental problem as it is currently identified is that of developing a new source of water supply. This is regarded as a matter primarily for county initiative, although the feeling is general that the problem cannot be solved without a generous measure of cooperation on the part of the city. Cooperation between the city and the county comes more easily when tax rates are not affected; nevertheless urban support for the county water district proposal may be expected in the end, if only because the city has a heavy investment in the well-being of the metropolitan area. The final decision regarding an expanded water supply, however, does not rest with the governing bodies of the city and the county, as have other metropolitan decisions in years past, but with the electorate. And capital indebtedness and tax increases for public works have never been popular with the voters of Onondaga County.

VI

Health and Welfare: Four Case Studies

THE brief cases to be examined here concern four efforts to move fragmented local services into the orbit of the county's government, or to place new ones there. Three were successful, one was not. Two involved public health and public welfare, familiar actors on the metropolitan stage; two had to do with mental health and a court for children, less well known as subjects of metropolitan action. Although the cases cover a period of more than 20 years, they are mutually interrelated in a variety of ways. Taken together, they provide material for useful hypotheses about metropolitan decision-making in the field of health and welfare.

The Children's Court

One of the earliest and most often cited examples of metropolitan action in Onondaga County centers on the creation of the county Children's Court in 1936. Although its name rightly implies a judicial function, the court serves a much broader purpose. It employs a large

---
Harold Herman prepared this chapter.

staff of counsellors and probation officers whose task is to aid children before it becomes necessary to bring them into court. In 1947, when State Youth Commission funds became available for child guidance centers, Onondaga County's center was attached administratively to its Children's Court.

The movement for a county-wide court was motivated by the desire to extend the non-judicial services of such a body to all the children of the county. Syracuse had long had a probation office attached to the Children's Division of its Court of Special Sessions. Judge Leo Yehle heard juvenile cases several days each week and devoted much of his time, both on and off the bench, to work with children. County Judge Barnum received additional compensation for hearing children's cases one day each week in the County Court, and in some instances children were brought before justices of the peace. Outside the city, however, probation and guidance services were not available.

Although the state had authorized the creation of county children's courts by general legislation in 1922, for some years Onondaga County had showed little interest in invoking this law. But in 1931 Richard Greene came to Syracuse to head its probation office. His experience with children's courts in other parts of the country had included close association with interested citizens' groups working actively with court officials. With Judge Yehle's concurrence, the probation chief set out to stimulate the organization of such a group in Syracuse. His opportunity came in 1934, when the League of Women Voters chose child welfare services as the topic for its major annual study. The league's study committee formed the nucleus of a group of citizens who in 1935 organized into the Children's Court Case Study Committee. The members of this committee dedicated themselves to supporting the activities of the Children's Division and to reviewing cases and adding their collective and individual efforts to its rehabilitation program.[1]

The immediate result of the league's study was to focus attention on the delinquency problem in Onondaga County and on the inadequacy of local resources. Not that Onondaga County was a hotbed of delinquency. There had been a slight increase in incidents and cases reported during the early years of the depression, but the juvenile delinquency problem of Syracuse and Onondaga County was still relatively mild when compared with those of other large urban areas in the state. Nevertheless, it was feared that unless adequate rehabilitation services were provided, the increasing numbers of children involved in reportable cases would become habitual offenders and so pose a greater problem of adult crime in future years. And existing governmental and private resources both were found to be insufficient. In fact, two private activities that had been of considerable help to the city, the Big Brother and Big Sister programs, had recently been discontinued.

It was perhaps inevitable that comparisons of the number of cases in Onondaga and other counties should invite discussion of the merits of their respective organizations for the prevention and treatment of juvenile delinquency. The league study group and the citizens' committee became convinced that Onondaga County needed a children's court. To promote their aim and to stimulate general community support, they sought the endorsement of the community chest and council and its affiliated social and welfare agencies. Their cause was greatly aided by a series of feature newspaper articles and by the editorial support of the *Syracuse Post-Standard*. By early 1935 the campaign had succeeded in generating the interest and support of large numbers of individuals and groups in the county. The time therefore seemed ripe for proposing governmental action. The court officials who had been largely responsible for the direction which the league's study and its subsequent activities had taken now stepped into the background, confident that the citizens' committee and its organized supporters could elicit the political support necessary to attain their objectives.

The political phase of the children's court campaign found support at the top of the political hierarchy. No attempt was made to "sell" individual members of the Board of Supervisors; instead, the chairmen of the citizens' committee and the community chest and council went directly to Clarence King, Republican County Chairman, seeking to enlist his support in the creation of a county children's court. King was a senior partner in the Syracuse law firm of Bond, Schoeneck, and King. During his lengthy term as county chairman, he had gained recognition for his ability to placate both city and town interests. King's rule was characterized by persuasion rather than force. It was known nevertheless that he had at his command the full resources of the highly organized Republican Party, and that he could and would use them in case of need.

King reportedly was sympathetic to the court plan, but there were factors that dampened his enthusiasm. Alerted by the newspaper publicity generated by the league's study, several supervisors had already informed him of their opposition to any new county expenditures. Furthermore, King was hesitant to adopt a course that would result in cutting off Judge Barnum's extra compensation. Since that official was expected to retire at the end of the following year, King told the court's supporters that the issue could not be presented to the Board of Supervisors until 1936. He did promise that he would use his influence at that time to have the proposal enacted.

True to his word, King initiated action early in 1936. In caucus with Republican supervisors, however, he met with considerable rural opposition. Town supervisors contended that delinquency was a city rather than a county problem, and that the entire proposal was designed to foist the financial burden of a city problem on to the townspeople. The town supervisors were joined by some city members, including the board's chairman, in resisting new expenditures, if only moderate ones, at a time when economic conditions necessitated governmental retrenchment. Under pressure from civic groups, King continued to press the Board of Supervisors. He was able to gain their approval in the end by suggesting a reduced salary for the new judge. The general enabling law stipulated that a children's court judge was to receive the same compensation as a county court judge, at this time $12,000 a year. To circumvent this requirement, King proposed that the court be created by a special act of the state legislature. Pursuant to this arrangement, Senator Fearon introduced a bill in the legislature creating a children's court and authorizing a $6,000 salary for its presiding judge.[2]

Local social and welfare groups were incensed at the salary called for in the bill. The citizens' committee regarded it as an attempt to undermine the purposes of the court by using the position as a mere source of patronage. It was no secret that local organizations hoped and expected that Judge Yehle would be transferred from the Court of Special Sessions to the proposed children's court; but Judge Yehle had already told Clarence King that he would not consider a change in post unless the new salary at least matched his current one, which was $10,000 a year.

Resolutions and letters of protest condemning the bill poured into the offices of Fearon and King. In self defense, the Senator called upon the Board of Supervisors to advise the legislature of the amount it wished to allocate to the position. While King worked behind the scenes to achieve a new compromise, the Board of Supervisors refused to assume any responsibility for the state's action. Under constitutional provisions then in effect, the legislature was not required to request advice from counties to be affected by special legislation. The supervisors insisted that the salary was a matter for state determination and declined to interfere in the state's legislative process. But Senator Fearon was equally unwilling to bear responsibility for the evidently unpopular salary provision. With the legislative session drawing to a close, he amended his original bill to leave the determination of salary to the Board of Supervisors.[3] The issue had come home to roost.

Four groups with varying interests and concerns sought to influence the decision. First were the court's active proponents, who, scenting victory, had by now reduced the issue to a choice between Judge Yehle and, as they put it, a political hack. A hard core of rural supervisors adamantly opposed to the creation of the court constituted a second pressure group. A third comprised a mixed group of town and city supervisors who ostensibly were not against the court but who were in favor of keeping its costs to a minimum. A fourth and new source of pressure came from several Republican lawyers who had not advanced far enough within the party organization to be considered for a well-paying judgeship but who might hope for appointment to a lesser position. One such was reported to have remarked that he would accept the job for $3,000. His statement did much to strengthen the determination of the advocates of a $10,000 salary.

The Board of Supervisors met to organize the court in special meetings on March 26 and 30, 1936. The meetings were highlighted by the largest public attendance many supervisors could remember. A parade of speakers from a number of organizations was introduced by the chairwoman of the community chest's welfare council. All supported the court and asked that a $10,000 salary be set. The board, however, was not considering salary at these meetings. Several supervisors had tried to inject the issue into their pre-meeting caucus, but had been cut short by Chairman King. The question was on creation of the court. With eight members absent and three abstaining, the board on March 30 established a county children's court by a vote of 26 to 1.

Two months later, a town supervisor introduced a compromise resolution calling for a salary of $7,500. It was tabled for two weeks' consideration. On June 18, the resolution and a proposed amendment increasing the salary to $10,000 were both put to a vote. Neither could secure the 20 affirmative votes needed for passage, failing by votes of 19 to 17 and 18 to 18 respectively. On July 7 the Board met once more to consider the question of salary. On the previous night Clarence King had confidently announced that the community's wishes would be respected. The $10,000 salary was approved by a vote recorded as 21 to 0. Among the 21 affirmative votes were those of four city Democrats, 14 city Republicans, and the Republican supervisors of Dewitt, Manlius, and Pompey. The vote therefore divided essentially along urban and non-urban lines, although the city Republican serving as chairman of the board did not vote. The bulk of the town supervisors likewise abstained, to allow the implementation of a new county function by what was in effect the vote of the city supervisors. Party discipline on the issue was not without flaw, but it proved adequate to the need. To conclude the account, it may be noted that in due course the children's court was established with Judge Yehle at its head.

Public Welfare

Clarence King was one of the more powerful leaders in a long line of strong Republican county chairmen. Next in succession was Rolland Marvin, whose methods contrasted sharply with those of King. Where King used persuasion and always gave the impression of considering all elements of his party, Marvin deferred to none, least of all to town supervisors. He was aggressive, self-assured, and blunt. Syracuse, the city that continued to turn out Republican majorities throughout the depression and the Roosevelt years, was Marvin's source of strength. He used it to rule the county organization with a firm hand.

Rollie Marvin was Mayor of Syracuse from 1930 to 1942. From 1937 to 1945 he was also county chairman, a position he assumed upon Clarence King's voluntary retirement. From his dual position Marvin effected a number of significant changes in city and county government, including the far-reaching welfare consolidation to be examined here. In the process, he discarded any pretense of using the party's legislative caucus as a means of evolving agreement, employing it instead as a vehicle for transmitting predetermined party policy to the legislators.

The Onondaga County Welfare Department was created in November 1938. It assumed responsibility for all the home relief programs previously conducted by the county's local governments. In recent years, the department has come close to exemplifying the organizational ideal of welfare administration—a single county agency administering all the diverse components of a complete public welfare program. The single agency ideal has yet to be achieved in full, but the 1938 action took a long step toward area integration. It set the pattern of county-wide sharing in the financing of relief payments.

Although the single-agency and shared-responsibility concepts have been essential features of the welfare policies of both New York State and the national government, and although the requirements conditioning participation in state and national welfare programs have had considerable impact upon local welfare administration, consolidation in Onondaga County was largely a product of local factors. For if the local action was made possible through permissive features of state and national legislation, nevertheless it represented a local solution to fiscal problems which, while not peculiar to Syracuse, had little to do with ideal methods of welfare administration or with state and national policies.

In 1929 the state of New York had replaced the State Charities

Law with the Public Welfare Law. The latter marked a reorientation of the state program which made it as different from its predecessor as the titles of the old and new law connoted. The new law divided the state into city and county welfare districts. The 57 upstate counties and the five cities of New York, Kingston, Newburgh, Owego, and Poughkeepsie were each designated public welfare districts. The city districts were independent of their counties for welfare purposes. Within county public welfare districts, program responsibility was divided among the county, town, and city governments. Special legislation still in force permitted several variations in the basic pattern, but essentially towns and cities were responsible only for home relief and medical care of individuals residing in their jurisdictions; cities had the additional option of administering their own old age assistance programs; and the county was responsible for all other programs, including home relief and medical care for county residents outside town or cities. County boards of supervisors were permitted to distinguish between "county poor" and "town and city poor." That is, a board could consider recipients of some county programs as a charge either upon the county or upon the town or city of residence. Through a charge back system, the county could require communities to reimburse it for its expenditures. If the county elected to make all its programs in the aggregate a general county charge, it could then assume responsibility for all welfare administration, abolishing city and town welfare departments.

In the early 1930's welfare administration in Onondaga County was the responsibility of 19 town welfare officers dispensing home relief and assistance for medical care; the Syracuse Welfare Department, conducting home relief, medical care, and old age assistance programs in the city; and an elected County Welfare Commissioner and several independent county boards directing a number of categorical programs, some of which were financed through charges back. In addition, the city and the county had both created emergency work bureaus in compliance with the state's Temporary Emergency Relief Act. The profusion of independent organizations and programs resulted in jurisdictional conflicts, varying administrative costs, complex intergovernmental financial arrangements, and serious discrepancies in the benefits provided by the several jurisdictions.

The depression caused fiscal difficulties for all local governments in Onondaga County, as it did for governments all over the country. Syracuse and the older industrial towns of Geddes and Salina were particularly hard hit. In addition to financing its own programs, the city at this time supplied approximately 80 per cent of the county's real property tax base. Because of the overlapping in welfare programs, Syracuse found itself the major supporter of a number of county activities that were not financed by charges back to the communities in which recipients resided but which operated predominantly, if not exclusively, for non-city residents. The work relief programs were a particular source of irritation to the city. Although the state contributed about 40 per cent of its total cost, the remainder of the county's work relief program was financed by a general county tax. The county emergency work bureau, however, employed only non-city residents. To offset this apparent inequity, the state had provided higher reimbursements for the city's work relief program and had conducted several wholly state-financed projects within the city. But these were hardly enough to employ the thousands of city workers on home relief.

Welfare administration became a tactical exercise in categorical classification. A successful welfare administrator was one who could manipulate his indigents into categories for which the state or another municipality was responsible. A common practice when marginal families moved into a town was for the supervisor to pay them a visit toward the end of their first year's residence and present a "welcoming gift" of food or clothing from the town. If the family applied for relief during the next year, the town could legally disclaim responsibility for support, since the family had not fulfilled the requirement of town settlement—a year's residence without receiving aid.

The Syracuse–Onondaga County system of welfare administration first became the object of serious attention with the completion in 1933 of a welfare study by the Syracuse Research Committee.[4] The resulting report was concerned primarily with the disparity in benefits provided by the many local units and agencies, and with their administrative efficiency. It recommended the consolidation of all welfare activities in a county department of public welfare. The report was taken up at a number of club meetings, but failed to excite any general interest. It was not noted in the newspapers, nor was it seriously considered by political leaders at the time. As an effort to provoke public discussion of welfare problems, the report achieved very limited success.

Five years later the whole subject of welfare administration broke into the open, so far as the public knew with little prior consideration. Mayor Marvin had been plagued by the problem, and more especially by welfare costs, since his first election in 1930. The city financed its welfare program through short-term borrowing, as did most of the towns. The city was rapidly approaching its debt limit, while the county had very little outstanding debt. The Mayor conceived the plan of transferring welfare responsibilities to the county, partially as a device for reducing city expenditures but also, and particularly, as a method of relieving the city's debt burden. Without fanfare, indeed in what the newspapers described as a surprise move, he caused two resolutions to be presented to the Board of Supervisors. The first proposed to make all welfare costs a general charge on the county government, the second to create a county welfare department to administer the programs then conducted by the Syracuse Welfare Department, a number of county agencies, and the town welfare officers.

The Mayor's move may have come as a surprise to the public, and even to the papers, but it was not made without careful preparation. His plan had the tacit approval of the city's leading bankers, who, while they did not become openly involved, viewed it with favor as a means of improving the city's general financial condition. The 19 supervisors from the city were easily persuaded to support the proposal, as were the members of the Common Council, which later would have to adopt similar resolutions to complete consolidation. Several supervisors from towns adjacent to the city also were favorably disposed, since the plan promised to enable them to shift to the county their relatively heavy welfare burdens.

The strongest opposition came from the towns with the lowest welfare costs. The town welfare officers, as could have been foretold, were overwhelmingly opposed to the plan. The County Welfare Commissioner and his staff were not happy at the prospect of being engulfed in an enlarged department dominated by former city personnel, particularly since the commissioner was slated to become deputy to the then city commissioner, who was to be named director of the new department. Whatever the reaction of the welfare employees, city and county, they remained silent. The city employees had recently completed the transition to civil service status, and the county employees were scheduled to follow in 1938. But civil service or no, they were for the most part Republicans; and Rollie Marvin was not only Mayor of Syracuse but also Republican county chairman.

The two resolutions came before the Board of Supervisors for action on June 6, 1938. They were handled as purely routine matters. The incipient resistance in the board had been taken care of in caucus. There had been no public discussion, nor had the civic and social welfare organizations of the community been consulted about the proposal. As the former Mayor puts it today, "I never needed a citizens' committee to tell me what to do." The vote in the board was 22 for, 12 against.

Public Health

In contrast to the speed and secrecy with which welfare administration was consolidated, the question of forming an Onondaga County health department has been publicly debated throughout the past 30 years. The dispute has involved many of the same organizations that participated in the creation of the Children's Court. In many respects, the proposal concerning health and that concerning welfare were strikingly similar; but town opposition, thwarted in its efforts to block welfare integration, has been able repeatedly to ward off the consolidation of health activities.

Onondaga County receives public health services through a system of administration developed largely in the last century. The 35 municipal subdivisions of the county are organized into 33 local health jurisdictions. Every city, town, and village constitutes a health district with its own health board and health officer, except for the Villages and Towns of Fabius and Tully, which have merged into two consolidated health districts. Several town and village boards employ the same health officer. In addition to the local districts, the State Health Department district office provides some direct services to non-city areas, and the county government supports a corps of public health nurses who operate exclusively outside of Syracuse.[5] This arrangement has been under attack by the State Health Department and several private organizations for a number of years. The State Health Department, reflecting a nation-wide movement for larger units of health administration begun in the 1920's, is now committed to promoting local reorganization on a county-wide basis.

In 1923 the City of Syracuse and Cattaraugus County were named recipients of health demonstration grants from the Milbank Memorial Fund. Both grants were administered by the State Charities Aid Association. Their purposes were to demonstrate the results that could be obtained from a well financed, well staffed municipal department in the one case and the advantages of a county department for the administration of rural areas in the other.[6] Both demonstrations were judged to be highly successful. The Cattaraugus experience led to the initiation of a series of state grants-in-aid acts to stimulate formation of county health departments. In 1930, the grants were extended to urban as well as rural counties. The success of the Syracuse demonstration stimulated a continued high level of local support for the city's public health program. By 1930 the city was rated as one of the nation's better communities in terms of a number of public health indices.[7] By this time, however, some of the problems occasioned by county decentralization were already becoming evident.

Administrative difficulties as well as humanitarian principles prohibited the Syracuse Health Department from following the law strictly by limiting its services to city residents alone. County residents increasingly came to depend upon the city's clinic and laboratory facilities. A contract with the county provided reimbursement for laboratory services; but it failed to cover fully the cost of these services, let alone the cost of others for which no payment was made. Moreover, the increasing cost of the county nursing program was supported from general county revenues despite the city's exclusion from the service. These two factors—the obvious inequalities in favor of non-city areas in the financing of the several programs and the availability of the city's facilities to non-city residents—nullified what otherwise might have been a potent argument for creation of a county department, namely the need for additional public health facilities in suburban areas.

The financial considerations that motivated Mayor Marvin to consolidate welfare activities were generally applicable also to health services. In one respect, there were even more compelling reasons for health than for welfare consolidation, since the city was not eligible for the 50 per cent reimbursement available to a county health department through the grant-in-aid program. There was, however, one significant difference: while the Mayor held the initiative on the welfare proposal, the impetus for a county health department came from state and private sources. The difference in tactics with respect to the two proposals was dramatic; for whereas Mayor Marvin nursed the welfare consolidation plan along virtually without public notice, the advocates of health administration reform made open declaration of their intention. The resulting publicity aroused immediate and vigorous opposition. Marvin did not care to test his strength on both fronts at the same time and chose to concentrate on the welfare issue, where he could operate with minimum interference from state officials and local volunteer agencies. His choice also reflected the much greater sums expended for welfare than for health.

A movement in support of reorganization of health services nevertheless gradually assumed form. From 1930 to 1938 a number of individuals and organizations added their voices to the State Health Department's suggestion that the county create a health department and absorb the city's health activities. A study of the considerations involved in establishing such a department was prepared by the research adviser to the Syracuse Research Committee in behalf of the Technology Club, an organization dedicated to the advancement of social and political life through application thereto of scientific principles.[8] The League of Women Voters supported the proposal, as did the Syracuse Chamber of Commerce. Spurred on by the State Health Department, the Onondaga Health Association and the Council of

Social Agencies conducted a continuing public information campaign in advocacy of a county department.

The major newspapers supported the proposal, but several village and rural weeklies were vigorous in their opposition. Their position generally reflected the rural tendency to minimize the need for a county agency and to view the proposal as an attempt to substitute state for local control. Prominent also was a native hesitancy to incur increased expenditures despite the state's assurance that grants-in-aid would absorb much of the additional cost.

The resulting urban-rural division led to a political stalemate which gradually hardened into a habit of thought and action. The equilibrium occasionally was threatened, but only briefly, by a resolution passed by some organization or by the local appearance of a State Health Department official. The Board of Supervisors, reflecting public sentiment, squared off about half-and-half on the issue. It was quite apparent that a dramatic event would be necessary to break the deadlock. Unfortunately the most dramatic occurrence of the period solidified rather than dissolved the spirit of mutual defiance. It might have been hoped that the welfare consolidation of 1938 would point the way to a solution of the health impasse. Far from providing a guide for further action, however, that event served only to stiffen the opposition; for when the rural folk saw "what Mayor Marvin had done to them" in the welfare merger, they resisted a like move in health more bitterly than ever. To this day resentment of the manner in which welfare reform was effected and of its increased costs (real or imagined) to the rural sections continues to plague those who favor creation of a county health department.

The issue of health reform was laid aside during the war years in favor of attention to more pressing matters. At the end of the war, however, the question was revived again, this time by the *Post-War Report,* which contained a strong recommendation for a county health department. At the same time the State Health Department reemphasized its policy of favoring county departments by making grants to such departments even more attractive than before. And for the first time, grants were made available also to city departments. Although this assistance relieved Syracuse of some of its financial motivation for support of consolidation, city health officials continued to favor integration of health services in a county department for professional reasons. For the most part, their position was supported by the city's political leaders.

Further in support of its policy, the State Health Department adopted a uniform procedure for stimulating local action. Boards of supervisors were urged to request the department to conduct health surveys of their counties. In each of the more than 20 surveys conducted between 1947 and 1950, the department's findings called for a county health department. A county requesting a survey therefore could generally foretell its conclusion. In Onondaga County, a movement for a survey was launched in May of 1948. The State Health Department's local representatives organized a local "strategy" committee composed of the regional and district health officers, the Dean of Syracuse University Medical College, the Health Commissioner of the City of Syracuse, the Chairman of the County Medical Society's Public Health Committee, and the Executive Secretary of the Onondaga County Health Association. The Health Association undertook a vigorous educational campaign, in which it was joined by the Council of Social Agencies.

Numerous conferences with members of the Board of Supervisors led to the introduction of a resolution on June 7, 1948, calling for a health survey. The resolution was supported by testimonials from the Health Association, the Council of Social Agencies, the League of Women Voters, the Technology Club, and the medical and dental societies. In view of the anticipated results of the survey, the Medical Society's position at this time almost constituted support of a county department. The Board of Supervisors directed its public health committee to consider the resolution. The committee submitted a report which reflected the party's inability to resolve urban-rural differences. It failed to propose a recommendation, suggesting instead that each supervisor "vote his conscience." On August 4, 1948, the consciences of all the city supervisors, supported by those of three town colleagues, joined to produce a resolution requesting a state survey by a vote of 22 to 14.

During the course of the survey local civic organizations, with the support of the State Health Department, conducted an active promotional campaign. Volunteer workers found, however, that many organizations, looking ahead to the conclusion of the survey, considered the county health department a topic too controversial for discussion. The Health Association tried especially to reach rural residents through the Grange, but that body would not endorse a proposal that promised to strengthen county government.

Within the Medical Society, a group of town physicians and health officers organized to combat efforts to "superimpose a county health department upon them." The society at this time was in the midst of a campaign against President Truman's plan to "socialize medicine," and there is some indication that the two issues were partially fused in the minds of some doctors. In any event, the town group succeeded in preventing the society from supporting the proposal. Although it never formally opposed the proposal, the Medical Society's failure to provide positive support was cited by several supervisors as justification for their own negative reaction to a county health department.

The town physicians were also successful in organizing opposition among townspeople and town supervisors. The plan's opponents repeated arguments heard in the 1930's, which emphasized (1) adequacy of existing facilities, (2) fear of centralization (bolstered by the welfare experience), and (3) excessive costs (strengthened by suspicions that the city was trying to push its costs off on the towns, as it was alleged to have done with welfare).

In an attempt to ward off open conflict within the party, several Republican supervisors persuaded their state senator to introduce an amendment to the Public Health Law to permit voluntary participation in a part-county health department. Existing legislation provided for either a part-county department exclusive of cities of over 50,000 population, or a county department including such cities upon their approval. The amendment approved by the legislature provided for a part-county department consisting only of those jurisdictions electing to join.[9] If any suburban towns should feel the need for more public health facilities, they would thus be able to join together or to cooperate with the city without committing the rural towns to a county health department. The State Health Department opposed the amendment. It would not consent to a plan that threatened further to fragment an already complex system of local organization.[10] The department's vigorous opposition caused the Governor to veto the measure.

Foiled in their attempt to develop an acceptable compromise plan, the town leaders fell back to a prepared defense position which called for resistance to the findings and recommendations of the survey. The survey report, as expected, proposed the creation of a county health department "to serve the metropolitan needs of Onondaga County." [11] The report was in fact greeted with widespread indifference, perhaps because its conclusion had been anticipated and argued out in the months and years preceding. In any event, the burden rested on the proponents, who proved unable to mount an effective campaign. The fate of the proposal may have been already decided when the State Commissioner of Health spoke in its behalf on March 24, 1950. Newspaper reports of his address were unfavorable, and a meeting sponsored by the Medical Society for a second talk provided a disappointingly small audience. The Board of Supervisors found it unnecessary to take action and the issue subsided. Because of a shortage of competent physicians aggravated by the outbreak of hostilities in Korea and of local resistance, the State Health Department advised local agencies to discontinue active promotion of the proposal for five years. It was hoped that by that time some of the leading opponents would no longer be practicing in the county, and that experience with a system of deputizing local health officials as assistants to the county health commissioner being developed in Erie County would help to soften the resistance of local health officers.

The initiative in reopening the health issue was taken by the Medical Society in 1954. The district office of the State Health Department had been expanding its local activities in environmental sanitation and subdivision control. Local medical and political leaders, somewhat resentful of the state's "intervention," were concerned with the state agency's relationships to local jurisdictions. In a resolution of October 5, 1954, the Medical Society called upon the Board of Supervisors "to work out a solution of public health problems," adding that it did not feel that an all-county health unit was the correct solution at that time.

The Medical Society's action was stimulated by the town health officer who had led the rural opposition to the county department proposal. In retrospect, his move proved to be an excellent counteroffensive. The Board of Supervisors responded by directing the County Department of Research and Development to study the county's public health needs. The department began its study in 1955, and shortly presented an objective report describing existing health facilities and the proposals for change that had been considered but containing no recommendations. The reactivation of health issues at this time served chiefly to revive and solidify opposition to the county department proposal. When local organizations considered renewing their promotional efforts, they encountered many of the older hostile local health officers and several new opponents who had been realerted to the reported dangers of centralization by the current discussion. The State Health Department was engaged in staff changes both in Albany and in Syracuse, and in view of its preoccupation again suggested deferring the campaign.

In 1958 the State Health Department advised the Onondaga County Health Association to renew its activities. A committee was formed to develop new estimates of the costs and benefits of a county health department, and to secure the Medical Society's support of the plan. The committee disbanded the following year. It had not received a statement of support from the Medical Society, and the new district health officer, who had agreed to prepare the report of estimated costs and benefits, had resigned before that task was completed.

In 1959 a Metropolitan Health Council was formed to coordinate the activities of the 28 private health organizations in Onondaga County. The council's first president was a former president of the Onondaga Health Association. One of his first acts was to ask the association to allow the new council to assume leadership of the promotional campaign for a county health department. The association readily assented, feeling that it had irritated many political leaders and that the new organization might be able more effectively to marshal support for the proposal. In mid-1960 the council was having difficulty in perfecting its organization, and indeed appeared to be on the verge of dissolution.

Most observers believe that a county health department is inevitable. Some feel that resistance by local health officers is lessening and that many town residents are now convinced of the need for more effective coordination of public health services. Even if these sources of opposition were won over, however, the Board of Supervisors probably would be slow to adopt the proposal. That body is reluctant to expand county activities, fearing that new programs might require the county to adopt a sales tax. This is an eventuality it is committed to avoid at any cost.

Mental Health

On July 5, 1955, at almost the same time that the public health issue received its last serious consideration, the Board of Supervisors unanimously resolved to create the Onondaga County Mental Health Board and authorized it to formulate a long-range county mental health program. There were certain obvious reasons for the board's approval of one program and its rejection of the other. Nevertheless, many of the promoters of a county health department who also participated in the events leading to the formation of the mental health board are still slightly puzzled by the relative ease with which the latter gained public and political acceptance.

The proposal to establish an integrated county mental health program had its roots in a number of independent actions taken by the state government and local private organizations. Prior to 1955 mental health programs in the county were conducted by a number of public and private agencies. Excluding state and federal hospitals, mental health services were furnished by four agencies: the Bishop Foery Clinic, supported by St. Joseph's Hospital and state mental health grants; the Syracuse Dispensary Alcoholic Clinic, supported by state, private, and Community Chest funds; the Syracuse Board of Education, which provided a combination of medical and nonmedical school-home services to children; and the Child Guidance Center, a branch of the Children's Court since 1947, which received 50 per cent of its funds from the State Youth Commission and the remainder from the county.

The community obviously needed additional adult services. The Foery clinic and the dispensary clinic were limited in their capacity to provide service and were forced to concentrate on those most in need of help and least able to afford it. Services for children were similarly limited. The Child Guidance Center provided county-wide coverage, but had a long waiting list and treated only obviously and seriously disturbed children. Within the city, the school programs operated only part time.

In 1953 the psychiatry department of the Medical College approached the Council of Social Agencies and the Onondaga Health Association with a proposal to staff a new adult psychiatric clinic. The proposal promised to provide a needed community facility while expanding the college's teaching program. It was favorably received, and a planning committee was appointed consisting of representatives of a number of interested organizations. The council and the health association sounded out their memberships, and also community leaders who were not affiliated with their organizations as well. Their report to the planning committee was favorable: the community need was generally recognized, and influential citizens could be counted upon to support the new facility through existing community organizations. Accordingly, plans were developed for creating the new clinic and attaching it to the Syracuse Dispensary Alcoholic Clinic. It would receive funds from the Community Chest, the Onondaga Health Association, and the State Mental Health Commission, if the impending reorganization of that agency's program permitted.

The clinic was scheduled to begin operations in the summer of 1954, but its inauguration was postponed. The psychiatry department meanwhile had undertaken to provide medical staff for the Syracuse Veterans' Hospital and found itself unable to take on further commitments. The possibility of the passage of a mental health services act by the state legislature also contributed to the delay.

Although the Medical College's proposal was eventually dropped in favor of county action, it served to alert the community to a medical need and to mobilize support for a community facility before the matter became a political issue. The Board of Supervisors could charge that the county health department proposal represented a scheme by the State Health Department and other organizations to saddle local government with an added burden; but when the board took mental health under consideration it found substantial community sentiment in favor of a new program—sentiment, moreover, that had already manifested itself in support of a private program. This impressed the political leaders as a fact of considerable significance. So also, it may be supposed, did the further fact that in the mental health field no violent opposition to a county program appeared.

Consideration of a mental health program by the Board of Supervisors was necessitated by the Community Mental Health Services Act, passed by the state legislature in February of 1955. The act created a formalized means of channeling state funds into local mental health services. It authorized the appointment of county, part-county, and city mental health boards, which were to integrate and provide leadership for community mental health programs. Their programs would be eligible for 50 per cent reimbursement by the state. To be eligible for state aid, however, the boards were expected substantially to increase services beyond those that existed before their appointment. Although the program was permissive, it contained one feature that virtually required some form of action in Onondaga County. Funds previously distributed by the State Youth Commission to Child Guidance Centers were now to be handled through the mental health program. The county stood to lose more than $18,-000 annually in state aid if it took no action. In addition, although the Bishop Foery and the Syracuse Dispensary Alcoholic Clinics would probably continue to receive aid in one form or another, the initiation of a new adult psychiatric clinic was tied to eligibility for state aid through mental health boards.

On passage of the act the State Mental Health Commission began an intensive educational campaign, utilizing its own resources and those of local volunteer agencies. Locally, the campaign centered almost at once upon formulating a county program. The city's Health Department was hard pressed for funds and had no desire to undertake a new program. Mayor Mead, who had recently successfully completed negotiations for the Metropolitan Sewage Treatment Plant, let it be known that he favored an expanded county program. The issue therefore came quickly before the Board of Supervisors.

Thomas Dyer, chairman of the board, took an active interest in the proposal and appointed a committee to review the effect of the state act upon Onondaga County and to consider the possibility of forming a county mental health board. Several members of the committee, including its chairman, had served on the public health study committee in 1948. This time there was no suggestion that "each supervisor vote his own conscience." Dyer and the chairman of the committee, Supervisor Ladd of Cicero, appeared at meetings and on radio and television broadcasts sponsored by volunteer agencies and spoke enthusiastically of the benefits to be derived from a county program. Ladd and Dyer worked closely with the committee, and conferred with the County Department of Research and Development in the preparation of a staff report to the committee. That report strongly urged appointment of a county board.[12] By spring it appeared that the proposal would have no difficulty in passing the Board of Supervisors.

During the committee's deliberations, the volunteer agencies canvassed many of the same people as in the earlier public health campaign. Volunteer workers reported little community understanding of the nature of a mental health program. More important, however, there was little prejudgment of or organized opposition to a county program, whose way was smoothed by the support of the county medical society. Lacking the preconditioning of an aggressive opposition, such as that supplied before by town health officers, people were receptive to reasoning showing the necessity for mental health activities. Volunteers reported that the discussions of mental health generated an interest that was absent in the presentation of mortality and morbidity statistics.

Town supervisors were similarly receptive. Some had financial reservations about undertaking new programs but financial considerations were not decisive, for the cost to the county was expected to be relatively small. State aid and private contributions would bear most of the cost of a new adult clinic and expansion of existing clinics. In all, the estimated cost to the county would be about $14,000 more than was already being spent for the Child Guidance Center.

Although he anticipated no substantial opposition in the Board of Supervisors, Chairman Dyer suggested that the volunteer agencies appear in force at the public hearing called on the mental health proposal. More than 150 agency representatives and individuals appeared at the hearing, and many spoke in favor of the proposal. No opposition was voiced. On July 5, 1955, the Board of Supervisors voted unanimously in favor of forming a county mental health board and submitted its resolution to the Syracuse Common Council, which subsequently approved participation in a county unit. The Mental Health Board was appointed in August. In October it submitted and received approval of a 1956 budget of $124,000, the amount that had been estimated as the cost of the program before its approval.

Within two years the Mental Health Board's budget had almost doubled. Its program was threefold: the Child Guidance Center; the new Adult Psychiatric Clinic; and board activities, including professional executive staff and contracts and consultative arrangements with the Bishop Foery and Syracuse Dispensary Alcoholic Clinics. Although state aid had increased with the expansion of program, economy-minded supervisors were becoming concerned about the board's ever-mounting demands. The program was already costing the county more than $100,000 a year.

The Mental Health Board's 1960 budget request brought into the open the conflict that had been building up between the board and the Board of Supervisors. Ostensibly, the conflict centered around requests for increased salaries. The board, which had been unable to hire a full-time psychiatrist to direct clinic activities, asked for an appropriation of $20,000 for the position. The supervisors refused to grant more than $15,000. There are some who say that Onondaga County and its legislators cannot conceive of any governmental employee's being worth such a salary as that requested. The supervisors defend their position on the grounds of economy and public resistance to high taxes. But the issue goes deeper. It reflects the lack of executive leadership in Onondaga County government; the Board of Supervisors' lack of experience in dealing with non-political, semi-independent boards; and the classic conflict between politically and professionally oriented governmental bodies.

Onondaga County has its share of boards and commissions. Most of them are politically oriented and are responsible to the limited executive oversight of the Board of Supervisors or, more important, to the integrating and controlling influence of the Republican Party. Legally and structurally there is little difference between the Public Works Commission or the Equalization Board on the one hand and the Mental Health Board on the other, but operationally they are miles apart. Political leaders in Onondaga County are not accustomed to dealing with policy boards that can command support from private health, welfare, and civic organizations in the face of a position taken by the Board of Supervisors. Although the Mental Health Board insists it has not done so, supervisors have accused the board and its staff of encouraging pressure group activity contrary to the supervisors' budget stand. The deliberately non-political, even anti-political, attitude displayed by the board's professional staff since its inception has also irritated political leaders. The absence of a dominant agency capable of representing community views, together with the fact that no county leader has appeared to take up where Tom Dyer left off when he failed to win reelection, has made agreement difficult to achieve.

Bluntly, the issue appears to be: who is to run the county's mental health program? In mid-1960 the answer could not be foretold. In protest over interference by the supervisors, the Mental Health Board had threatened to resign. Staff vacancies had forced it to curtail activities. After months of indecision the Metropolitan Health Council, beset by its own organizational difficulties, had reluctantly stepped in to appoint a citizens' committee to conciliate political differences. The prospect for success, however, did not appear bright.[13]

Conclusions

Of the four decisions in the field of health and welfare examined here, three favored metropolitan solutions to the problems posed— metropolitan solutions, that is, in the sense that in each area a number of fragmented programs were consolidated into a single program under the direction of a newly created county agency. Success in establishing the Children's Court resulted from conversion to that cause of the Republican county chairman, who then by patient and skillful negotiation built up the political support necessary to adoption. The County Department of Public Welfare grew from the conviction of another Republican county chairman (who was also Mayor of Syracuse) that such an agency would be a good thing, notably in that it would save the city money. The second chairman, by contrast with the first, disdained the soft touch and rammed his proposition through to adoption in a display of naked political power. The tactics employed were different, but Republican discipline was paramount in both cases. The proposal for a county health department, though strongly supported, failed to generate the political strength necessary to overcome the rural opposition which rose against it. The Mental Health Board slipped through without serious resistance, though its subsequent history warrants the expectation that any proposal for future functional integration in a county agency will be examined with special care.

Key considerations in determining the success or failure of functional consolidation at the county level would appear from these instances to be four. First, the urban-town conflict, always latent in rural suspicion and distrust of the city and its ways and urban impatience at rural "obstructionism," must be anticipated and dealt with, else the cause is lost. The city has proved itself more willing to consider functional consolidation than the county; hence the problem with respect to any given proposal is that of persuading the towns to go along on an expansion of county functions. It is a crucial problem, for there are as many non-city as there are city (Syracuse) supervisors; and the exact balance in the Board of Supervisors in normal circumstances works in favor of the *status quo*. Second, the county and town bureaucracies in a given program area, which from professional considerations might be expected to welcome an expansion in activities, frequently oppose instead because of the threat to their position and power. They are particularly prone to opposition if the proposed expansion comes as a result of functional integration; for in any such move they are likely to lose in status as compared with the opposite-number staffs in City Hall. Third, the reactions of professional organizations and their leaders may play an important role in a move for functional consolidation. The failure of the county medical society to come out strongly for a county health department was a grave blow to that proposal; so also was the almost uniform opposition of the town health officers, whose motivation, however, was probably at least as much political as professional. Fourth, the position adopted by the Republican organization in the past has been crucial to the success or failure of a proposal for functional integration. Given firm direction by a strong and resourceful county chairman, the party's traditional discipline normally has been sufficient to bring the organization through to the decision predetermined by its managers. Only in the most unusual circumstances has the cardinal rule of Republican control failed to hold.

VII

Education: The Special District Solution

STUDIES included in this volume deal with several types of attempted solutions to metropolitan problems. Notable by its absence is a device widely employed in other areas, the special district. The cause of this omission is not oversight, but rather the fact that, with one principal exception, the special district is not used to relieve metropolitan pressures in Onondaga County. Special districts are numerous, but in most instances they are not separate governments; instead their affairs are administered by the regular units of government and they are merely special-benefit assessment districts.

The major exception to this generalization lies in the field of education. Here the use of the special district has been authorized since a state law of 1812 provided for the organization of common school districts. The focus of this chapter will be not on the school district as such, but on the aspect of educational administration most analogous to a favorite metropolitan solution: the creation of central school districts out of smaller districts.[1]

Frank J. Munger prepared this chapter.

Organization for Education in New York State

Education is usually treated as a special case among government functions. This is true also in New York, where the legal provisions surrounding educational administration differ markedly from those relating to other governmental fields. One of the principal points of difference is the greater authority exercised in educational matters by the state government. In his study of New York State government, Lynton K. Caldwell concludes: "In New York the control and supervision of public education is centralized to a degree greater than is common in most states."[2] This extends to both the organization of education and the setting of educational policy.

It is difficult to describe briefly the local structure of educational administration in New York State, for the course of history and successive statutes have produced a variety of types of educational districts. Caldwell catalogues five types—common school districts, union free districts, city school districts, central school districts, and central high school districts—and with further subclassifications more could be distinguished. All, however, are headed by locally selected board members and trustees and all are units of local government. With some exceptions these local school districts are grouped together into state supervisory districts, each headed by a district superintendent. Although locally selected, the district superintendent is a state employee: his base salary is paid by the State Education Department, his duties are prescribed in the state education law, and he reports to an Assistant Commissioner of Education for Finance and School Administrative Services.[3] No comparable state supervision is provided in any other functional area.

The extent of state control can be seen also in the making of educational policy. State policy toward school centralization is a case in point. Consolidation of the excessively numerous common school districts has been an objective of state educational policy since the mid-nineteenth century, but it was not until 1925 that an effective tool for the achievement of such consolidation was provided. At that time the existing law authorizing the creation of central school districts was amended to provide financial incentives for centralization in the form of additional state aid. The principal amendments authorized payment by the state of 50 per cent of the transportation costs and 25 per cent of the construction costs of the new central district, whether the latter consisted of enlarging and remodeling existing buildings or erecting new ones. Subsequent legislation extended these incentives still further.[4]

The revised law was soon put into use in Onondaga County as elsewhere, and central districts were organized in Elbridge in 1928; in Fabius, Onondaga, and Tully in 1930; in Marcellus in 1935; and in Lafayette in 1937. Significantly, these were the rural sections of the county. At the time of the outbreak of war no centralizations had been accomplished in the suburbanized districts to the north, east, and west of the City of Syracuse.

Increasing dissatisfaction with the course taken by centralization developed at the state level during this period. Under the provisions of the educational law the initiative for the formation of the central district came from the local residents, who developed a proposal for centralization and submitted it to the State Education Department for approval. Many of the central districts developed in this way were considered by state officials to be poorly planned in relation to one another and too small in size. By the mid-1930's, therefore, there was widespread support for the preparation of a general, state-wide plan for the centralization of school districts. In 1939 the Regents Inquiry into the Nature and Costs of Education proposed a procedure to prepare a mandatory plan, but the proposal was dropped.[5] Instead, the preparation of a comprehensive but voluntary centralization plan was initiated by a joint resolution of the state legislature in 1940, vesting the necessary authority in the Joint Legislative Committee on the State Educational System.

The joint committee was widely known as the Rapp Committee after its chairman, Assemblyman Herbert A. Rapp, and the plan the committee ultimately prepared was generally described as the "master plan." Central school districts were laid out a county at a time, public hearings held on each, and the results published in reports issued in 1944, 1945, and 1946. In 1947, every county in the state outside of New York City having been covered, the results were published in a single volume.[6] The master plan, revised from time to time since, still provides the basis for state education policy on centralization. It does not constitute a plan for compulsory centralization, but it is thought to define the boundaries of the central school districts likely to be approved by the Commissioner of Education when and if local sponsors appear.

Detailed consideration will be given here to four efforts to effect centralization in Onondaga County: in North Syracuse, Solvay, East Syracuse, and Elbridge-Jordan. The locations of the four central districts (or proposed districts) are shown on Map 2. Of these districts one, North Syracuse, has the distinction of being the largest central district in the state; it may be appropriate, therefore, to use it as a first illustration of the forces affecting centralization proposals.

Creation of the North Syracuse Central School District

The first consideration of centralization in the North Syracuse area came long before preparation of the master plan. In 1929 the Board of Education of the school district including the Village of North Syracuse approved a resolution for a survey of the schools in the towns of Clay and Cicero to determine the practicability of creating a central district. The school board viewed centralization as a means of financing an expanded educational program with equal or lower taxes by taking advantage of the available state aid.[7]

Dr. Harry P. Smith of Syracuse University was commissioned to conduct the study. Smith's report noted that the population of the area had increased by 20 per cent during the 1920's and would continue to grow. He recommended three alternative plans: (1) a central district generally comparable in area to the present North Syracuse Central School District; (2) a central district somewhat smaller in size; and (3) a "much inferior" substitute, a district encompassing only a small area around the Village of North Syracuse. Smith noted four advantages of a central school: additional state aid would keep taxes low, transportation could be provided for all distant pupils, a central district would justify establishing a junior high school, and elementary schools in the outlying districts would still be maintained in operation.

Encouraged by this report the North Syracuse Board of Education in 1931 prepared petitions for a centralization vote. Committees of two board members each were assigned to circulate petitions. Numerous signatures were obtained in the Cicero 9 School District, close by the village, which was struggling to educate an expanding pupil population in a small, one-room schoolhouse. The voters in the more distant districts proved uninterested, however, and the plan was dropped.

The following year petitions were circulated for a smaller central school district, but again the voters of the would-be district proved passive or hostile and the petitions were withdrawn. The distrust shown for the centralization plan was the product in part of fears of increased taxation and loss of local control of the school, but resulted even more from a general lack of awareness of the significance of centralization, particularly in the absence of any systematic effort to promote and explain the idea. The State Education Department did little at the time to encourage centralization apart from providing the incentives described above.

The North Syracuse area continued to grow through the 1930's and a substantial addition was made to the high school plant. The North Syracuse High School provided instruction for numerous students from outlying districts on a tuition basis, but it was not until 1944 that the subject of centralization was raised again. On May 23 of that year the District Superintendent, Earl L. Asselstine, submitted an application to the State Commissioner of Education requesting him to lay out a central school district comprising 18 existing districts. The central district proposed by Asselstine was substantially different from that originally conceived by Smith. Where Smith's plan had included most of the Town of Cicero and part of Clay, Asselstine proposed to leave out most of the Cicero school districts and to place the Village of North Syracuse in a central district oriented to the west and encompassing much of the Town of Clay plus the Pitcher Hill district of the Town of Salina.

Frederick R. Sears, a member of the Clay School District Number 12 (North Syracuse) Board of Education since 1938, assumed the chairmanship of a Committee for Centralization, calling together periodically the trustees of the various districts. The 18 districts had shown an actual decrease in enrollment from 1940 to 1945, and the principal argument for the centralization rested on an anticipated post-war population explosion in view of the plans for a large General Electric plant in the area.

No immediate action was taken on Asselstine's proposal. Conversations and correspondence between local school officials and representatives of the State Education Department explored the possibility of alternative combinations of districts for centralization. Three modifications of the 18-district plan were considered; two made only limited adjustments, but the third changed the Asselstine plan radically, moving it back in the direction of the district outlined by Smith. The third proposal resulted primarily from the fact that the Board of Education of Liverpool—to the west of North Syracuse—had begun consideration of a central district of its own and there was danger of overlap. It may be noted that two central districts, one in North Syracuse and one in Liverpool, were included in the master plan published in 1947.

By this time more than three years had passed without decisive action. Asselstine, growing impatient with the delay, came forward with a new, more grandiose proposal for a central district that would include North Syracuse, Lyncourt, Mattydale, *and* Liverpool, and would swallow up 30 districts. On October 1, 1947, he forwarded an application to lay out such a district. Since no action had been forthcoming on either the Liverpool or the North Syracuse centralization scheme, he proposed to combine the two, adding for good measure the Mattydale and Lyncourt districts, left as orphans "for future determination" by the master plan. By December 12 the State Education Department had agreed that such a plan might be possible and had begun preliminary financial planning. Early in January of 1948, representatives of various districts around Liverpool voted "by a large majority" to consider the plan. Preparation of a financial plan proved time-consuming, however, and a full year had passed before the long-term financial plan was completed.

In the meantime local officials continued their contacts with the State Education Department, seeking at the same time to educate the people as to what was involved. A meeting called to consider centralization brought out 71 representatives from the 30 districts of Clay, Cicero, and Salina, and resulted in the appointment of a committee representing all 30 districts to study the proposed new central district.

Shortly after completion of the final financial plan in January of 1949, Asselstine presented it to a joint meeting of the Liverpool and North Syracuse Boards of Education. The board members expressed interest but within a short time opposition began to appear. The vocal opponents of the plan, chiefly from Liverpool, included several members of its Board of Education and a school principal. The major criticism advanced was that the district's enormous size would destroy any sense of community identity with the school, but at least two other reasons for opposition were involved. Creation of a central district was bound to subordinate some administrators and board members to others; and since the North Syracuse area was larger than the Liverpool area, it was likely that the former would attain greater influence. Secondly, the true valuation of property on a per pupil basis in the Liverpool area was substantially higher than that elsewhere in the proposed district. The centralization of the 10 districts surrounding Liverpool previously under consideration would have provided a per pupil property valuation of $8,804; by contrast the ratio was $5,854 in the 30-district proposal made by Asselstine; $5,317 in the final revision of an 18-district, strictly North Syracuse centralization; and $4,727 for a 19-district centralization which added Mattydale to North Syracuse.

Faced with these contrary influences, the Liverpool Board of Education was not prepared to act. It did agree to join with North Syracuse in publication of a booklet explaining the 30-district plan, but was not ready to choose at once between the 30-district plan and its own 10-district centralization. If centralization was to be effected in 1949, however, the North Syracuse Board of Education faced a deadline for petitions of May 15. And the rapid increase in school enrollments—which bore out Asselstine's earlier predictions—made immediate action imperative.

With Liverpool unwilling to commit itself, the North Syracuse board voted to proceed with a centralization plan for its own area alone and so notified the Liverpool board. Asselstine was asked to call a meeting of the trustees of North Syracuse and the surrounding districts. Publicity materials were prepared and distributed. The plan now called for a central district consisting of 19 districts, extending east from North Syracuse through Cicero but including also Mattydale to the south. Each of the districts had been included by request of a majority of its voters, or so the plan's proponents claimed. The Mattydale district had not originally been scheduled for inclusion, but requested and received permission to enter in view of the many Mattydale pupils attending North Syracuse High School. Large numbers of signatures were obtained for the petitions requesting a vote on centralization. Of the eligible voters, 73 per cent signed in the Town of Cicero, 85 per cent in Clay, and 98 per cent in Salina. On June 6, 1949, the State Commissioner of Education gave his approval, and a meeting was scheduled for June 29 to conduct the vote.

In the brief campaign that followed the proponents of centralization offered a number of justifications. These can be summarized in three points: (1) Centralization would make possible an improved educational program by facilitating supervision and special instruction in the elementary school and by permitting a reduction in the pupil-teacher ratio. (2) The business affairs of the district could be run more efficiently and economically under professional management, with duplications of program eliminated. (3) Tax rates could be reduced despite the extensive building program required because of the additional aid provided by the state to central school districts.

One of the strongest incentives for approval of the central school district was the fact that rapidly expanding populations made necessary the construction of new facilities in many of the districts. The creation of a new central district did not impose an additional burden, but promised rather to ease the job of building that was inevitable in any case. The centralization proposal was not without opposition, but it was approved at the June 29 meeting by a vote of 1,725 to 446. Although State Education Department procedures do not permit a breakdown of the vote by districts, the distribution of petition signatures cited above would seem to suggest that such opposition as remained was found in the more rural sections of Cicero. Approval of the centralization plan even among this group was encouraged, however, by the contrast with the earlier 30-district scheme. In comparison, the smaller North Syracuse central district was regarded by those skeptical of all centralization as the lesser of two evils.

Opposition to Centralization

Creation of the North Syracuse Central District, if not in the form at one time preferred, illustrates the success of the state's policy of encouraging centralization. Numerous other examples of successful centralization could be offered, including the creation of the Liverpool Central District from the remainder of the original 30-district North Syracuse plan. The state program, however, has not always achieved its goal; three brief studies of failures may serve to illustrate some of the forces working against centralization.

The Solvay Centralization

By the early 1950's the development of the Liverpool Central School District to the north, the Baldwinsville Central School District to the northwest, and Camillus Central School District No. 1 (West Genesee) to the west and south had left isolated a tier of still uncentralized school districts running along the southwestern shore of Lake Onondaga and extending from the Syracuse city boundary to the New York State Thruway. These were the Cherry Road, Solvay, Lakeside, and Lakeland Districts of the Town of Geddes, plus Onondaga District No. 3, the so-called Avery district. Together they made up a relatively small area, 8.1 miles at its greatest length and 2.8 miles at its greatest width.

The four adjoining schools for many years had sent their junior and senior high school pupils to the schools of the Village of Solvay. A study in 1923 had recommended that the other districts be brought into the Solvay School District, but the master plan of 1947 had left the four districts in Geddes "for future determination" while assigning the Avery district to the proposed Camillus Central District. In 1951, however, another study was made in cooperation with the State Education Department of the possibility of a consolidation of the districts. The following year an amendment to the state education law permitted the Solvay village school system to enter a central school district, and in May, 1954, a taxpayers' meeting of the Solvay

District unanimously approved an investigation of the advisability of centralization.

The Bureau of School Service of the Syracuse University School of Education was employed to conduct a study. The survey, directed by Dean Virgil M. Rogers of the School of Education, produced a recommendation for the creation of a central district from the five separate districts. The survey report urged the adoption of a junior high school program for the district and the construction of a new junior high school building, and concluded that such a program would be impossible without the larger enrollments that would result from centralization. An incidental advantage of the creation of a central district would be a state contribution of 32 per cent of the construction cost of the new building.[8] The proposal was taken up by the State Education Department and incorporated in an amended version of the master plan.

The proposal for centralization was opposed strongly in Solvay, however. One source of opposition was fiscal. By most standards the Solvay School District is very wealthy. Of the four districts of substantial size involved in the proposed centralization, the Solvay District in 1953–54 reported an assessed valuation per pupil of $10,910; comparable figures for the other three districts were Cherry Road, $5,614, Lakeside, $4,465, and Lakeland, $4,334. The president of the Solvay School Board, John O. Martino, opposed the plan on the ground that it would increase school taxes "beyond proportion to its requirements" and insisted that the village would not relinquish control of its schools to any other district.

Other elements of conflict were also present. One of the most significant was a sensed cleavage between the two neighborhoods to be united. Although Solvay is actually a heterogeneous community with some well-to-do residential areas, many of the original settlers were European immigrants and it possesses the reputation of being a working-class, industrial neighborhood. Many Solvay residents, who felt that the residents of the suburban residential areas to the south of the village (the so-called Westvale section) "looked down their noses" at Solvay, were unwilling to join them in a central school district.

The education law provides for a referendum on centralization among all the districts involved, with the result determined by a majority of all those voting without distinction as to district. Without following this procedure, an advisory public referendum was held in Solvay in 1956 on the centralization plan, and the proposal was overwhelmingly rejected, 2,163 to 257.

The State Education Department reacted to this expression with a revised centralization plan that would place the Cherry Road, Lakeland, Lakeside, and Avery districts within the already created West Genesee Central District, thus isolating the Village of Solvay. This was the danger of which the Syracuse survey had warned: that Solvay might find its enrollments cut by the centralization of the adjoining districts and that the quality of its educational program might suffer thereby. Before action could be taken on this proposal, the Solvay Board of Education abruptly offered to annex the Lakeland District and the Lakeside District, the two districts accepted, and the state discarded its plan. When the West Genesee District displayed a lack of interest in absorbing the two remaining areas, a new central district was created by combining the Onondaga Hill District (originally scheduled for inclusion in the Onondaga Central District) with the Cherry Road and Avery districts. Approved by a 1,149 to 279 vote on July 1, 1958, the new district was called Westhill since it served the combined communities of Westvale and Onondaga Hill.

The East Syracuse–Minoa Centralization

Somewhat different problems were raised by the proposal to create a new central school district extending east from the Village of East Syracuse through Minoa. This district, incorporated in the 1956 revision of the state master plan, was put to referendum in the 15 districts involved in June of 1958.

The centralization plan faced criticism on two major counts. First, opposition resulted from the proposal to construct a single senior high school for the area. Although no location for the high school was definitely determined, it was assumed it would probably be located in East Syracuse. On this expectation centralization was opposed in Minoa. Second, opposition arose from the fact the new central district would include two school districts which had operated as tax havens for industry. One, the Courtview District, is discussed below in the chapter on Industrial Park. The second, Dewitt District 6, includes the plant of Bristol Laboratories. Under a 1926 law the district was sending its few children to the Syracuse schools and paying a school tax of 50 cents per $1,000 of assessed valuation. It was estimated that centralization would result in an increase in taxes to $40 per $1,000.

In the first vote taken centralization was rejected 2,630 to 1,685. The proponents of the plan continued their campaign, however, and under the provisions of the education law a second referendum was held April 25, 1959. The negative vote remained almost constant, but the advocates of centralization turned out a substantially larger vote and the plan was approved, though by only 48 votes (2,731 to 2,683).

The vote did not produce a final solution to the controversy, but on the contrary was followed by a series of court tests. A group of taxpayers charged procedural irregularities; the Courtview District alleged its inclusion in the merger was "arbitrary and capricious" because it had no need of additional educational facilities; and the Bristol Lab district appealed on the special ground that the act by which Eastwood was annexed to the City of Syracuse in 1926 exempted the residual school district from centralization. Although the state courts eventually rejected all these pleas, the confused legal situation precluded expeditious implementation of the decision.

The Elbridge-Jordan Unification

In the case of the proposed merger of the Elbridge and Jordan Central Districts, centralization had already been accomplished. The Elbridge Central District was in fact the oldest in the county, while a central district was created around Jordan (in the northwestern corner of the county) in 1950. The State Education Department was dissatisfied with the small size of the two districts, however, and proposed they be combined in a single district.

The question was put to a vote in May of 1960, and rejected 875 to 601. Among the reasons for rejection were a record of controversy within the Elbridge District that made Jordan reluctant to affiliate, the possession by the Jordan District of land for future building that would no longer be valuable in a combined district, and differences between the two districts as to the emphasis to be given academic vs. extracurricular activities. Although both areas were overcrowded and confronted by building problems, as central districts they were not under the same compulsion to accept the state policy as non-centralized districts; the favorable state aid quotas applied to them in any case, or so they thought.

In their assumption that they would in any case receive state aid for construction of needed new facilities, the opponents of centralization proved to be in error. The State Education Department took the position that unification was the only proper solution to the needs of the two districts, and concluded that it would therefore be wasteful to finance construction of separate facilities. Accordingly, state aid for the proposed new buildings was refused.

An explosion followed in which residents of the districts charged officials of the State Education Department with "deception," "distortion," "dictatorship," and "contempt for the people." The charges were taken up by the two state legislators from the area, Senator Lawrence M. Rulison and Assemblyman Don H. Brown. The two men appealed to the Governor to investigate the matter, enclosed 49 pages of letters protesting the action, and noted: "Frankly, it is our opinion that if all the residents of the Jordan-Elbridge School District voted on the question, 'Have you confidence in the State Education Department?' the majority would answer no."[9] Governor Rockefeller's answer was courteous but noncommittal. He promised to urge the Education Department to review the manner in which it handled the merger, but indicated he had no jurisdiction over the matter. He noted that the department was following its master plan, which meant that it must examine all building proposals for all districts scheduled for future reorganization with the "purpose of avoiding any building that will not be completely useful *when the district reorganization is finally secured*" (italics supplied). Whether intended or not, the Governor's reply contained the implication that the State Education Department would have more to say on the subject. It also indicated his support of the department's centralization policy.

Centralization and the Federated School District

School district centralization involves many of the problems confronted in merging governmental units, though none of the proposals for centralization so far discussed involve more than a small part of the total metropolitan area. Inevitably some attention has been given to the creation of a metropolitan educational unit. Recent discussion of this subject has turned largely upon the proposal made by Governor Rockefeller in 1960 for a so-called federated school district.

One of the first endorsements for an enlarged school district was made in March of 1959 by the State Commissioner of Education, James E. Allen, Jr. In a speech at Columbia University Allen asked: "What is more logical than to explore the possibility of bringing groups of school districts conforming to metropolitan areas into federation for financial purposes?" Governor Rockefeller picked up this idea, and in his annual message to the legislature of January 6, 1960, proposed a plan for the creation of federated school districts that would include several central districts and might cross county lines. Such federated districts would possess power to levy non-property taxes impractical of administration by a single school district. In this fashion additional school revenue could be secured on the local level. Rockefeller indicated that such a plan was the only feasible alternative to two equally unacceptable proposals for meeting the needs for increased revenue for education: (1) a further increase in property tax levies and (2) increased state aid for education. The Governor's proposal was sketchy and almost wholly lacking in relevant detail.

Even in the absence of details, battle lines began to form on the proposal. The Democratic legislative leaders promptly attacked it, opposing the levy of a new tax and insisting that the state budgetary surplus would permit an increase in state aid to the school districts. Some Republican legislators also indicated suspicion of the plan, based upon fears that school board members—perennially suspected of permitting themselves to be dominated by the professional educators—would be too quick to levy additional taxes.

Nor were the school board members and the educators themselves excessively enthusiastic concerning the plan. Onondaga County educators, like those elsewhere, were divided in their reactions. Dr.

Paul A. Miller, superintendent of the Syracuse city school system, hailed the proposal as a "forward step in principle" that would broaden the tax base and modify "the highs and lows" from one district to another; but several educators from poorer districts expressed fears that the federated district might dilute the "equalization" principle of state aid. Although the presidents of the school boards of the North Syracuse and the Fayetteville–Manlius Central Districts suggested that use of the sales tax as a supplement to the property tax merited consideration, the president of the Liverpool Board of Education flatly opposed a sales tax and called the plan an "attempt on the state's part to shirk some of its responsibilities." More general across the state than the localized sales tax issue was the fear that a federated district would endanger "equalization." State aid is offered under a formula to provide additional assistance to districts with limited property resources of their own. Many rural officials feared that the federated district plan would result in reduced state aid in the future and would undermine the principle of equalization since poor districts would be forced to federate with adjacent poor districts.

Despite such opposition, the Rockefeller plan was taken up by the State Education Department and the New York State School Boards Association, which assisted in working out specific details and drafting the necessary legislation. The Education Department clearly hoped the federated district might be the opening wedge for districts defined by "economic areas," with steadily expanding functions that would ultimately include the power to borrow; administer school bus transportation, educational television, and vocational education; and exercise central control over the construction of capital facilities.

The full Rockefeller plan on educational finance was submitted to the legislature on February 14, 1960. The special message of that date at last offered a detailed presentation of the federated district proposal. Even as expanded, however, the proposal was incomplete; for example, it offered no indication of the non-property taxes to be available for use by the new districts, or of the relationship of such taxes to existing municipal and county taxes. But the federated district plan was lost from view in any case in the controversy surrounding the other educational proposals contained in the same message, for the entire Rockefeller program was predestined to arouse vigorous opposition. Indeed, Speaker of the Assembly Joseph Carlino, in collaboration with a group of Long Island Republican legislators, had already prepared a counterplan to the Governor's, the so-called "Nassau Plan," which called for much more substantial increases in state aid.

By late March the *New York Times* was reporting the federated district plan as "in serious trouble" in the legislature. One *Times* report declared that "At last count there were not enough Republican votes to pass it, and the Democrats were disinclined to do anything about it." The prospects for approval were not heightened by a proposal initiated by Senator John H. Hughes of Onondaga County calling for creation of a joint legislative commission to study the problems of educational finance. A study commission seemed a good reason to postpone action, hence the proposal was adopted and the legislature adjourned without acting on the federated district plan. Governor Rockefeller subsequently attributed this lack of enthusiasm to fear that the superdistricts would be given additional authority and told the State Mayors Conference in June: "At the next session we've got to develop the means to permit local authorities to increase their contributions toward the cost of education."

One central point is clear from this account: although the federated district plan was fraught with consequence for Onondaga County, the significant struggle over its adoption was waged in the state capital. Onondaga County educators, political leaders, and interested lay citizens had an opportunity to influence the decision reached, either directly through contacts with the legislators or indirectly through participation in the educational associations involved; but the decision to shelve the plan was made in Albany, not in Syracuse. Had it been approved, that decision, too, would have been made in Albany.

School Centralization and Metropolitan Government

It has been noted that, education is the most distinctive of all governmental functions. In numerous respects it is accorded special treatment in the organization and practice of government. Nonetheless, there are points of similarity between decisions within the metropolitan area concerning education and those concerning other subjects of governmental attention. Educational experience therefore has much to teach the student of metropolitanism. Among the lessons to be learned from the case studies above, three in particular may be noted here:

1. Many of the forces favoring or opposing centralization of school districts can be identified also in the struggles over the metropolitan treatment of other governmental functions. The desire to create a new unit that will conduct a more vigorous functional program, that will reflect changes in population and in public needs, that can reach beyond existing governmental boundaries to tap revenue sources previously underutilized, is found in education as in other program areas. Similarly, common bases of resistance can be identified: the desire to retain tax advantages, the preference for local control (often reflecting a preference for lower, and less expensive, levels of service), the opposition of existing bureaucracies to changes that threaten their security, the fear of larger units and more effective government.

2. Not only are many of the same forces involved in education and general local government: many of the actors are identical. The manufacturing interests found, for example, in the metropolitan sewage treatment plant case appear again here. There is, however, one critical difference: the industrial interests, which often favor the geographical expansion of government, appear primarily as opponents of educational change. The difference would seem to spring from the fact that the former is held to represent improved service, the latter increased costs. The proponents of higher service levels in education are found primarily among groups not otherwise involved in local community decision-making: the members of the many school boards, the officers and active members of parent-teacher associations, and the school administrators and teachers.

3. Of the educators involved in the centralization movement, the most influential are those who are a part of the state educational system. For it is in the amount of power wielded at the state level that education differs most materially from other functional areas. State policies are important in other fields, but in education the language of state officials is blunter and their weapons more powerful. The tone of Governor Rockefeller's reply to Senator Rulison and Assem-

blyman Brown is significant. When the State Education Department determines upon a reorganization move, it possesses a number of weapons it may employ and is highly likely to win. Under special circumstances it may fail, as when the Village of Solvay had sufficient tax resources to ignore the incentive of state aid. But the structure of decision-making in the realm of local educational policy cannot be understood in local terms alone, for in this functional area the most significant members of the Syracuse community power structure live in Albany.

VIII

Reorganizing County Government: Proposals for Reform, 1934-1943

THE emergence of the county as a unit of general government is a well-told story, which need not be recounted here. Onondaga County fits comfortably into the broad history of county government. For more than a century it pursued a placid course, discharging the duties imposed by law and serving almost exclusively rural needs and purposes; then, caught up willy-nilly in the advancing flood of urbanism, it assumed more and more functions appropriate to government in an industrial-urban society. Since 1930 Onondaga County has taken on responsibility successively for parks, sewage facilities, welfare, civil service, a public auditorium, civil defense, a children's court, regional planning, and mental health; and other expansions are on the horizon. The stories behind many of these developments are recited in the preceding chapters. Two propositions, reverse sides of the same coin, assert themselves over and over in these cases: first, county functions expand chiefly in response to metropolitan needs; second, when a metropolitan problem arises which can no longer be ignored or put off, the county is the most logical unit for dealing with it.

Lewis P. Welch prepared this chapter.

The Onondaga County Regional Planning Board, in its 1960 preliminary report, put it this way: "Because of the existence of effective county government with jurisdiction over the bulk of the rapidly urbanizing area, there appears to be no need for trying to create a new intermediate level of metropolitan government between county and city." [1]

To identify Onondaga County as the logical repository of the power to make metropolitan decisions, however, is not to suggest that it is well equipped in point of organization and outlook to assume new decision-making responsibilities. On the contrary, there is an abundance of evidence that the county is ill fitted to perform its traditional modest chores, much less to undertake the imposing new obligations of an urban age. There is evidence, moreover, that this fact is widely understood locally. For half a century there has been intermittent criticism of the county's government, and for 25 years there have been recurrent efforts to modernize that government. The earlier reorganization moves tended to stress economy and efficiency; the later, reform to make the county government more effective in the discharge of its expanding responsibilities. While the difference in approach was significant, the end-product sought was the same: the sponsors of reorganization have labored for the creation of a county executive (by whatever name) throughout the lifetime of the reform movement.

It would seem useful to examine the efforts to tool up Onondaga County's government for the assumption of responsibilities and the administration of programs appropriate to modern government. This chapter and the next are devoted to that subject. As the story unfolds, it will be interesting to note the complete absence of reference to metropolitan problems. This is an extraordinarily significant omission, one to which we shall return subsequently.

Background

The non-judicial sector of county government in New York State developed largely without rationalized general pattern from its formal recognition in the Duke of York Laws of 1665 through the early

1900's. Side currents of the government reform movement, dating from the turn of the century, stimulated interest in county government; and the resulting pressures to make the county a more effective instrument of government produced a series of legislative responses in the form both of studies and of new laws.

The legislature sponsored large-scale studies of local government by the Special Joint Legislative Committee on Taxation and Retrenchment during the early nineteen-twenties, and by the Commission for the Revision of the Tax Laws in the early thirties. Both groups recommended a constitutional amendment to permit the legislature to establish optional forms of county government and to allow counties to draft and adopt their own charters or to adopt an optional form devised by the legislature.

Among the relevant legislation, statutory and constitutional, passed during these two decades were:

1. A law permitting any county (outside New York City) to create a charter commission, either upon initiative of the board of supervisors or by popular petition, and to draft and adopt its own charter (1934).[2]

2. An amendment empowering the legislature to provide alternative forms of county government which could be selected by voters by referendum (1935).

3. Four laws, each embodying several optional forms of county government, including a number of plans establishing county chief executives with varying amounts of independent powers and authority: (a) The First Buckley Act (1935);[3] (b) The Fearon Law (1936);[4] (c) The Desmond Law (1937);[5] (d) The Second Buckley Act (1937).[6]

Interest in county government reorganization was prevalent in a number of counties during the 1930's. Monroe, Nassau, and Westchester electorates approved new county executive plans in 1935, 1936, and 1937 respectively. Optional forms were rejected, however, by the voters of both Erie and Schenectady Counties in 1937. Interest was also evidenced during this period in Onondaga, where efforts to reorganize county government constitute a significant chapter in the history of attempts at metropolitan adaptation.

The Onondaga County Bar Association Report

In January, 1934, some days after Governor Herbert Lehman spoke to both legislative houses in Albany on the need for a thorough reform of local government, a similar message was delivered to the people of Onondaga County through the local press. Crandall Melvin, President of the Onondaga County Bar Association, declared that governmental reform was "imperative and inescapable," and held out little hope for national recovery until the "enormous and overwhelming waste of public funds" should be stopped by the elimination of "antique, outgrown, ox-cart mechanisms" of government. He concluded by announcing the appointment of a seven-man committee to make a study of local government and report to the Association.

Named chairman of the committee was Charles Major of Skaneateles, who had just retired from the Board of Supervisors after serving six years. In the course of a long public career Major had gained a reputation as a tireless, willing, and dedicated public servant who was also known to favor county government reform. Given neither staff nor financial resources, the chairman set out virtually single-handed to accomplish the task given his committee. It is apparent that Major did not take counsel of any source during the study; no hearings of any type were held, no public officials were invited to offer opinions, and the committee as a whole rarely met. During the course of the study through most of 1934, there was no evidence of interest in or awareness of the nature of the inquiry on the part of the leaders of either major political party.

About ten days before the committee report was to be submitted to the bar association and released to the newspapers, Major received a call from Attorney Clarence King, Chairman of the Republican County Committee, who invited him to come and discuss the forthcoming report. Major brought a draft copy to King, who asked permission to keep it a day or so for study. A few days later, King returned the report to Major with a few noncommittal comments, but voiced no objection to its release.

The result of the ten-month study was submitted to the Board of Directors of the Onondaga County Bar Association in late November 1934.[7] The report dealt with city, county, town, and village government organization, and generally suggested a reduction in the number of public officials and a consolidation and centralization of governmental functions to reduce "duplication and overlap." It made the top local headline of the day's Syracuse papers.

Among Major's far-reaching recommendations was one calling for the outright abolition of town government and the transfer of town functions to the county. Another proposed the establishment of a county executive branch headed by a president elected by the voters for a three-year term, with power to appoint and remove certain department heads and with veto power over acts of the Board of Supervisors. Still another suggested that the board be reduced in size to ten supervisors, five from the city and five from the area outside, apportioned on the basis of population and assessed valuation. Other recommendations called for the abolition of some offices and the transfer or consolidation of others. The report was withal strong medicine, and offered small comfort to the traditionalist.

It failed to provoke any significant response. Major's former colleagues on the Board of Supervisors were publicly unimpressed, though a few privately conceded merit in several of the proposals. Editorial comment was scant. The author of the report grants in 1960 that it was "idealistic" and without serious prospects for adoption, but maintains that it was an intellectually honest effort which contained but slight compromise of principles. Whatever its claim to academic distinction, the politicians passed it by, thus interring in near-silence the first proposal for extensive governmental reorganization in Onondaga County.

Plan B

There was little talk of county government reform during the next three years; but in 1937 the League of Women Voters of Syracuse and Onondaga County, which had earlier supported the city manager plan for Syracuse, added a new plank to its local action program calling for study of the problem of county government reorganization. In early 1939 the League released a report highly critical of the county's government, which it characterized as "outdated, archaic, and outmoded." Professor Robert S. Steadman of Syracuse University, a professor of political science and prominent member of the liberal wing of the Democratic Party, saw the issue of county government reform as "good politics," more especially because the League of Women Voters, always a good prospective ally, had been developing sentiment for county reform over a period of two years. He succeeded in impressing the Democratic leadership with the attractiveness of this issue, and a plan of action was agreed upon in early June 1939.

The Democrats opened the fall campaign June 13 with the announcement that the Democratic County Committee had unanimously endorsed the chairman's proposal for securing a referendum on the county manager plan. On that day Cornelius J. Nugent, Syracuse postmaster and Democratic County Chairman, appeared at the office of the county clerk and filed a formal notice of intention to circulate the necessary petitions requesting a referendum on the county manager option (Plan B) of the Desmond Law.[8] This plan would establish a county manager to be appointed for an indefinite term by a reconstituted board of supervisors, five of whom would be elected from the City of Syracuse as a separate district and five from the remainder of the county as a separate district, all by proportional representation. All county administrative officers would be appointed by the manager or his subordinates except the district attorney, who would be named by the Board of Supervisors. The plan coincided with the principles of ideal county government as set forth by the program of the League of Women Voters of New York State.

Faced with the prospect of collecting over 13,500 signatures within a month, the Democrats dispatched two petition forms into each election district in the county. With the number of enrolled Democrats in the county approaching 30,000, the petitions conceivably could be filled without leaving Democratic ranks. The volunteer petition bearers succeeded easily. Chairman Nugent filed 8,100 signatures with the county clerk on June 23 and turned in an additional 8,400 names on July 12, thus assuring that the question would appear on the November 7 ballot. Nugent claimed that analysis showed that more than 35 per cent of the signers were not registered Democrats.

At the October 2 meeting of the Board of Supervisors a resolution was introduced calling for the submission of Plan B to the electorate, as required by law upon receipt of valid petitions. The motion was passed unanimously, but the GOP board leadership hastened to "clarify" the situation. City Supervisor Tyminski, acting majority floor leader, explained that, while the board had no alternative but to put the proposition on the ballot, this should not be construed as indicating board approval of the plan. He stated that many supervisors opposed the plan in the Republican caucus which preceded the board meeting, with most of the opposition centering on the proportional representation feature which, it was felt, would be "too complicated" for the voters to readily understand and would cause a delay in reaching election results. Tyminski himself termed it an unsound plan which would cost more money and would deprive the citizens of the right to vote for several county officers.

It was not made clear whether Supervisor Tyminski was speaking for the party or merely for himself in his criticisms of Plan B; but Democratic Chairman Nugent accused "Boss" Marvin of opposing the plan through the "machine-riddled Second Ward Supervisor" because the Mayor himself, knowing it to be a popular proposal, did not want to come out against it. The Democrats called for minority representation, proclaiming that "one-party rule is evil and one-man government is intolerable."

Five days before the election, the Republican County Committee released a pamphlet to be distributed throughout the county. Titled "Vote No on Plan B," the tract summarized the now familiar critical theme: Plan B would

deprive the towns of direct representation on the Board of Supervisors; abolish most elective offices and make them appointive; install PR which is understood by only one in a thousand voters, which wipes out majority rule and forces minority representation, and under which first choice votes for a particular candidate may be nullified and given to the second choice; create a condition where political bossism might thrive at its worst since control of six supervisors would control the manager who directs important officials; not insure savings since no jobs are abolished and, in fact, the Board would cost $25,000 instead of $19,000, and towns would have to pay for another supervisor. It also would mean the return to paper ballots and the costly voting machines would be discarded.

The pamphlet noted that Plan B was a proposal of the Democratic party, and characterized its introduction as merely an attempt to create an election issue by the Democrats. No other New York county had adopted a "ready-made or canned" system, according to the brochure.[9]

The *Post-Standard* took an editorial stand against Plan B in late October.[10] Attacking "Fancy Dan" PR because it would give minorities the power to block governmental action, the editorial claimed that PR had led to the rise of Hitler. Under our democratic system, it went on, the protest vote goes to the minority party, which "may not be sound" but is in general committed to support American institutions. Under Plan B, the editorial held, the protest vote would be directed to more radical groups because the Democratic Party "has no strong leaders and sound principles which appeal to the voters." The newspaper capped its opposition campaign the day before election with a fictitious interview with an imaginary Syracuse University professor, who promised a revolutionary new order of things after Plan B was adopted.

The first hint of formal League of Women Voters support for Plan B came in a letter to the *Post-Standard* on November 1 from Mrs. Harold Dyke of Syracuse, a state director of the league. Mrs. Dyke protested the *Post-Standard* editorials against PR, maintaining that the non-partisan league endorsed PR because study had shown it to be democratic. Far from destroying the two-party system, the letter concluded, it prevented one-party monopoly. Three days before the election the local League of Women Voters organization went on record in favor of Plan B. Indicating that the optional plans themselves were non-partisan in origin, the league expressed the opinion that such an important step as changing the form of county government should not be allowed to become a party issue, notwithstanding both parties had made it one. The announcement stated that the league's stand was based on a vote of its membership.

Democratic candidates for office tended to concentrate their efforts on their own election and to soft-pedal or ignore Plan B. The major burden of campaigning for Plan B therefore fell by default on Professor Steadman, who attempted to promote the innovation and to rebut its critics in numerous speeches throughout the county

PROPOSALS FOR REFORM, 1934–1943   183

and by radio. Shortly before election, however, the Democratic Party rose to its Plan B responsibilities by releasing a barrage of letters to county residents urging adoption of the plan and prophesying that it would save $500,000 a year. Endorsements of PR by state and national leaders of both parties were quoted with approval. Chairman Nugent ascribed GOP opposition mainly to the fact that the Democrats had beaten the Republicans to the punch in proposing a manager plan.

Suspicions that Chairman Marvin would employ the same strategy he had used in combating the city manager movement a few years before were borne out three days before the election when the Mayor finally took to the air waves. He explained that the Republicans had not taken issue with the Democrats over Plan B because the latter were simply trying to stir up a fight to obscure "the real issue —the record of the GOP." Chairman Marvin concluded with a "solemn pledge" that if Plan B were defeated, "the Republicans would go to the Legislature for authority to study the problems of county government and to provide for changes needed." [11]

The generally quiet contest over Plan B came to its climax in the election of November 7, 1939. According to the terms of the County Home Rule Amendment, an alternative form required a double majority for approval: that is, one majority in every city containing more than 25 per cent of the county population, another and separate majority in that part of the county outside of such cities. The vote on Plan B divided thus:

	For	Against	Blank	Majority Against
Syracuse	17,791	30,545	29,244	12,754
Towns	4,973	16,595	13,925	11,622
County	22,764	47,140	43,169	24,376

Source: *Official Canvass*, Onondaga County, 1939.

Nearly 62 per cent of those participating voted on Plan B, with the towns recording a vote of more than 3 to 1 against the proposition and the city rejecting by somewhat less than 2 to 1. The countywide vote was more than 2 to 1 against Plan B. The plan carried only the (city) Eighth Ward, which also elected a Democratic supervisor by 13 votes.

The Manager Plan Bill

An interesting postscript to the county manager campaign was provided shortly after the election by the political columnist of the *Herald-Journal*, who revealed that Mayor Marvin had been considering county government reform before the Plan B proposal was broached by the Democrats. At the 1939 session of the legislature, a special act had been passed for Erie County under which a new official, the comptroller, became the chief coordinator and financial officer of the county government.[12] This plan caught the attention of Mr. Marvin, who arranged for the county attorney to look over the Erie County set-up with an eye to its adaptation to Onondaga County. The deputy assigned to this task was Charles Major, who, after a short period in political retirement, had been appointed Assistant County Attorney in 1938. Major was familiar with the Erie County law and was well acquainted with the incumbent comptroller. Proceeding to draw up a county manager law modeled closely after the Erie example but substituting a manager for the comptroller, he completed the draft plan in late spring of 1939 and submitted it to Mayor Marvin. Before Marvin could take action on it, however, the Democrats had launched their Plan B campaign and the Mayor quietly put aside the draft until a more propitious time.

A special meeting of the Board of Supervisors was called for January 20, 1940. The purpose of the meeting was not stated, but brief reports in the local press indicated that the Mayor would present a county reorganization plan. At 2:00 o'clock in the afternoon the Republican members of the board went into secret caucus with County Chairman Marvin. There they were informed that the county manager bill drafted by Major was to be introduced and approved at the board meeting, then submitted to Albany for enactment by the legislature as a special local law. Sharp exceptions to the proposal were taken by the supervisors, particularly those from the towns, many of whom were learning the contents of the plan for the first time. Mayor Marvin vigorously supported the proposal, however, and after extended discussion succeeded in gaining agreement among the majority party supervisors.

The bill established the office of county manager and outlined certain powers and duties. The manager, who must have been a county resident for at least three years, would be appointed by the Board of Supervisors for a four-year term. He was empowered to supervise and coordinate county departments and agencies and to oversee all financial affairs not specifically delegated to the auditor and treasurer. He was to prepare the annual budget and maintain control of expenditures. He was authorized to recommend to the board organizational and procedural improvements and personnel appointments. The existing departmental structure, however, was left untouched. The bill also included a provision which permitted the board to authorize virtually unlimited deficit spending.

The Republican caucus adjourned at 3:45 P.M., whereupon the meeting of the Board of Supervisors was called to order. On hand for the little-publicized meeting was a large number of spectators, including several prominent Democrats and members of the League of Women Voters. The majority leader immediately moved approval of a resolution endorsing the county manager plan and requesting the state legislature to enact it into law. The deputy clerk of the board read the resolution, following which the chair called for discussion.

Several Republican supervisors spoke briefly to urge adoption of the motion, but Democratic Supervisor John J. Young filed formal objection to the resolution under Rule 5 of the board, which provided that a "resolution . . . shall lie over at least one day before final action is taken thereon if objected to by any member. . . ." Young posed a series of questions which elicited the information from the chairman of the board that there would be no public hearing on the resolution, and from the county attorney that there would be no referendum on the measure after enactment by the legislature and signing by the Governor. Supervisor Young, now convinced that there was a steam-roller movement under way, requested that the motion be held over and that a copy of the resolution be furnished those desiring it. The assistant Republican floor leader thereupon moved the suspension of the rules under Rule 16, which provided for such suspension upon a two-thirds majority of those voting. Following defense of this procedure by majority spokesmen and criticism by Young, the motion to suspend was carried 29 to 1, with Young's two Democratic colleagues abstaining. The county manager resolution then was passed 29 to 2, with one Democratic member again failing to vote. The resolution was certified by the chairman and quickly dispatched to Albany.

A small flurry of protest greeted the procedure followed by the Board of Supervisors, but it quickly subsided.

The Onondaga County manager bill was introduced in the legislature two days later by Senator William Martin and Assemblyman George Parsons, both Syracuse Republicans. The Parsons bill cleared the lower house and on February 5 the Martin bill advanced to final reading in the Senate. As it happened, the Democratic minority in the Senate could have blocked passage, since the absence of three Republican senators had evened off both parties' ranks at 24. But the minority leader had received no information on the bill from Onondaga County Democratic leaders and so granted the courtesy usually extended to local legislation requested by a board of supervisors.

Opposition to the measure from Onondaga County, however, came to life after the bill received legislative sanction. Democratic spokesmen, League of Women Voters members, and disgruntled citizens from all parts of the county flooded the Governor's office with letters and wires urging a veto. Criticism centered both on the manner in which the resolution was rushed through the Board of Supervisors and on the substance of the act. Republicans, moreover, proceeding on the assumption that the Governor would sign the measure, added fuel to the fire by bandying about the names of prospects for the managership. Prominently mentioned for the job was William Lane, Syracuse Common Council President and former executive secretary to Mayor Marvin. Republican members of the Board of Supervisors had their own candidate: they presented a petition urging Mayor Marvin to name Chairman of the Board Edward O. Yackel as manager, even though the act provided that the board itself should appoint the manager. But Marvin preferred

Lane, a close associate and, as he said, a "known quantity," and so Lane was designated for the job. As a concession, the Mayor was willing to go along on Yackel for the post of deputy county manager. This arrangement to some degree pacified the supervisors, though the conviction remained strong among them that a "Court House Republican" should get the managership. The local press, well aware of Onondaga's political imperatives, bannered Chairman Marvin's decision. All that was wanting was gubernatorial approval of the act under which the appointments could be formalized.

With the "naming" of Lane as manager, the communications to the Governor mounted in volume and intensity. Charges of patronage, extravagance, and bossism were leveled against the plan and its sponsor, GOP County Chairman Marvin. Democrats, independents, and indeed a number of Republicans, including both proponents and opponents of the earlier proposed Plan B, joined together in opposition. The Syracuse League of Women Voters lodged a formal protest against the manager bill with the Governor, and stimulated its membership to dispatch telegrams to Albany.

Professor Steadman, with the concurrence of County Democratic Chairman Nugent, submitted a detailed analysis of the proposed county manager plan and its background to Lieutenant-Governor Charles Poletti. Steadman stressed a number of points. There was no need for special legislation when five general statutes permitted practically any conceivable scheme of organization to be adopted on local initiative. The Democrats in 1939 had sponsored a fundamental optional reorganization plan which was defeated after the Mayor had promised a study; but this bill was a snap proposal presented with no advance publicity, no public hearing, no opportunity for discussion, and no referendum. The measure would not give the manager any effective authority, and further would permit manipulation of the budget to produce a floating debt. Several days later, Steadman sent a letter to the Governor's Counsel, Nathan Sobel, with a copy of his letter to the Lieutenant-Governor attached. There he advanced the further argument that if the bill were signed it would prevent the adoption of sound reform for many years. He also stated that the candidates for the managership were "quite devoid of training or experience" which would permit them to become an effective force in future reforms.

Soon after the legislature approved the manager bill, Democratic Supervisor Young dispatched a wire to the Governor asking him to defer decision on the measure; and on February 12, he mailed the Governor a detailed account of the session of the Board of Supervisors which had approved the manager resolution. He also arranged for an appointment with the Governor and his Counsel, on which occasion he emphasized that the establishment of a manager would simply mean more Republican jobs. The Governor, however, was obviously more concerned with the fact that the people would have no opportunity to pass on the plan, while Counsel Sobel was critical of the fiscal "loophole" in the bill which authorized deficit spending by the board. Young returned to Syracuse confident that the Governor would veto but uncertain as to the ground on which he would rest his decision.

The only communication from Syracuse even beginning to approach support for the manager bill was a letter from County Attorney Preston to Counsel Sobel. The letter spoke of the "clearinghouse" functions to be served by the county manager, who, it averred, would provide a point of "general contact" between departments and officials. The coordination to be furnished by the manager, it held, promised greater economy and efficiency. It went on to say that, at the same time, the bill reserved to the Board of Supervisors the power which the law vested in it, refraining from setting up an executive who could usurp powers and authority which the "framers of the Constitution" wished left with the people through the Board of Supervisors. Counsel Sobel asked Chairman of the Board Yackel, both directly and through Assemblyman Parsons, to furnish his office with an expression of the opinion of the Board of Supervisors on the merits of the bill. There is no evidence that Yackel responded to this request.

A second document essentially favorable to the proposal was added to the record when a memorandum from Harry T. O'Brien, Director of the Division of Municipal Accounts in the State Department of Audit and Control, reached the Counsel's desk. (Comment by this division, the State's "local government office," was requested by the Governor's Counsel as a matter of routine on bills dealing with local affairs.) O'Brien pointed out the parallel of the instant bill with its model, the Erie County Comptroller Law, which had been largely drafted by an examiner from his division. He noted that the bill aimed to remedy the deficiency of the lack of an executive in county government, and recommended its approval by the Governor. Counsel Sobel was struck by the absence of any reference to the provision permitting the funding of deficits and checked with O'Brien, who admitted that he had overlooked the provision in his review but added that he was not completely out of sympathy with it. He noted that state law was extremely restrictive on deficit financing except with respect to relief and certain emergencies, and observed that during the preceding year the Governor had signed several bills authorizing such financing. He conceded, however, that the provision in the bill at hand was "extremely dangerous" because of its practically unlimited scope.

Thus armed with expressions of popular sentiment, political evaluations, and expert testimony, Counsel Sobel submitted his recommendations to the Governor. In his memorandum, Sobel distinguished this plan from the several optional forms already available under the law, which provided for initiation by the voters, referendum, and establishment of a strong executive. He attached the Steadman letter, with the comment that he could not improve on it. The Counsel went on to analyze the nature and legal status of the "budget joker." He concluded with a recommendation for veto, and attached a draft of a veto message.

On February 20 Governor Lehman vetoed the county manager measure in one of his longest veto messages. Drawing liberally upon the arguments and even the phraseology of the Steadman letter, the Governor recounted the series of acts passed to facilitate basic reorganization. With these alternatives available, he concluded, "there is no longer any excuse for makeshift legislation of this type."

Public reaction to the Governor's veto was immediate and almost uniformly favorable. The Executive Office was flooded by a second wave of telegrams and letters from Onondaga County residents commending the Governor for his action. Mayor Marvin, in the only negative comment recorded, dismissed the veto as "purely political."

The major alternatives now available to Marvin were several. He could: (1) request Republican legislative leaders to try to override the Governor's veto, or (2) have the bill amended to meet the objections of the Governor and request the legislature to pass it again, or (3) devise an appropriate optional form for approval by the Board of Supervisors and submission to the voters, or (4) take the Governor's advice and have a commission named to prepare an optional form for submission to the voters, or (5) put aside the matter of county government reorganization. The Mayor's course of action turned out to be an unexpected combination of two of these possibilities.

The Charter Plan

The uneasy quiet following the Governor's veto lasted only five weeks; it was broken on March 27, when Democratic County Chairman Nugent announced the appointment of the nucleus of a five-member "non-partisan" committee to study plans for county government reform. This news produced a hurried call from Mayor Marvin to GOP ward and town leaders and supervisors to meet with him two days later. The meeting of the GOP leaders was a stormy affair, with many town representatives opposed to any further action on reorganization. Others, though, believed that the party had committed itself to some measure of reform by backing the vetoed manager plan. With Governor Lehman's veto centering public attention on the issue and with the Democrats threatening to establish their own charter committee, it was apparent that the Republican Party had to make some move or risk losing the initiative in the next reform campaign. Under strong urging by the Mayor, it was finally agreed that a charter commission would be created under the auspices of the Board of Supervisors to study the problems of county government organization and to report its recommendations to the board.

At the regular monthly meeting of the Board of Supervisors on April 1, 1940, a measure was introduced creating a commission "to prepare and recommend a draft of a county charter prescribing a form or plan of government for the county," providing for the manner of appointing the commission, and appropriating funds for its work. The nine-member commission, to be appointed by the Chairman of the Board of Supervisors, was directed to complete its study and present to the board a draft of a new county charter by July 15, 1940. Assigned to serve as commission staff were the clerk of the board, County Attorney Preston, and Assistant County Attorney Charles Major. The resolution was approved by a 33 to 0 vote, including the three Democratic supervisors.

Chairman of the Board Yackel immediately requested the Democratic minority to submit the names of two nominees for appointment to the commission. A week following receipt of the Democratic recommendations, Chairman Yackel announced the membership of the full commission of seven Republicans and two Democrats. The individuals proposed by the Democratic Party had been passed over in favor of appointees otherwise selected.

The first three sessions of the commission, held during April, sought to provide an informational base for its deliberations. County officials representing every department and agency appeared before the body to describe their duties and functions, working interrelationships, and lines of responsibility. Beginning in May, the commission opened its Syracuse sessions to citizens and organizations. In late May it went on the road, holding meetings in several towns where citizens and officials added their voices to the record. In mid-June it invited testimony from outside experts on reorganization. In all, some 18 public hearings were held during the two-month period April 16–June 17, at which appeared more than 120 witnesses. A near-verbatim record of the hearings, running to five volumes, was compiled. It would be impracticable to summarize the hearings, but it may be stated that arguments both for and against every prospective change were presented, with varying degrees of articulateness, rationality, and emotion. Scholars called for fundamental reform, while town supervisors testified that no citizen of their acquaintance wanted any change whatever. Mayor Marvin urged limited changes, "coordination more than consolidation," citing the distractions of the international scene as reason for a moderate course.

Beginning on June 19 the Charter Commission commenced a series of executive sessions designed to delineate the features of the new charter. In its initial executive session the commission expressed itself as being unanimously in favor of the establishment of a county executive; it also recorded its opposition to any reduction in the size of the Board of Supervisors. At its second executive session the commission voted on the question whether the executive should be elected or appointed. The vote split on party lines, the two Democrats favoring popular election, the seven Republicans appointment. A second motion, to the effect that the manager should have the power to appoint all department heads under his jurisdiction and supervision, was carried unanimously. By consensus, the commission favored proceeding under either the Desmond or the Second Buckley Act, and requested Counsel Major to prepare a synopsis of the provisions of the latter for the next meeting. On that occasion the commission addressed itself mainly to Major's summary of the Second Buckley Act, which, he suggested, "most nearly filled the requirement [of] creating an executive plan" with minimum changes otherwise. Following considerable discussion, which failed to produce a consensus, Counsel Major was asked to prepare a report on the Desmond Act for the next meeting.

With less than two weeks remaining before the July 15 deadline, Major presented a chart comparing the respective provisions of selective Plan E of the Second Buckley Act and Plan B of the Desmond Act, the latter being the basic form rejected the previous year. Again considerable discussion ensued, at the end of which a motion committing the commission to proceed under the Plan E selective form of the Buckley Act was carried by unanimous vote. Major was directed to prepare the option in correct legal form. A second resolution named a committee of three to draft a set of recommendations to accompany the plan of reorganization. At its final executive session on July 11, 1940, the commission discussed and approved unanimously its report, which was received and "placed on file for further consideration" by the Board of Supervisors at a special meeting on July 13.

Three courses had been open to the commission, according to its report.[13] One would have been to recommend a "complete and drastic overhaul" of county government. Another would have been to defer action in the face of critical national and international events. The third was found in the middle course of proposing "entirely obvious and desirable" improvements in the existing system, improvements in no sense "dangerous or radical." The commission decided on the third course. The report pointed out that under the county charter commission law, the Board of Supervisors could refer the recommendations of the commission to the voters without change or comment or with revisions, or could refrain from submitting a proposition in any form. The report went on to enumerate and support the major features of the organizational plan. The essence of the selective form recommended was a county manager appointed by the Board of Supervisors. The manager in turn would appoint a director of finance, a welfare commissioner, and a coroner. The sheriff and county clerk would continue to be elected independently. The county auditor would be replaced by an elected comptroller, who would head a department of audit and control. A strong budget system would be set up under the manager, who would become the chief administrator of the county.

The next regular meeting of the Board of Supervisors was scheduled for August 5. At the usual pre-meeting caucus of the Republican majority, several town supervisors opposed submission of the charter to a referendum vote. The GOP leadership and most of the supervisors, however, believed that a commitment had been made to the community and to the charter commission itself to place the proposal before the electorate; and a resolution to that effect was approved. Subsequently, the Board of Supervisors formally adopted a referendum resolution by a party vote of 29 to 3, rejecting a series of Democratic amendments, including one to make the executive elective, on the way to the final vote. Following this action several Republican town supervisors indicated their personal dissatisfaction with the reorganization plan notwithstanding their acquiescence in the referendum vote. It was clear that a number of board members meant to take advantage of the caucus decision to refer the charter to popular vote without endorsement.

For some weeks following the action of the Board of Supervisors little was heard of county reform. Then, in mid-September, the County Democratic Committee took an official stand of indifference on the issue, complaining that the proposed charter did not go far enough but disclaiming any plan to organize a campaign against it. In late September the Board of Supervisors provided for the publication of 10,000 copies of the Charter Commission report to be distributed to the voters through the ward and town supervisors. With time running out, the traditional spirit of conservatism reported strong in the towns, a double majority required for adoption, and no energetic sponsorship, the new charter faced bleak prospects indeed. In an effort to stimulate some interest the county League of Women Voters went on record as favoring the proposal, and scheduled a meeting of its membership on October 27 to discuss county reorganization. The pro-charter *Herald-Journal* tried to inject spirit into the issue by hailing any news about the charter proposal as the harbinger of a "lively campaign," but the simple fact was that the charter evoked no organized support and very little interest.

The *Post-Standard* took no official stand on the charter question, but Don H. Brown of Baldwinsville put his chain of eight county weekly newspapers on record against the plan by running a front page editorial and several critical letters to the editor in each paper. Among the letters was one from Crandall Melvin, who as President of the County Bar Association in 1934 had appointed a committee to study local government reform. Melvin attacked the charter vigorously. Meanwhile anti-charter groups which had sprung up in Fayetteville and Jordan merged to become the Committee to Retain Our Present Form of County Government. The GOP took no formal position, but individual Republican office-holders, including particularly town supervisors but numerous other village and town officials as well, were quoted as opposing the charter. The official Democratic stand of "indifference" also permitted its spokesmen to oppose the plan, and many did so.

Dean William E. Mosher of the Maxwell School of Syracuse University censured both parties for their "indifference and evasiveness" on the matter of county reform. He charged that "the order had gone out" to squelch the plan and maintained that the insincerity of both parties on the issue had been demonstrated the year before when neither conducted an educational campaign on Plan B, and when poll watchers of both parties advised citizens to vote "No"—the Republicans in order to defeat a Democratic plan, the

Democrats in order to be able to blame the Republicans for the failure of reform.

On election day, November 5, the county charter proposal was defeated in both city and towns. A summary of the vote follows:

	For	Against	Blank	Majority Against
Syracuse	10,678	15,258	86,364	4,580
Towns	3,346	13,811	32,079	10,465
County	14,024	29,069	118,443	15,045

Source: *Official Canvass*, Onondaga County, 1940.

Only 27 per cent of those voting bothered to record their opinions on the charter question, turning in a 2–1 vote against the proposition in the county as a whole, with margins of 3–2 in the city and 4–1 in the towns. The charter did carry two city wards, 16 and 17, by narrow pluralities.

In retrospect, the charter proposal and the referendum vote seem to have been a pointless exercise. Those favorable to county reorganization had no organization around which to rally their support, and anyway they were tiring of the issue. Those satisfied with the *status quo* did not feel compelled to organize in serious opposition, depending instead on the natural resistance of the electorate to change. The result might be characterized as death of the charter by suffocation.

The Board of Supervisors Special Committee on County Government

There was to be one more reorganization flurry before local concerns gave way finally to preoccupation with the war. Early in 1943 the League of Women Voters announced that it would recommend to the Board of Supervisors a series of reforms in the government of Onondaga County. At its regular meeting of February 1, the promised action came before the board in the form of a letter which strongly supported the creation of an appointed, qualified county manager with broad administrative powers. Chairman Yackel responded by announcing the appointment of an eight-man special committee to "study and investigate into the merits of a possible change in the form of the present county government" and to report its findings to the board at some later date. In naming the committee, Yackel noted the absence of many citizens from the county in the service of the nation, and suggested that it might be well to postpone action until they should return.

For three months following its appointment the committee dallied with the subject of county reform. As before, the issue, if issue it could be called in the face of massive indifference, provoked little public interest. A series of hearings failed to produce anything approaching excitement although a few faithful partisans did appear to repeat well-worn arguments. The League of Women Voters did what it could to generate support for action; and both daily papers favored the county manager plan editorially, while exhibiting less than unrestrained enthusiasm for this particular proposal at this particular time.

At the regular monthly meeting of the Board of Supervisors on May 3, its chairman presented the majority report of the special committee on county government. The report, noting public preoccupation with world affairs and particularly with the war effort, recommended against immediate action; instead, it proposed that at "the proper time" a reorganization proposition again be submitted to the people at referendum. The report went on to suggest that for the present the chairman of the board act as an intermediary between the board and the various county institutions and departments. At the next (June 7) meeting of the Board of Supervisors, the Democratic leader presented a dissent criticizing the majority report and proposing that the people be given the opportunity at the next election to vote on an elected county president form of government. The majority report was approved and ordered "placed on file" by a straight party vote of 32 to 4. In an anticlimactic vote, the minority report was defeated by 30 to 3. Thus was county reorganization laid to rest "for the duration."

IX

Reorganizing County Government: The County Director Proposal

AFTER five years of obscurity, the subject of county government reorganization emerged once more, and again it was the League of Women Voters which assumed the lead in proposing basic reforms. Again, too, as though in replay of an old and familiar record, the Board of Supervisors passed a resolution on July 12, 1948, providing for a special five-man committee to "study the form of county government." Appointed as chairman was Supervisor Fritz Campbell of Elbridge, who had publicly opposed the county manager charter five years before. The committee accomplished, and so far as the record reveals sought to accomplish, nothing; it merits mention solely because it was subsequently incorporated into yet another committee which did take significant action.

The Syracuse Governmental Research Bureau and Its Early Plans

In early 1948 the City of Syracuse, faced with teachers' salary increases mandated by the state legislature and approaching its con-

---
Lewis P. Welch prepared this chapter.

stitutional debt limitation, adopted a city sales tax. The general unpopularity of this measure soon prompted consideration by the city of other levies which might be substituted for the sales tax. Among the alternatives discussed was a business excise levy. Unhappy with the sales tax and even more concerned over the prospect of an excise tax, the Syracuse business community, led by the Chamber of Commerce, sought a means by which organized business might gain an enlightened and articulate voice in local governmental affairs. After an unsuccessful experience with an *ad hoc* committee of accountants, the chamber decided to establish a private research bureau and pledged a three-year financial guarantee for its support for a trial period. The Syracuse Governmental Research Bureau was incorporated in late 1948 with Robert G. Soule, head of the Chamber of Commerce, as its President. Selected as its first Executive Director was Richard A. Atkins, who came from the same position with the Boston Bureau of Municipal Research. No stranger to the city, Atkins had received a Master's Degree in Public Administration from Syracuse University's Maxwell School in 1935.[1]

When the Bureau opened on January 1, 1949, there was initial suspicion among city officials that its primary purpose was to keep an eye on city financial activities. In order to dispel possible antagonism on this score as well as to provide background for the new staff, Atkins and his assistants devoted much early attention to county government. The culmination of this preliminary research took the form of a memorandum circulated in August 1949 to members of the Board of Directors of the Bureau, and proposing that Plan B of the First Buckley Act of 1935 be adopted by Onondaga County.[2] The document characterized Plan B as "well adapted to the purposes of Onondaga County" for several reasons: it could be approved by a simple majority of the voters of the county, it would not change the membership or the method of election of the Board of Supervisors, it would not transfer any functions, it had been tested successfully in Monroe County, and it would provide the essentials of a manager plan.

The county manager memorandum was favorably received by the Executive Committee and Board of Directors of the Governmental Research Bureau, and Atkins was authorized to prepare an expanded brochure for public distribution. This he did, and in mid-February 1950, the research bureau released a brochure titled *Executive Management for Onondaga County: A Plan for the Manager Form of County Government.*

The reception of this pamphlet by the city press, the Chamber of Commerce membership, and civic leaders from both the city and the suburbs was encouraging to Atkins, who presently proposed to his Executive Committee that the bureau either take the lead itself or establish a separate organization to promote a manager plan for Onondaga County. He was prepared to make the bureau's first major effort the reorganization of the county government. The bureau's Executive Committee was impressed with Atkins' proposal, although several remembered well the ill-fated history of Onondaga County reorganization and were cautious about staking the new agency's future on this issue. It was agreed, however, that the earlier efforts had failed largely because of the lack of a campaign organization, which was a basic element in Atkins' suggestion. The Executive Committee gave its support to the proposed plan for a county manager campaign and to the creation of an organization to guide it. Then the committee turned its attention to the matter of locating a chairman to head up the campaign organization. Meanwhile Atkins moved along on campaign preparations, hoping to be able to bring the manager proposition to a vote in November 1950.

A Change in Approach

Warning signs, however, were appearing on the horizon. The bureau brochure proposing Plan B had been submitted to the Board of Supervisors at its March meeting and had been referred to the special committee on county government, which had largely lain dormant since its appointment in 1948. Rumors of unhappiness over the prospect of a county manager were emanating from some of the towns and from the Court House. In order to clear the lines to the county government and to prevent the wrecking of the campaign on the first shoal, a delegation from the research bureau, including among others former Republican Mayor Thomas E. Kennedy and Stewart F. Hancock, prominent attorney and reputedly an influential community leader,[3] called on Chairman of the Board George Traister and County Attorney Charles Major.

Traister and Major were not optimistic over the chances for Plan B and frankly predicted its defeat if submitted to referendum. Traister proposed that a joint committee of supervisors and citizens be formed to draft an acceptable manager plan for Onondaga County. The research bureau, he suggested, could nominate the citizen members of the committee. Atkins considered the joint committee device simply a delaying action, but most of the bureau delegation accorded weight to the criticisms of Plan B which Major and Traister believed would cause its defeat. The upshot was general agreement on the joint committee proposal. The plan to be drafted by the committee would be presented to the Board of Supervisors, then, on approval by that body, to the legislature for passage as a special law. Presumably it would also be voted on by the electorate. County Attorney Major and Bureau Director Atkins were to assist the committee in its drafting effort.

President Soule and Director Atkins of the research bureau strove to assemble a list of ten private individuals who were committed to reform for consideration for appointment to the joint committee. On July 21 Soule submitted to Traister the names of 10 persons characterized as "broadly representative of the public" and who had "devoted time and effort" to the study of county government organization. Of these Traister selected five to join the study committee of five supervisors as members of the new joint committee. Supervisor Fritz Campbell, chairman of the old committee, was designated chairman of the new one as well.

After the legislature and the Governor had approved the new county law formulated by the Uniform County Laws Commission at the 1950 session,[4] the commission's life was extended an additional year for the purpose of studying the variety of alternative forms of county government passed in pursuance of the County Home Rule Amendment of 1935. It was noted that these options had been little used and the commission was instructed to determine if they should be revised or simplified. The commission launched into its new assignment in early 1950. In the spring, however, the commission counsel was taken seriously ill; and in June

THE COUNTY DIRECTOR PROPOSAL

Onondaga County Attorney Charles Major was invited to assume his responsibilities and to rework the existing alternative forms.

The newly appointed joint committee decided to await the result of Major's work instead of proceeding to draft a new plan for Onondaga County. At a fall meeting of the committee, it was tentatively agreed that the 1940 charter manager plan would be used as a basis of the joint committee proposal, and an understanding was reached that County Attorney Major would develop an option similar to this plan which would be included in the new alternative forms bill he was drafting. It was hoped that this latter legislation would be enacted at the 1951 session; if it was not, the option appropriate for Onondaga County would be introduced as a special bill.

During the remainder of 1950 Mr. Major worked on the new options in relative seclusion. By the end of the year, with no report from Major on his progress, Atkins and Soule (who had been appointed to the joint committee) were growing anxious lest no option for Onondaga County be ready for introduction at the 1951 legislative session; and Soule wrote to committee chairman Campbell expressing his concern. Failing to elicit a response from the committee chairman, in early January Soule wrote to the other four citizen members of the joint committee. His letter stated that, since there had been neither word of progress nor action in months, he had had a draft bill prepared, and invited them to meet to discuss the plan and their next move. By the date of this meeting, however, it was learned that an optional forms bill would be introduced in the legislature in February; so the citizen members of the joint committee deferred action until a copy of the bill should become available.

A copy of the proposed new Alternative County Government Law was not received in Syracuse until shortly before its introduction on February 20, 1951. The staff of the research bureau were disappointed with the measure as a whole, and with the county director option (which was designed to be employed locally) in particular. Moreover, the bill was introduced for study only, which ruled out any prospect of invoking it in Onondaga County that year even if it were considered a good instrument. To add to the uncertainty was a local event which gave no cause for optimism: in January, 1951, the Board of Supervisors chose as its new chairman Supervisor Fritz Campbell, who as chairman of the joint committee had done little and who as representative of a rural town outside the suburban ring was generally regarded as opposed to county reorganization. In the circumstances, Atkins and the Governmental Research Bureau resigned themselves to a delay of an additional year.

The Alternative County Government Law

The introduction of the Alternative County Government Bill in Albany brought a variety of reactions, mostly unfavorable, in its wake. During the remainder of 1951 the Uniform County Laws Commission held hearings across the state, collecting comments, criticisms, and suggestions regarding the new law. A revised measure, incorporating a number of changes, grew out of these deliberations; it was introduced in the legislature in February, 1952. There was wide agreement that it had been much improved though still subject to criticism on a number of points.

During 1951 the Alternative County Government Bill and the whole subject of county government reorganization continued to hang over the Syracuse Governmental Research Bureau. Bureau Director Atkins desired to be relieved of this burden which had now consumed more than two years, so that bureau efforts could be directed more fully to other projects. The bureau could either give up on the whole subject of reorganization, or it could drive on to resolution of the issue as quickly as possible, whatever the outcome. In early 1952 the bureau's Executive Committee decided that the reorganization question should be pursued to its conclusion.

The chances for passage of the Alternative County Government Bill at the 1952 session were not overly bright, and Atkins set out to help improve them. Beginning in late February, the bureau launched a massive letter campaign aimed at securing passage of the new law. Letters over the signature of President Soule went to the Governor, the Chairman of the Uniform County Laws Commission, Onondaga County legislators, and the state Comptroller, urging favorable consideration of the legislation. In addition,

Soule dispatched notes to prominent Syracuse business and civic leaders outlining the importance of the alternative government measure to Onondaga County and asking that they send letters to the Governor and the Onondaga County legislative delegation urging passage.

Keeping Atkins posted on developments in Albany was Homer E. Scace, Director of Governmental Affairs for the Empire State Association of Commerce. On March 12 came a telegram to Atkins from Scace, informing him that both houses had passed the Alternative County Government Act and advising that letters be sent to the Governor urging him to sign: the measure had been put in jeopardy because of hesitancy on the part of the Governor's Counsel to recommend signature. (The Counsel was irritated because his office had not been briefed on the bill before its passage.) A second round of letters seeking favorable executive action immediately went to the Governor from local business, professional, and civic leaders closely associated with the research bureau. Atkins sent letters to the local bureau's counterparts in other upstate cities requesting support from them for the bill. Favorable editorial comment on the measure was also induced from several upstate newspapers, including the Syracuse *Herald-Journal*. There were local stirrings of dissidence even while this campaign was in progress, but they were largely overlooked in the drive to put the measure on the statute books.

Governor Dewey signed the Alternative County Government Law on April 19, 1952. It provided four basic executive forms of county government, all of which continued the Board of Supervisors with all existing legislative functions, powers, and duties. Each alternative form created an executive or administrative head of the county, with powers of supervision, direction, and control of all county administrative agencies. The status and responsibilities of the executive, however, differed somewhat from one option to another. The County Administrator form, designed primarily for use by smaller counties, represented but a slight variation from the existing form. The County Manager form provided for a manager to be appointed for an indefinite term and to be removable by the board at will, while the County Director form established a director to be appointed for a four-year term and to be removable for cause by the board. Both manager and director were to have similar supervisory and managerial powers, but the latter was to be more subject to the board on matters of personnel appointments and administrative reorganization. The director must be a county resident, while no such restriction applied to the manager. The County President form provided for a strong executive elected by the voters for a four-year term from among county residents.

During the late spring and early summer the joint committee held a series of meetings for discussion of the new law and the options it offered. These conversations provide the basis for three significant conclusions. First, the marked hostility to county reorganization existing earlier in important places had not been dispelled or allayed. Chairman of the Board of Supervisors Campbell made this plain at the first meeting, which he attended. Second, there seemed little chance that the board would order a popular vote on an optional form; instead, the official attitude communicated to the committee was that those who had been active in drafting the law and procuring its passage should petition for a referendum.[5] Third and most embarrassing of all, it became increasingly clear that the committee itself was hopelessly divided, not only on which option to recommend but on the fundamental question whether reorganization was timely and therefore whether there should be a referendum at all. As a result of this schism two reports went to the Board of Supervisors. The majority report, signed by seven committee members, recommended that the board submit to referendum at the 1952 general election the county director form without advice as to its adoption or rejection. The minority report, submitted by three members (two of them nominees of the research bureau), voiced firm opposition to all optional forms and therefore to a popular referendum. The minority group stressed a new point of contention in its opposition to a referendum on county reorganization in a presidential election year. Both reports were received by the Board of Supervisors and filed without action at its July meeting.

Meanwhile, representatives of the research bureau had informally discussed with board Chairman Campbell the prospects for future action on reorganization, and the chairman had agreed to appoint a special committee of the board to review the alternative forms law and work out suggestions for its amendment to be conveyed to the Uniform County Laws Commission. At the board meeting of November 20, Campbell took the step indicated. The committee chairman forthwith arranged a meeting with representatives of the Syracuse Governmental Research Bureau. The ensuing discussion produced agreement on a number of amendments, which were laid before the Uniform County Laws Commission when that group visited Syracuse on December 10. The commission introduced proposed amendments to the Alternative County Government Law in the 1953 legislative session. Included among them was one restricting a referendum on an alternative form to odd-year elections. Both Assembly and Senate passed the bill quickly and Governor Dewey affixed his signature to the act in April.

The Campaign for the County Director Plan

Here at last was something definite which local partisans, opponents as well as supporters of county reorganization, could count on. The law left many dissatisfied, but at any rate some effort had been made to accommodate its provisions to Onondaga County conditions. The time for haggling over legal requirements or limitations was past, for the issue now was clearly drawn: proceed under the law as amended, or abandon thought of county reorganization for an indefinite period.

The Syracuse Governmental Research Bureau meant to proceed, and took steps to that end. At a May meeting of the Board of Directors, Atkins put forward his view that the Board of Supervisors was quite unlikely to initiate a referendum on the county director (or any other) form. The unwelcome corollary was clear: if the bureau wished a popular vote on the subject, it would have to undertake a petition campaign. This would require considerable effort, for the number of signatures needed approximated 15,000 and the deadline for filing was September 3. Three months was a limited time in which to organize and conduct the kind of campaign that would be necessary to ensure success.

The research bureau nevertheless decided to push ahead, and Director Atkins devoted most of his energies the first half of the summer to putting together the skeleton of an organization to conduct the petition campaign. The officers and board of the bureau gave him full support in these efforts, attending meetings on call, lending their influence whenever and wherever it promised to be useful, and serving as members of special committees to explore alternative courses. One such special committee made yet another attempt to persuade the county GOP leadership to initiate the referendum, but to no avail; those in places of power refused to modify their expressed opposition to that course. The task of building an organization for the circulation of petitions proceeded, and by midsummer most of the leadership spots had been filled. Hardly a beginning had been made, however, toward recruiting a corps of workers. News of the formation of a Citizens' Committee for Progressive County Government was released to the papers for the editions of Sunday, July 19. It was then less than six weeks to the September 3 closing date.

Meanwhile the bureau and its supporters kept a close eye on developments in another sector. It was of course widely known that Chairman Campbell did not speak for all its members in opposing instigation of a referendum by action of the Board of Supervisors. Four supervisors, indeed, as members of the majority faction of the joint committee, had recommended adoption by the board of a referendum resolution and there were others who were known to favor such action. Among these were the Democratic supervisors, who, though numerically insignificant, nevertheless had considerable nuisance influence. Late in July an announcement from Democratic headquarters stated that the three Democratic supervisors from the city would introduce a referendum resolution at the August 3 meeting of the Board of Supervisors. Ordinarily such an announcement would have been ignored, but these were not ordinary times. For one thing, the citizens petition campaign was gathering momentum, and it was more and more evident that its backers meant business. For another, the Republican supervisors were split pretty well down the middle on the issue of a board-inspired referendum.

This fact was emphasized in the GOP caucus which preceded the board meeting of August 3. There Republican County Chairman

Traister found the majority badly split on the referendum issue. A few favored the county director plan and wanted to get on with its adoption, others had reservations about the plan but did not object to a popular vote on it, still others were adamantly opposed to both plan and referendum. There was little sentiment for a Republican resolution to be introduced in place of the one to be proposed by the Democrats, hence little prospect for positive action by the majority. The caucus decision, reached after lengthy discussion had produced nothing approaching consensus, was that each Republican supervisor should be free to vote as he wished.

Freed of party restraints, most majority supervisors chose to initiate a popular vote. The Democratic resolution authorizing a referendum on the county director plan, placed before the Board of Supervisors for action on August 3, passed by a vote of 29 to 7. Thus was the board relieved of the odium of obstructing a popular vote on county reorganization.

Thus, too, was the nature of the task confronting the citizens' committee completely changed; for whereas before it had faced the chore of procuring 15,000 signatures on referendum petitions, it was now free to devote its energies to a campaign for popular approval of the county director plan. Its altered status was reflected by a change in title by which the "Citizens' Committee for Progressive County Government" became the "Citizens' Committee for the County Director." Otherwise the organization remained essentially unchanged, with Donald Pomeroy, Syracuse realtor and civic leader, who had agreed to serve as chairman of the first committee, staying on as chairman of the second.

Throughout the remainder of the summer the committee worked at broadening its organizational base, appointing new town, ward, and district chairmen until the network covered most of the county. The educational campaign also began to take form around the twin themes of the archaic character of the county's government and the county director plan as a move toward reform which would at the same time preserve local home rule. Formal launching came with a series of "kick-off" luncheons held September 15. There workers heard division chairmen set the tone for the campaign and received copies of a campaign handbook prepared by Atkins. The handbook described the basic idea behind the director plan, analyzed the plan in relation to Onondaga County needs, summarized Monroe County's experience with its county executive, and provided a series of questions and answers for the worker. It was to become the basic campaign document for the county director forces.

The daily newspapers lent their support to the reorganization effort both through news coverage and through editorial comment. This was particularly true of the *Herald-Journal,* which from the beginning advocated a county-called referendum and which subsequently gave warm support to the county director proposal. The *Post-Standard* pursued a policy which caused the plan's proponents considerable uneasiness, but ultimately it, too, gave the proposition its editorial endorsement. The issue was removed from the Syracuse mayoralty campaign when both Republican and Democratic candidates announced their support of the county director plan. Neither the Republican nor the Democratic organization took an official stand on the matter.

If the opponents remained generally silent during the summer they did not at the same time remain idle. On the contrary they sponsored an educational campaign of their own which was not less effective because subterranean. The strategy was simple: it consisted in passing the word among selected townspeople that the county director plan would substitute an autocratic for a democratic system and that their supervisors therefore opposed it. The *Herald-Journal* took note of this whispering campaign in a late summer series of editorials which denounced as "contemptible fabrications" some of the more far-fetched charges being employed to combat county reorganization.

The undercover opposition to the county director proposal began to come to the surface in the early fall. Weekly newspapers throughout the county carried an increasing volume of letters and articles attacking the director plan, and spoken criticism became more open. The *Post-Standard* took cognizance of these rumblings, reporting strong resistance in many parts of the county and prophesying the early launching of a vigorous opposition campaign. The first step toward realization of this forecast was taken when attorney Alan Flattery invited all known opponents to an organization meeting on

October 15.⁶ Nearly 50 persons appeared at the organization meeting. Several major campaign themes were decided upon for emphasis: one, that the existing county government was functioning satisfactorily and that minor modifications could be made to meet its critics' objections without a drastic change; another, that the director plan offered a potential dictatorship which would subvert traditional local self-government. The name selected for the organization was "Voters for Democracy not Dictatorship."

The new organization employed for the most part standard campaign techniques. Conceding the daily papers to the pro-reorganization camp, the opposition group nevertheless received good press coverage through the channel afforded by the Don Brown chain of weekly papers, which also came out editorially against the county director plan in the last week in October. During the same week the Voters for Democracy not Dictatorship mailed an unsigned four-page tabloid to county residents which emphasized its "Dictatorship or Democracy?" theme in a way to bring strong protest from the Citizens' Committee for the County Director. The leaflet received wide publicity, thanks in part to the stir made about it by the pro-director group. Both sides achieved a good hearing through a series of joint debates carried to all parts of the county by both radio and live appearances.

The facts at hand warrant the judgment that the two committees achieved considerable success in their drive to place the county director proposal before the voters. At the same time, the subject-matter level of the campaign was far from impressive. Most of what was new was supplied by the Syracuse Governmental Research Bureau, which sought to inject into the contest objective data both about the government of Onondaga County and about manager government elsewhere. The issue, however, had to be fought out on common ground; and since the pro-director group were the attackers and the opposition group the defenders, the latter chose the field of battle. And for all the bureau's preoccupation with facts, government reorganization is a battleground where emotion often counts for more than intellect. The arguments in favor of a chief executive officer for the county, irrefutable in the logic of scientific management, must have seemed empty to a rural resident who was assured by a neighbor that the county director plan stood for centralization which would spell the doom of the towns and town officials, that it was the very embodiment of dictatorship, that it represented an attack on the American system of grass-roots government, that it was a ruse to transfer the city tax burden to the towns, that it was designed to permit Syracuse bankers and industrialists to seize control of the county ("Look who's backing it!"), that it would cost the taxpayers an additional half million dollars a year. These were the charges leveled by the opposition, and these became the controlling issues of the campaign.

The prosecution and defense rested their hard-fought cases, and on November 3, 1953, the people returned the following verdict on the county director plan:

	For	Against	Blank	Majority for (+) or against (−)
Syracuse	19,657	17,042	39,445	+2,615
Towns	8,709	19,103	18,909	−10,394
County	28,366	36,145	58,354	−7,779

Source: *Official Canvass*, Onondaga County, 1953.

Notwithstanding the vigor of the campaign, a minority approaching half of the voters (41 per cent in the towns, 52 per cent in the city) expressed no judgment on the question. The towns voted against the plan by better than 2 to 1, the city favored it by a safe if not robust margin. Over-all, the ratio of unfavorable to favorable votes was of the order of 5:4—a close vote.

The figures available show the costs of the campaign to have been somewhat more than $15,300, with $12,500 spent for the county director plan, $2,800 against. Both committees depended largely on contributions of $100 or less. The principal contributors to the pro-director campaign fund were banking, business, and manufacturing executives, with a sprinkling of former Republican county officials. Most of the financial support for the opposition campaign was said to have come from Crandall Melvin and his immediate associates. There were, of course, a number of smaller donations made to both sides.

Aftermath

The sound defeat of the county director plan was accompanied by a convincing victory by Fritz Campbell over his Democratic opponent for the position of Elbridge town supervisor. The prospect of having Campbell as chairman of the Board of Supervisors for another two years was not viewed with enthusiasm by those influential elements in the Republican Party which had supported the county director proposal. Further, it was doubted that Campbell was sympathetic to the idea of improving management in the county government by strengthening the office of chairman of the Board of Supervisors—a move which many heavy contributors to the party regarded as minimal. The party leadership responded to expressions of these feelings by looking around for a position to which Campbell might be appointed in lieu of board membership. The spot settled upon was a deputy directorship of the County Department of Welfare.

With the chairmanship of the Board of Supervisors to be filled by board election, the choice of the successor was an obvious one to both the pro-director and the anti-director wing of the Republican Party. The plan's supporters believed that Supervisor Thomas Dyer of the Town of Onondaga, the chairman of the late joint committee, had been sincerely convinced of the need for improving executive management in the county government and had been initially sympathetic to the director plan. True, he had modified his stand during the campaign, but there was a disposition to forgive and forget this defection; after all, heavy pressure had been brought to bear on the town supervisors. On the other hand, Dyer was highly regarded by the county director opponents for his articulate criticism of the director plan. His suggestion for strengthening the office of chairman of the county board was viewed as a compromise around which both factions could rally. Thus Dyer was confirmed as chairman of the Board of Supervisors at its organization meeting in January 1954.

The new chairman responded to the challenge by designating the county auditor as the county budget officer. Further in reaction to a recommendation by the chairman, the Board of Supervisors created a County Department of Research and Development to conduct studies of government operations and make recommendations thereon to the board. The quality of political and managerial talent brought to the board by Chairman Dyer was judged to be outstanding almost uniformly by Republicans and Democrats alike. However well he succeeded in toning up the existing structure of the county government, a real executive nevertheless was still lacking. Moreover, one of the obvious deficiencies of the chairman-executive system asserted itself when Supervisor Dyer was defeated for reelection by the voters of the Town of Onondaga in November 1957, primarily on local issues.

Conclusion

The most significant single feature of the reorganization movement in Onondaga County during the last quarter-century is found in its almost complete lack of substantial achievement. Wave after wave of reformers (including many who would wince at that appellation) have been cut down by the defending forces. There have been gains, to be sure, most of them resulting from state legislative action; but measured against the demands recurrently made for reform they have not been great. The county's government in its essential organization remains substantially as it was a century ago.

A second arresting feature of the county reform movement is that the increasingly metropolitan character of the county has received no notice as a reason urged for reorganization. Each new reorganization campaign has been characterized by the time-honored appeal for economy and efficiency in local government. The integration of functions, the rationalization of departmental structure, the elimination of duplication and overlap, the centralization of financial administration, the establishment of a county executive officer—these have been the battle cries of those who would reform the county's government. Functional accretions palpably growing from metropolitan needs have almost never been justified in metropolitan terms; instead such accretions normally have been regarded as nothing more than an expansion in county functions bound to cost the taxpayers more money. Notwithstanding the area's increasingly urban character, no responsible spokesman has come forward to identify the demands for new services with new opportunities, to embrace the fresh responsibilities of an emergent urban society, to equate the Syracuse metropolitan area with Onondaga County in fact as well as in name.

This is a sad concluding note for a comment on the obligations and opportunities of an urban county. Happily we do not have to end on this note—quite. Late in 1960 an official charter commission was appointed to draft a new basic document for Onondaga County.[7] It is significant that the discussion preceding the establishment of the commission emphasized the need of a metropolitan county for a modern governmental structure. Moreover, public comment since has played on the same theme: the newspapers in particular have taken up the cry. So has the Metropolitan Development Association, which from its inception has dwelt on the need for rendering the county's government adequate to the metropolitan demands made (and to be made) upon it.[8] There are signs that metropolitan needs may be superseding administrative efficiency as an argument for county reorganization. A conclusion that the county has turned the corner and is now willing (and able) to think in terms of new opportunities would, however, be premature. The habits of thought of half a century are not easily changed.

X

Cooperation, Contract, or Consolidation?

IN AN appearance before the New York State Joint Legislative Committee on Metropolitan Areas Study,[1] Donald H. Mead, then Mayor of Syracuse, discussed a number of problems of the Syracuse Metropolitan Area and the methods by which solutions have been or might be sought. Describing eight forms of metropolitan action, the Mayor cited five as having been used in the Syracuse area: annexation, special districts, functional consolidation, functional cooperation, and transfer of function. He reported that annexation had had little recent application and that it possessed even less possibility of future use, while the special district device had been used extensively outside but not within the city.[2] This left functional cooperation, transfer of function, and functional consolidation as the principal devices employed locally for dealing with metropolitan problems.

While the distinctions among the several methods of metropolitan action are useful, applying them to specific situations is often difficult. The construction of the Metropolitan Treatment Plant, for example, was variously described by the Mayor as an example of functional consolidation, transfer, and functional cooperation. Fortu-

---

Harold Herman prepared this chapter.

nately, precision in classification is not required. The significance of the categories lies not in their descriptive accuracy but in the attitudes toward problem-solving that official familiarity with them reflects, and in their impact, actual and potential, upon governmental organization and practice in the metropolitan area.

Informal and Formal Action

Cooperation, transfer of function, and consolidation represent different degrees of formalization of solutions to metropolitan area problems. In the less formal arrangements between independent fire districts and the county for joint training, mutual aid, and maintenance of a centralized fire control center, and in the completely informal exchanges of information between governmental agencies (such as the sharing of radio frequencies by counties and municipal police forces), adaptations to metropolitan conditions have come not through organizational change but through the cooperation of existing governmental units. On the other hand, the Onondaga County Water Authority, a financially independent, interjurisdictional, single-purpose agency, was established to administer a new (or newly embraced) metropolitan activity. The County Welfare Department and Children's Court exemplify transfers of functions from the city and the towns to the county government. Both these devices have already affected and promise further to alter the structure, interrelationships, and relative strength of the several governments in Onondaga County.

Metropolitan action in Onondaga County appears to be contributing to two divergent trends. The first reaffirms the traditional role and responsibilities of local governments through informal and contractual methods of interlocal cooperation. The second diminishes the stature of local units through transfer of older activities or delegation of new ones to the county government, or, as in the case of water, to a new interjurisdictional unit.

Informal cooperation is usually conceived, initiated, and maintained by the professional and administrative staffs of governmental units. Many cooperative arrangements predate the contemporary concern for metropolitan problems. They are, moreover, often cited as adequate solutions to such problems; hence they supply a powerful counter-argument to incipient demands for more drastic approaches to metropolitan action. It is not surprising that an occasional newspaper article or editorial commenting upon the possibility of police or fire consolidation is immediately followed by glowing accounts of the benefits derived from cooperative arrangements already in effect. The fire and police departments (and their chiefs) are quick to counter an expression of interest in their activities which might threaten their continued independent existence. Voluntary cooperation is an easy, painless, and usually effective antidote to any such expression.

Although the use of city public health facilities by non-city residents represents in some part involuntary "metropolitan cooperation," the availability of city facilities illustrates the negative effect that even limited cooperation can have upon proposals to consolidate or transfer functions. Not only does a cooperative arrangement minimize the need for formal metropolitan reorganization; it also poses a ticklish strategical problem for the proponents of more positive action. It is one thing to criticize an obvious lack of coordination in the conduct of similar activities by a number of governments, but it is quite another to criticize the adequacy of steps taken in the direction of coordination. The latter can easily be interpreted as an attack on the sincerity and even the motives of local officials. In a relatively small metropolitan county, where social and political relationships are comparatively uncomplicated, such aspersions may serve only to rally the community to a defense of the *status quo*. Nelson Pitts, Judge Yehle, and the town health officers, in different ways and under varying circumstances, each figured centrally in manifestations of this phenomenon. The town health officers were especially successful in exploiting a hurt defensiveness to prevent an organizational change that would have abolished their positions.

The suggestion that the less formal types of cooperative action are often the product of internal bureaucratic decisions designed to prevent more drastic changes in structure and power is not intended to imply that they occur without the involvement and consent of the official organs of public decision-making. On the contrary, such arrangements can rarely be concluded without political endorsement or without legislative and executive approval. The point is not that the bureaucracies engage in informal cooperation in a manner unknown to the responsible authorities, but that they are the initiators of such action and that normally they can obtain approval for their proposals. The formation of the Mutual Aid Association and related fire coordination activities provide an instance of a cooperative undertaking in which the role of the county's formal decision-making body was that of ratifier of decisions previously made by the chiefs of the several fire departments. The formation of the Planning Federation of Onondaga County Municipalities in 1947 similarly can be traced to action taken by the Board of Supervisors with the concurrence of local planners. The advisory federation has since been overshadowed by the creation of the slightly stronger Regional (County) Planning Board; but for some years it represented the sole local agency participating in metropolitan planning, if only on the voluntary cooperative basis agreed to by its members.

The choice of a formal over an informal course of metropolitan action is of course not accidental. At times it is not even a choice, but a result of irresistible forces generated by previous local (and even distant) decisions, economic pressures, and factors inherent in the alternatives available. Nelson Pitts' suggestion that metropolitan sewage treatment be undertaken by the city and neighboring towns through contractual agreement was inherently too modest a proposal to satisfy the intense interest in sewage treatment and its political and economic ramifications after the war. Nothing less than a formal and permanent arrangement would have been acceptable. Similarly, the Governor's veto of a local proposal to found metropolitan health programs on a voluntary part-county basis reflected a state commitment to a county form of health organization. Public interest vigorously expressed also acts as a stimulus to the selection of formal devices of metropolitan action. Once a problem is publicly identified and accepted as metropolitan in scope, it becomes difficult to confine its solution to the relatively undramatic realm of interprofessional cooperation, informal agreements, and contracts. More striking action at that juncture is both more natural and more feasible.

The cases examined in this section all deal with formal organizational change. Several factors appear to differentiate these decisional situations from those which were satisfied with informal undertakings in other functional solutions. Each of the decisions studied involved one or more of the following elements: (1) large capital or operating expenditures; (2) a clear stimulus or mandate to local action in the form of state policy; (3) active public or political participation, or both. It will prove useful to analyze the role played by each of these elements in metropolitan action.

Economy and Metropolitan Action

In recent years economists have vigorously challenged the earlier tendency to assume that metropolitan action is synonymous with increased efficiency and economies of scale. Nevertheless the promise of economy, in the sense of a prospective reduction of costs through the transfer or the consolidation of activities, continues to provide a major source of support for formal metropolitan undertakings. Financial considerations also continue to serve as a reason for opposition to metropolitan action. The savings attributable to such action are measured in terms of the aggregate expenditures of several units of government, but are usually achieved through one unit's assumption of the total reduced cost; and the net result may be an increase in expenditures by the assuming unit. Whether or not a metropolitan solution is economically beneficial may depend, therefore, on the point of view from which it is evaluated. Thus the economies claimed for the welfare and children's court consolidations failed to impress many members of the Board of Supervisors, who saw in these moves the threat of increased county expenditures and corresponding tax increases. The millions of dollars expected to be saved through construction of a metropolitan treatment plant were similarly unimpressive to political leaders of Solvay and Geddes, who balked at helping their neighbors save money at the price of involving themselves in a costly and, to their way of thinking, unnecessary program. The contradictory nature of the claim of economy is similarly reflected in the failure of the state's stimulative grant-in-aid for county health departments to overcome rural opposition to increased health expenditures, although that consideration was only partially responsible for the proposal's rejection.

Economy is a factor bearing significantly on metropolitan solutions only when the expenditures affected are relatively large; and if the experience with school district centralization can be generalized, the economic argument appears to be most effective when substantial new expenditures are in prospect. Even then, economy does not appeal equally to all groups within the community. The absence of financial arguments in the campaigns of civic and social organizations indicates both their attitudes toward government activities and their reasons for supporting metropolitan action. The adequacy of programs and the availability of responsible governmental agencies with which they can deal are the issues that command their participation.

To ascribe industrial interest in metropolitan solutions solely to concern for financial savings is to overlook other significant motives for industrial participation in public decision-making. Although company spokesmen and the Governmental Research Bureau (which is favorably predisposed to considerations of economy and efficiency) stressed the economic advantages of metropolitan water supply and sewage disposal action to industries in Onondaga County, cost was only one factor contributing to industrial support of water supply and sewage disposal programs. The saving of several million dollars in the disposal of waste into Onondaga Lake was of immediate concern to the Solvay Process Company and less directly to Crouse-Hinds, a city taxpayer. Significantly, officials of these companies played a leading role in developing the metropolitan proposal. But to Carrier and General Electric (and several other industries as well), which were included within the Ley Creek District, the difference in costs between separate city and west side facilities and a metropolitan plant was inconsequential. They were far more interested in the stability of the sewage disposal program, and in the future opportunities for area development expected to result from elevation of the Public Works Commission to a prominent position in metropolitan affairs.

Underlying industrial support of a metropolitan treatment plant and a county water authority was the concept of the metropolitan area as an economic community. Economy in this sense implies far more than the mere counting of dollar savings attainable through metropolitan action. It embraces the idea of a favorable environment, which industries consider essential. Water supply, waste disposal, transportation, and other governmental service activities that affect industry's physical environment are the functions in which they have a clear and vital concern. Although professing a continuing interest in holding public expenditures and tax rates to a minimum, industrial leaders and their organization, the Manufacturers Association, rarely become involved in programs of only indirect moment to industry. Organized industry's comparative neglect of non-industrial community problems contrasts markedly with the policy pursued by the Chamber of Commerce, which participates actively in the resolution of a wide variety of public issues. It follows that community health, social, and welfare organizations depend upon the Chamber of Commerce and its more locally oriented commercial and service business executives for support in their continuing efforts to improve governmental services.

In the light of this interpretation, it is interesting to speculate on whether the transfer of city welfare administration to the county government and its consequent redistribution of large costs could be effected today, even under Rollie Marvin's leadership, without industrial support of the proposal, much less in the face of industrial opposition. In 1938 most industrial plants were still concentrated in downtown Syracuse; of recent years there has been a marked movement of industry from the city to the suburbs. A functional transfer from city to county that was clearly to the advantage of industry in 1938 would just as clearly be to its disadvantage in 1960. Thus has the suburbanization trend affected the environment of metropolitan decision-making in one important area.

In the final analysis, any metropolitan proposal involving large capital or operating expenditures will probably attract the interest of most organized groups in the community; but as motivation for metropolitan action, dollar savings are secondary to other considerations. In educational finance, for example, the need for large accumulations of capital for construction of new schools is a greater incentive for consolidation and centralization than any reduction in costs to be derived from the construction of one school rather than several. The two largest functional transfers to date, welfare and sewage treatment, were made not so much to effect savings as to maintain what was regarded as a sound fiscal position for the city in the light of necessary bond issues.

The State and Metropolitan Problems

Notwithstanding the increasing pressures occasioned by urbanism and its consequences, Onondaga County still requires external stimulation to help in translating felt needs into governmental action. The most frequent source of external stimulation is Albany, the seat of New York State government.[3]

The state's impact on local decision-making takes many forms, but is basically derived from its ultimate authority to prescribe the number and kind of local governments and to distribute powers, duties, and limitations among them. State approval is required for a wide variety of decisions, whether they result in little or great changes in the structure and duties of local governments. In general, in order to cooperate and contract with one another, local governments must obtain prior permission from the state. This may take the form of specific advance permission to consolidate welfare activities or create a county children's court. Permissive authority may be accompanied by other legislative and executive action that seeks to influence local units rather than merely to offer them a choice of alternatives. Preferential grants for county health departments and centralized school districts exemplify this type of action. Mandatory reorganization and distribution of functions are the most severe and least used means of state influence.

Except for its active role in general educational reorganization, the passage of special legislation upon local request is probably the state's most significant contribution to the reorganization of local governments to adapt to metropolitan conditions. In time, the provisions of such legislation are often incorporated into general legislation and so made available on a local option basis throughout the state. To illustrate, permissive general legislation of 1954 authorizing the creation of county sewer agencies was patterned after the

Onondaga County Public Works Act of 1933 and its Public Works Commission. If state policy leaders feel strongly enough about the merits of the new legislation, pressures may be exerted to stimulate local governments to choose the new option. Thus the state's role varies at different stages in the historical development of a metropolitan device.

The present state policy in regard to county health departments represents the most advanced form of permissive action. Starting with the successful experimental development of a county department in Cattaraugus, the state subsequently authorized its general use, supplied financial incentives, and, more recently, put its full resources into a campaign to promote county-wide departments. Continued resistance may yet compel the state to resort to its ultimate weapon, the mandating of county departments. Experience with the state policy of encouraging school district centralization is instructive in this connection.

In addition to approving local decisions and making available new alternatives for local selection, with or without additional stimulation, the state acts in several ways to provide positive leadership to local units. Even at the stage in which it merely approves local decisions, the state is often instrumental through some prior action in shaping the course of a decision. For example, although the decision to treat Onondaga Lake pollution on a metropolitan basis was locally made, the Water Pollution Control Board, and before that the Departments of Health and Conservation, had contributed greatly toward articulating the problem in metropolitan terms. In this instance state policy acted as a stimulator of local initiative and ingenuity. Significantly, the Water Pollution Control Board is often criticized for threatening local officials with legal prosecution while failing to provide them with funds or with suggestions of methods for solving their financial problems. To date, the state's suggestions for metropolitan sewage disposal programs are contained in permissive legislation authorizing interlocal contractual arrangements and the creation of county sewer agencies; it has done nothing more to compel or direct metropolitan action by local units.

State legislative and administrative policy often sets the boundaries by which local decisions are limited. Moreover, such policy frequently stimulates local reevaluations. The Water Power and Control Commission's ruling that Syracuse does not have sufficient reserves to permit it to continue the sale of water to neighboring towns was a major factor precipitating consideration of a new metropolitan water agency for Onondaga County. The outside boundary of state intervention appears virtually limitless, for Onondaga County historically has had little difficulty in securing legislative approval of its requests for special legislation. The lengthy tenures of office enjoyed by Onondaga County Republican members in the state legislature have led frequently to their assuming positions of leadership in state councils. During his term of office, Senator Fearon served at different times as both Majority and Minority Leader of the Senate. Assemblyman Charles Schoeneck, a nephew of former Lieutenant-Governor Edward Schoeneck, recently acted as Majority Leader of the Assembly. When Onondaga County representatives have not been officers of the two houses, their requests have generally been granted by the legislature, even though the resulting action incurred departmental opposition and sometimes a gubernatorial veto. Amiable relations with the legislature also enable local political leaders occasionally to shift the burden of responsibility for unpopular local decisions to Albany.

The state's capacity to develop, or to participate effectively in the development of, new forms of urban organization and action is severely limited by its lack of a metropolitan policy. If the major avenues of state action *vis-à-vis* the localities could be brought into reasonable focus in support of a concerted policy (or nexus of rationally related policies) respecting "the metropolitan problem," those concerned with that problem in New York could face the future with considerably more assurance. Establishment of the Joint Legislative Committee on Metropolitan Areas Study gave evidence of a feeling on the part of some state leaders that all is not well. It represented, however, little more than a gesture, a token pebble of state interest cast into a large and expanding pool of unavoidable state concern. The state of New York has yet to come to grips with the metropolitan world of the nineteen-sixties.

The Politicians and the Party

With the county assuming ever greater importance in the solution of metropolitan problems, the Board of Supervisors has come increasingly to serve as the agent for making and voicing formal metropolitan decisions. In view of the board's new-found responsibility, a number of questions about that body come to mind. What values does it (or do its members individually) seek to advance? To what extent does it *make* decisions, to what extent does it merely *ratify* decisions taken elsewhere? What is its position in the political power structure?

The values underlying the political orientation of the Board of Supervisors are a unique product of its organizational and representative structure. Members of the board, the town and village boards, and (somewhat less vigorously) the Common Council share a common compulsion to resist change. Like most members of most representative bodies, they tend to view with suspicion any proposal that threatens to upset the political order as they know it, though in Onondaga County the threshold of suspicion seems unusually low. They are equally loath to sanction increased expenditures and regard political success—that is, their ability to gain reelection—as contingent on maintaining existing tax rates. Thus motivated, the legislators, and indeed other local officials as well, rarely act as initiators of new programs or proposals for reorganization.

These values motivate the Board of Supervisors with even greater intensity because of its confederative structure. Supervisors, city as well as town, tend to think of themselves first and foremost as district representatives. Indeed, in recent city campaigns, more than one candidate for ward supervisor has addressed himself exclusively to municipal issues over which the board has no control, a fact the candidates either did not understand or chose to ignore. To county residents outside the city, the town or village is still a more meaningful entity, political as well as social, than the county; and town supervisors reflect this traditional predilection in their grass-roots approach to county problems. Their parochial allegiances cause them to evaluate every county program in terms of its comparative benefits and costs to their individual constituencies. To some extent, all legislative bodies are of course moved by this form of allegiance, but the representative base of the Board of Supervisors has the effect of elevating local loyalty to the status of the primary political virtue. The Syracuse Common Council is composed of representatives elected in part at large, in part from districts; seldom, however, is a district councilman heard to complain that a city expenditure financed from general revenues will benefit another district at the expense of his own. Such a complaint is common among the supervisors. This difference in attitude well illustrates the weakness of the county legislative body, as presently constituted, as a metropolitan decision-maker. A county-wide consensus rarely emerges from the deliberations of the Board of Supervisors, and then only as regards issues either well insulated from local interest or influence or subjected to the coercive force of Republican Party discipline.

The board suffers further from a lack of executive leadership.[4] That this reflects an institutional defect may be seen from a comparison of the offices of mayor and chairman. Syracuse has a strong mayor type of government, which enables the mayor to seize and enlarge upon the opportunities inherent in his office. The chairman occupies no such position; he is in fact precisely what his title indicates, Chairman of the Board of Supervisors. Occasionally a chairman or even an individual member can play a positive role regarding an issue in which he is particularly concerned; but ordinarily the board turns to outside sources for leadership, as did the (Republican) Common Council during (Democratic) Mayor Corcoran's administration.

A tradition of cohesiveness and broad community awareness differentiates both officials and citizens of the city from their non-city counterparts. Their broader perspective, however, ordinarily does not extend to the towns. Attempts to instill in urban residents a sense of town needs must combat a spirit of separatism bolstered by a deliberately cultivated urban consciousness as opposed to the rural attitudes of the countryside. City officials in the past have often been frustrated in their attempts to gain cooperation from the county in bringing about what they regarded as a more equitable distribution of services and resources. The towns' reluctance to admit that public welfare, public health, and juvenile delinquency are rural as well as urban problems may now be matched, ironically, by a similar attitude on the part of the city with regard to the problem of providing additional water for the growing suburban areas.

The differences in attitude toward their governments by city and town residents are in part a reflection of differing forms of financial administration. With some few exceptions, the special benefit form of taxation is not used in the city. Its residents have long been accustomed to pay taxes without regard for the neighborhoods that will derive advantages from their expenditure. This is as true for the city's fiscally dependent school system as for the traditional municipal programs. The county and towns, in contrast, have employed the special benefit assessment district widely as a device for extending services to particular areas at no expense to non-benefited territory. The impact of these differing methods of financing upon community consciousness is nowhere more evident than in the dispute over construction of the metropolitan treatment plant. In contrast to the bickering among towns and villages as to who would gain most at the least cost, there was no appreciable resistance from the areas serviced by existing plants, despite the fact that city residents in these sections would have to contribute through the general fund to the cost of a new plant from which they would receive no direct service.

When their values are not in conflict with those of the initiators of metropolitan proposals, and when the issue of increased cost can be rationalized, supervisors tend to accept and approve the proposals formulated by others. In at least the early stages of the Children's Court deliberations, the Board of Supervisors seemed content to go along with what appeared to be a worthy League of Women Voters project. Similarly, with respect to proposals for inter-local cooperation, the board often perfunctorily lends its approval to schemes developed elsewhere. But when its values and those of a plan's proponents seriously conflict, as they did in the case of the proposed county health department, in the absence of other factors the board may either assert a position of its own and refuse to approve the proposal or adopt another course of action.

In the majority of cases in which the board and the initiators of metropolitan proposals find themselves in conflict, a third force comes into play to compromise and resolve the differences. This force is leadership. In the sense in which it is used here, leadership is defined as the ability to influence the selection of one alternative from a number available to the board. It is, or may become, a coercive force, for the natural inclination of the board is to take no action. To some, leadership is an inclusive term applicable to all who participate in the process of articulating a problem and planning and undertaking its solution. In the vague and indiscriminate manner in which the term "community leader" is normally used, little distinction can be drawn between the William Maloneys and the Rolland Marvins. But it is evident from the cases studied that a great gulf separates the articulation of a problem and the initiation of a proposal from the actual decision to adopt a metropolitan solution. The state, interest groups, community volunteer agency leaders, and individual citizens are all sources, jointly and severally, of articulation and initiative. In Onondaga County, the Republican Party supplies the leadership which cajoles or extracts decisions from the bodies officially charged with policy determination.

What and who is the Republican Party? It is the one political organization (discounting the Democratic Party—and it is always discounted locally) that encompasses all of Onondaga County. It is the one fountain of direction and decision to which the party faithful can look with complete assurance, for if an issue is politically important its views will be made known. For many years the Republican Party was personified by Clarence King and Rolland Marvin, successive county chairmen. At times they acted on their own initiative, but more often they reacted to the political pressures of the community. When the pressures assumed the proportions of a threat to the party, the chairman did not hesitate to take a decision and enforce it upon all appropriate officials. The campaign for a county health department in the 1930's did not pose a threat sufficiently great to induce King or Marvin to involve the party in the issue; the danger, real or fancied, of the city's financial collapse if it continued to incur debt for welfare purposes did.

After Marvin's decline local resentment at his tactics, together with social changes throughout the country which modified the nature of political participation, led to the selection of county chairmen who would not continue in the tradition of strong leadership. That the health department proposal has languished in recent years is due partly to the absence of a leader upon whom the proposal's sponsors could call for aid. When that issue was reactivated in the late 1940's, volunteer agency leaders were compelled to approach individual supervisors in the hope of convincing them of the proposal's merits. In this effort they failed. They were more successful in mental health, where they found an ally in the articulate and persuasive chairman of the Board of Supervisors. But Thomas Dyer's role was much different from Marvin's or King's. In the final analysis the supervisors followed Dyer's lead not from fear of reprisal nor from considerations of party loyalty, but because they believed his position was sound. Persuasiveness and logic were indeed his only weapons.

If the few cases examined here can be taken to indicate a trend, decision-making in Onondaga County is as dependent as ever upon the Republican Party. But the approach to the party has altered markedly in the last 15 years; for whereas previously all that was necessary under normal conditions to assure the success of a proposal was the support of the party's county chairman, now there is no such easy and convenient access. It has become difficult today to find a man, county chairman or other, who can throw the party's united resources into a battle.[5] Industrial leaders spent months trying to pin the Republican Party down to a position on the metropolitan treatment plant issue. In the end, the industrialists themselves had to step in and direct the progress of the proposal through the required hearings and other processes to a decision. The political party was the mechanism through which agreement was evolved, but its action was stimulated, guided, and supplemented by the activities of industry. Few initiators are in a position to set this process in motion.

The change in Republican Party organization and leadership is symptomatic of the growing threat to political stability posed by the metropolitan problem. Local leaders have learned to weigh well the possible consequences of metropolitan action, which often has meant to them centralization of activities at the county level and increased taxation. The welfare experience continues to serve as a dramatic reminder of the price paid for party loyalty. Even without that reminder, new forces of divisiveness are generated daily as local leaders strive to resist the pressures for change that, in the nature of the political process as it is known in Onondaga County, must eventually be resolved within the Republican Party.

The party's traditional city-town split has been intensified rather than relieved as a consequence of the increasing urbanization of the county. In the past, local leaders were willing to compose their differences at the urging of a strong party leader. Now a centrally directed party would pose threats to their security more serious than ever before, and it is to their interest to retain independence in party as well as governmental affairs. The absence of a strong county chairman since 1945 is more than coincidentally related to the emergence of the metropolitan problem.

City leaders are particularly affected by the growing separatism within the Republican Party. The financial advantages of transferring urban functions to the county provide a compelling motivation for such action. In the past city officials have tended to view a transfer of program control not as a loss to the county but as a switch to another branch of the Republican organization. The delays involved in the treatment plant negotiations suggest that the branches are becoming more than a little suspicious of one another.

With respect to decisions concerning metropolitan problems, the argument may be reduced to a few basic propositions. First, in the Syracuse metropolitan area Onondaga County is the most likely center of metropolitan action. Second, the county is ill equipped in point of organization and executive leadership to come to reasoned decisions regarding metropolitan issues. Third, such decisions for area-wide action as have been made in the past—and they have not been inconsiderable—have resulted chiefly from vigorous political leadership residing in the Republican Party outside the formal structure of government. Fourth, the conditions making for such leadership no longer obtain, with the result that that party now operates without the firm direction it had for so long. Fifth, and as a consequence of the foregoing, the main traditional channel for metropolitan decision-making in Onondaga County has been so drastically modified as to be available only under new and largely untried conditions. What these conditions will mean for metropolitan action in the future cannot be foretold, but the way ahead looks considerably more rocky than that recently traveled.

Concluding Comment

In essence the approaches to metropolitan decision-making may be reduced to two. The first, which emphasizes the metropolitan character of the problems to be dealt with, in principle favors an area-wide agency with power of decision. The achievement of a general metropolitan government, an implicit and sometimes a stated goal in other days, has since been abandoned as impractical by the rationalist school, which nevertheless continues to stress the importance of institutional arrangements. Recognized channels for bringing up issues, established agencies and stated procedures for their consideration, accepted methods for their resolution—these are held to be the hallmarks of logical action for the disposition of metropolitan problems.

The second approach elevates the values resident in existing institutions and procedures. The pragmatic school is concerned not with form but with results. Its adherents find no cause for taking metropolitan issues out of context by establishing novel area-wide institutions, which, they aver, would create more problems than they would solve. In the long run, they argue, metropolitan problems, along with most others, do get solved, whether or not by neat and orderly procedure; and the process by which they are solved allows most interested individuals and groups ample opportunity to express themselves. Citizen participation in the making of decisions is a fundamental characteristic of the democratic process. Involved here, then, the argument concludes, is nothing less than the preservation of democratic values. (It is hardly necessary to observe that the rationalists do not accept this interpretation of the issue.)

The cases analyzed in this section reveal the Syracuse metropolitan area caught up in the conflict between the rationalists and the pragmatists, the former urging institutional reform as the only logical approach to metropolitan decision-making, the latter demanding that metropolitan problems be treated within the framework of existing institutions. Whatever the merits of the quarrel, there can be no doubt where the advantage lies up to this time. Governmental reorganization has failed on a number of fronts over the last three decades; most particularly, it has failed in respect of the county's government, which looms at once as the ultimate repository of the power to make area-wide decisions and as an embattled stronghold of resistance to change. Institutional reform will come, but there are no indications that its advent will be abrupt or dramatic.

Meanwhile metropolitan decisions in some miraculous fashion continue to be made. The problems called up for consideration depend upon the interests of those with the power of initiation, as the disposition of each depends upon the strength of the forces marshaled in favor of or against a proposed course of action. In all this there is little that appears orderly or logical. In the labyrinth of public decision-making that prevails in the Syracuse metropolitan area there is no predicting when or where or how a problem will originate, by what governments or agencies or by what methods it will be considered, or how it will be disposed of. In this respect, it may be surmised, Onondaga County does not differ materially from other metropolitan areas; for almost nowhere has there been substantial institutional reform to substitute systematic arrangements for the process of improvisation described for the Syracuse metropolitan area.

Part 3

PUBLIC-PRIVATE DECISIONS

Introduction

THE pattern of economic activity in regions can be studied from a number of vantage points. In economics the oldest approach is by way of location theory; von Thünen was the original architect and his first work was published in 1826. First for agriculture and later for industrial activity von Thünen and followers in this tradition have constructed models to show the patterns of economic activity that will occur within a region as a consequence of the operation of market forces. Given the desire of entrepreneurs to maximize profits and therefore minimize transportation costs, the resulting location of economic activity can be described in a pattern of spatial relationships.[1]

In the last several decades, the techniques of economic analysis have been applied to the metropolitan region for quite a different purpose. The recent emphasis is not on the "natural" forces of the market and their outcome, but on the constraints that public policy should impose on the private market in the interests of long-run efficient use of resources. City planners must describe the economic structure of an urban area as a basis for judging the adequacy of land use for transportation facilities, water, sewerage, and other municipal services. Such descriptions are invariably undertaken with a view to forecasting. The planner will be faced with the necessity for anticipating the future of population growth and employment, and hence of residential, commercial, and industrial location patterns and land requirements. In such cases, the planner-economist undertakes to project historical trends, as modified in accordance with his informed judgment.[2]

Another type of contemporary economic analysis of the metropolitan area may be termed the "impact study." Here the objective is to trace through the probable consequences of a specific addition to economic activity, for example the establishment of a large industrial plant. One of the techniques developed for this purpose is the economic base study.[3] Working with readily available data on employment patterns, it is possible to calculate ratios of persons employed as producers of goods and services consumed within the metropolitan region in relation to employment for production to be consumed outside the region. This ratio of "domestic" to "export" employment can then be used to approximate the total employment pattern that may result from a new "export" industry. The base ratio technique can also be employed for more general projections of a region's economic activity.

Another approach, which may be termed "the analysis of strategic factors," is well illustrated in the work of Edgar M. Hoover and the recent study of the New York metropolitan region by Hoover and Vernon.[4] Here the starting point is the national economy and anticipated changes in the composition of national output. Then an effort is made to select the industries in a specific metropolitan region that are critical for its development in relation to national trends, and within these industries to examine cost factors, such as transportation, space requirements, access to raw materials, etc., that determine patterns of location. The analysis of these strategic elements permits a general forecast of the probable economic development of the region. A similar but more limited approach starts with the computation of regional shares of national economic activity in a base period and seeks to analyze the factors that will change the magnitude of such "localization coefficients."[5]

More elaborate descriptions of economic activity within the metropolitan region are developed as part of a structure of regional accounts. These may take a number of forms. One is the regional income and product account, along the lines of national income accounts.[6] Another is the balance of payments account, whose principal objective is to show the relationship between intra- and extra-regional activity.[7] The most complete description of economic activity within a region is provided by the input-output matrix. This is a tabular presentation of inter-industry relationships to show the patterns of final demand for goods and services within a region, and the transaction patterns among industries that make up the region's aggregate flow of goods and services. Leontief is the major contributor to this development; Isard and others have developed its application to regional studies.[8]

In spite of the very large volume of work that has been done in the examination of economic activity in metropolitan regions, both at the conceptual and at the measurement level, there are great gaps in our knowledge and in the application of known techniques. Coleman Woodbury, who is a pessimist in these matters, has said, "From our admittedly poor knowledge of current metropolitan growth and our even poorer understanding of what lies behind it no one can see, clearly and unmistakably, all or nearly all of its economic implications."[9] Most of the work that has been done by economists and city planners has been macroeconomic in character, that is, it has sought to measure and project regional aggregates or industrial aggregates within regions to meet specific problems at hand. This is a promising research frontier where efforts now under way will yield substantial improvements in concepts and techniques for the measurement of regional economic activity. Much less attention has been directed to the economic decision patterns of specific business firms and government units within the metropolitan region, although one aspect of this complex, business decisions in the context of community power structure, has come in for recent examination.[10]

The chapters that follow are essentially microeconomic in character. The first unit for investigation is the business firm which is engaged in one or more phases of real estate development. A second category of units for study comprises public agencies and officials—the complicated pattern of bureaucracy that characterizes the governmental structure existing in metropolitan regions. A third group consists of the intermediaries—the law firms, engineering firms, and

SOME REAL ESTATE DEVELOPMENTS IN THE SYRACUSE METROPOLITAN AREA

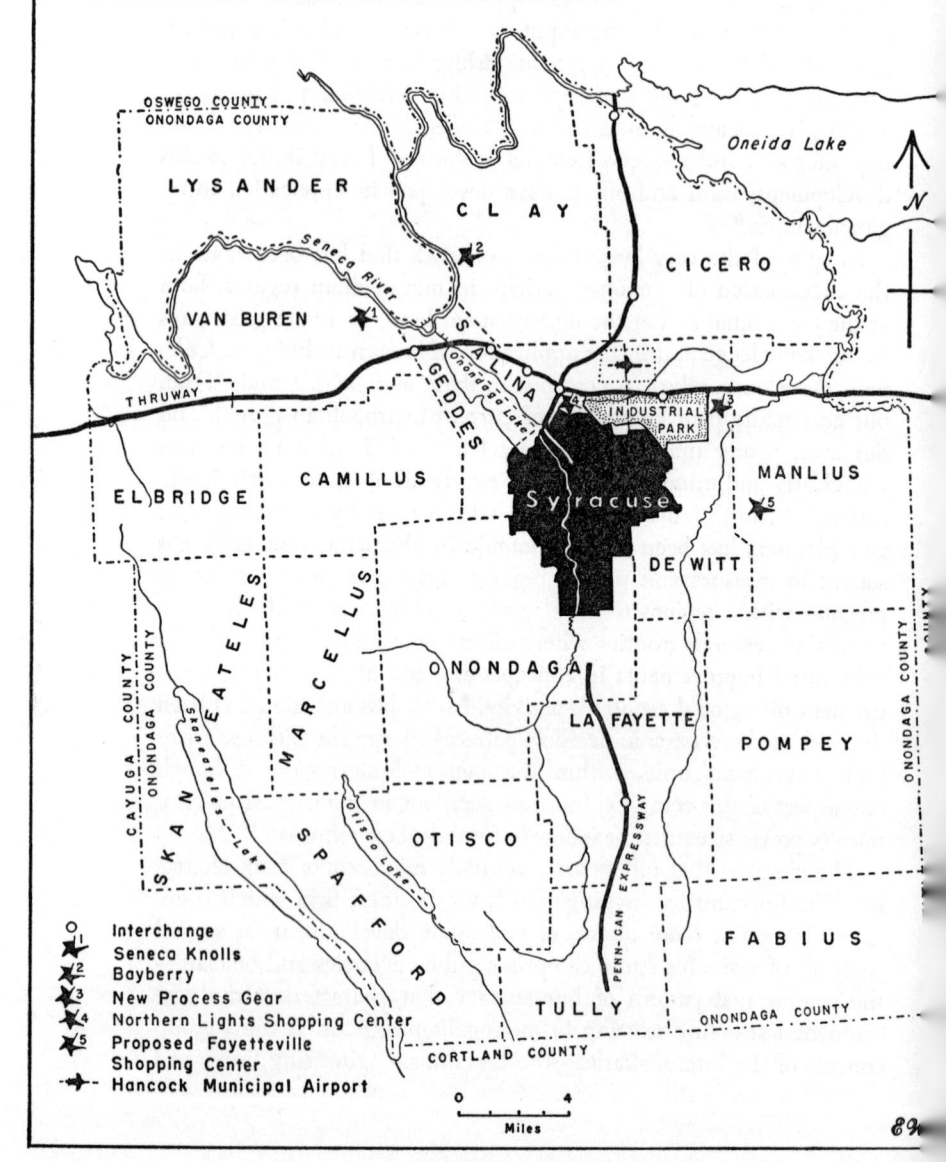

Map 3

○ 1 Interchange
★ 2 Seneca Knolls
★ 2 Bayberry
★ 3 New Process Gear
★ 4 Northern Lights Shopping Center
★ 5 Proposed Fayetteville Shopping Center
✈ Hancock Municipal Airport

INTRODUCTION

real estate brokers that discharge the functions of communicating, bargaining, and mediating between the public and the private sector in matters of local economic development.

The spatial context is the Syracuse metropolitan area, which for purposes of this study is viewed in isolation from its larger fabric— the pattern of state or national public and private influences that affect the locality's growth and development. Only occasional references are made to extra-regional or national forces. It may be hoped that an examination of the interplay of public and private interests at the local level will provide at least limited insights into regional patterns of public and private decision-making.

Chapter XI presents five brief case studies of specific development projects. Chapter XII examines in greater depth the promotion of an industrial park in the county. This venture has been and continues to be of the greatest importance in shaping the area's economic development. Map 3 indicates the location of the developments described. Chapter XIII builds on these investigations of specific real estate developments, and on scattered literature drawn from such diverse fields as urban land economics, public finance, public administration, urban planning, and political theory, to describe a behavior pattern in the relations between private economic development and public agencies in the metropolitan region.

XI

Real Estate Development: Five Case Studies

ONE who would engage in real estate development in the Syracuse metropolitan area must be prepared to deal with a wide variety of governmental units and agencies. The federal government is represented principally by the Federal Housing Administration and the Veterans Administration. Among state agencies the Conservation Department, Department of Public Works, Health Department, Water Pollution Control Board, Public Service Commission, Department of Audit and Control, and Traffic Commission are those most frequently involved. The City of Syracuse is so close to the scene that its Mayor and Common Council sometimes take a direct hand; while its Planning Commission, Board of Zoning Appeals, Engineering Department, and Department of Public Works may figure in a developmental project in a number of ways. The same may be said of Onondaga County and its Board of Supervisors, and of such county agencies as the Regional Planning Board, Water Authority, and Public Works Commission. The 19 town and 15 village governments

---

Herbert M. Kagi prepared this chapter.

REAL ESTATE DEVELOPMENT: FIVE CASE STUDIES 241

take an active interest in such developments as may concern them, notably (though by no means exclusively) through their 23 planning boards and 25 boards of zoning appeals. Finally there are 417 special town improvement districts, among which in the present context the water and sewer districts are most important. There is, then, no dearth of governments concerned with such developmental factors as planning, zoning, and subdivision regulations, water supply, sewage disposal, and streets and roads.[1]

The complex involvement of governmental agencies in the procedures, processes, and end products of real estate development requires the entrepreneur-promoter, whether builder, real estate agent, banker, or lawyer, to negotiate continuously with public officials. At the same time, the development entrepreneur must conduct his operations in the private sector, where he deals in a market relationship with the landowner, the construction firm, the supplier of building materials and the ultimate purchaser of the property. Real estate development is therefore intrinsically interesting for its semi-public and semi-private character.

The five short case studies examined here are intended to suggest the intricacies of these public-private relationships. They embrace the three major types of development projects—residential, commercial, and industrial—and they represent both large and small developments. The first study (Fayetteville) illustrates the reactions of citizen groups and their influence in modifying or restraining a project. The next two cases (Seneca Knolls and Bayberry) relate to residential projects; in one instance the developer is a relatively small local firm, in the other a large interstate company. The fourth case (Northern Lights) concerns a shopping center development and the fifth (New Process Gear) a large industrial project. The last case is intimately related to the following chapter, which examines in greater detail the background and promotion of a major industrial park. Map 3 shows the location of the several developments.

Fayetteville: Development Denied

It has been said that, given a free choice, upper-income suburbs typically develop to the east of the central city so that commuters may drive to and from work with the sun at their backs instead of in their eyes. This preference for pleasant driving may or may not explain the location of residential suburbs in the Syracuse metropolitan area, but in fact most of the upper-income residential suburbs are to the east of the city. Fayetteville is an incorporated village six miles east of the city boundary with some streets of stately homes that are as well kept as in Grover Cleveland's boyhood. New subdivisions in other sections of the village have not outwardly altered the character of the community nor destroyed an essentially "village" psychology.

In 1956 Gulf Oil Company concluded that a filling station would be profitable in this growing area and selected a site across the village line on a state highway—Route 5. The property in question was within the Town of Manlius, in which the Village of Fayetteville is located. The company optioned the necessary property and retained an attorney from neighboring Dewitt, Mr. John Humpleby, to proceed with a zone change from residential to commercial. Humpleby had been Dewitt Town Supervisor in the late 'forties and had been active as a real estate attorney with more than ordinary success in negotiations with local officials. He talked with three acquaintances on the Manlius Town Board and received their assurance of an affirmative vote for the necessary zoning modification. The Town Board is composed of six members plus the Town Supervisor, who votes in case of a tie. This meant that, given the probable opposition of the other three members, the deciding vote would be cast by the supervisor, whose tentative approval Humpleby had secured before the hearing.

The hearing on the resolution for zone changes was held February 7, 1957. About 75 people appeared to register opposition, including the North Burdick Street Mothers Club; residents from points as far as two miles away; an attorney from the Syracuse law firm of Estabrook, Estabrook, Brooks, and Hancock; and C. S. Estabrook, Sr., who headed that important firm and was a long-time resident of Fayetteville. His position in town and village affairs had been of considerable importance in years past. Coincidentally, the site in question was just across the state highway from his home.

At the meeting, various people spoke about the disadvantages of commercial development, particularly gas stations. The attorney from the Estabrook firm identified himself as the representative of Syracuse University, which owned a golf course about one-half mile west on Route 5. That institution, he stated, opposed the building of a gas station. Humpleby's argument emphasized the tax contribution that would be made by a small commercial development. One of the Town Board members who had agreed to vote for the zone change could not appear at the meeting; the final vote, therefore, was 3 to 2 against the resolution for the change.

This activity served as a backdrop for a much larger real estate project planned by two Syracuse attorneys, George Peluso and Michael Koplovitz, who had purchased not just a site for a filling station but a 72-acre tract (including that site) at a price of about $125,000. A third investor, a contractor, participated by extending a $70,000 mortgage to Messrs. Peluso and Koplovitz. The principals then filed an application with the Town of Manlius for a zoning change which would permit construction of a medium-sized shopping center. The site was considered ideal for such a project in view of its location, the cost of the land, the income levels of residents in the area, the condition of the site itself, and the fact that the property was serviced with both water and sewer lines.

Peluso and Koplovitz did not attempt any preliminary negotiation, but proceeded directly to the public hearing stage. The local paper, the Fayetteville *Village Eagle,* voiced strong opposition in advance of the hearing, which was held in August 1957. The same forces that opposed the previous zone change application appeared at the shopping center hearing; but this time Estabrook, who had remained silent before, made his view clearly known. Discussion was heated, but the opposition of Fayetteville residents held firm. The vote of the Town Board was 6 to 0 against the zone change.

Fayetteville, Lyndon, and Manlius residents continue without the facilities of a suburban shopping center. Some real estate developers feel that the Town Board may one day permit the zone change, with an appropriate control over physical design and landscape planning for the area. The principals in the shopping center proposal continue to control the site and have been unwilling to grant options to other potential developers.

Seneca Knolls: The Private Financing of Public Facilities

Most of the mass home building in the Syracuse metropolitan area has occurred north of the city. The terrain there is relatively flat, with large amounts of open acreage available and with easy access to the network of superhighways and interchanges. The area's proximity to a number of new industrial plants has also contributed to its development for mass subdivision.

The Town of Van Buren lies on the suburban fringe of the central city. By 1954 it had gained only a small fraction of either the population or the industrial growth of Onondaga County. Town officials had had almost no experience in adjusting to the pressures and demands created by new and large-scale real estate activity. Early in 1954, however, Peter Cappuccilli acquired control of 170 acres of farm land in Van Buren to build some 500 middle-income homes to be priced from $11,000 to $13,000. A part of the acreage was originally assembled by Eagan Real Estate for an industrial park development. A New York State Thruway interchange is located one mile to the south of the site and a four-lane road from the interchange to the city line was already projected. The land cost was relatively low, ranging from $600 to $1,200 per acre. A water district had been organized the previous year closely approximating the area planned for development, with a water main reaching almost to the tract. The site posed no major land fill, drainage, or clearance problem.

Preliminary plans were drawn for the project, to be known as Seneca Knolls. These included the subdivision plats, road layouts and specifications, drainage facilities, individual sewage disposal units (septic tanks), lateral water lines, a school site, and park and recreational areas to be ultimately transferred to local governmental units. At about the same time, the Van Buren Town Board was in the process of rezoning areas previously designated as farm or open land to residential, commercial, or industrial use. These changes included the proposed site, which was to be redesignated Residential I with large lot size minima. This move would have frustrated Cappuccilli's plans for low-priced homes constructed for a specific market. With his attorney, therefore, he talked with the Town Board and reached agreement that the area would be zoned Residential II (which carried smaller lot size minima) if water and sewage facilities were provided for each lot. The preliminary plans were filed and approved by the Town Board without any major difficulty.

Relations between the town officials and the developer may be described as good. Such delays as occurred were largely attributable to the lack of administrative experience on the part of the town. A sort of reliance relationship was developed in which the town officials "trusted" Cappuccilli's attorney in matters of common concern between town and developer.

Plans were also submitted to the State Health Department, Federal Housing Administration, and Veterans Administration. Approval was granted by the latter two agencies with some minor revisions concerning street layout, park areas, and the planting of trees. None of these was objected to by the developer. Approval by the Health Department posed more of a problem.

The water district, known as the Seneca Water District, did not include the whole of the tract and it became necessary to induce the town to extend the district to cover the total development acreage. This was accomplished without undue difficulty; but the extension of the district's water main, to be financed by a new bond issue, presented a problem. The developer's engineers concluded that the proposed trunk line to the tract would be too small to provide adequate hydrant pressures for the fire protection system. The bonding had been set, but the contract had not yet been let nor materials purchased. Under these circumstances Cappuccilli, rather than have his plans delayed by the time required to float a new bond issue, agreed to pay the water district the difference in cost for a larger main—approximately $15,000. All lateral water pipes were to be installed by the developer and the additional costs reflected in the purchase price of each home. Water was to be furnished on contract by the Village of Baldwinsville, north of the tract, from a well supply which engineers agreed would provide sufficient water for the completed tract for the time being.

The Seneca Knolls project encountered its greatest difficulty in providing sewage disposal. In fact, sewage treatment continues to be partially unresolved, although by the early summer of 1960 more than 300 families were occupying homes in the tract. As noted above, the original plans called for a septic tank for each home. At about this time, however, the State Health Department established a policy of approving septic tanks for sewage disposal only in tracts with more than half-acre sites.[2] Cappuccilli's plat plans did not meet this standard. This meant that the local governing body must either extend sewer trunk facilities to the tract or build a treatment plant for the newly-formed district. Another alternative, if the local government unit would not act, was for the builder to construct his own treatment facilities. Rather than wait for governmental action, Cappuccilli began making plans to build a treatment plant as well as laterals. (Laterals from the house to the street, although not laid for immediate use, were shown on the original plans.) These plans met with the technical specifications of the State Health Department. Because of the lack of experience in the construction of private sewage treatment plants locally, however, no clearly defined approval and control procedures had been worked out; hence it was not clear whether the developer must seek permission from the town, the State Health Department, or the County Public Works Commission. Eventually it became necessary to secure the approval of all those agencies, and in addition that of the State Department of Public Works and the Water Pollution Control Board (since the plans called for pumping sewage effluent into a branch of the Barge Canal located on one side of the tract).

The Public Works Commission, operating under broad policies established by its basic law, asserted jurisdiction over private treatment facilities. Its program embraced plans for the eventual take-over of sewer facilities for the whole county. Moreover the commission required the developer to build a treatment plant with enough capacity to take care of future area needs, which would increase the cost of the proposed Seneca Knolls plant by 30 to 40 per cent. The net effect of this requirement, if applied, would be to confront Cappuccilli with a capital expenditure approximating $250,000 for sewage disposal facilities before he could sell a single home. And apart from capital construction costs, there was the problem of protecting an investment made unsure by the capacity requirement, along with the obligation to turn the facilities over to a public agency upon completion. After such transfer another developer could presumably tap into the plant without assuming any of the risk or the financial obligations of initial construction. Conceivably this might take place even before Cappuccilli had realized any return on his capital outlay.

The chief advantage of a private sewage treatment plant to the developer, if these complications could be overcome, was that facilities installed and paid for would serve as a selling attraction to a tax-conscious public. Further, private development would be less costly than public because of the savings on attorney fees and bond flotation charges, and this could represent substantial cost advantage to the home purchaser.

The Public Works Commission did not immediately approve the developer's proposal because the projected facilities did not meet the commission's capacity requirement. After extended negotiations, however, Cappuccilli secured approval of his plans with the understanding that that requirement would be met subsequently. Upon completion of the facilities and construction of the first group of homes in Seneca Knolls, a tentative agreement for transfer was drafted in the form of a lease between the developer and the Town of Van Buren. The lease called for control, operation, and maintenance by the town at town expense. Other subdivisions or large-scale developers utilizing the plant would be required to pay a fee proportionate to their use, such payments to be remitted to Cappuccilli. The lease was to be terminated and title to the treatment plant assumed by the town when Cappuccilli had built and sold enough homes to cover his investment or when another developer had paid sums which, together with Cappuccilli's returns, would meet the capital construction costs. This arrangement has not yet been consummated, for the Town of Van Buren is not anxious to take over the added burden of maintaining the facilities. Meanwhile Cappuccilli has been paying the service and maintenance costs, which have amounted to about $700 per year. Meanwhile, too, the State Health Department and the County Public Works Commission continue to press for transfer to a public agency of the plant that nobody wants but the residents need.

An additional complication arose from the fact that public sewage facilities would not, of course, be subject to assessment for property taxes; while the value of private facilities would be reflected in the market value of the homes, which would carry correspondingly higher valuations. The developer has had some (though not complete) success in convincing the town assessors that, in the special circumstances which prevail in Seneca Knolls, private facilities should be treated as public facilities in the determination of assessed values.

School sites and park areas set aside by the developer have not been transferred to government jurisdiction because of reluctance on the part of public bodies to assume maintenance and ownership costs. Moreover, the developer's plans for a mall at the entrance to the tract were abandoned because the town highway superintendent was unwilling to agree to maintain the area. A volunteer fire house site, however, has been transferred to the appropriate fire protection district.

The foregoing negotiations, all preliminary to building, took approximately nine months. Current construction plans call for adding 350 homes to the 300 initially built. The rate of construction will, of course, depend on market demand since only a few homes are built at any one time in order to avoid accumulating an inventory of unsold structures. A small shopping center with a supermarket and five stores has been constructed on the main road that runs through the tract.

The school district that includes Seneca Knolls is now faced with the need for an increase in physical plant to accommodate the additional children. Town officials have reacted to this need by zoning most areas of Van Buren with larger lot requirements and higher cost minima for future developments in the hope of precluding low-middle income home building and its attendant decline in assessed valuation per pupil.

Bayberry: The Interaction of Public and Private Interests

One of the major residential projects developed in the last six years in the Syracuse metropolitan area is the Bayberry Tract. Located in the Town of Clay to the north of Syracuse, the area is on the fringe of the post–World War II residential growth. Original plans for Bayberry called for construction of more than 1200 homes. The investors, developers, and attorneys who conceived, negotiated, and developed Bayberry were "outside" people; that is, they were not from central New York. The organizing group did, however, employ a local engineering firm (O'Brien and Gere) for site planning and local subcontractors for construction. Further, the major portion of the financing, beyond equity in the initial purchase of the land, was arranged through the locally owned Merchants National Bank.

The developers, organized as the Bayberry Corporation,[3] had past experience in mass subdivisions in Long Island and New Jersey. Their approach to residential tracts was to acquire a minimum of 500 acres of raw land and design a "total community" in one large project to include homes, a small shopping center, recreation and playground areas, and school, church, and fire-house sites. The actual selection of a site in the Syracuse area was made after consideration of such conventional factors as site condition, price, proximity to the metropolitan road system, and availability of public facilities. Land use possibilities in Onondaga County had been studied by some Cornell University students of architecture in 1952, and the tract finally selected by the developers was classified in that study as prime residential land. In addition to reviewing the Cornell study, the developers also consulted with Sergei Grimm, Executive Director of the Syracuse City Planning Commission, who recommended the area as appropriate for mass subdivision. Finally, the developers undertook investigations of market demand for homes with respect to price and quantity. These surveys were made in part to support plans submitted to the Federal Housing Administration for mortgage finance approval.

Three major changes in plan were necessary before approval by the various public agencies was forthcoming. First, the homes were originally designed without basements. This met with objection by both the FHA and the mortgage department of the Merchants National Bank on the basis of their understanding of buyers' preferences. Second, the road layout originally called for a design featuring superblocks and dead-end streets. Town officials objected to this because of the difficulties of snow removal—a major problem in central New York. The plans were changed accordingly to eliminate dead ends. Third, the size of the lots was increased from a 60-to-70 to a 75-to-90 foot frontage, again in the interest of saleability.

The provision of sewage disposal facilities for the Bayberry Tract was complicated by the fact that it was outside the service area of established sewer systems. The developers therefore drew their own plans both for a sewage treatment plant and for laterals, by contract with O'Brien and Gere. The Town of Clay, with county approval, established a sewer district to acquire title to the system of laterals upon completion.

The negotiations for the sewage treatment facilities were more intricate. As noted above, the County Public Works Commission was committed to a policy of public construction of such facilities. Following negotiations with the developers and the attorney for the Town of Clay (who was also a member of the law firm associated with the Merchants Bank), the commission asked the town to request it to survey the possibilities of construction with public funds. This maneuver was necessitated by the fact that the commission normally initiates action only at the request of municipalities, and not at the behest of private developers.

The Town of Clay thereupon initiated the request, the Public Works Commission undertook the survey, and a sanitary district was eventually established to build, maintain, and operate sewer trunk lines and a treatment plant. This permitted the commission directly to control construction standards, and assured public operation of the facilities. At the same time, the private developer was relieved of the capital financing difficulties encountered by Cappuccilli in the Seneca Knolls project. To protect the public's interest, the commission required the developer to post a performance bond for the completion of 100 homes within 18 months. This was estimated to be the minimum development necessary to avoid financial hardship on the residents of the sanitary district, who would be faced with disproportionately high costs in the event that few homes were built and sold. The performance bond was also thought appropriate because the Bayberry developers were without previous financial history and experience in Onondaga County.

Arrangements were made with the Village of Liverpool, which purchases its water from the City of Syracuse, to supply water to the tract one-and-one-half miles to the north. The developers organized a private water distribution company for Bayberry in accordance with New York State Public Service Commission rules. As a result of a petition from new residents in the tract, however, the water system was purchased by the Town of Clay—for somewhat less than the actual cost estimated by the developer. For both water and sewage disposal, O'Brien and Gere acted as the engineers for the developer, the town, and the County Public Works Commission in both the designing and approving stages.

The developers set aside specific acreages for park, recreational, and school sites. No transfer for park or recreation sites had occurred up to mid-1960. Part of the proposed 10-acre site for a school was declared unusable by the State Department of Education. This action precipitated further negotiations which eventually led to the transfer of a 17-acre tract to the Liverpool school district. A bond issue was approved by the school district voters in April 1960; construction proceeded, and the facilities were expected to be in operation by September 1961.

In spite of careful private planning based on studies of the general growth of the county, practical economic forces came to play a major role in determining the rate at which homes would actually be constructed. The arrangement with the Merchants National Bank for building loans was that two-thirds of the sale price of each house would be advanced to the developer as construction proceeded. This placed the control of the rate of development in the hands of the bank, which exercised its judgment on the basis of new homes sold and unsold in Bayberry and the rate of home-building and sale elsewhere in the metropolitan area. In the 1958 recession the bank, in reflection of these considerations, cut back the supply of funds. Since 1959 construction rates have been somewhat closer to the original development schedule. As of June 1960 approximately 400 homes were occupied in the Bayberry Tract, with about 75 more under construction for the completion of that year.

Northern Lights Shopping Center: Typical Commercial Development

The New York State Thruway has been the proximate parent of many real estate developments. The location of its exits and entrances has shaped development patterns and land use in ways that could hardly have been anticipated at the time the Thruway was planned. Northern Lights Shopping Center is the direct result of the economic, technological, and demographic forces released by the location of Thruway interchanges in the area to the north of the city. In more prosaic terms, Northern Lights had its beginning in a land fill operation.

D. W. Winkleman, who heads a large general construction firm in Syracuse, needed fill to complete work on portions of the Thruway for which he had subcontracted. He purchased land for obtaining fill near the Thruway. A part of the acreage was low and marshy and generally unsuitable for development. Winkleman, however, filled this area to usable levels with left-over hard fill from other parts of the site. At the time he apparently contemplated that a warehouse or other small industrial building might be constructed there.

Once it was brought up to development standards, the value of the site became more and more apparent. It was located on Route 11, the major north-south artery leading into Syracuse. Just to the north were the expanding suburban areas of Clay, Salina, and North Syracuse. To the immediate south were Mattydale and Hinsdale, both residential. The potential use of the site for a shopping center was evident to some of the national chain stores looking for locations outside the city. Since Winkleman had no interest in promoting a commercial venture he sold the property to Eagan Real Estate. The development of the center was assigned to an Eagan employee, William Porter, who put in motion the procedures necessary for planning, developing, and constructing the shopping center.

Porter's first contact with local government officials was with Fred Kies, Salina town supervisor, to discuss matters related to zoning of the site. Mr. Kies had been elected to office in 1950 as a Republican in a traditionally Republican town. Salina enjoyed the highest total property valuation of any town in the county. Within its jurisdiction are such industrial concerns as Crouse-Hinds, General Electric, General Motors, Will and Baumer Candle Company, and Onondaga Pottery. Nevertheless, the town did not then and does not now have a zoning or planning board. It was zoned in the early 1930's by a short-lived zoning board, after which land use classifications and planning were controlled by the Town Board on an *ad hoc* basis.

After discussion Porter obtained from Kies an agreement that because of soil condition and topography it would be appropriate to rezone the site from residential to commercial. Porter also met with the town assessors to discuss the tax burden that might be anticipated if projected plans were carried through.

At this point, Porter left the Eagan firm with the Northern Lights site under his control. He soon returned to Salina to meet with Kies, apprising him of the fact that he was "on his own." Kies again gave him verbal approval of the zone change. Shortly thereafter, the change was voted by the Town Board without registered opposition.

During the same period Porter began closing leases with major tenants, the first of which was American Stores (Acme Supermarkets). Plans expanded from a small "food and services" shopping center to a district type when a downtown department store, Chappell, along with Woolworth and W. T. Grant, decided to locate in Northern Lights. The surrounding residential area was growing rapidly, and needed a major retail shopping center since the only shopping facilities were in downtown Syracuse or in a limited strip commercial development along Route 11. Other smaller leases were negotiated and the center assumed its final design when a Howard Johnson Restaurant and Motel decided to locate there. The location looked attractive for these facilities because preliminary plans for the new Penn-Can Highway showed an intersection with Route 11, with an interchange directly in front of the site. The expansion to incorporate a motel tenant required Porter to obtain a further zone change from commercial to multiple dwelling classification. A proposal to this effect was submitted to the Town of Salina, which granted the zone change for the area within the shopping center to be occupied by the motel.

During the period of lease negotiations there were other decisions to make possible the servicing of the site with sewers. A Ley Creek Sanitary District main ended in Mattydale approximately one mile to the south of the Northern Lights property. The plans of the County Public Works Commission (which operated the Ley Creek district) called for eventually extending the main to the residential sections of North Syracuse if enough lateral sewer districts should petition for service to warrant the cost involved. But the commission had on file a petition for a $350,000 lateral sewer district covering the Hinsdale area, just south of the site. Leaning heavily on the proposal of the Hinsdale district, Porter arranged for the Public Works Commission to extend the main (at a cost of about $1,000,000) to his property in exchange for easement rights. Whether or not the main would have been extended without the Hinsdale district, already established but unserviced, is difficult to determine. It is clear, however, that the Public Works Commission was convinced that the North Syracuse area would need ultimately to be served; the move to Northern Lights was a step in that direction.

Water for the site posed no problem, for mains were available within a short distance. During planning and construction Porter, who employed O'Brien and Gere as consulting engineers, negotiated water contracts with the then New York Water Service Corporation. The sale of the NYWSC to the Onondaga County Water Authority did not alter any previous arrangement except that Porter was asked for an easement for a water main, to which assent was readily given.

With zoning changes secured, water at hand, a sewer main arranged for, preliminary plans for ingress and egress to and from the center approved, and tenants committed, Porter was ready to begin construction. The final product was a shopping center with approximately 200,000 square feet of rentable space and a 3,000-car parking area.

New Process Gear: Million Dollar Meeting

The loss of a major employer in a metropolitan region may be a matter of critical concern. Jobs and people and property values are involved. Immediate dislocation may be severe, and there is always the fear that one loss will be followed by others. Sometimes the fears are warranted, sometimes not; but the threat, to say nothing of the actuality, of a major industrial relocation will often bring a concerted community response to ward off the move. Such is the case that culminated in the decision of the New Process Gear Corporation, a division of the Chrysler Corporation, to remain and expand its facilities in the Syracuse metropolitan area.

New Process Gear had been located in Syracuse since the early years of World War I. By 1959 it occupied three plants in various sections of the city and employed about 1,300 persons. Early in that year Chrysler decided to expand the New Process Gear facilities by a deadline date of July 1, 1960, for production of component parts of 1961 automobile models. None of the three existing plants had sound expansion potential; they were old, and two of the three were multi-story. New Process therefore began investigating various sites in the Syracuse area and in Auburn, a city of 35,000 about 40 miles southwest of Syracuse, where the company operated a foundry. Eventually the investigation reduced the location possibilities in the Syracuse area to three sites: Milton Avenue in Camillus, the newly assembled Woodard Industrial Tract in the Town of Clay, and a tract in the Town of Dewitt just east of Industrial Park.[4] All three locations had direct and easy access to the New York State Thruway.

In spite of the availability of these sites, New Process found that in no instance were there definite assurances that the properties under consideration could be serviced with sewers, water, roads, and drainage facilities by the deadline fixed by Chrysler for expansion. The real estate brokers responsible for the several sites were unable to provide the coordination among the numerous governmental jurisdictions necessary to meet the New Process demands. The company, unable to obtain commitments for service facilities, therefore approached the city of Auburn, which responded by guaranteeing all facilities and offering free land.

Early in September 1959 a few Syracuse community leaders became aware of New Process Gear's serious intention to move. The Syracuse Chamber of Commerce and the Manufacturers Association held a series of meetings with Alvin T. Hanson of New Process to discuss the difficulties of expanding in the Syracuse area. Problems relating to specific sites were examined and the difficulties in each case identified. It was impossible to provide the Woodard Tract site with a sewer sufficient for industrial needs until the middle of 1961 —twelve months too late. The facilities at the Camillus and Dewitt sites were discussed, but little progress was made in securing agreement for the provision of facilities. The citizen leaders meeting with New Process officials apparently had no one to whom they could turn for the staff work required to arrive at specific agreements. The meeting did serve to inform community leaders as to the details of the facilities required. Kenneth Bartlett, President of the Metropolitan Development Association,[5] Vice-President of the Syracuse Chamber of Commerce, and Vice-President of Syracuse University, attended this meeting and became familiar with the factors influencing New Process Gear's plans.

Further discussion accomplished little except to induce the real estate brokers controlling the Camillus and the Dewitt sites to express a willingness to lower the price of their land. Then on October 5, 1959, New Process Gear prepared press releases announcing its intention to move to Auburn. At this point state Senator John Hughes, who numbered the New Process Gear Corporation among his clients, asked Bartlett to talk further with Hanson on behalf of the Metropolitan Development Association. Hanson informed Bartlett that Syracuse was a "tough place" to get decisions of an important operational nature. There was no one place the company could go to for action on such matters as water, drainage, sewage, and assessments; so it was moving its plant to Auburn, where such matters could be (indeed had been) ironed out. Nevertheless Hanson arranged for Bartlett, John D. Williams, David Jaquith, and John McCarty of the Metropolitan Development Association to visit Detroit the next day (October 7) to meet with officials of the Chrysler Corporation. A preparatory session was held in the offices of the Manufacturers Association with representatives of the Chamber of Commerce and real estate firms present. There the problem was analyzed with care, as background for the discussions with Chrysler. Leo Eagan, who controlled the Dewitt site, went to Detroit ahead of the committee, which he met at the Chrysler offices with an offer to reduce the land cost from $450,000 to $375,000.

At the meeting with Chrysler officials, Bartlett, as spokesman for the MDA and other Syracuse interests, gave assurances on facilities and promised that a full-time man would be assigned to work with New Process Gear in taking care of the details. In Bartlett's words:

> The committee received a fine welcome and were told they could have all the time needed to present their case. As I entered my home on my return, a Chrysler official called to say he had been authorized

by his Detroit supervisors to report that the Syracuse situation had been greatly improved and the odds against Syracuse had changed from 15–85 to 45–55. The official said company representatives would come to Syracuse the next day to talk about facilities and schedule.

Following this call Bartlett called Senator Hughes, apprised him of the impending visit by the Chrysler team, and urged that a meeting be arranged to be attended by all government officials involved. Hughes thereupon called George Traister, Onondaga County Republican Party chairman, and suggested that arrangements be made to have these officials meet in his law office at 9 A.M. the next morning (October 8). Every official invited was present. Besides Hughes, Traister, Hanson and Bartlett, these included principally the chairman of the county Board of Supervisors, the Mayor of Syracuse, the supervisors of the Towns of Dewitt, Clay, and Camillus, the director of sewer plant operations for Onondaga County, the county Superintendent of Highways, the District Engineer of the New York State Department of Public Works, the Vice-President of the Niagara Mohawk Power Company, a member of the county Public Works Commission, and the chairman of the Onondaga County Water Authority. The Chrysler representatives of course attended as well.

The Dewitt site was settled upon for New Process Gear, since it appeared to pose fewer problems than the others and since Eagan's proposal of that site had been tentatively accepted in Detroit. Having made this decision, the meeting concentrated on the following matters:

Zoning: The supervisor of the Town of Dewitt assured the Chrysler officials that he did not anticipate any serious opposition to the necessary zoning change.

Assessments: The Mayor of Syracuse agreed that assessments on New Process Gear's vacated city plants would be lowered in order to facilitate sale. The Dewitt supervisor assured New Process that after the initial assessment on the proposed new multi-million dollar plant there would be no major assessment increase.

Sewers: The chairman of the county Board of Supervisors agreed to furnish a fifteen-inch full-flow sanitary sewer to the property line, and to procure the necessary easements. The cost of construction of the new facilities was not to be charged to the New Process Gear property as a special assessment, but rather was to be financed by a general charge on the Ley Creek Sanitary District.

Water: The Onondaga County Water Authority and the Town of Dewitt agreed to provide a sixteen-inch water main to the property at no charge to New Process. Also, fire hydrants and related facilities to assure minimum fire insurance rates were to be installed. The Town of Dewitt (the Thompson Road Water District) agreed that its share of the cost of servicing the site was to be charged against all the property in the Thompson Road District. The amount of the charge was expected to be about $2 per thousand of assessed valuation.

Roads: Fly Road, which was inadequate to handle large amounts of traffic, was under the control of New York State. Arrangements were made by the county highway superintendent and the New York State District Engineer whereby the county would take over a portion of the road. The county, in turn, agreed to make such improvements as would be necessary to meet traffic needs. The county also agreed to construct a four-lane concrete highway westward from the site along Court Street to the Thruway interchange. Court Street was to be closed and abandoned at the property line.

Drainage: The chairman of the Board of Supervisors and the county highway superintendent agreed to assume responsibility for the improvement of existing drainage facilities and any problems that might arise as a result of plant expansion in the future.

Power: The area's gas distribution was under the control of the Suburban Gas Company, which held franchise rights from the Niagara-Mohawk Corporation. The Suburban Gas Company refused to provide a rate schedule that New Process would agree to. Niagara-Mohawk therefore agreed to lower its price to Suburban in order to make it possible to meet New Process Gear's demands. Further, Niagara-Mohawk agreed to bring a specified amount of electric power to the proposed site at no cost to New Process. Right-of-way procurement for electric transmission lines was to be coordinated with the county highway superintendent.

The conference divided into groups meeting in separate rooms to discuss each problem area. Hughes and Bartlett circulated from room to room throughout the day "breaking log-jams." The gas price arrangement was the last to be consummated in the 12-hour session. At the conclusion of the discussions letters of commitment to New Process were provided by the officials responsible for governmental action in each sector. The long day of negotiating finished at last, the meeting adjourned and the Chrysler team returned to Detroit.

The next day brought victory in the form of a call to Bartlett from Detroit announcing a decision in favor of the Dewitt site. The local newspapers headlined the success story with praise for all public officials and private citizens involved. An editorial began: "A group of Syracuse and County men deserve gold helmets for their work in influencing the Chrysler decision."[6] All of the many decisions that could not be reached by individual negotiations in the months preceding were made in a matter of hours under the pressure of acknowledged crisis and with the aid of the dominant political party organization. The cost of public improvements committed at the conference to meet New Process Gear's requirements exceeded one million dollars.

As a follow-up to this meeting the General Electric Company loaned David O'Brien, of its public and employee relations department, to the Metropolitan Development Association. He was assigned as full-time coordinator on all matters agreed upon between New Process Gear and government officials. Shortly thereafter he was named by the chairman of the Board of Supervisors to the post of county research director, with continuing responsibility for follow-up and coordination work. All commitments made by public officials were kept on schedule, and New Process Gear began production at the new plant in the fall of 1960.

Conclusion

The five abbreviated cases summarized above illustrate in a variety of ways the richness and complexity of the process of metropolitan decision-making as it relates to private real estate development. They indicate first that such development is not private in any restrictive sense, but rather private-public, or perhaps in the end public-private. Thus what begins as a purely private proposal concludes with such a large public component that it takes on the character of a partnership operation. It is not strange that it is sometimes difficult to discern where one leaves off and the other begins, or to discover what representative is working in whose behalf. Indeed it may appear in some instances that a private entrepreneur is in fact acting as (or in place of) a public official, while a public officer acts as a businessman. The dividing line between public and private sometimes becomes so blurred as to be virtually lost in these negotiations.

The cases also shed light on the nature of the decision reached in any particular development. To begin with, the decision normally is not a clean-cut yes-or-no action on a specific proposition. It is much more likely to emerge as a number of decisions taken in series on a sequence of issues, the later decisions (and the necessity for making them) sometimes foreseen, sometimes not. Moreover, a decision-situation frequently arises from fortuitous and often seemingly unrelated circumstances: a new expressway interchange seems to provide an opportunity for a shopping center, with its attendant train of arrangements for zoning variances, water, and sewage disposal facilities and its consequences—some anticipated, some not—for schools, traffic congestion, fire protection, and so on. Finally (to observe the reverse side of a coin examined above), a particular decision may appear on close approach to have been pre-formed: that is, in view of steps taken earlier, no alternative is available in the instant case.

With respect to community power and its exercise, the cases illustrate the modest level of involvement of most elements in the community power structure in a typical case. It simply was not worth the while of any very important "influentials" to become involved in the Fayetteville filling station/shopping center imbroglio. Clearly this issue primarily concerned individual citizens in a private dispute, and the community power structure did not have to take a significant part in its resolution. With one exception, these remarks are applicable to the other cases examined as well. The exception is the New Process Gear re-location. There the issue was conceived to be of fundamental importance to the community, which threw its full resources into the fray. Civil and industrial spokesmen, political leaders, public officials—all joined in one grand show of cooperation to keep New Process in the area. Significantly, the Republican organization rose to this challenge as it has seldom been able to do in recent years. The New Process Gear case commanded as nearly complete commitment of the community power structure as any decision taken in perhaps a decade. It is not a matter for wonder that success followed.

XII

Syracuse Industrial Park

FOR most urban areas economic growth is heavily dependent on both the expansion of old and the attraction of new industry. In many communities and not a few states there are organizations, public and private, to promote a "better business climate" and to compete aggressively to attract firms. In the years since World War II many of these efforts have centered on the promotion of industrial parks—specifically designated areas appropriately zoned, adequately sited for water, sewage disposal, and drainage, and possessed of suitable transportation facilities.[1]

These areas are typically located within the metropolitan region but outside the boundaries of the central city. They provide space for the technological requirements of contemporary industrial architecture, along with parking areas for the commuting employees. They attract firms from central city locations and thus contribute to the continued economic and physical deterioration of that city. In many areas, and Syracuse is no exception, almost all new industrial plants come to be located outside the city, but they have affected the economy and government of the metropolitan region.

Industrial developments are one type of real estate development,

---

Clyde J. Wingfield prepared this chapter.

and some of the relationships between the developer and local government are not sharply different from those prevailing in commercial and residential ventures. In other respects, however, industrial real estate calls for different patterns of public-private decision-making. The industrial developer and promoter has a stronger bargaining position in relation to public agencies, for the economic future of the area depends in large part on the success of his efforts. The development examined here is not the only industrial park in Onondaga County, but it is the largest and most complex.

The term "Syracuse Industrial Park" is employed by the Eagan Real Estate Corporation to describe that part of the park developed by Eagan and affiliated corporations. To the man on the street or to the Syracuse Chamber of Commerce, however, the term has a far wider meaning; it is generally applied to the modern (post-1940) industrial area lying in the Town of Dewitt adjacent to the City of Syracuse. The Eagan dimensions generally are accepted for this study, though the influence of the broader development cannot be ignored. Map 3 indicates the location of the park.

Background

While formal planning for the Syracuse Industrial Park did not get under way until the 1950's, several prophetic events occurred much earlier. At the time, these occurrences had no known connection with the later park development. Nevertheless they are a part of the pattern of public and private action which influenced the course of metropolitan development. The point of departure for a study of this kind is always somewhat arbitrary. There seems to be general consensus, however, that the story of Industrial Park should begin in the 1920's when H. H. Franklin, president of the now defunct motor car company which bore his name, became dissatisfied with his multi-story downtown factory and proposed the construction of a suburban automobile assembly plant. A tract of farm land of approximately 1,000 acres, lying to the north and east of the city, was assembled; and a subsidiary company, the Syracuse Land Development Company, took title. Unfortunately, before Franklin's vision could bear fruit, his motor car company went bankrupt and the real estate holdings of its subsidiaries passed to creditors. The proposed industrial property, which had become known as Franklin Park, went to New York City investors, the principal of which was the Chase National Bank. The new owners had little interest in developing Franklin Park and set about selling piecemeal such of the property as was saleable in order to recoup losses. Some acreage was sold for small enterprises but no sales of a substantial nature were made during the prewar period.[2]

With the coming of World War II the Defense Plant Corporation, formed as a subsidiary of the Reconstruction Finance Corporation, was authorized to enter into agreements with private firms for the construction and operation (under lease) of certain essential war plants. Under these provisions the General Electric Company undertook to construct and operate a steam turbine plant on the Franklin Park tract. Several factors accounted for GE's choice of Syracuse as the site. Perhaps most important was the fact that, during a period of scarce labor, Syracuse had an adequate supply. Transportation facilities were particularly good and an ideal site existed in the properties already assembled as a result of Franklin's earlier enterprise. Moreover, the Ley Creek trunk sewer line cut through the heart of the area. The Defense Plant Corporation secured title to an 80-acre tract of the former Franklin property and General Electric's turbine plant became the first substantial industry to locate in what was to become Industrial Park. World War II also produced an airport (now Hancock Field) on the northern periphery of the park.

With the end of hostilities in 1945 General Electric, confronted with a decreased demand for steam turbines, decided not to exercise its option to buy the facility it had operated during the war years. The plant was turned over to the War Assets Administration and in 1946 was sold to Syracuse University. For a short period it was used by the University's engineering college. Then the Carrier Corporation, which was operating an increasingly inadequate downtown plant, began negotiations with the University and the War Assets Administration for the purchase of the old GE plant; and in the fall of 1947 Carrier took title to the plant and the original 80-acre tract. Simultaneously, Carrier was acquiring title to (or options to buy) adjacent acreage to protect plans for future growth. In all Carrier acquired approximately 300 acres, much of it within the old Franklin Park tract. A small part of this acreage Carrier has since released from option or sold for other industrial uses, but it has employed the greater portion in its own growth. At present Carrier's 300 acres hold buildings with a total of nearly two million square feet of plant, office, and warehouse floor space.[3]

The decision by General Motors to relocate its Syracuse Brown-Lipe-Chapin installation in the suburbs, contributing as it did to the industrial atmosphere, was significant to the area's ultimate development, although the site chosen was not actually included within the limits of Industrial Park as described here. With this 1953 relocation the area became bounded by the Carrier and General Motors properties on the east and west and by the New York Thruway and New York Central Railroad tracks on the north and south.

One of the most significant events shaping the pattern of Industrial Park's development was the construction of the New York State Thruway from New York City through Albany, Syracuse, and Rochester to Buffalo and on to the Pennsylvania state line. The original announcement of the proposed expressway was made in the midst of the war, and few people took time to reflect on its significance for the Syracuse metropolitan area. When in 1949 actual surveying and construction began, however, alert real estate men and industrialists took note. Enthusiasm was perhaps a bit excessive. Some visualized a "strip city" stretching the 427-mile length of the new billion-dollar road, with industrial concentrations and residential suburbs and "green belts" in between.[4] The more conservative were willing to settle for occasional industrial parks at key interchanges marking the major cities.

Even in retrospect it is difficult to assess the part the Thruway has played in the development of Industrial Park, but it has been a significant one. To illustrate, some park land near the Thompson Road interchange (Thruway Exit 35) could have been bought in 1950 for $500 to $700 per acre; today the property usually cannot be bought, but if it could the price would probably approach $30,000 per acre. The Thruway is of course not the sole enhancer. The general industrial development of the area and the resulting scarcity of land are equally or perhaps even more important. Nor should the significance of the availability of public utilities be underestimated. Nevertheless land prices all up and down the Thruway have soared since that facility's construction. A good average price for choice land near intersections, according to *Fortune* magazine, is about $20,000 per acre. General Motors paid some $300,000 for three acres adjoining the Thruway in Tarrytown.[5] With increasing scarcity, value in all likelihood will continue to go up.

The reasons for locating industry along the Thruway are obvious. It provides a means for quick distribution of manufactured or processed goods and rapid transportation for workers and executives, many of whom commute as far as 50 miles. A factor often overlooked is advertising. The new, modern factories are viewed by thousands of passing motorists daily. For the new garden-type industry a Thruway site carries as much prestige as a downtown Manhattan location for its home office.

The Principal Promoters

Of the principal parties involved in the formal stages of the Industrial Park development, those who are associated formally or informally with Eagan Real Estate, Inc., predominate. Three corporations, Midcourt Builders Corporation, Midler-Court Realty, Inc., and Midler Land Development, Inc., have been responsible for the planning, land improvement, and, in many instances, building and plant construction which have been the *sine qua non* of Industrial Park. In all transactions involving these corporations the Eagan firm has been the sole agent and promoter.

Even the most cursory examination of the relationships between Eagan and the title-holding organizations suggests that ties exist beyond those of real estate agent and client. In the case of Midler-Court Realty, Inc., and Midler Land Development, Inc., the officers and directors were salaried employees of Eagan. Midcourt Builders, the last incorporated and most active in the park project, was formed in 1952 with Matthew V. Byrne, Jr., a local attorney (often for Eagan), Frederick S. Christy, and William P. Christy, Jr., of the accounting firm of Christy & Christy, signing as the incorporating directors. The principal subscribers have remained anonymous but there is a logical inference that Floyd Stover, a vice-president of Eagan and promoter of the park, has an interest beyond that which can be documented. The link between these "dummy" corporations and the Eagan firm is clear from even the most casual discussion of the park with Eagan owners or employees. The properties developed by the corporations are usually referred to as the "Eagan portion of the park," and negotiations in all cases have been handled or supervised by Stover. In numerous reports relating to the park's development, the Syracuse press has seldom alluded to the paper corporations, attributing credit and responsibility to Eagan direct.

Eagan Real Estate, Inc., was incorporated December 29, 1931, by Leo T. Eagan, Edward Eagan, and Floyd H. Stover. Leo Eagan had started in the real estate business earlier in literally a broom closet operation. Edward Eagan, a graduate of the Syracuse University School of Law, practiced law in Syracuse until 1929. Stover moved east from Milwaukee to organize the industrial branch of the business in 1933. Over the years the firm has grown until today it is one of the largest real estate operations in New York and ranks well up in national ratings. As head of Eagan's industrial department, Stover initiated and guided the various negotiations which in total account for much of the formal development of Industrial Park.

There were, however, other participants worth noting. Among them may be mentioned Robert Lynch and William Marshall of the New York Central's Industrial Development Division; John Brockway and later Calvin Hamilton, Supervisors for the Town of Dewitt; Earl O'Brien, who on occasion was project engineer for both Eagan and the Town of Dewitt; and a number of Syracuse investors with a passion for anonymity who financially underwrote critical phases of the enterprise. Syracuse Supply Company, interested in relocating its operations, purchased 137 acres in and adjoining the area. Later all except 25 acres of this plat was sold to other firms. The Eagan, Potter, and Pomeroy real estate firms handled the marketing of these properties. Further, a number of private purchases have resulted in a significant growth on the periphery of the park, although they have little bearing on the focus of this study. Such locations can generally be explained by the magnet-like attractions of the well planned and eye-catching park, together with the availability of small parcels of land which were passed by in the major land acquisitions of the larger developers.

Planning for Industrial Park

In the summer of 1951 the head of the real estate department of the Kraft Food Company came to Syracuse seeking a site for an 11,000 square foot building for his company. After inspecting several possible locations with Stover, he remarked that he was surprised Syracuse had not undertaken the development of an industrial park similar to those Kraft had found elsewhere. This comment has been credited with having fired Stover's imagination; in any event it was about this time that he set about to locate vacant land suitable for such development. After making a number of land surveys with Robert Lynch, then traffic manager of the New York Central Railroad and Earl O'Brien and William Gere of the engineering firm O'Brien and Gere,[6] he hit upon the property known as the Courtview Heights section. This plot had been originally surveyed in 1920 for residential use and had been subdivided into blocks. The development never materialized, however, and by 1952, when Stover became interested, most of the property was tax delinquent.

On May 15, 1952, the Midler Land Development, Inc., and the Midler-Court Realty, Inc., were formed. Under their certificates of incorporation the firms espoused the purposes of acquiring and improving real estate and other property, and erecting buildings for sale, lease, etc. The directors filing for the certificate were all salaried employees of the Eagan firm. Immediately, Midler-Court Realty set out to acquire the Courtview property, and in a short time the original 33-acre tract was assembled. On August 19, 1952, several lots in the northeast corner of the plot were sold to a Syracuse building contractor, who constructed a 20,800 square foot commercial building. Half the building was leased for 15 years to the J. S. Woodhouse Company; the remainder was sold outright to LeValley-McLeo, Inc. These were the first firms to locate in the Eagan section of the park, and both were new to the Syracuse area.

Midler-Court Industrial Park, as the tract was first called, developed rapidly. It was soon to include a number of small firms employing for the most part 25 to 50 workers each. Development was along two lines. In some cases lots owned by the Eagan subsidiaries were sold to new enterprises which did their own construction. In other instances buildings were constructed to specification and leased to the locating concerns. While these early developmental activities frequently were discussed in terms of a planned industrial district or park, they really amounted to little more than a real estate promotion. Little or no control was exercised over the development except in the selection of buyers.

Formal declaration of intention to initiate a planned industrial complex of magnitude came on May 20, 1953, at a Hotel Syracuse luncheon meeting sponsored by the New York Central Railroad and attended by some 50 representatives of local manufacturing and real estate interests. The public announcement was issued as a press release from the New York Central's news bureau in New York City. It proclaimed that the railroad, in conjunction with Eagan Real Estate, Inc., and the Syracuse Supply Company, had prepared plans for a diversified industrial development. On May 21, 1953, the *Post-Standard* carried a story of the luncheon announcement headlined "Plans for Industrial Park East of City Revealed."[7] So far as can be determined, this was the first time the term Industrial Park was applied publicly to the project. The new plans, as outlined at this time, took little notice of such major industries as Carrier and General Motors already located in the area. The park property included some 570 acres located between these two major plants.[8] It was bounded by the Thruway on the north, Thompson Road on the east, Town Line Road on the west, and the New York Central tracks on the south.

At the same time the park plans were announced, Eagan's Floyd Stover stated that 16 national concerns were negotiating for 175 acres out of the 400 acres his firm was developing. The Pomeroy Real Estate firm, as the selling agent for Syracuse Supply Company, announced that seven industries were negotiating for 90 of its 137 acres and that Syracuse Supply intended to retain and develop most of the remaining acreage for its own purposes. As these public announcements of the new park were made, four companies had already located in the park and were occupying 16 acres in the southwestern corner, where the New York Central had recently completed an industrial lead siding and supporting tracks. Each employed fewer than 50 workers.

As the ultimate dimensions of the new industrial site began to be realized, it became apparent that public service problems existed which in the haste of early action had been overlooked or ignored. As the host jurisdiction, the Town of Dewitt fell heir to these liabilities. Perhaps no public official played a more active role in furthering the park's progress than John Brockway, Supervisor of the Town of Dewitt from 1945 until his death in October, 1954. From the early planning stage Brockway was kept closely advised and conferred frequently with Stover and others involved in the project. Convinced that additional industry was in the best interest of the town, he worked hard to provide the public services the developers required, whenever possible on their terms.

The existence of the Ley Creek trunk sewer line resolved in advance what otherwise would have posed a difficult problem. Still there remained the matter of lateral sewers. After the Eagan project was under way, Stover petitioned the Dewitt Town Board for the creation of a special sewer district which would service property of Midler-Court Builders, Inc. The board evidently foresaw the eventual sewage requirements of the area and declined Stover's petition, but provided instead for the creation of the Court Street Area Sewer District. The formal proposal was submitted November 6, 1953. The district includes the whole of Industrial Park and extends east to include the Franklin Park residential area as well. Lateral lines have been provided within the district as required, and on occasion have been laid before the construction of new developments. Town officials in this matter as in most others have evidenced a willingness to cooperate fully with the promoters. Costs are met by assessments laid on a benefit basis, as determined by the Town Supervisor and Board.

For a time it appeared that water might become the limiting factor in the development of the park. How that problem was solved, temporarily, at least, has been told elsewhere (see Chapter V) and need not be repeated here. It is, however, worth noting that the interest exhibited by Eagan and the industries in and adjacent to Industrial

Park weighed heavily in the chain of decisions through which the Onondaga County Water Authority emerged as the agency principally responsible for water supply in the industrial suburbs. It is alleged, indeed, that Carrier "underwrote" the authority's initial bonding by pledging water consumption in advance, thus ensuring approval of the bond proposal by the state Comptroller.

Phase Two of the Eagan Project [9]

While development of the Courtview Heights area was still under way, Stover, through Attorney Myron Melvin, was able to obtain options to purchase the Gilbert Mautz farm of approximately 140 acres lying immediately to the north. The problem of capital to purchase this property and proceed with its development, however, brought a temporary impasse. Stover first attempted to interest Edward and Leo Eagan in the enterprise, but at the time they were too preoccupied with residential and commercial property in the city to be enthusiastic about a farmland venture out in the country. Stover thereupon went outside the Eagan firm and secured from other unidentified Syracuse investors the sum necessary to promote the development. On October 22, 1953, this group of local investors, through the vehicle of the Midcourt Builders, Inc. (incorporated December 13, 1952), took title. This was the third new corporation involved in the development. In every case Eagan was the exclusive agent.

Before significant industrialization could be achieved in the new tract, key transportation problems had to be resolved. William Robinson, District Engineer for the New York State Department of Public Works, cooperated with the developers to bring about significant highway changes and improvements. By 1953 the first steps had been taken to widen to four lanes what was then Court Street between Barton's Corners and the city limits. Plans were also developing for an elaborate Thruway access pattern based on a traffic circle located on the western side of the park near the Brown-Lipe-Chapin plant. In the midst of these successes an obstacle arose.

The New York Central from the beginning had played a very active role in the development of the park property.[10] William J. Marshall of the Central's Industrial Development Office in New York

City, with Robert Lynch of the Syracuse office, worked closely with Stover and other developers, and in the early days proved perhaps the most tangible source of support. The railroad provided lead sidings at its own expense for the new concerns locating in the heart of the park. This posed little difficulty in the original 33-acre tract; but in order to extend rail service to the second phase of the Eagan development both Court Street and State Highway 672 had to be traversed by a grade crossing. Under the provisions of a state law dating back to the 1920's, grade crossings of state highways were to be eliminated. A sizable appropriation had been expended pursuant to that end. As a matter of legislative intent and Public Works Department policy, new grade crossings were generally not permitted.

Fortunately for the future of the park, a number of related problems were under discussion by local, state, and federal officials. On May 21, 1953, this group, headed by District Engineer Robinson, met in Syracuse. Under consideration was the construction of the above-mentioned traffic circle, a six-lane Court Street underpass, the general development of a Thruway interchange, and matters relative to Oswego Boulevard and the North-South Thruway. Robinson, at the urging of Stover, supported a proposal that a permit be granted to the New York Central to construct a grade crossing across State Highway 672. It was already evident that when the new Thruway interchange was completed, State Highway 672 would be rerouted over the new interchange highway and that portion of old 672 to be crossed by Central's new line would become surplus. With abandonment of the controverted portion of Highway 672 a virtual certainty, and with the blessing and support of the District Engineer, Central's petition was eventually approved by the Chief Engineer of the Department of Public Works and the State Public Service Commission.[11] Eagan immediately deeded right-of-way property to New York Central and a crossing was constructed by mid-1953, long before the siding tracks were linked on either side.

After resolution of this issue the Mautz farm tract developed rapidly. Immediately after acquiring the property, 19 acres were sold to the John Deere Plow Company. At the time the tract was purchased, Stover was already negotiating with General Electric for space to locate that company's Heavy Military Equipment Division;

and in May, 1954, arrangements with GE were completed and Midcourt Builders Corporation signed a lease to become effective on completion of an office and shop building. General Electric's first two buildings were completed in 1954. They totaled over 104,000 square feet of floor space. In 1955 another 75,000 square feet of space were leased to General Electric and in 1956 78,000 square feet were added. To date eight major structures totaling over 800,000 square feet of floor space have been built to specifications and leased to GE, whose Heavy Military Division is the largest single enterprise in the Eagan-developed section of the park.

Of particular interest in the negotiations between General Electric and Eagan is the fact that in this transaction Stover was in a sense competing with GE's own real estate department. It is General Electric policy to purchase land and build its own facilities when locating a new plant. In the case of the Heavy Military Division, however, the company's real estate people were evidently less optimistic over growth prospects than the local managers. Space requirements requested by J. J. Farrell and Joseph Barrett, Manager and Production Manager respectively for Heavy Military, were deemed excessive and risky by the home office realty officials. It was into this breach that Stover moved with a proposal that Midcourt Builders construct the facilities desired by Farrell and Barrett and lease them to GE on a 10-year agreement. General Electric's real estate people readily agreed.

While General Electric occupies the most imposing position in the later Eagan development, Graybar Electric Company, Pepsi Cola, J. I. Case Company, Swift & Company, Continental Can Company, Whitehead Metals, Inc., and other well known names contributed significantly to its over-all development. A wide variety of other enterprises have located in piecemeal fashion around the periphery of the Industrial Park area, making difficult a clear-cut delineation of boundary, but the properties described here represent the heart of the park and all of the "planned" area.

Opposition

Although the Industrial Park plan was heralded by community leaders, the press, the Chamber of Commerce, and many private businessmen, it was not without its critics. Most prominent among these was the Manufacturers Association of Syracuse.[12] Nothing of record has been found to suggest outright opposition. Officially, the Manufacturers Association was never involved in the project in any way, and the principals in the park development insist they were not aware of any criticism stemming from this source. The nominal reason for the association's critical view was that the park developers had completely ignored the Syracuse Post-War Report, which it regarded as providing the framework for long-range industrial planning in the metropolitan Syracuse area. (See Chapter III.) The post-war plan called for comprehensive coordination by the City Planning Commission of all development within the Syracuse city limits and all subdivisions within the three-mile planning jurisdiction. But when Eagan and the other developers set about to build a new park, they saw little need for coordination. Instead they viewed their project as a real estate venture of a strictly private nature. Eagan's attorney advised that since the park was not subdivided the City Planning Commission had no jurisdiction, hence it did not seem necessary to consult that body. For that matter the commission is not on record as having expressed an interest. The Town of Dewitt, the other governmental jurisdiction with regulatory authority, eagerly welcomed the project. Dewitt had no zoning ordinance at the time of the park's initiation, but an ordinance adopted in 1957 classified the whole park area as industrial.

It seems likely that the issue here goes beyond lack of coordination or a breakdown in planning. Manufacturers' associations are frequently at odds with incoming industries. As an organization representing established local enterprises, the Manufacturers Association of Syracuse and its sponsors view fearfully any new activity which may compete for labor, force wages up, or otherwise disturb the *status quo*. On the other hand retail merchants, bankers, and the Chamber of Commerce usually welcome new manufacturing concerns with open arms.

It is significant that, whatever the feeling of discontent within the Manufacturers Association, it was not sufficiently well crystallized to warrant a declaration of opposition. Moreover, if there were reasons for objecting to the location of the park or the manner of its development, the responsible public officials in Syracuse and the Town of Dewitt failed to voice them. All in all, Syracuse probably reacted to the Industrial Park project as would the average middle-sized industrial city. The majority of the citizenry took little note beyond a casual glance at a newspaper headline or at the skeleton of a new plant building. Those actively aware of the park for the most part seemed to regard it as an asset to the community—as an added safeguard against the threat of unemployment.

Impact

It is difficult to assess accurately Industrial Park's impact on the Syracuse area. To the Town of Dewitt it represents a windfall of major proportions. The total 1958 assessed valuation for the town was $38,387,216, based on an equalization rate of approximately 35 per cent or a full valuation of $109,677,760. About 30 per cent of this valuation is accounted for by Industrial Park. County, state, and special property tax revenue increased from $703,178.67 in 1953 to $1,413,110.27 in 1958. During the same period the tax rate, apart from the school tax, actually decreased. In 1959 Dewitt had the lowest property tax rate on equalized value in the county.

Visible direct costs to the town resulting from the park consist of the assumption of approximately six miles of new town highway built by the developers but turned over to the town for maintenance. This may entail some unanticipated costs resulting from population increases induced by the new industry. Some hidden costs may also be involved in the creation and maintenance of new sewer and water districts, although such special districts nominally are self-sustaining. The indebtedness on special sewer facilities, constructed initially by bonding, is retired by benefit assessments. Once the revenue bonds on a specific sewer project have been retired, assessments drop to a minimum level reflecting maintenance and service costs. Water districts purchase water from the County Water Authority and charge users at a commercial rate. There are obviously other public costs arising from the industrialization of a suburban town, such as the additional burdens imposed for public education. No attempt has been made to evaluate these on an area-wide basis.

The Courtview School District, in which Industrial Park is almost wholly located, had an assessed valuation of $11,676,512 for the year 1959 with an equalization rate of approximately 35 per cent.[13] Total school revenue for the tax year 1959 was $168,735.[14] Town Supervisor Calvin Hamilton estimates that of the property assessments in the district a little over $4,000,000 come from residential property. The remainder derives from industry in or adjacent to Industrial Park.[15] Since nearly all of the vacant property in the Courtview District is zoned for industry, little residential growth can occur. The school tax advantages for industry are obvious. The Courtview rate is $16.00 per $1,000 of assessed valuation, the county average school tax is between $40 and $50 per $1,000.

Defining the park's boundaries liberally to include all enterprises in the general area, over 160 manufacturing, wholesale, retail, and service concerns can be identified. Of these only 13 employ over 250 workers. Informed estimates place the total working force in the park area at between 12,000 and 20,000. The indefiniteness of boundaries in part accounts for the variations in estimates. Using the restrictive definition employed in this study, the lower figure perhaps would be more accurate. If peripheral concerns are included, the 13 largest firms employ approximately 16,600, or between 80 and 85 per cent of the total park area's working force. It is important to bear in mind that this figure represents very largely a net accretion in suburban employment since 1945.

The largest employer is General Electric's Heavy Military Equipment Division. Including the Tube Division warehouse and the X-Ray Division, GE employs over 5,000 workers. Following close behind is the Carrier Corporation with about 5,000 employees. In order of size of working force (figures approximate) come the Brown-Lipe-Chapin Division of General Motors with 1,200 to 1,500 employees; Bristol Laboratories, Inc., with 1,000; Onondaga Pottery Company, 900; Western Electric Company, Inc., 750; Lamson Corporation and Oberdorfer Foundries, Inc., 600 each; Electric Auto-Lite Company, 500; the New York State Thruway Authority, 350 (including road crews); and American Stores Company and Lennox Industries, Inc., 250 each. Syracuse Supply Company employs close to 375 persons. Probably fewer than two-thirds of the work force accounted for here actually work in the park if the conventional dismensions are applied. There are a number of other firms employing from 25 to 200 which have added significantly to the park's development.[16]

On the basis of these crude data one might tentatively conclude that Industrial Park can be linked casually with perhaps 30 per cent of the total employment in the Town of Dewitt. Clearly the park has played an important part in the growth of the Syracuse metropolitan area in the last ten years.

As for impact on governmental jurisdictions aside from Dewitt, two factors can be cited with some certainty. First, there has been an increase of population in some jurisdictions attributable in part to Industrial Park's working force, though as a rule this increase, as it affects the over-all metropolitan area, is overestimated. Some of what seems to be general area growth represents a shifting of population instead. Second, the working force employed by Industrial Park enterprises is generally dispersed throughout the metropolitan area with the central city probably harboring the largest portion of the non-skilled and semi-skilled workers and the suburbs a majority of the highly skilled and professional. There are various residential districts which seem to attract the respective categories employed in the park. Obviously, those closest to the park bear the heaviest load, but with adequate parking space provided for any worker who wishes to drive and with the Thruway and other good access routes available, dispersal of the working force is wide. It is therefore very difficult to assess any added burden they may place on the various governmental jurisdictions.

Apart from a few surface generalizations, it is difficult to talk meaningfully about tax levels in Industrial Park or the Town of Dewitt as a whole. The town has 112 different taxes, the majority of which are assessed by special districts. Rates on one side of the street frequently are quite different from those on the other side. And within the park like conditions prevail. A look at a fairly typical property in the park will serve to illustrate this point. Building #1 (valuation $178,000) of the General Electric Heavy Military Equipment branch (under lease from Syracuse Industrial Park Corporation, built originally by Mid-Court Builders, Inc.) was assessed the following rates per $1,000 valuation in 1958:

State and county taxes	$23.20
Health district tax	.20
Highway tax	3.40
Zoning and planning tax	.45
Fire district	1.05
Water district	2.20
Ley Creek Sewer District (disposal)	4.04
Thompson Road Sewer District (laterals)	2.75
School district (Courtview)	16.00
Total	$52.99

In the Town of Dewitt the property tax equalization rate was 35 per cent in this year, hence the effective or full value rate on the foregoing property was $18.55 per $1,000. According to the chairman of the Onondaga County Board of Equalization, residential and industrial properties in Dewitt are assessed at about the same proportion of current market value, and industrial property in the town thus has no important relative advantage as compared with other property.[17] In the City of Syracuse the tax rate on the same building would have approximated $62.50 in 1958; application of the city equalization ratio, which was 56 per cent in that year, produces a full value rate of about $34.00 per $1,000. Thus Industrial Park properties have a significant property tax advantage as compared with city properties. Almost all of this advantage is attributable to the school district taxing pattern. The Courtview District is essentially an industrial tax haven.

The level of property taxation has long been regarded as an important determinant of industrial location, and beyond doubt the favorable tax status of Industrial Park has been a factor making for its development. But the relative importance of the property tax advantage as compared with other considerations and its actual influence on the decisions of firms to locate in the park are impossible to determine.

Conclusion

The decisions summarized here probably represent, in subject, scope, and sequence, actions which are fairly typical of the private industrial development process. They are typical in the sense that identifiable public and private decisions regarded as separate and perhaps trivial when made inadvertently shape the course of private action over a span of time and circumstances. A specific decision made today may have long-range implications for matters at the moment completely unrelated.

The Syracuse Industrial Park was not the product of a single decision, or even of a number of decisions either made simultaneously or logically connected. On the contrary it resulted from a long and discontinuous history of public and private actions. On the public side there were the Ley Creek sewage treatment plant and trunk line construction of the 1930's (a major factor in the area's favorable tax situation in the 1950's), the wartime decisions which produced a major defense plant and an airport, the developments which led to building the New York Thruway, and the events leading up to the establishment of the Onondaga County Water Authority and its acquisition of a temporarily adequate source of supply. Of significance also were the various actions by the Town of Dewitt creating special districts, enacting a favorable zoning ordinance, and providing agreeable tax assessment patterns; and the numerous passive decisions not to act by both Syracuse and Dewitt officials.

On the private side there was also a chain of identifiable decisions: the early assembly of land into Franklin Park; General Electric's wartime preference for Syracuse as a turbine plant site; Carrier's decision to buy the GE plant from the War Assets Administration; General Motors' decision to relocate its Brown-Lipe-Chapin plant in the suburbs; separate decisions by Eagan's Stover, the New York Central Railroad, and others to develop a common area; and many more individual and personal decisions relative to locations, investments, options, sales, leases, etc.

Many decisions of greater or lesser importance for the park's development have of course been overlooked or ignored. The decisions, both personal and corporate, emphasized here, however, would seem to represent the benchmarks shaping the course for industry in the Town of Dewitt. Such omissions as there may have been would not in any important way alter the logic of the conclusion: that a history of individual and seemingly unrelated decisions by private and public representatives in this instance shaped the pattern of suburban land use and industrial development.

Despite the recognized dangers of generalizing from a particular experience, some speculation about the nature of suburban industrialization seems in order. As might have been expected, most of the conventional determinants of industrial location come to bear here. Transportation facilities, public utilities, a compatible general "business climate," favorable tax levels, availability of labor, and satisfactory sites are all included among the factors influencing industry to locate in Industrial Park. Yet it is equally clear that all these locational factors are in some sense marginal.

For example, it would appear that one of the central factors behind the success of the park was the existence of a near-ideal transportation arrangement. The construction of the Thruway seems to have provided the initial impetus, although the proximity of the park property to the New York Central Railroad was a consideration of very great importance. Almost without exception planned industrial districts are situated adjacent to railroads, trucking terminals, airports, waterways or some combination of these means of transportation.[18] All industries producing a product for distribution require transport facilities, but the kind of transportation may vary and the facility does not necessarily have to be in place at the time the site is selected. This case clearly demonstrates the reciprocal aspects of the industry-transport relationship. Since industrial freight accounts for the bulk of the transportation industry's revenue, it is not unusual for the transporter to take the lead in development. Thus where the locating industry finds a satisfactory site minus transportation it may be able to arrange for provision of the needed facilities in return for prospective future freight revenue. Or where roads, streets, and highways are required, the locating industry is in a bargaining position *vis-à-vis* the public sector and may be able to negotiate for such facilities at public expense.

Similar negotiations are possible, indeed likely, where other public services—water supply and sewage disposal facilities, for example—are concerned. Since industry seeking a new location has a wide variety of alternatives, the governmental jurisdiction recruiting new plant is often willing to make concessions at public expense in expectation of future payroll growth and additional tax base. Even tax concessions may be made in the expectation that the economic growth of the community will eventually augment the public coffers. There is abundant evidence that industries are on occasion able to extract similar concessions with respect to zoning and subdivision modifications. It is in no sense clear, however, that it is to the advantage of industry to break down public protective devices. Many industries seem to realize that, once they are located, the requirement for strict compliance affords a measure of protection. In fact, the Association of State Planning and Development Agencies has for some time contended that rigorous (as opposed to rigid) zoning is welcomed by progressive industries.

In the Syracuse Industrial Park there were no controls when the initial development was planned; indeed, the developer employed a restrictive covenant as a controlling mechanism long before there was a public zoning ordinance. Some feared that locating industries would balk at such restrictions, but such fears seem to have been less than well grounded.

Finally, it should be pointed out that the private industrial district or park serves a peculiar function as a focus for public action even where public planning is non-existent. The private planning of a park necessitates a great deal of public activity in order to provide water, sewage disposal, streets, and the like. Such public facilities are typically negotiated for by the developing interest on a much wider and more uniform basis than would generally be the case in a piecemeal development. The privately-planned park is an inadequate substitute for conscious public planning for industrialization simply because private firms center attention on the promotion of a specific area and cannot be expected to survey the complete range of regional alternatives. Private decision-making therefore will be less rational than public because it is more narrowly focused.

Conscious public planning for industrialization for the whole of a metropolitan region could be expected to bring about a more efficient allocation of public and private resources because it would result in assessment and evaluation of a larger part of the region's complex interaction pattern than normally receives consideration. But in metropolitan communities such as Syracuse, where regional planning is underdeveloped, the privately planned industrial park can serve as a useful mechanism for the focusing of public and private planning actions.

XIII

Private Economic Development and the Metropolitan Problem

VIEWED in terms of decision-making most of the real estate development in metropolitan areas belongs in the category of what may be termed "lesser policy." Residential, industrial, and commercial development projects typically proceed outside the center of public discussion and debate. There are, of course, notable exceptions. Development projects that are initiated in the public sector, such as low-income housing, urban renewal projects, and the construction of arterial highways, may become area-wide issues of "big policy" with grave resulting conflicts.

Projects initiated in the private sector in most circumstances attract less attention. The exceptions include the location of a major industrial establishment with substantial economic impact. Such a development may require a wide mobilization of both public and private resources and arouse corresponding area-wide interest. Another exception, at the other end of the spectrum, is the isolated real estate project that threatens the established property values of neighborhood residents. Here public attention usually centers on a

---

Jesse Burkhead prepared this chapter.

proposed change in the zoning law, with the issues hotly debated and culminating in a public hearing. The social and political conflict generated in such a case may be far out of proportion to its long-run impacts on the income and wealth of the residents of the affected neighborhood.

Whether or not specific real estate developments become major policy issues in the metropolitan area, the sum total of their impact clearly determines many of the basic conditions of urban existence. The aggregation of decisions concerning residential, commercial, and industrial development both reflect public and private policy and in turn influence patterns of growth and change, thus shaping the entire social, political, and economic environment.

There is no unified pattern of public control over real estate development in any metropolitan area in the United States. This is the inescapable reality that emerges, not from the inherent incapacity of local government but from the nature of the local economy. Ours is an economic system in which the great bulk of activity is conducted in the private sector, with public authority providing a framework of regulations. This is the case with urban real estate development. Business firms initiate the action; public authority, reacting to the needs or desires of private interests, responds to restrain, modify, or implement private decisions. With notably few exceptions, in real estate development the private firm provides the initiative to which public agencies respond.

The Character of the "Market" in Real Estate Development

The organizational structure for planning and executing real estate projects will be examined in the next section. As a preliminary, it may be appropriate to investigate the character of the market for real estate development. In the terminology of economics, the end product of this development is private investment as an addition to the capital stock of the economy. Once this investment is in place, whether as commercial, residential, or industrial construction, it will require the continuing services of local government in the provision of transportation facilities, water supply, sewage disposal, and other public facilities. Thus every real estate development, in greater or lesser degree, affects the nature and scope of local government activity. Local government is shaped by real estate development to a greater extent than by most other private economic activity.

As a producer of investment goods, the real estate business is subject to a wider range of economic fluctuations than most other industries. This industry in most urban areas is characterized by a very large number of firms; two or three major concerns may dominate the field but there are many small firms. In times past new construction firms could be organized almost overnight by those with experience as craftsmen or foremen or supervisors in existing firms. Of recent years, entry into the industry has become more difficult for the newcomer. Instability continues to be the industry's dominant characteristic. A decline in the volume of construction will bring an almost equivalent percentage drop in the number of firms. As Ratcliff says, "The building industry has developed into a system that lacks the strong management and the integration of functional groups that are found in other industries." [1]

The end result of real estate development is not a standardized product that permits ready price comparisons. There are many sub-markets and many market imperfections. Legal complications arise continuously in securing title to property appropriate for development, with resulting inefficiencies and distortions in the effective use of urban land. Outmoded building codes and trade union regulations, local monopolies in building supplies, and a low level and rate of technological development in construction generally contribute to market imperfections and distortions. [2]

The relatively free entry into the construction game invites developers who are known as "speculative builders," a phrase that carries a sense of opprobrium in the minds of many local government officials. The speculative builder, moving into and out of the industry in response to changing market conditions, is often regarded as the villain of the piece. He competes with established firms which are both more permanent and more responsible. Operating on a thin financial margin, he is held to be the natural enemy of building codes and zoning regulations. He makes life miserable for local government officials, lacks a sense of social responsibility, and occasionally defrauds purchasers.

The large, established firms are also thought by some to be enemies of orderly development. Here the popular image is that of a manipulator, an operator, one who can persuade local government officials to overlook the regulations. The extent to which the popular images of the large and the small developer conform with reality is, of course, impossible to ascertain.

But in spite of the monopoly elements and the frictions and imperfections in the market for real estate development, considerations of efficiency are by no means absent. The developer will, of course, seek to maximize his profits in a market in which certain types of behavior are set by the forces of competition, and to do this it will be necessary for him to calculate costs carefully with appropriate attention to selection and planning of the site, market analysis, and protection of the future of the development. The successful developer no doubt acquires his own techniques for analysis of costs and markets, but even the inexperienced have access to a literature that will contribute to economic rationality.[3]

The pervasive characteristic of real estate development that marks it off from many other types of private activity is the overriding presence of benefits and losses to third parties. What makes a market transaction private in character is that the transaction is of significance only to the buyer and the seller; the housewife's purchase of a loaf of bread at the grocery store is the textbook case. But the end product of real estate development, whether it be a factory, a commercial property, or a residence, is a commodity that remains in existence and continues to influence the economic position of many who were not party to the transaction. The construction of a large factory, with its consequent impact on the welfare of large segments of the community, is the obvious example; but even a small residential development will affect third parties by the way that it influences the residential "character" of the community, by its impact on neighboring land values and land uses, and by its influence on the distribution of the costs of local government.

The point of particular concern here is the relationship between real estate development and local government. The dominant and relevant characteristics of urban government viewed in relation to real estate development are (1) its fragmented nature, (2) its fiscal inadequacy, and (3) the attendant pattern of commingled public and private interest. Unfortunately, the first two of these characteristics reinforce one another. The multiplicity of governmental units in the metropolitan area drastically reduces the possibility for effectively reaching, through the taxing mechanism, the wealth and income of the whole region. At the same time, the thin fiscal base on which urban governments operate necessitates recourse to special districts, service charges, and more fragmentation. The tax base is obviously "there;" indeed, the wealth and income of the whole nation is increasingly concentrated in urban areas. But the often observed lack of homogeneity between the economic region and the governmental region in metropolitan areas produces a perpetual state of fiscal imbalance. It has been appropriately stated that "Under the economic conditions which prevail in the twentieth century, the right to develop property proves profitable only if someone else is taxed to pay the cost of public improvement needed to support urban services."[4]

Governmental fragmentation is of course not the only factor that gives rise to fiscal imbalance in the relationship between real estate development and urban government. In case studies in three Massachusetts cities it was discovered that builders' capital costs for similarly priced homes might vary as much as $1,200, depending on the location of the construction.[5] From the standpoint of the builder, such factors as the scale of development and the presence or absence of unused capacity in existing water and sewerage systems will have the greatest impact on his development costs. From the standpoint of the community, the possibilities for securing state and federal aid, the presence or absence of unused capacity (especially in school facilities), and the distribution of public service capital requirements over time will determine whether residential developments will or will not pay their way.

The great range of variation in the capital costs that may confront the builder puts him in a position where he bargains with local government officials for the provision of community services. This bargaining process has many diverse and conflicting elements. For industrial and commercial development, unless there are specific neighborhood objections, local government officials will extend a welcoming hand. Nearly every local government official in a metropolitan area is certain that commercial and industrial development adds more to the tax base than it costs in government services. Moreover, this is probably a correct assumption viewed from the standpoint of a single governmental unit in the region. A new factory located in a suburban town is likely to draw its employees from the whole metropolitan area, hence the town in which the factory locates will not be faced with the burden of providing community facilities for all the employees and their families.

The burden of servicing residential development is quite another matter, and gives rise to a different pattern of relationship between the developer and the local community. The developer must negotiate his way into the suburban town; sometimes this is easy and sometimes it is difficult. The Connecticut towns that are successful in resisting any but high-priced residential construction are well known. No doubt every large metropolitan area has communities that, to a greater or lesser degree, attempt to pursue similar ends.

The fragmented government of the metropolitan area widens the range of effective bargaining available to the residential developer. If one community resists his efforts, he may seek development possibilities in another community. In suburban areas in New York State the separation of school governments from other local government offers a distinct advantage to the residential developer. The town board, the zoning board of appeals, the planning board, and the town supervisor—these are the officials with whom the developer deals; and the school board, separately organized, must adjust its operations to the results of decisions over which it has no control.

This kind of market structure for the end product of real estate development may well be reasonably efficient in allocating resources, from the viewpoint of a specific community that is in a strong bargaining position. It cannot, however, be expected to produce a general social efficiency in terms of effective land utilization and rational patterns of growth.[6] On the contrary, by any definition of rationality the imperfect market for real estate development yields many perverse effects. Some of the most serious distortions, from the standpoint of social efficiency, emerge from the influences generated by the combination of technology and interest groups. Robert C. Wood points out in *1400 Governments* that the interests supporting the rubber tire dominate all transportation planning in the New York metropolitan region.[7] Patterns of economic activity and of residential living would be substantially altered if mass rail transportation were promoted with the same zeal as the use of the private automobile and truck. It seems reasonable to suspect that in the New York metropolitan region economic activity and patterns of land use would be more efficient if different transportation policies were adopted.

Public policies, then, have a major impact on the real estate market and on real estate development. In the metropolitan area the agencies of government exercise three functions with respect to such development. The first is procedural. There is an established routine that the real estate developer and all who are linked with him must follow. This starts with observance of the rules for the acquisition of title to property and extends through routines for building permits, the provision of public facilities, and adherence to inspection procedures intended to safeguard building codes, and culminates in the legal transactions that accompany the final transfer of title to the purchaser. The second function of public agencies is to provide governmental services to the end product of the development —water, sewerage facilities, roads, schools, and the like.

The third function involves the reconciliation of the conflicting interests that surround the development process. This function is most obvious where community residents oppose a specific project and local government officials are called on to promote the development, modify its character, or prevent it. The mediation and conciliation and ultimate resolution of real estate development problems, like all other such governmental processes, affects property values and redistributes income to a greater or lesser extent among households and neighborhoods and within the business community.

Public agencies in the metropolitan region do not control real estate development, but only modify it at specific points. As Ratcliff has said, "The area of social control to accomplish corrective planning is small in comparison with the area over which control cannot effectively be exercised. The basic forces and processes of city growth move inexorably forward, and the efforts of man to modify them are puny and ineffective in comparison."[8] Puny and ineffective as such efforts may have been in the past, in most metropolitan areas the influence of public decision-making with respect to real estate development is surely growing, however slowly. Social and community values are coming increasingly to influence development decisions.

The Parties at Interest

Private Parties

The Developer. The central role of the developer as entrepreneur in the classical sense has already been stressed. In the words of a Canadian developer, he is "the catalyst [which] melds the planning and the sociological concepts with the hard realities of economics and human nature."[9]

The developer is the promoter and may emerge from almost any part of the real estate industry. As noted above, the condition of relatively free entry makes it possible for carpenters and other craftsmen to come up through the ranks as builders and to undertake small residential developments. Such developers may, over time, accumulate sufficient experience and financial backing to undertake large residential developments, or even commercial ventures. Real estate firms may organize separate corporations and arrange financing for such builders, or may themselves take the initiative in organizing a residential development and contracting for the services of a builder. Large commercial developments such as shopping centers are typically put under way by substantial real estate firms. Such firms may derive the bulk of their income from real estate brokerage, but maintain a commercial division with responsibility for the systematic promotion of new ventures.

Industrial real estate development is the most difficult of all to characterize. Here the builder is almost never the developer. Real estate firms, chambers of commerce, metropolitan development groups, banks, and public utilities may each and severally act to organize and promote a specific industrial development.

All real estate development must start, of course, with the

acquisition of land: a site is the initial raw material. The case studies in the two preceding chapters suggest that the developer looks for a site with certain characteristics, some more important than others. For a residential development the requirements are a favorable topography, the possibility of access roads, and facilities for water and sewage disposal. The absolute requirements and the marginal requirements are difficult to demarcate sharply. Water supply and access roads come close to being absolute, but even here the developer may be able to negotiate with public agencies to make potential sites available and feasible. At the same time, decisions of public agencies may alter the possibilities of development almost overnight. This occurred in Onondaga County in 1955, when the District Office of the New York State Department of Health ruled that septic tanks could be used in residential development only for lots that exceeded one-half acre in size. This forced development activity into areas with access to established sewer systems, and recourse to the private development of sewage treatment plants as described in the Seneca Knolls case. The point stressed here is that respecting all elements affecting the value and availability of sites the developer has access to a wide range of bargaining possibilities.

Law Firms. The testimony embodied in the foregoing case studies, together with evidence gathered from discussions with persons familiar with local development patterns, suggest that in Onondaga County lawyers, and in particular a small number of large established firms, exert a profound influence on the economic development of the metropolitan area.

A large real estate development will require legal services at almost every point. The lawyer must participate in the acquisition of land. He will typically be asked to carry the burden of negotiations with local government officials on zoning, access roads, and the provision of water and sewer facilities. He will negotiate with financial institutions to secure funds. When construction is completed and properties are transferred to their ultimate owners, he will arrange final settlements. Mortgages are recorded and titles are cleared under legal supervision. Small developers will retain a lawyer who is knowledgeable in real estate matters. A large development firm, as in the Bayberry case, may bring in its own legal staff, but even so that staff will work out a pattern of cooperation with established local firms.

Some of the most important and remunerative work undertaken by lawyers with respect to real estate development arises from the formation of special districts. Even a small residential development may require the organization of a sanitary, water, or lighting district. Capital financing will be arranged, a bond issue will be prepared, the securities will be marketed. In short, a new governmental unit will be created. This is expensive, and a large part of the expense consists of legal fees.

In Onondaga County the large, well-established law firms provide legal counsel to city, county, town, and village governments and to school districts within the metropolitan area. Counsel may be employed on a retainer or paid fees in accordance with the volume of legal work. It is by no means unusual for a single large firm to provide legal counsel to a number of these parties at interest: the town in which the development is to take place, the financial institution handling the mortgages on the property, the school district that must finance construction of the new capital facilities necessitated by the development, and county agencies that must approve capital facilities. A single law firm may thus serve, in a private capacity, as a mediator and conciliator of various public interests. The nonpartisan character of the firm will be preserved by the varying political affiliations of the senior partners, some of whom will be prominent Republicans, some prominent Democrats, in a pattern not unknown to other firms that deal with public agencies.

Real Estate Firms. Except where real estate firms are also development entrepreneurs, their role in the total process is more limited than might have been expected. In a commercial development, real estate brokers may be active in seeking tenants or lessees; in a residential development, the real estate firm is, of course, deeply involved in the sale of the final product. In Onondaga County exclusive listings are sometimes employed (that is, a developer may contract with a single real estate firm as sales agent for completed homes); but more typically any licensed real estate broker may sell in a development. Although fees are fixed, there is relatively free entry to this activity. The industry has a typical oligopoly structure, with a few dominant firms and several hundred small ones.

Observations in Onondaga County suggest that the large real estate firms are very much subject to that vague interplay of forces commonly described as "public opinion." Real estate brokers must be sensitive to the market demands of their customers with respect to the provision of public services and so must establish a pattern of continued working relations with local government officials, who themselves are particularly sensitive to the feelings of neighborhood groups. The real estate broker's role as middleman may well provide a significant element of self-discipline. The home-owner may deal only with the real estate agent and not at all with the builder; the developer-builder may transfer his operations elsewhere, but the real estate firm stays on. The firm is thus required to exercise a measure of responsibility not only over private construction standards but over the maintenance of community values in aesthetics and convenience as well.

Engineering Firms. Engineering firms have major responsibilities in real estate development in the planning, design, and construction of community facilities. Both the planning and the effective utilization of space within the metropolitan area depend measurably on the physical characteristics of specific sites, and engineers must be employed to assess the physical possibilities and estimate the costs of alternative possibilities of development. The decisions of engineering firms with respect to real estate development thus reflect a larger element of measurement and a smaller element of judgment than do the activities of the other private parties at interest. Unfortunately, the recommendations of engineers for the "one best way" in real estate development may often overlook the presence of feasible alternatives and obscure the value judgments that are implicit in the proposal. Engineers can make policy without appearing to do so.

Engineering firms, like law firms, can acquire a semi-monopoly position within a metropolitan area by virtue of successful practice and experience. Such established positions reduce the possibility for an effective independent check on engineering cost estimates and on feasible alternatives. In Onondaga County such a monopoly exists; for a single firm typically serves as consulting engineer to a real estate developer, as design engineer for the suburban town that may be constructing water or sewage facilities, and as consultant to the Onondaga County Public Works Commission and the County

Water Authority with responsibility for reviewing the plans submitted. This firm's reputation for competence is no doubt a major factor in the perpetuation of the multiple roles it is called upon to play.

In some communities architectural firms may be in a position to exercise an influence on the development process similar to that ascribed here to engineers. This is not the case, however, in Onondaga County, where there are a great many architectural firms, no one of which concern has a position approaching that of semimonopoly.

Financial Institutions. Every real estate development must be financed at successive stages from acquisition of land to the sale of the finished product. A single commercial bank or group of banks may provide credit to the developer for acquisition of land and initial construction. The same institutions may then be in a position to extend mortgage credit to the ultimate purchaser. The Federal Housing Administration and the Veterans Administration must approve subdivision and construction plans for residential developments so that mortgages may eventually be insured. The mortgage market is a national one and funds for development may come from far outside the region. The financial institutions in any one area typically arrange for participation with other institutions outside the community.

The interest of financial institutions in residential real estate development centers on the need for liquidity, and, in this context, for marketability. The houses that are constructed must be saleable and therefore must meet the expectations of buyers with respect to price, construction, aesthetics, and the availability of public services. This is both a short- and a long-run marketability. In the short run, financial institutions may control the rate of development by controlling the availability of credit to adjust construction rates to the volume of demand for completed units. In long-range terms, there must be reasonable expectation that the investment can be liquidated eventually, to protect the solvency of financial institutions.

Citizen and Neighborhood Groups. In suburban America it is possible to arouse overnight a more intense interest among citizens in the proposed location of an arterial highway or the threatened construction of an apartment building than over issues of war and peace. Both within the central city and (to an even greater extent) in suburban areas, real estate development is subject to influence and sometimes control by the veto of neighborhood groups. The ownership of private property may carry with it the right of development, but this development is very often sharply restrained by adjacent property owners. The Fayetteville case, explored above, is representative of developments that have been denied countless times in urban and suburban areas.

It has been observed that a compromise requires a more highly developed pattern of communication than an outright conflict or struggle,[10] and this fact adds to the difficulty of negotiating acceptance by the neighborhood of a development plan. But in any case the local government official must perforce operate within a pattern of compromise and conciliation. Such are the requirements of this pattern that it often seems that, in suburban areas, decisions are made not on the basis of majority agreement but on that of unanimous consent, or at the least of consensus.

There are a number of credible explanations of this phenomenon —the grass roots approach to governmental decisions in suburban areas.[11] Some communities, and indeed some counties in large metropolitan complexes, have established a firm consensus with respect to the proper path of economic development which they are able to enforce by zoning laws and subdivision regulations. Such communities truly shape the development forces that play on them.[12] Now and again, as in some Connecticut suburban and ex-urban communities, these exclusionist practices are undertaken with a view to preserving a "distinctive" community living pattern. More often, considerations of "financial efficiency" will be applied to limit hospitality to those activities that will provide more in property tax revenue than they cost in public services.[13] In other cases, less pleasant to contemplate, denial of access is directed squarely against minority religious and ethnic groups.

The most typical case of neighborhood or community action and reaction emerges from the threat of a new factory or a new commercial development. In this situation the beleaguered home-owner organizes his neighbors and his neighbors' neighbors, circulates petitions, transports delegations to meet with the zoning board of appeals, calls protest meetings, and writes letters to local newspapers. As a consequence, the factory or shopping center may be forced to move to another site. This kind of agitation may not be necessary for the communication of neighborhood viewpoints. The threat of agitation may do the trick, or town officials may be sufficiently sensitive to neighborhood feelings to discourage the developer at the outset in a project that is likely to encounter opposition.

The cases of exclusion and denial, however, are less numerous than those of modification and change as a result of vigorous expression of views of citizen and neighborhood groups. The developers of the apartment house agree to limit the height of the building, or to provide better off-street parking facilities, or to dedicate and maintain a neighborhood playground. The new factory establishes a buffer zone with trees and shrubbery between the plant and the nearby residential area. The developer's costs are modestly increased by such concessions, neighborhood antagonisms are ameliorated, and officials continue to enjoy the support of their constituents.

The Special Case of Industrial Location

Real estate development for industrial purposes differs rather sharply from residential and commercial development in terms of the parties at interest. For a sizable employer, as described above in the New Process Gear case, the pattern of initiation and response is reversed. Major interests within the community are anxious for the employer to locate his activities somewhere within the area, and some towns and villages will be anxious to provide the location. Here local government officials and business and civic organizations work together for a common purpose. Further, the enterprise may require the participation of the top echelons of the metropolitan area power structure. Again in the New Process Gear case, the political party structure was utilized as an instrument of decision-making to provide a cohesive and interrelated pattern of action. The leadership that emerged to negotiate with the Chrysler Corporation could apparently operate effectively and on short notice only by employing this established framework.

The differences between commercial and residential real estate development and industrial development are underlined by the phenomenon of the industrial park. Here, as Chapter XII shows, a single large real estate firm can organize a whole area and provide the facilities and services that are necessary for the attraction of industry, particularly small and medium sized establishments. An industrial park development thus becomes a kind of mechanism for making advance decisions about public services and for achieving a kind of prior community consensus. This device permits the real estate firm to negotiate with prospective concerns without the necessity for treating each location project individually, subject to a special pattern of negotiation with local government officials.

It seems likely that industrial parks will come increasingly to characterize industrial real estate development in urban areas. The park device brings order out of what can otherwise be near-chaos in the relations between a firm seeking a location and the multitude of local governments with which it must deal. Moreover, industrial firms of many (but not all) types are almost certain to continue in the pattern of the last 15 years, with relocation outside the central city and a resulting dispersion of the urbanized area.[14] Certainly the rate of industrial relocation is substantial. A study of the attitudes of Detroit firms toward location and relocation found that 23.1 per cent of all industrial firms in the central city preferred sites outside the city, while about 18 per cent had plans under way to move from their present locations.[15] There is no reason to believe that Detroit is unusual in this regard; other urbanized areas would undoubtedly reveal similar patterns of movement and change. Syracuse is among the cities which this description fits.

Local Government Agencies

It is difficult to generalize about the competence and effectiveness of the dozens of local government agencies that are involved in real estate development in the metropolitan area. Syracuse is no doubt typical of other metropolitan areas in that the central city planning staff has accumulated a substantial competence and expertness, and enjoys a considerable degree of prestige in the governmental structure of the city. Its role in the private real estate development of the metropolitan area as a whole, however, is almost negligible, because most major development occurs outside the boundaries of the central city. Under a special statute described above, the city Planning Commission must approve all subdivisions within a three-mile radius of the city limits, but inadequate staff and lack of effective working relations with town boards and other agencies in this three-mile zone handicap the planning agency in the discharge of this responsibility.

It is a reasonably good nation-wide generalization that suburban governments in metropolitan areas are not adequately staffed to meet their responsibility in economic development.[16] The governments of Onondaga County are certainly no exception to this rule. Suburban government agencies concerned with real estate development are manned largely by lay citizens. Town boards, planning boards, and zoning boards of appeal are typically made up of citizen-volunteers who devote endless hours to the consideration of local problems but who lack the assistance of qualified technicians to provide a professional examination of the whole range of available alternatives. Modest improvements on this score are in sight as an occasional suburban town retains the services of a planning consultant for the preparation of a master plan, but these changes come slowly.

In general, there is little formal linkage between the citizen-volunteer appointee and the organized political party structure in the suburban towns. The town supervisor may appoint or approve the appointment of the citizen-volunteer, who is likely to be chosen on the basis of geographical representation or by the simple criterion of willingness to devote the necessary time to the task. Community development problems are thus "kept out of politics," with no formal channel between the officials who propose policy and a voting constituency.

The case studies of the preceding chapters suggest that the patterns of relationship between real estate development and local public officials are by no means static. Each new development is an individual and different thing. The problems it poses in its requirements for public services will be solved in a pattern conditioned by previous developments that may or may not be comparable with the one at hand. By the same token, each new experience in development will shape the attitudes and reactions of public officials toward the next set of problems. The inexperience of local government officials in dealing with a major development, as in the Seneca Knolls case, permits wide leeway for bargaining and negotiation. But it may also act as a deterrent to the developer, who may himself be inexperienced and so may find it easier to negotiate with local government officials who are accustomed to established routines.

It is evident from the material examined that the parties at interest in real estate development are not discrete market units dealing with each other at arms' length in a competitive situation. On the contrary, decision-making in this field is characterized by a very high degree of interlocking among participating interests. A developer will approach an established law firm that has a reputation for "getting the job done." This means that the firm has a successful pattern of dealings with local government officials; that it is sensitive to the points of friction in the development process; that it knows how to persuade and conciliate; and that it has well-established channels of communication to architects, engineers, and suppliers of building materials. Moreover, ownership of the law firm may overlap with that of financial institutions that are parties to the development. Partners in the firm or stockholders in the bank may have financial interests in the real estate that is being developed, or even in the development firm itself. The patterns of relationship and communication may extend vertically to all parties at interest in a given development and laterally to firms and agencies engaged in similar activities in the metropolitan region.

It would not, however, be accurate to describe all government agencies as helpless in the face of such patterns of interlocking development. The district office of the New York State Department of Health, for example, has had considerable influence on development patterns in Onondaga County in spite of substantial opposition and with no very strong public support for its actions. Well organized neighborhood groups can block almost any development project by summoning to their aid "an aroused public opinion." At the same time, local government officials can utilize the support of such groups to strengthen their hand in dealing with developers. In almost every metropolitan region a variety of public control mechanisms are available, and they can be applied with reasonable effectiveness if there are political leadership to invoke and community attitudes to support their utilization.

The Outlook for Central Control over Real Estate Development

Although social controls over real estate developments are coming increasingly to be exercised in urbanized areas, both the case studies presented here and the opinion of observers suggest that fragmented urban government and essentially unplanned private development will not soon yield to a centralized metropolitan area authority. For the immediate future the outlook is for a modestly larger scope for public decision-making with major emphasis remaining on private controls. Rannels has commented: "Planning of land uses, to be effective, must work the separate interests into a larger scheme with enough flexibility and scope for unplanned adjustments to keep on occurring."[17] Although this prescription was directed to the central business district, it could be applied equally well to the whole metropolitan area.

Real estate development is essentially private-market and hence unplanned economic activity. For private enterprise there must be scope for the assumption of risk, flexibility for adjustment to an unstable economy, and adequate profits from investment. The developer himself has almost no stake whatever in a greater degree of centralization of public control over the developmental process. The fragmentation of local government in the metropolitan area may increase the number of parties at interest and hence multiply the number of officials with whom the developer must deal, but it also provides a broad scope for bargaining and compromise that the developer finds useful to his operations. There are, of course, occasions when even the most individualistic real estate developer will wish for a greater measure of public planning. For example, at a meeting held in one of the suburban towns in Onondaga County to discuss the relationship of land use planning to real estate development, the builders were unanimous in agreement that advance planning for trunk line sewers would introduce an element of certainty into what is now a near-chaotic situation. They were much less sympathetic, however, to other aspects of land use planning. Since public controls frequently entail delays in development and since developers are always anxious to proceed with a rapid liquidation of their investment, the development firms are not likely to be partisans of public control.

There are parties at interest in real estate development that have a substantially greater stake in metropolis-wide action than do individual developers. Large real estate brokerage firms can probably operate more effectively in an urban environment where the fragmentation of government is reduced, and where the rules of the game are more uniformly applied. Certainly there are many cases on record where real estate firms have supported region-wide planning and region-wide provision of water and sewerage facilities in the metropolitan area. Financial institutions similarly may be expected to favor a more uniform application of building and zoning regulations and a metropolitan approach to the provision of public facilities.

It would appear that the established law firms that play such an important part in real estate development have almost nothing to gain from a reduction in fragmented government through the institution of a larger measure of central decision-making. The client interests of law firms support the *status quo* in governmental organization; this would appear to be particularly important in the organization and financing of the multiplicity of special districts established to accompany residential real estate development. It is more difficult to assess the position of engineering firms, although their interests would seem to be found in a larger volume of public works regardless of the number or character of the sponsors. It may be conjectured, however, that such firms would not view with favor a strong metropolitan government that would maintain its own professional engineering staff.

It may be predicted that, as it becomes more and more clear that a series of unrelated and uncoordinated real estate developments largely shape the economic character of urban areas, an increasing measure of public control will be sought in an effort to bring about a more orderly development. The growth of such control will not occur easily or automatically. In the field of real estate development, the forces making for division and conflict are stronger than those making for metropolitan unity. Nor is there any existing pattern of political leadership that can serve to bring the diverse economic elements of the metropolitan community into an area-wide working relationship. If the business community is not united in support of metropolitan action, neither is it unified in opposition. Indeed, some leadership possibilities may be expected to emerge here, particularly from the ranks of financial institutions and public utilities with an immediate stake in the regularization of the development process.[18] If this seems a forlorn hope, it may help to remember that there are so few forces in either the public or the private sector that have a "natural" interest in the metropolitan region that persons, groups, or programs that appear to possess this attribute must be nurtured with tender care.

Part 4

CONCLUSION

XIV

Community Power and Metropolitan Decision-Making

IN THESE accounts of decision-making in the Syracuse metropolitan area we have reviewed some 22 cases or points of decision or action. Obviously they are not equal as regards breadth, depth, time span, importance of the participants, or significance of the issues; on the contrary, they vary greatly when appraised by these and other relevant criteria. They vary, too, in their pertinence to the subject and their contribution to achievement of the announced purpose of the study. Yet because of their common environment and subject-matter focus all contain suggestions for useful hypotheses. These may be examined under the dual headings of community power and metropolitan decision-making.

Community Power

The mythology of community power in Syracuse today is very clear. Any number of observers, including many knowledgeable in

---

Frank J. Munger prepared this chapter.

local affairs, will assert that a single man stands at the top (or, some might say, behind the top) of community affairs and runs things. This is Stewart F. Hancock, lawyer, banker, gentleman, spokesman for the old-line aristocracy, without whose consent, tacit or explicit, nothing of importance can be done. One writer refers to Hancock as "Mr. Syracuse."[1] Harking back to the categories advanced in Chapter I, Syracuse is commonly believed to have a slack, monolithic, pyramidal power structure with a businessman-attorney as its dominant figure. Many who hold this view concede that Hancock's power is now declining. The time spanned by this study, however, covers the period of his greatest reputed power, and the cases examined should demonstrate his leadership if in fact it possessed substance.

These analyses of actual decisions taken with respect to public problems in the Syracuse metropolitan area do not support an interpretation based on the concept of monolithic power. What is clear from the cases is that the pattern of decision-making in Syracuse has changed markedly over the last 30 years. The cases suggest that at one time the current myth had a solid foundation in fact, for earlier there was a high concentration of community authority in the hands of a single man, simultaneously a political leader and a public official. Expanding the already substantial powers vested in his predecessor as Republican County Chairman, Rolland Marvin consolidated those powers with his authority as Mayor to wield an unprecedented influence over public decisions. Moreover, he exercised his control with a minimum of public oversight. His ultimate rejection resulted partly from reaction against his autocratic methods, but more from the bitter opposition of Governor Thomas Dewey, still smarting over Marvin's support of Wendell Willkie at the 1940 Republican national convention.

After Marvin's defeat, a disintegration of political power took place. It was during this period that Stewart Hancock maximized his influence, and community leadership passed from a combined political boss and elective public official to a lawyer-businessman with no pronounced inclination for public notice. In the process, a change occurred in the process of leadership itself. Partly in reaction to the tight control exercised by Marvin, partly perhaps as a result of the example set by the Post-War Planning Council, the circle of participants in community affairs broadened. Such a change was no doubt inevitable in any case in view of the steady growth in the size of the metropolitan community and the complexity of its interests; nevertheless it accompanied, perhaps as both cause and effect, a significant change in the pattern of leadership. Since more persons were involved in community affairs and more individuals therefore had to be consulted, no successor's influence could be as unequivocally dominant as that of Marvin. Indeed, in the cases examined here Hancock appears only as one among several leaders.[2] A notable consequence of Marvin's fall was the collapse of central control over the Republican party organization. Lacking this essential part of Marvin's arsenal, subsequent community figures have never been able to force through measures over town opposition with Marvin's abandon. Whether the power system can at present be regarded as polylithic or whether it is in transition to monolithic control by some new individual leader is clearly an open question, although the fact that the change in the type of community leadership has accompanied changes in social forces would seem to suggest the former.

Even during the period of monolithic control, the case studies demonstrate the point that broad areas of public policy were left undirected by the dominant leaders of the community. That fact does not necessarily destroy the monolithic concept. As noted before, some distinction between major and minor policy must necessarily be made. So long as the top leaders continued to exercise tight control over such focal concerns as city and county budgets they might properly be considered to be dominant even though they failed to assert control at all points of decision-making. The establishment of a children's court, for example, might be offered to interested citizens' groups as a minor concession which would not affect substantially the central financial concerns of local government.

Although this abdication of control over certain areas of policy-making may be accommodated to a monolithic interpretation of the exercise of community power, it nevertheless has important consequences which are particularly evident within the real estate field.

Chapters XI through XIII make clear that in this area especially many lesser decisions are continually being made without reference to the power structure at its top levels. These decisions may be minimized as affecting only minor policy, but the fact remains that their cumulative impact has tremendous effect in shaping the course of development of the metropolitan area. The only recognized tool that might give the community leaders effective control over the accumulation of these decisions would be area-wide planning of land use, and either through tradition or through their own laissez-faire inclinations the leaders have been slow to grasp this weapon.

With respect to local-state relations, the cases clearly reveal the legislative advantages enjoyed by Syracuse and Onondaga County. By reason of their Republican affiliation both city and county are accorded a friendly reception in the perennially Republican legislature. When they ask for a special law, the legislature is quick to oblige. The only law sought from the state that provided any difficulty involved passage of the Alternative County Government law, a statute of general application. Two measures were indeed blocked, but both by gubernatorial vetoes.

The cases also demonstrate the difficulty of obtaining popular approval of a proposal for governmental reorganization. Three referenda were held on variations of this proposal. The first, supported by Democrats and opposed by Republicans, failed in both city and towns. The next, supported by neither party but opposed by neither, suffered a like fate. And even the third proposal (the county director plan), which was supported by both newspapers, a banner list of city leaders, and numerous party officials, failed to receive a county majority though carrying the city. The uniform lack of success of these efforts attests the conservatism of the electorate, the influence of the county bureaucracy, and the strong opposition of the towns (and more particularly their supervisors) to change.

Of the 22 cases examined, 14 are found on examination to have involved decisions at the county level. Isolating these 14 in order to obtain greater comparability through greater uniformity, it is possible to make an analysis of the effectiveness of exercise of power from an examination of the decisions reached. Robert Dahl has suggested a possible formula for such a calculation in his definition of a community leader in terms of ability to (1) initiate proposals and carry them through, (2) override substantial opposition on behalf of a proposal, and (3) veto a proposal initiated by others. Making some rather arbitrary groupings of the interests involved in the cases at hand, the power demonstrated in these terms assumes the following pattern:

	Won	Lost	Did Not Participate
Republican Party	5	2	7
Democratic Party	1	3	10
Manufacturers Association	2	0	12
Chamber of Commerce–Governmental Research Bureau	2	2	10
CIO	0	1	13
Real estate interests	3	0	11
League of Women Voters	2	5	7
Community Chest/Council of Social Agencies/Onondaga County Health Association	2	2	10
Town government officials	5	2	7
Post-Standard	3	2	9
Herald-Journal	2	4	8
Village weekly newspapers	3	0	11

Such a listing, while of course not conclusive, nevertheless has high suggestive value. It demonstrates clearly that, in terms of community decision-making, the Democratic Party is not very important in Onondaga County; the lone Democratic victory represents the party's success in persuading Governor Lehman (Democrat) to veto a Republican county reorganization measure. The tabulation likewise shows that the League of Women Voters concerns itself with many problems, but is not very effective in winning acceptance for its proposals. The League's chief value obviously lies in the service it performs in calling problems up for consideration. The list also instances the ineffectiveness of organized labor in local decision-making. It indicates that labor does not lose: it simply fails to participate. Likewise less effective than might have been expected are the daily newspapers, which together lost oftener than they won.

The group with what appears to be the best record of effective action is the Republican Party. In only two cases, however, can the party be said to have initiated the action it supported, and both of those involved Rolland Marvin as leader. The party organization therefore was rather a vehicle through which other interests sought to attain their goals. Success in obtaining party support usually guaranteed victory; but the party's own role was passive or instrumental, consisting in most cases of embracing decisions made elsewhere and seeing that the county government carried them out. The town officials were equally successful with, perhaps because often indistinguishable from, the Republican Party. The industrialists and the realtors had a low rate of participation, but were uniformly successful where they elected to commit their resources.

The most striking feature of the tabulation is the low level of participation in the decision-making process. No group tested its strength in a majority of the decisions, and most were involved in only a few cases. This warrants the conclusion that separate clusters of decision areas exist, each with its own distinct group of participants.[3] It effectively eliminates the notion of an all-sovereign wielder of community power, and it attacks (though it does not necessarily destroy) the concept of a monolithic power structure as applied to Syracuse. Under such circumstances it is meaningless to say that group A is more powerful than group B when A and B have never tested their strength against each other and because of their differing interests are not likely to.

The tabulation provides no clue concerning the problem of differential commitment, which as observed earlier is central to an appraisal of power and its exercise. The Chamber of Commerce, to illustrate, may take a mild interest in one measure and satisfy itself with a simple endorsement; in another case more tangibly related to the economic interest of its members, it may throw all its resources into a life-and-death struggle. It is manifestly unrealistic to regard the two commitments as being in any wise equal, for neither the rates nor the efficiencies of use of influence are comparable.

In summary, the decisions analyzed in this study afford no basis for easy generalizations about the structure and exercise of community power in the Syracuse metropolitan area. Only three overall conclusions seem warranted by the materials examined. First, the myth that significant decisions in Syracuse emanate from one source does not stand up under close scrutiny. Second, there tend to be as many decision centers as there are important decision areas, which means that the decision-making power is fragmented among the institutions, agencies, and individuals which cluster about these areas. Third, in reality there appear to be many kinds of community power, with one kind differing from another in so many fundamental ways as to make virtually impossible a meaningful comparison.

Community Power Roles

The cases clearly indicate that a full model of the decision-making process would have to take into account the fact that decisions do not eventuate from single, individual choices but from a flow of choices. Who raised the issue and brought it to public attention? Who formulated the alternatives and marshaled the facts employed by the decision-makers in reaching their conclusions? To what extent were the decision-makers free to choose among these alternatives? A series of acts are involved in a decision to take or not to take a particular public action. It will prove useful to examine the process briefly. This may be done by identifying the roles involved in the exercise of community power.

The Initiators

Innumerable problems calling for remedial action can be identified within a metropolitan area, for urban life is never perfect. Of these, however, only a limited number are—or in normal circumstances can be—brought forward for consideration. At times the process by which action is initiated may be almost automatic. Thus when an event occurs which sharply changes existing conditions to the detriment of a vocal group, a demand for action can be confidently expected. When the Big Sister and Big Brother programs were closed, the way was opened for creation of a county children's court. When a legislative act cut off child guidance funds to Onondaga County, establishment of a mental health board followed. The city's fiscal crisis of the late 1930's produced the county welfare consolidation. And so on.

More difficult to explain is the process by which action is initiated to remedy long-existent evils. Onondaga County's government structure is notoriously outdated; it has undergone no important change, much less anything approaching basic reorganization, for more than a century. As county agencies and functions have multiplied, the resulting problems have become steadily more severe. Only within comparatively recent years, however, did the League of Women Voters pick up the problem and make it an issue. What defines the point past which men (and women, too) are no longer disposed to endure?

The exercise of leadership by which action is initiated has come most frequently from the professional members of the governmental agencies. State Health Department officials initiated consideration of a county health department; Richard Greene of the city probation office launched action looking toward a children's court; Sergei Grimm, director of the City Planning Commission, inspired the Post-War Planning Council; the psychiatry department of the State College of Medicine proposed the creation of the mental health clinic.

This fact in itself may not appear surprising; for a widely popular belief holds that governmental agencies continually seek to expand their powers and budgets, and this might appear to be evidence substantiating that view. But contrary evidence appears in the fact that the county, whose agencies were to be expanded, has most frequently resisted growth. County supervisors have shown little desire to engage in empire-building. They personify the town governments, and they prefer to keep county taxes low. An example is provided by the County Public Works Commission, which accepted only reluctantly operating responsibility for the metropolitan sewage treatment plant. State and city governmental officials have served as initiators of county action, but seldom have county spokesmen done so.

This undoubtedly is one factor in the difficulty of effecting a reorganization of the county government. If there were a county manager or other executive he might be expected to attempt to strengthen his own powers, much as the strong mayor seeks to grow stronger in the city. With no county executive to make a beginning, however, there is no place at which to begin; and leadership of the county reorganization movement therefore falls to such groups as the League of Women Voters.

The Experts

Providing an idea concerning something that needs to be done is, however, only the beginning. An idea may be sufficient to start the ball rolling, but sooner or later the central idea must be fleshed out into a plan for action. If the need is for county reorganization, a proposal in detail must be offered. If it is for sewage treatment, the response must be a carefully conceived scheme for meeting it. If the need is complex, so also will be the plan. This means that a need for technicians arises early and insistently in the decision-making process.

The most obvious source for expert assistance is the reservoir of local government employees. In practice this means the professional people in the various functional fields.[4] On occasion they may be the initiators of action themselves, but in any event they are likely soon to be consulted. Their availability is undoubtedly one reason why unifunctional changes are easier to accomplish than general reorganizations, a phenomenon often noted. In Onondaga County the most commonly employed source of expert assistance is quasi-governmental. The engineering firm of O'Brien and Gere provides professional advice on virtually every major public works project in the county.

There are limits, however, to the opportunities for utilizing governmental experts. If the public employees are inert, incompetent, or suspected of seeking opportunity to feather their own nests, an alternative source of expertise must be found. It is this dilemma that was responsible for the creation of the Governmental Research Bureau. In effect the business and industrial interests hired themselves a rival set of experts in whom they felt greater confidence.

Not all groups concerned with government problems can afford to hire their own experts. In this more normal situation several possibilities exist, any or all of which may be utilized. One alternative source of knowledge lies in the state administrative departments, which may find options that have been missed locally. In one sense this is what the state legislature attempts to accomplish in such a measure as the alternative government law. Options by themselves are not enough, however, and experts are needed to point out and facilitate their local applications. This function is performed by the state Health Department and the state Education Department, among others.

An additional source of professional assistance resides in Syracuse University and, to a lesser extent, LeMoyne College. The significance of the role played by the Syracuse University faculty lies particularly in the technical support it provides for programs outside the area of economic interest of the business and industrial communities, and in the assistance it gives to minority interests in the formulation of policy alternatives. In such fields as mental health, education, youth development, county planning, urban renewal, and, quite recently, metropolitan matters, university personnel are active participants. The agitation for county reorganization in the late 1930's was sparked by a Syracuse University faculty professor, and other faculty members have rendered expert assistance on all manner of community issues called up for public decision.

The Publicists

It is not enough, however, to have an idea—even an expertly prepared one—in order to have an issue. As the 1934 Bar Association plan for county reorganization demonstrated, a proposal must be known to the public to become an issue. This is peculiarly the province of the newspapers. In an objective measurement of community power the two Syracuse dailies would not rank particularly high; more often than not, as we have observed, the measures they support are defeated. But they are capable of forcing consideration of an issue. By reports of events, feature stories, and editorials they are able to push the decision-makers into hard choices on matters they might prefer to ignore. In other language, they can compel items to be placed on the community's public-action agenda. Television likewise plays an increasingly important role in this respect.

There are limits to the newspapers' freedom of choice, for certain groups and individuals by their position or prestige can force newspaper copy. High public officials, the Chamber of Commerce, the Medical Society can command newspaper coverage. Even here, however, the choice of the newspaper to report minimally or to "play up" a news event may make a good deal of difference. And newspaper publicity is likely to prove indispensable to the success of lesser causes.

The only serious rival to the newspapers in this respect is, curiously enough, the Democratic Party. Rarely does that party sit in the seat of power, and when it does nothing much may happen: the only Democratic mayor in three decades was ineffectual as a party spokesman. But the Democratic Party can force issues on the attention of the community. Ordinarily the party does not initiate issues, but rather chooses among those initiated by others. By offering resolutions and debating them within the Common Council and the Board of Supervisors, the Democrats command newspaper space since party conflict is good copy. Beyond this, through campaigns for office Democratic candidates mobilize other means of communication—television and radio time, advertising, rallies, word of mouth, etc.—to make issues of the matters chosen for discussion.

The Influentials

The nominal target of this publicity is the general public, which may indeed be the real target if an election for office or a referendum is at stake. More frequently, however, the proponents of a program address the public in order to attract the attention of a limited number of persons believed to hold the power of decision. The purpose is to convince them that something that affects them is at stake, and so to enlist their support. Key public officials are an obvious target of such a campaign. So also are the major economic groups with stakes in the community. Gathered together in the Chamber of Commerce and the Manufacturers Association, they are important individually as well—Niagara Mohawk, General Electric, Carrier, the banks, etc.

Depending on the issue, the target also includes the major institutionalized social welfare and professional groups, such as the Community Chest, the Council of Social Agencies, and the Medical Society. Members of such groups may be drawn from the same social class as the leaders of the economic organizations, and indeed may sometimes be the same individuals; but their interest in social welfare, plus the effect of professional contacts, influences their behavior in different directions and makes them useful for different causes.

The struggle to win acceptance for a proposal may revolve largely around the effort to gain support among such groups without much attention to the formal governmental process, and a defeat here may end the tale. This was the case with the post-war version of the county health department plan. When it failed to command the support of the Medical Society the proposal was dropped by the supervisors, who were only too glad to be relieved of the responsibility for making a decision.

The Brokers

As has been suggested, the core of the influentials consists of the economic groups with the most substantial stake in the community. This does not mean, however, that the heads of the corporations are themselves involved in the decision-making process. Normally they are hidden behind an intervening curtain of community representatives. These may be public relations men, or in the more recent jargon of General Electric, a "community relations team." But most frequently they are drawn from local law firms.

It is customary for a major corporation, though employing national legal advisors, to retain local counsel to represent it within the community. Similarly, if a real estate developer wants to rearrange or facilitate his relations with government, he goes to one of the principal law firms. And if a town government wants something, it too is likely to turn to a lawyer. In the cases examined in the previous chapters, the names of two law firms recurred frequently: Melvin and Melvin, and Bond, Schoeneck, and King. At least two others might be added, but, in so far as these cases reveal, they are not especially active in the negotiation of metropolitan decisions.

Community conflicts—and those involving economic interests in particular—are rarely fought out between the principals, but are handled by their legal representatives. And since it is the legal counsel who tells the principal what is possible and what is not, the latter's vision of political reality is shaped accordingly. In the process the lawyers, though brokers of power, wield substantial power themselves. And because the hostilities are conducted through intermediaries, community conflicts rarely erupt as open warfare but simmer along as protracted negotiations. Accommodation and compromise are emphasized in place of the all-or-nothing rewards of outright victory or complete defeat.

Less well-financed interests (that is, those of a non-economic character) usually must serve the representative function themselves. As a result they may stumble, or suffer costly delays. As another result the decisions they seek are far more likely to be made in public, and to be couched in the extreme terms the skilled broker is able to avoid through negotiation and compromise.

The Transmitters of Power

Just as the true leaders of the economic interests are masked in the process of community decision-making by their representatives, so too are the final decision-makers, the governmental officials, concealed by a cover. Instead of dealing directly with, for example, the Board of Supervisors or its members, the representative of an economic group seeking action from the government is likely to go to the Republican party leader. And since both representative and leader are usually lawyers, the task may be no more complex than talking the matter over with his law partner. Under some circumstances, the representative may find himself talking to himself as party leader. The New Process Gear case provides an illustration of the manner of operation of—and the results achieved by—the transmitters of power.

Republican party leaders ordinarily do not initiate action: in the cases presented above only Rolland Marvin could be said to have done so. But by possessing the capacity to issue orders to subordinates that will be obeyed, they enormously simplify the task of political contact for those with access to the party leadership. The clearest evidence of the effort and time they save is provided by the difficulties attending those groups—the League of Women Voters, for example—which have dealt with supervisors and the like on an individual basis, winning their support one by one.

The Authority of Government

Only the final step in the process of decision-making is the act of government itself, the approval or rejection of the proposal by the officials formally vested with the authority of office. Because the individual members of the Common Council or the Board of Supervisors are rarely persons of prominence in the community—customarily they consist of young men making their reputations and older men of long experience in the limited world of party affairs—it is conventional to minimize their role. When the time arrived for official action, Clarence King secured the votes he needed from them. With less persuasion and more power, Rolland Marvin did the same.

It is possible, however, to understate the role of the Common Council or the Board of Supervisors as well as to overstate it. The approval of the supervisors is essential since, for better or worse, they are the government of the county. Some supervisors, especially those from the rural towns, show a substantial capacity for independent action. Their resistance to change can be seen in the recurrent city-town struggles described in the cases above. Stubborn supervisors have at times delayed board approval for long periods, and when their own positions seem to them to be at stake, as in the case of a proposal for county governmental reorganization, they may exercise an effective veto over action. The role of the supervisors in decision-making is negative, but negative power may be as effective in its way as positive. Substantially the same may be said of the Common Council and its members.

Interrelationships among the Roles

The traditional approach to the study of community power has been to emphasize the role of the community influentials. Under the concept of power as a process, however, other roles become important. It is the argument of this analysis that isolation of the possessors of power from the participants in the flow and process of decision-making has little meaning. Power has value and substance only as it is used for something. The "powerful" community leader without idea men to suggest possibilities to him, or experts to package his program, or publicists to put wheels under it, or brokers to facilitate its consideration, or transmitters to bring it before the nominal decision-makers, can do little with his power. [Community power is a network of action, not a locus of residence.

It is meaningless to try to measure these strands of community power against one another, to argue that the lawyer is more influential than the corporation executive who in turn is more influential than the consulting engineer. Their power roles are not competitive, but complementary; they are links in a chain. When none of the partners to the process is expendable, none can truthfully be described as the inferior of any of the others.

The Environment and Freedom of Choice

One final aspect of the power process in relation to local decision-making remains to be considered: the degree of choice exercised within the community. The earliest studies of community power structure assumed a high measure of freedom for the individual community to choose its own course of action. A more recent line of inquiry, however, has opened the question of the degree to which decisions attributed to the local community are in fact determined by the unavoidable impact of such environmental factors as the population of the community, its resources, its taxable property, its ongoing commitments, its position *vis-à-vis* the state, etc. A striking part of Robert Wood's recent study of the governments in the New York City metropolitan area was an attempt to determine the extent to which local governmental expenditures in New Jersey are fixed by such factors, and to delimit the residual, unexplained variations in expenditures that might be attributed to the actual decisions of local governments. A similar study, concerned with expenditures for education, is now under way at Syracuse University.

In so far as these cases may be held to provide a guide, the realistic choices available to the Syracuse metropolitan community appear to be substantial. The size, growth pattern, and composition of the population would seem to offer no special problem. There is considerable unused or under-used space within the city, with land to accommodate great growth outside; moreover, there are no physical barriers to expansion, either residential or industrial. The multiplicity of local governmental units serves as a complicating factor, but this is a normal obstacle to metropolitan action. The community's reserve resources are substantial, for while there are constitutional limits on both taxes and public debt, these have not usually proved to be a serious damper on government spending.[5] The state has embraced certain policies which have the effect of limiting local choice, but for the most part these have not been pursued rigorously. The most serious trammel is found in the native conservatism of the people, and even that yields before the blandishment (or the bludgeoning) of the Republican Party. In short, there are few environmental limitations on decision-making in the Syracuse metropolitan area which cannot be overridden where there is a combination of need and will.

In another sense, however, it is necessary to indicate a limit upon the conception of a decision as a free choice among alternatives by a determinate set of decision-makers. This concerns what might be called the "inadvertence" of decisions. The cases make clear that many decisions are made partly by accident, that chance factors may play an important role, that sometimes a decision is the inevitable end product of past decisions that were made without anticipation of their consequences. Particularly in the real estate field this inadvertence of decision-making is evident. The Industrial Park was made possible by a confluence of seemingly unrelated past decisions —the forehanded accumulation of land, the provision of sewage facilities, the convenient location of a Thruway interchange, the laying of railroad trackage, etc. It might be argued that some of these decisions—as that of the Public Works Commission to provide sewerage—were taken in anticipation of some future industrial development, if not in foreknowledge of the Eagan project. This cannot be said, however, of Franklin's decision in the 1920's to obtain title to the lands involved. Yet without his action it is unlikely that an industrial park would have been created in this particular form or at this place. Industrial Park, then, was made possible by a series of individual actions taken over a period of 30 years without contemplation of any such eventuation as ultimately occurred. The cases examined here warrant the hypothesis that this is characteristic of community decision-making in general.

Metropolitan Cooperation and Its Components

So far the analysis has been concerned with community power and the process of decision-making generally; it is now necessary to relate the subject to the metropolitan context of multiple governments. For many types of public decision within a metropolitan area it is necessary to secure favorable action from two or more governments, each subject to its own particular and peculiar combination of pressures. The schematic representation offered in Figure 1 will illustrate the point. There a hypothetical proposal that requires the support of three governments is presented, along with certain assumed combinations of pressures that admit of various courses of action. From the drawing, it is possible to identify three types of situations in which cooperative action becomes possible.

Parallel Action

The first and simplest of these is portrayed in diagrams A and B of Figure 1. A particular interest group seeks action from the three governments. So far as Government A is concerned, it may find that competing or conflicting interests are pushing in other directions, some favorable to action but of a modified character, others opposed to the program sought. Government B may present a somewhat different situation, with a new combination of interests playing upon the government officials and influencing their behavior, while Government C may involve a still different pattern. In diagram A the assumption is made that the interest group favoring action is sufficiently influential within each governmental jurisdiction to produce identical decisions among the three governments. In this instance metropolitan action is secured through the ability of a single interest (or coalition of interests) to bring pressure on each of the separate governments adequate to procure parallel action. Diagram B shows how a similar situation may produce contrary results. Although Governments B and C are responsive to the pressure from the group

METROPOLITAN DECISION-MAKING
A SCHEMATIC REPRESENTATION

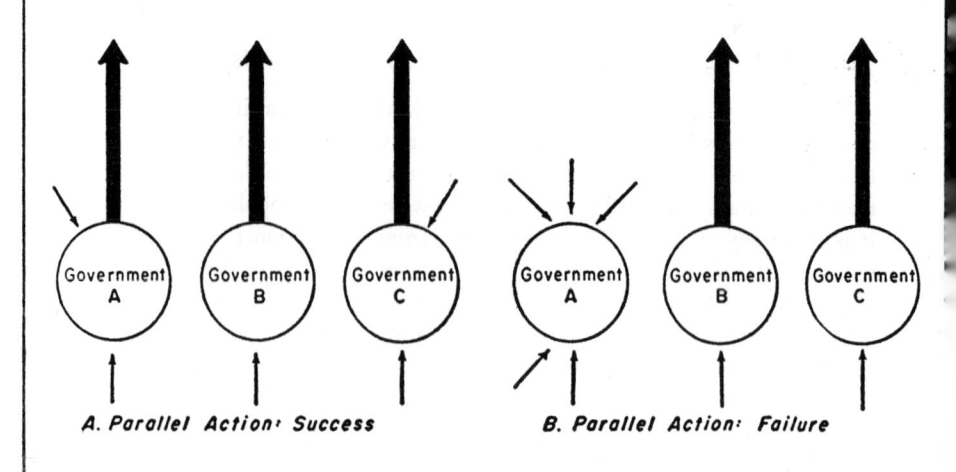

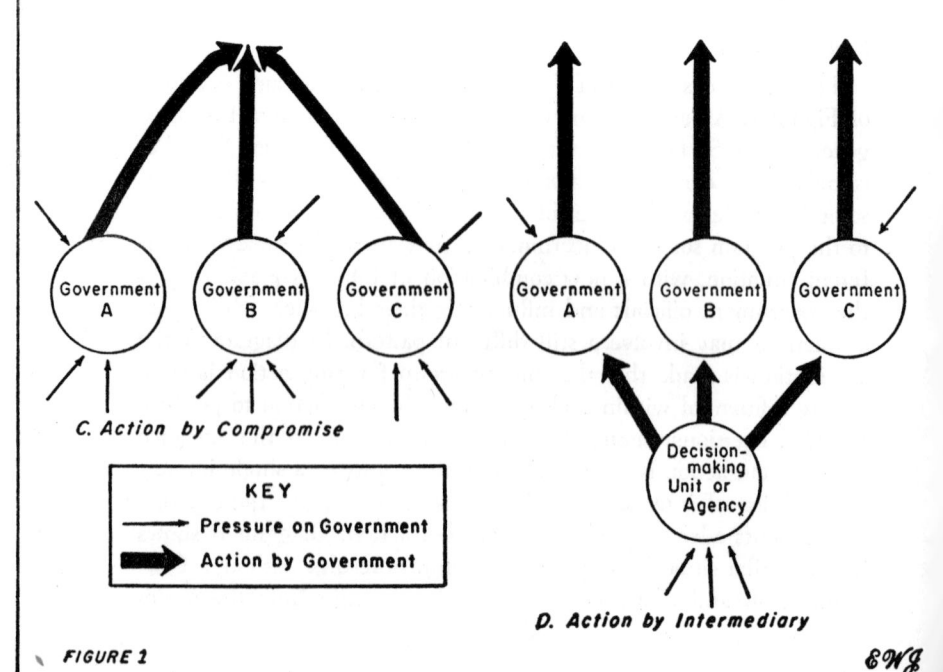

A. Parallel Action: Success

B. Parallel Action: Failure

C. Action by Compromise

KEY
→ Pressure on Government
➔ Action by Government

D. Action by Intermediary

FIGURE 2

seeking action, the weight of the influences brought to bear upon Government A is such that it refuses to cooperate. Since the cooperation of all three is assumed to be necessary to adoption of the proposal, failure ensues.

All this may seem obvious, but the nature of the forces affecting the application of community power to governmental decision-making in a metropolitan context is ignored with astonishing frequency. When numerous governments exist within a metropolitan area, it is not realistic to assume that the same constellation of interests will exist or will exert equal weight in each. Consequently, when the cooperation of two or more governments is required differences are more to be expected than agreement, and deadlocks of the variety depicted in diagram B may easily develop. In this context it is wholly natural to expect that the influence of a particular community interest will vary with the nature and organization of the governmental unit called upon to act. The structure of government within the metropolitan area thus becomes a dynamic factor in the analysis of community power.

Situations requiring parallel action are particularly common in the field of real estate development. Ordinarily action or at least approval by several governments and governmental agencies is required in advance of development. Frequently, however, there is no particular opposition to the proposal in any of the governmental units. A developer who lacks the necessary personal contacts may find it necessary to hire a representative to make the arrangements for him—most probably, as observed above, a legal firm with prior experience in this type of work—but once this is done the project is likely to proceed smoothly.

There are exceptions, of course. A shopping center, like that proposed in Fayetteville, may be adequately endowed with water supplies and sewerage and yet fail to win the necessary rezoning from a local government dominated by hostile interests. Faced by such an obstacle, the entrepreneur must choose between the alternatives of abandoning his project or modifying it and trying again. And this is equally true whether the promotion is a real estate development or a new inter-town park or other metropolitan cooperative program.

The hostile forces that block action may originate with rival interests possessing superior influence or with the local government officials themselves. It would be a mistake to forget that governmental units—in the sense of their personnel—have lives of their own and are not always easily pushed about by the pressures brought to bear on them. Equally, of course, positive leadership in a cooperative undertaking may be provided by the public official, either because of his conviction that action is needed or because the bold and imaginative exercise of leadership is at times an effective political gambit. The argument has been advanced above that cooperative programs are often the result of the desires of public officials to head off pressures for governmental reorganization and consolidation. This is simply to restate the point made in Chapter I, that public officials and governmental bureaucracies must themselves be regarded as participants in the contest over governmental decision-making.

Action by Compromise

A second type of situation also may produce cooperative action at the metropolitan level. This situation is portrayed in Figure 1-C. Again parallel action by three governments is regarded as essential to the success of the proposal. Again it is assumed that the influences brought to bear upon the three governments differ; these pressures, however, are so distributed as to produce a desire for action in each of the three governments, though action in differing forms. By negotiation and compromise an agreement is reached and parallel action is thus finally secured.

This type of cooperation seems to be relatively rare in the metropolitan area, and the reasons why this should be so are important to understanding the dynamics of the metropolitan power structure. It will already have become evident that this analysis of the means by which several governments can be brought into harmony on a common program is not necessarily peculiar to the metropolitan area. The same type of analysis can be applied to cooperation among the officials of a particular government. Each member of a city council is likely to be subject to different pressures: if a measure is to pass the council, it is necessary that agreement be reached among its members. The city council and the mayor in turn are subject to different pressures, and they must be brought into agreement. The same could be said of the president and the two houses of congress on the national level.

There is, however, a difference. Cooperative action in the city and in Washington is continuous; the negotiating and bargaining never stop, and a concession on one issue can be balanced upon the next. But metropolitan bargaining involves the negotiation of agreement between two or more governments that have perhaps never cooperated before and may not again for years. Sayre and Kaufman have pointed out the sporadic and *ad hoc* character of both cooperative and competitive interrelationships between New York City and its neighbors.[6] It is clear from the case studies that the same can be said of relationships among the multiple governments of the Syracuse metropolitan area. In the absence of either a tradition of negotiation or diplomatic skills in bargaining, it is hardly surprising that agreements are reached but slowly and that insoluble deadlocks frequently block any action.

Action by Intermediary

In the absence of effective procedures for negotiated compromises, recourse must be had to some other device when powerful pressures for metropolitan action are blocked by one or more obstinate local governments. The third type of arrangement may be labeled action by intermediary. It may take the form of an appeal to some higher level of government, as the county or the state, for intercession when cooperation among towns, villages, and cities has failed. Or it may be found in an appeal to an extra-governmental organization capable of exercising control over the several local governments involved, as when the power of the political party is used to compel acquiescence in a decision. The common factor in both cases is that the issue is taken to some single, superior forum where the pressures for and against action can be assessed and a decision reached without the risk of veto within each of a series of local governments. A schematic representation of the direction of the pressures involved is suggested in Figure 1-D. Instances of both kinds of cooperative action by intermediary can be found in the cases above. Particularly interesting are the decisions in which the political party has been employed as a device to secure cooperation from governmental units that showed reluctance to act.

Within the Syracuse metropolitan area the Republican Party might be described as a kind of superstructure for decision-making which is called into action only on certain occasions. These include action on (1) issues that involve the party interest as such, e.g., nominations for office (not explored in this study), governmental reorganizations, etc.; and (2) issues that concern individuals in a position to ask the party's help. Such individuals include the top industrial leaders who, it seems plausible to say, can secure party help when they need it regardless of the magnitude of the issue as measured, say, in dollars and cents. Presumably some relationship exists between the fact of access and campaign contributions to the party. Reversing this, it does not appear that the party leadership intervenes in an issue because it is big in thousands of dollars, but because it is big to persons who are important to the party.

Thus the Republican Party organization became the basic mechanism by which those interested in the relocation of the New Process Gear plant secured the cooperation of the local governmental officials. In an earlier quite similar case, not related in detail in this study, the Republican Party leadership intervened to prevent Solvay Process from moving when a zoning regulation by the Town of Camillus blocked the use of property for dumping sludge that the corporation considered essential for that purpose. In this case, which was remarkably similar to the New Process Gear incident, the initiative for action came from the Chamber of Commerce, whose leaders, working through party officials, arranged the complex intergovernmental trades necessary to persuade Camillus to rescind its zoning ordinance. On the other hand the establishment of the mental health board, involving very large expenditures, was determined without apparent intervention by the top political party leaders.

This last illustration is, of course, different in that it involved action by the Board of Supervisors rather than by several individual local governments. In an important sense, however, action by that body on intergovernmental issues may be regarded as metropolitan action, and has been so treated here. The members of the board actually are the heads of the significant local governments outside the City of Syracuse, the towns, and a major decision by the Board of Supervisors is therefore suggestive of group action by the towns. It is true that the institutional structure creates a somewhat different situation, since the rule of unanimity is replaced by one of majority vote; but in practice this has little effective meaning since all decisions are reached first in caucus and the Republican supervisors, who represent all or almost all of the towns, vote as a block.

This suggests that all actions of the Board of Supervisors might be termed action by intermediary, since all are taken through the Republican caucus. In a sense this is true, but there is an important distinction between two types of issues taken to caucus. Some groups with sufficient access to the top party leadership will take their case directly to these leaders, who will then convey orders through the caucus to the individual supervisors. Others will take their plea directly to the individual members of the government. They may do this because (1) they do not know any better; (2) they consider it more democratic to "contact everyone" (and boast that they do); or (3) they are unable to gain access to the superstructure. Ordinarily their requests will necessitate party action too, since the party caucus is dominant in decision-making; but the caucus in the latter case will play the role of a decision-making unit rather than a vehicle to convey orders from the top.

Emphasis on the role of the political party as an intermediary in reaching metropolitan decisions should not becloud recognition of the fact that the state government often performs the same role. A common thread running through the cases is the ease with which problems of local cooperation within Onondaga County have been resolved when necessary by special legislation. Time and again when the provisions of the General County Government Law do not fit the perceived needs of the county, or when a local agency (e.g. the Public Works Commission) is to be created, or whatever the need may be, the legislature has smoothed the way by a special act.

This role played by the legislature is not, however, unrelated to the political party considerations treated above. Both phenomena result from the same cause: that Onondaga County differs from the usual image of a metropolitan area in that the central city, its surrounding suburbs, the county, and the state legislature all are Republican. It is highly significant that this identity of partisan affiliation exists in a state in which party names are not nominal (as they might be in the South with reversed party labels), but in which instead party organizations are relatively tightly structured and capable of exercising discipline over their members. It is this concurrence of party membership that makes it possible for a Republican Mayor of Syracuse, who is also Republican County Chairman, to integrate welfare functions in the county, as Marvin did in the 1930's, and it is this concurrence further that makes the Republican legislative leadership so readily responsive to the wishes of Onondaga County. It is not meant to suggest that such coincidence uniformly makes for metropolitan action, for legislative responsiveness may be to a negative as well as to a positive stimulus.

The reverse of this proposition also is valid. A report for Utica (in Oneida County) suggests that the absence of partisan identity between the central city administration and the county board—a far more frequent occurrence than in Syracuse, since Utica is more often Democratic than not—has produced conflicts that have sometimes acted as barriers to metropolitan cooperation.[7] That partisan differences between the central city and the surrounding areas, as well as between the city and the legislature, hamper the resolution of problems in the New York City metropolitan area is so evident as hardly to require documentation.[8]

The conclusion seems inescapable therefore that one of the potent forces encouraging and facilitating metropolitan action in the Syracuse metropolitan area has been the existence of a universal and disciplined party allegiance that has united central city, suburban governments, county government, and state legislature in common cause.

Metropolitan Decision-Making and Institutional Change

In Chapter I a model of metropolitan decision-making was presented; one ingredient was missing from that model, however, which is included in the pattern of decision-making described by Sayre and Kaufman. In their model the contest over the control of governmental action occurs within an institutional framework characterized as the "rules of the game." These consist partly of rules laid down by law determining the structures and jurisdictions of governments, partly of rules emanating from social consensus. The rules of the game are not unvarying, but are subject to change.

Study of metropolitan governmental reorganization consists in essence of an examination of the circumstances under which the rules of the game in the metropolitan contest over decision-making actually do change. In general two kinds of circumstances can be identified under which changes are made in that part of the rules of the game consisting of formal governmental institutions. In the first place, an institutional change may occur as the result of an effort by one of the contestants in the decision-making struggle to secure an advantage for himself. An individual or group may seek advantage by tinkering with the governmental institutions, by using control over some of the powers of government to introduce changes in order to make easier control over other parts of the government. This sort of maneuver occurs constantly in government, particularly with respect to the rules affecting the selection of government personnel. Election laws are altered, election dates changed, electoral districts reapportioned, changes made in terms of administrative officials, etc.

"Reform" movements of this sort are likely initially to possess only a narrow basis of support; if they were strong, they would not need to seek such advantages. The permanence of such a change, therefore, is likely to depend upon its effectiveness. If the strategy succeeds in securing a monopolistic power position for the contestant who profits by it, then the change will be retained. On the other hand, there may be circumstances in which the change has unexpected consequences and groups that feared they would be injured come to approve it. Sayre and Kaufman suggest that the creation of the City of Greater New York in the 1890's occurred somewhat in this fashion. One of the prime movers in the consolidation of the Cities of Brooklyn and New York, the greatest metropolitan governmental reorganization in American history, was Thomas C. Platt, Republican leader in New York State, who anticipated that the position of the regular Republicans in the combined municipality would be improved. He was wrong, but the new system proved sufficiently flexible to accommodate itself to the interests of other groups who, initially opposed, ultimately came to support it.

The rules of the game can be changed for a second reason also, namely that the contestants agree generally that the existing institutions are incapable of producing solutions to the problems of society. Explanation of what is meant will require consideration of a model different from that which views decision-making as a contest. For while governmental policy-making may legitimately be regarded as a contest, government at the same time must be recognized as a social institution with a social purpose. Its purpose is the solving of problems of conflict among groups within the society, and its efficacy in accomplishing that purpose depends in considerable part upon its internal organization. If the institutions of government are hopelessly disorganized, they may fail completely in the solving of problems. In the language of the contest previously used as a model, no major group will find it possible to achieve a significant innovation in governmental policy, and as new problems arise the failure to find solutions will produce a steady accumulation of tensions. This is the precise charge leveled against the government of the Fourth Republic in France, which was generally characterized by the term *immobilisme*. *Immobilisme* is not, however, a national disease that can be suffered only by Frenchmen; it can also affect other governments, including those of metropolitan areas within the United States.

Such a formulation suggests the existence of three variables which determine the likelihood of substantial governmental reorganization: (1) the number of problems facing the society; (2) the expectations of its members as to how many of their problems should be resolved through the instrumentality of government; and (3) the capacity of the governmental institutions to resolve problems. Variation in any one of the three factors or any combination of the three may generate demands for reorganization. A movement for reform may therefore result from: (1) new problems introduced by technological developments; (2) demands by substantial parts of the population for higher levels of governmental service; (3) a relative decline in the efficiency of government (for whatever reason); or (4) some combination of these factors. Reform movements of this kind are distinguished from those aimed at creating advantages for one of the parties to the contest both by the generality of the support they receive and by the greater durability of any changes they may bring about.[9]

It is commonplace to cite the role of crisis in encouraging experimentation with governmental institutions. A flood that leads to creation of a flood control district is an obvious illustration. Or the crisis may be felt secondhand: John Gaus has called attention to the effects of the disastrous Cocoanut Grove fire in Boston in tightening fire regulations generally across the country. The fatal school fire in Chicago in the late 1950's had something of the same effect, at least so far as school buildings were concerned. In the present context, a crisis may be defined as a rapid multiplication of the problems faced by government. Although a slow accumulation of problems of similar magnitude eventually may produce much the same overloading of the problem-solving capacity of the governmental institutions, it appears that a rapid decline in governmental ability to meet public expectations produces a greater psychological readiness to make changes in the institutions themselves.

This analysis has relevance to the Syracuse metropolitan area. If Onondaga County faced crisis, more incentive for change might be found; but the metropolitan area has not experienced a real disaster and there is no reason to expect that it will. A breakdown in government could provide the occasion for drastic reorganization, but no such event has occurred. If the governments of Syracuse and Onondaga County are not spectacularly good, neither are they dramatically bad; and there has been no public evidence of gross mismanagement or other emergency to provoke significant structural change. The physical environment has been the source of only minor annoyances. Onondaga Creek, which runs through the heart of the city's central business district, overflowed its banks for a century but the largest flood of record caused damage of no more than $100,000. This is not the stuff of which governmental reorganizations are made. Rather the floods led to a succession of minor ameliorative measures —the straightening and deepening of the channel in 1868, extensions of the improved channel from time to time—and finally to a federally financed $4,252,200 flood control project in 1950. The only stringency that might have forced any sort of governmental reorganization was the cost of the 1950 project, and the assumption of responsibility by the federal government eliminated even that mild compulsion.[10]

Today the disaster most likely to precipitate substantial governmental action would be a major exodus of industry. Both exodus and drastic action, however, seem highly unlikely eventualities. Individual industries have moved or threatened to move from the city, but public reaction to such threats has been for the most part sporadic and piecemeal. As individual problems, such as sewage or water, have emerged, they have been dealt with on an *ad hoc* basis. Little enthusiasm has been shown for the creation of new governmental institutions to deal on an area-wide basis with the multiplicity of metropolitan problems.

In this Syracuse deviates little from the national norm, for it is universally observed that multi-functional reform, that is, general governmental reorganization, is far more difficult to secure than a redistribution of individual functions among existing governments. Probably the most significant reason for this lies in the character of the different interest groups involved. Elevation of a single program to the metropolitan level is ordinarily sought by an economic interest group which finds a new governmental service necessary to its economic well-being. In the standard situation, this means that local industry has been brought face to face with the problem of a shortage of water, an oversupply of pollution, an undersupply of transportation, or whatever, and demands—successfully—that government take a hand in the matter. Although economic interests may be alleged to be at stake in government reorganizations (which are often sold as moves to save money by eliminating "waste"), the monetary gains involved are more diffuse, less certain, and often suspect. The industrialist or businessman may fear that a rejuvenated government, even if more efficient in its use of tax moneys, might seek to justify itself by embarking on new and more expensive programs. The cause of metropolitan reorganization is therefore likely to be supported only by individuals attracted by its rational simplicity, but without either an established position of influence within the community or the kind of economic commitment that will produce vigorous action.

An additional factor which encourages the piecemeal approach to metropolitan problems in the Syracuse area is the coincidence of the county boundary with what has long been regarded as the metropolitan area. On the positive side this has facilitated the handling of metropolitan problems by their transfer to the county government, a procedure frequently employed. Solution of individual problems in this way, however, relieves the pressure for a more general reorganization. On a limited scale this phenomenon was encountered in the proposal for a county health department. Because the most serious of the rural health needs have been met by state programs, private action, the county mental health program, etc., insufficient incentive has been found to support a drastic change. In words appropriate to a formula proposed above it may be said that, although both the number of problems and the expectations of what government should do about them have been increasing in the Syracuse metropolitan area, the existence of a county with a metropolitan jurisdiction has made possible a problem-solving process effective enough to head off serious metropolitan governmental proposals.

The build-up of functions at the county level has in turn created a further problem by making more serious the consequences of the failure to reorganize the county government. There seems little reason to doubt that Onondaga County will follow the other metropolitan counties of the state within the next few years and reorganize.[11] If we are to learn from history this will entail the creation of a county executive, who will immediately become the center of a move for expanding the county government's powers. County reorganization thus will result in a growth in county authority, and in the relaxation and ultimate abandonment of the tradition of minimal local government.

In the long run, the most effective practical argument for the transfer of urban governmental functions to the county is likely to emphasize not the increase in the problem-solving capacity of government but the preservation of party advantage. Syracuse has long been a citadel of Republicanism. It seems improbable, however, that the Republican Party can do more than delay the partisan realignment likely to occur within the city as a result of population change. In local elections in the past the Republicans have succeeded in maintaining their hold on the Negro vote. By national standards such a situation is unnatural, and the vote of the rapidly increasing Negro population may be expected eventually to tip the balance within the city to the Democratic Party. Another prospective development pointing in that direction is the growth in the political strength of labor. The approach of equality and the threat of superiority in the city by the Democrats is likely to encourage a rapid transfer of functions to the county by the Republican leaders, secure in the conviction the county government constitutes a stronghold from which they cannot easily be routed. If such a transfer does not take place, indeed, it is logical to anticipate a steady accumulation of metropolitan conflicts as the unifying force of Republicanism relaxes its grip. In such a twilight of the *Pax Republicana*, the resulting tensions would erupt in violent party warfare. He would be rash who would prophesy the outcome in terms of possible solutions to metropolitan problems.

APPENDIX

Principal Participants in the Decision-Making Process in the Syracuse Metropolitan Area

I. PUBLIC OFFICIALS AND PARTY CHAIRMEN

Chairman of Onondaga County Board of Supervisors, 1930–61
  Virgil Clymer, 1930–37
  Edward O. Yackel, Sr., 1938–47
  George L. Traister, 1948–50
  Fritz Campbell, 1951–53
  Thomas H. Dyer, 1954–57
  Gerald W. Ladd, 1958–61

Onondaga County Attorney, 1930–61
  Truman H. Preston, 1930–43
  Charles T. Major, 1944–52
  Julian W. Edgcomb, 1953–61

Mayor of Syracuse, 1929–61
  Rolland B. Marvin, 1929–41
  Thomas E. Kennedy, 1942–45
  Frank J. Costello, 1946–49
  Thomas J. Corcoran, 1950–53
  Donald H. Mead, 1954–57
  Anthony A. Henninger, 1958–61

Syracuse Corporation Counsel, 1930–61
  Frank P. Malpass, 1930–31
  Edward L. Robertson, 1932–34
  James C. Tormey, 1935–45
  Lyle L. Hornbeck, 1946–49
  George L. Richardson, 1950–53
  George T. Driscoll, 1954–61

City Engineer, 1928–61
  Nelson F. Pitts, 1928–53
  Potter W. Kelly, 1954–61

City Planning Director,* 1928–61
  Sergei N. Grimm, 1928–58
  Joseph M. Heikoff, 1958
  Arthur Reed, 1958–61

State Senator from Onondaga County, 1921–60
  George R. Fearon, 1921–36
  Francis L. McElroy, 1937–38
  William C. Martin, 1939–40
  G. Frank Wallace, 1941–44
  Richard P. Byrne, 1945–46
  John H. Hughes, 1947–60
  Searles G. Shultz, 1955–58
  Lawrence M. Rulison, 1959–60

Assemblyman from Onondaga County, 1923–60
  Horace M. Stone, 1923–36
  Richard B. Smith, 1924–37
  Willis H. Sargent, 1925–33
  George B. Parsons, 1934–44
  Frank J. Costello, 1937–45
  Leo W. Breed, 1937–46
  Clellan S. Forsythe, 1945–48
  Lawrence M. Rulison, 1946–58
  Searles G. Shultz, 1947–54

* The Planning Commission gave way in 1958 to a Commissioner of Planning appointed by the Mayor. Arthur Reed was named to the new position.

APPENDIX

Donald H. Mead, 1949–53
Philip R. Chase, 1955–60
Charles A. Schoeneck, 1955–60
Don H. Brown, 1959–60

Chairman of Republican County Committee, 1925–61
Clarence L. King, 1925–37
Rolland B. Marvin, 1937–45
Charles A. NcNett, 1945–51
George L. Traister, 1951–60
John H. Hughes, 1960–61

Chairman of Democratic County Committee, 1930–61
Frank J. Shaughnessy, 1930–33
George M. Haight, 1933–34
Ambrose D. Ginnelly, 1934–38
Cornelius J. Nugent, 1938–40
Francis L. McElroy, 1940–42
Myron J. Parkinson, 1942–46
Charles J. Hogan, 1946–56
John J. Young, 1956–57
Charles H. Keene, 1957–61

II. OTHER INDIVIDUALS

Alberts, Clarence. He was chairman of the Public Works Commission in 1952 when it proceeded to assume greater responsibility for sewage treatment in Onondaga County.

Asselstine, Earl L. As District Superintendent of Schools, he began a campaign in 1944 to create a large central school district to the northeast of Syracuse. The district was formed in 1949.

Brockway, John. A Town of Dewitt supervisor who worked for the necessary town, county, and state activity needed to establish Industrial Park.

Brown, Carlton. Named chairman of the Ways and Means group of the Syracuse-Onondaga Post-War Planning Council, he was at the time President of the Syracuse Chamber of Commerce and Vice President of the L. C. Smith-Corona Typewriter Corporation.

Clary, F. Ware. Selected as chairman of the Public Participation group of the Syracuse-Onondaga Post-War Planning Council, he was Advertising Manager of the Crouse-Hinds Company and President of the Board of Education.

Crawford, Finla G. He served as chairman of the Research and Planning group of the Syracuse-Onondaga Post-War Planning Council. He was Vice-Chancellor of Syracuse University and one-time Democratic candidate for mayor of Syracuse.

Greene, Richard. Coming to Onondaga County in 1931 as head of the Syracuse Probation Office, he worked for the creation of a children's court. Recently retired from his position, he is now an associate of the Youth Development Center of Syracuse University.

Grosso, Joseph. This Republican councilman opposed a metropolitan solution of the sewage treatment problem in favor of a separate Syracuse solution. Grosso, a physician, later ran for mayor as an independent.

Haight, Alfred. As President of the Common Council in 1950–52, this long-time Democrat worked for the acceptance of a metropolitan solution of the county's sewage problem.

Hamilton, Calvin. He was a Town of Dewitt supervisor during the latter phases of the development of Industrial Park.

Hancock, Stewart F. Past Corporation Counsel and reputed influential community and civic leader, he is the son of a former Republican Attorney General of New York State and long-time Republican party leader.

Jones, Alexander F. Chairman of the Joint City-County Water Committee (later the Onondaga County Water Agency), Jones is Executive Editor of the *Herald-Journal*.

Kies, Fred. Town of Salina supervisor during the development of the Northern Lights Shopping Center (located in that town), he acted as liaison between the developer and the town.

Lane, William T. Past executive secretary to Mayor Marvin and Mayor Kennedy and President of the Common Council (1938–41), Lane was later appointed chairman of the Syracuse Parking Authority. He is president of his own advertising agency.

O'Brien, David. Formerly connected with the public and employee relations department of General Electric Company, he was appointed County Research Director in 1960.

Tolley, William P. Chancellor of Syracuse University, Tolley was appointed by Mayor Kennedy to be chairman of the Syracuse-Onondaga Post-War Planning Council.

Yehle, Leo. He is a former assistant Corporation Counsel and Justice of Special Sessions; he was appointed first Children's Court Judge in Onondaga County.

III. PUBLIC AGENCIES

Board of Estimate. This three-man board prepares the Syracuse city budget. It is made up of the Mayor, President of the Common Council, and Director of Finance (who is appointed by the Mayor).

Board of Supervisors. This is the combined executive-legislative body of Onondaga County; it is composed of 38 elected members, one from each town (19) and one from each city ward (19).

Board of Zoning Appeals. A five-man body created in 1958 when the City Planning Commission was abolished, it hears appeals seeking variances in zoning regulations.

Charter Commission. This nine-man commission was appointed by the Chairman of the Board of Supervisors in 1940 to draft a new county charter.

Charter Commission. This latest official commission to study and make recommendations for a new county charter was appointed in 1960.

Children's Court. Created as a separate court for juvenile offenders in 1936, this court also serves as a central agency for county guidance, probation, and counseling personnel.

City Planning Commission. This body, created in 1914, existed under a variety of names until 1958. It was appointed by the mayor and had supervision over zoning and planning.

Common Council. This legislative body for Syracuse comprises nine members: a President and four elected at large and five elected by districts.

Joint Citizens-Syracuse Charter Committee. It was appointed in

1950 to draft a county charter for the Board of Supervisors to consider.

Joint City-County Water Committee. The Mayor and the Board of Supervisors appointed this body in 1959 to study the problem of new sources of water for the metropolitan area.

Ley Creek Sanitary District. This sewage district is operated by the Public Works Commission.

New York State Thruway Authority. This is a state agency which administers the toll road known as the Thruway.

Onondaga County Department of Research and Development. This agency was created by the Board of Supervisors in 1954 to conduct studies of government operation and make recommendations to the board.

Onondaga County Water Agency. By a resolution of the Board of Supervisors in 1960 the Joint City-County Water Committee (see above) was transformed into this official body which was empowered to make recommendations to the board concerning a proposed water district.

Onondaga County Water Authority. Created by the state in 1951 to assume responsibility for the operation of a county water system, it acquired the New York Water Service Corporation's property and operating rights in Onondaga County in 1955.

Public Works Commission. Created in 1933 by the state to construct sewage treatment plants for Onondaga County, it was not until the 1950's that it began to use its authority to serve as a truly metropolitan agency.

Syracuse-Onondaga Post-War Planning Council. This was a body created in 1943 to coordinate and develop post-war plans for the city-county area.

Water Pollution Control Board. This is a state agency which has responsibility for water quality. Its work was drawn more closely into the orbit of the Department of Health by a recent statute.

Water Power and Control Commission. This state agency is primarily concerned with regulating the supply and use of water in the State. A recent statutory change in status did not materially affect its functioning.

APPENDIX 341

IV. PRIVATE ORGANIZATIONS AND ASSOCIATIONS

Bond, Schoeneck, and King. This is a prominent Syracuse law firm some of whose members are active in local public and party affairs.

Brown-Lipe-Chapin. This branch manufacturing plant of the General Motors Corporation is located to the east of Syracuse.

Carrier Corporation. A locally-owned air conditioning equipment manufacturer and one of the county's larger employers, Carrier is located in Industrial Park.

Chamber of Commerce. The Syracuse Chamber does not differ markedly from its counterparts in other typical American cities. It takes an active part in civic affairs, and has been a participant in a number of significant metropolitan decisions.

Civic Development Committee. This body was organized as a citizens' group in 1948 as a successor to the Syracuse-Onondaga Post-War Planning Council.

Community Chest. This is the fund-raising agency for voluntary organizations; it was organized in 1921.

Council of Social Agencies. This body, organized in 1930 to work with the Community Chest, has become the agency which allocates the funds raised in behalf of the Chest.

Crouse-Hinds. This long-established, home-owned company, which manufactures electrical equipment and supplies, was intimately involved in water development plans.

Eagan Real Estate, Inc. Incorporated in 1929, this firm is one of the state's larger realtors. It has been behind many of the residential, commercial, and industrial developments of Syracuse and Onondaga County.

General Electric Company. G.E. leased a facility constructed by the Defense Plant Corporation to build turbines in 1942, and later returned as a builder of heavy defense equipment. One of the county's larger employers.

League of Women Voters. This is a non-partisan women's group active in the promotion of better government in Syracuse and Onondaga County.

Manufacturers Association. This group, founded in Syracuse in 1913, has been active in promoting political participation by businessmen. It serves the manufacturers as the Chamber of Commerce serves other sectors of the business community.

Melvin and Melvin. The partners in this Syracuse law firm are also active in banking and real estate. The firm represents both private and government clients.

Metropolitan Development Association. This citizen group, whose purposes are suggested by its title, was formed in 1959.

New Process Gear. This branch plant of the Chrysler Corporation, whose retired president became Mayor of Syracuse in 1958, located in Syracuse in World War I. It moved to a suburban location in 1960.

New York Water Service Corporation. A holding corporation operating water companies in several New York counties, it acquired the Onondaga County Suburban Water Company in 1929.

O'Brien and Gere. This consulting engineering firm supplies professional advice to many governmental units and private concerns. It has been active in the county for many years in the domain of public works.

Onondaga County Suburban Water Company. This was a private water company authorized in 1907 to use Otisco Lake as a source for its franchise area. (See New York Water Service Corporation.)

Onondaga Lake Reclamation Association. This was a citizen group formed in 1945 to combat further pollution of Onondaga Lake and restore it to its former purity.

Solvay Process Company. This branch of the Allied Chemical Company, located in the Village of Solvay, formerly provided sewage treatment facilities for Syracuse as part of an agreement setting up areas for the disposal of its own waste.

Syracuse Governmental Research Bureau. Organized by the Chamber of Commerce in 1948 to act as a citizens' watchdog agency on municipal finance, the bureau has substantially broadened both its conceptual framework and its influence.

Notes

Preface

1. A separate but kindred study, financed by the Fund for Adult Education through University College, was conducted simultaneously with this one at Syracuse University. It had for its purpose identification of the principal community leaders currently active in the Syracuse metropolitan area. Inasmuch as both projects were staffed by members of the social science faculty of the Maxwell Graduate School, it was a simple enough matter for the two research groups to maintain close contact with one another. The report of the other undertaking has been published; see Linton C. Freeman and others, *Local Community Leadership* (Syracuse: University College of Syracuse University, 1960, pp. 29).

I. Power Structure and Its Study

1. Floyd Hunter, *Community Power Structure: A Study of Decision Makers* (Chapel Hill: University of North Carolina Press, 1953).
2. A catalogue of criticisms of Hunter's methodology can be found in Raymond E. Wolfinger, "Reputation and Reality in the Study of 'Community Power,'" *American Sociological Review*, October, 1960, pp. 636–644. Probably the most serious flaw in Hunter's book, as in many studies of political elites, is its tendency to divide the community into active and passive elements, without consideration of the continual interaction involved in decision-making. David Easton, *The Political System: An Inquiry into the State of Political Science* (New York: Alfred A. Knopf, 1953).
3. For useful commentaries see Maurice Stein, *The Eclipse of Community* (Princeton, New Jersey: Princeton University Press, 1960); and the articles by Gordon Blackwell on "Community Analysis" and Peter Rossi on

"Community Decision-Making" in Roland A. Young, *Approaches to the Study of Politics* (Evanston, Illinois: Northwestern University Press, 1958).

4. The author's indebtedness to the stimulating papers and discussions at the Conference on Metropolitan Leadership, sponsored by the Social Science Research Council and held at Northwestern University in April 1960, is obvious throughout the following sections.

5. An extensive literature has developed employing the decision-making approach. A convenient summary will be found in Richard C. Snyder, "A Decision-Making Approach to the Study of Political Phenomena," in Roland Young, *op. cit.*

6. Wallace S. Sayre and Herbert Kaufman, *Governing New York City* (New York: Russell Sage Foundation, 1960), pp. 87–91.

7. The point is made by Norton E. Long, "The Local Community as an Ecology of Games," *American Journal of Sociology*, November, 1958, pp. 251–261.

8. Sayre and Kaufman, *op. cit.*, pp. 39–66. The second type of reward, money, includes both the seeking of opportunities for financial gain through politics and the protection through political action of economic advantages secured outside politics. The fourth category of political prizes, clearly a residual one, involves the complex psychological question of why people participate in politics. As Sayre and Kaufman note, however, the question of what people *get* through political action is somewhat easier to answer than the question of what motivates them to go into politics. For the purpose of a decision-making model, it is sufficient to note the existence of this fourth category of rewards.

9. Robert A. Dahl, "Leadership in a Fragmented Political System: Notes for a Theory," a paper presented at the Conference on Metropolitan Leadership held at Northwestern University, April 1960 (duplicated).

10. This listing is taken from Robert A. Dahl, "The Analysis of Influence in Local Communities" (May 1959, duplicated). A somewhat different tabulation is contained in Dahl, "Leadership in a Fragmented Political System," *op. cit.*

11. Dahl, "Leadership in a Fragmented Political System," *op. cit.*, p. 5.

12. Hunter, *op. cit.*, p. 62.

13. This interpretation follows the argument of Rossi, "Theory and Method in the Study of Power in the Local Community" (paper presented at the Conference on Metropolitan Leadership, Northwestern University, April 1960, duplicated). Rossi notes that it is also possible to identify potential power from the simple fact of ownership; thus the attribution of influence to the "X" family in Middletown by the Lynds rested in large part on legal ownership by the "X's" of a substantial part of the potential resource base of the community. Robert S. and Helen M. Lynd, *Middletown* (New York: Harcourt, Brace, 1937).

14. This rests on the logical assumption that a man will be influential so long as those who deal with him think that he is and are influenced by him. One limitation on such an assumption, as based on Hunter's and similar studies, rests in the fact that the interviews in which power is attributed have typically been with other business leaders, rather than with the government officials on whom power must finally be exerted if it is to affect government action. It is interesting that we have few equivalents on the municipal level of the state legislative studies of Oliver Garceau, Corinne Silverman, and others, in which state legislators have been asked to express their own opinions as to the relative importance of the interest groups that purport to wield power; lacking such studies, we have little evidence as to the perceptions of community power of the governmental officials themselves. *Cf.* Oliver Garceau and Corinne Silverman, "A Pressure Group and the Pressured: A Case Report," *American Political Science Review*, September, 1954, pp. 672–691.

15. The argument that follows is suggested by Rossi's work, although the author has taken numerous liberties with Rossi's classifications and added to them. *Cf.* Peter H. Rossi, "Theory and Method in the Study of Power in the Local Community," *op. cit.*, pp. 21–43.

16. Robert A. Dahl, "The Analysis of Influence in Local Communities," *op. cit.*, p. 15.

17. *Ibid.*, p. 16.

18. The monolithic power structure is often also described as a "pyramid of power." Guthrie Birkhead has proposed facetiously that the visual imagery might be carried farther by conceiving of the polylithic power structure as a Stonehenge.

19. Floyd Hunter, *op. cit.* It is not difficult to present Hunter's description of a monolithic system in such a fashion as to make it appear absurd and unrealistic on its face. This has been done by some of his critics, who assume that Hunter's definition requires that all top business leaders always agree and always get their way. Actually it would seem clear that Hunter has in mind a community where on major matters of policy the top leaders are ordinarily united, and when united they *almost* always get their way barring rare contingencies. It might also be noted that Hunter does not claim Regional City to be the prototype of an American community, but indeed offers some possible explanations for its atypical character.

20. These definitions are borrowed from "Political Decision-Making in North Carolina Cities," *Research Previews* (Chapel Hill: Institute for Research in Social Science, University of North Carolina, Vol. 7, No. 2, January, 1960), pp. 15–20.

21. This assertion can, of course, be turned squarely around; that is, it can be argued that political competition *results from* (rather than *produces*) a system of countervailing elites.

22. In practice, an attempt to distinguish major from minor policy is likely

to introduce a high degree of subjectivity on the part of the observer. The things that seem important to him are likely to be defined as involving major policy. Nonetheless, there would appear to be some objective criteria for such a distinction. In fiscal questions, the magnitude of the sums involved is an obvious point of difference. In other matters, the ability of the community leaders to "call up" controversial minor decisions for review may serve to distinguish the relative power of the groups.

23. For one exception see Charles R. Adrian, "Leadership and Decision-Making in Manager Cities: A Study of Three Communities," *Public Administration Review*, Summer, 1958, pp. 208–213. A second exception to this generalization can be found in the paper by Rossi previously cited; in seeking to explain some of the variables affecting the existence of a polylithic rather than a monolithic power structure, he notes the importance of the legal status assigned to the city government. If the municipal government is sharply restricted in its powers and many decisions are made by the intervention of officials from the state or national governments, it is far more likely that the agents of these governments will act as a separate force within the local power structure. Rossi notes, for example, that the studies of English cities, where the central government possesses more authority in municipal affairs, attribute vastly greater influence to public officials. *Cf.* Delbert C. Miller, "Decision-Making Cliques in Community Power Structure," *American Journal of Sociology*, November, 1958, pp. 299–310; and Delbert C. Miller, "Industry and Community Power Structures," *American Sociological Review*, February, 1958, pp. 9–15. The extreme situation is that found in Mexico and referred to above, where the authority of the central government may be so great as to make the exercise of power in the local community completely unpredictable. See Arvin E. Klapp and Vincent L. Padgett, "Power Structure and Decision-Making in a Mexican Border City,"*American Journal of Sociology*, December, 1959, pp. 400–406, and William H. Form and William V. D'Antonio, "Integration and Cleavage Among Community Influentials in Two Border Cities," *American Sociological Review*, December, 1959, pp. 804–14.

24. Boston appears to be clearly in this position, for example, and New York City, while not so completely hobbled, is affected by similar restraints. It may well be that the fragmented decision-making structure described by Sayre and Kaufman results partly from this fact. Sayre and Kaufman, *op. cit. Cf.* William H. Brown, Jr., and Charles E. Gilbert, "Capital Programming in Philadelphia: A Study of Long-Range Planning," *American Political Science Review*, September, 1960, pp. 659–668.

25. Herbert Kaufman and Victor Jones, "The Mystery of Power," *Public Administration Review*, Summer, 1954, pp. 205–212.

26. Compare Hunter's report, for example, with the account of events in Cleveland, St. Louis, and Miami in Norton E. Long, "Some Observations Towards a Natural History of Metropolitan Politics" (paper presented at Conference on Metropolitan Leadership, April 1960, duplicated).

27. This is the major project, sponsored by the Ford Foundation and directed by Professor York Willbern, mentioned in the Preface.

28. See Harold Stein's discussion in *Public Administration and Policy Development* (New York: Harcourt, Brace, 1952), pp. ix–xlv.

29. Herbert Kaufman, "The Next Step in Case Studies," *Public Administration Review*, Winter, 1958, pp. 52–59. The Board for the Inter-University Case Program, heedful of this criticism, has arranged to produce concentrations of cases in certain special areas (state government and natural resources, to illustrate) in an effort to meet it.

II. The Syracuse Metropolitan Area

1. The Metropolitan Development Association of Syracuse and Onondaga County recently published a very useful summary of salient facts about the Syracuse metropolitan area. See *A Profile of Onondaga County* (Syracuse: January 20, 1961, mimeographed).

2. Information for this section of the chapter has been taken from Eric H. Faigle, "Syracuse: A Study in Urban Geography" (unpublished doctoral dissertation, University of Michigan, 1935); and Eric H. Faigle, *Regional Relationships: Syracuse and Onondaga County* (Syracuse: Syracuse-Onondaga Post-War Planning Council, no date).

3. The prior existence of these earlier villages is still evident, however, in the street map of the city. Most city streets are established on a gridiron pattern, but the grids of the West Side (formerly Geddes), the North Side (formerly Salina), and some other parts of the city lie at angles to the principal street pattern.

4. If the reclassification made by the census bureau in 1960 of the Syracuse metropolitan area as a three-county unit is used, the city is already a minority within its metropolitan area, providing only 38 per cent of the area's population. All this, of course, is in accord with trends elsewhere.

5. William C. Lehmann, *Preliminary Report on Population Characteristics, Trends, and Prospects* (Syracuse: Syracuse-Onondaga Post-War Planning Council, 1943).

6. Much of the material that follows is drawn from Syracuse Department of City Planning, *A General Plan* (1959).

7. Syracuse-Onondaga Post-War Planning Council, *Economic Characteristics of the Syracuse Area* (1943, mimeographed).

8. *Ibid.* A similar conclusion is presented in the Report of the Economic Research Council of Metropolitan Syracuse, *Business Stability and Opportunities for Growth in the Syracuse Area* (Syracuse University, 1956).

9. *A General Plan, op. cit.*

10. *Economic Characteristics, op. cit.*

11. Onondaga County Regional Planning Board, *Regional Planning for the Onondaga-Syracuse Metropolitan Area*, Report 1 (Syracuse: January, 1960, mimeographed).

12. This trend is treated in detail in Marilyn Gittell "The Role of the Urban County in Solving Metropolitan Problems in New York State" (unpublished doctoral dissertation, New York University, 1959).

13. *A General Plan, op. cit.,* VIII, pp. 1-2.

14. The difficulty of maintaining a Democratic island in a sea of Republicanism is indicated by the reversion of Solvay to Republican control in the village elections of 1961.

15. The voting behavior of the upstate area is considered in greater detail in Ralph A. Straetz and Frank J. Munger, *New York Politics* (New York: New York University Press, 1960), pp. 39–67.

16. *Cf.* Lyle M. Hanson, "Status Attitudes of City Councilmen: A Case Study of the Syracuse, New York, City Councilmen" (unpublished doctoral dissertation, Syracuse University, 1958).

17. A statistical verification of the dominance of this group within the state legislature can be found in Albert J. Lipson, "Analysis of Roll Call Voting in the New York State Assembly, 1953–54, 1957–58" (unpublished M.A. thesis, Syracuse University, 1959).

III. The Post-War Report

1. Syracuse–Onondaga County Post-War Planning Council, *The Post-War Report* (Syracuse, 1945).

2. Mr. Greer had formerly worked in the Federal Housing Authority.

3. A. H. Hansen and Guy Greer, "Toward Full Use of Our Resources," *Fortune,* November, 1942.

4. It was never clear just how substantial a role in counter-cyclical spending was envisioned for localities by Mr. Greer or by *Fortune's* board of editors. Only in later years did it begin to seem that little could be expected from localities in this regard.

5. *Syracuse Herald-Journal,* December 18, 1942. It is worth noting that no target date or specific time period was widely used by the council, although often debate centered on the 12 months right after the war.

6. The chairman is a town supervisor, elected to the post by his fellow supervisors.

7. *Herald-Journal,* November 19, 1943.

8. Mayor Kennedy of course shared this view with many other Americans, who recalled the staggering municipal debts of the early twentieth century and the subsequent fiscal agonies cities experienced in the 'thirties. Their mental set was toward depression and not post-war boom. Years later Mayor Kennedy changed his mind and accepted the need for some local borrowing.

9. Just two years later the legislature passed the well known "cafeteria" tax plan, under the terms of which municipalities were able to choose from among ten alternative sources of revenue. This idea doubtless came from the discussion of sources of local revenue that was carried on in Syracuse and many other cities during the late war years.

10. The firm was suggested to *Fortune* by the lawyers serving as counsel to the City of Syracuse.

11. For example, the Ways and Means Group reported that the city's total debt had decreased from a top of $42 million in 1938 to $25.5 million in 1944, far below the statutory limit. Other local governments were also in comparatively sound fiscal positions.

12. *Syracuse Post-Standard*, April 25, 1944.

13. It is reported that 2,000 copies of the report were printed, of which 1,000 were circulated in Onondaga County. About 4,000 copies of the shorter document "Program for Progress," appeared, of which 3,000 were distributed in the county.

IV. The Metropolitan Sewage Treatment Plant

1. Although it contains some highly subjective comments on the pollution problem, Walter L. Welch, *The Onondaga Lake Reclamation Problem* (Onondaga Lake Reclamation Association, May 15, 1953), is the most complete history of Onondaga Lake.

2. Chapter 568, *Laws of 1933*, as amended.

3. "Water Supply, Sanitation, Drainage and Flood Control," Report to the Syracuse-Onondaga Post-War Planning Council by the Onondaga County Public Works Commission, May 1, 1944.

4. "Report of the Onondaga County Pollution Commission," July 12, 1948.

5. "A Study of Pollution of Onondaga Lake and Its Tributaries," Department of City Engineering, January 24, 1948. Pitts served as city engineer for almost 40 years. In that time he built a reputation for personal integrity and non-partisan technical competence and enjoyed very favorable relations with the press, particularly with the *Syracuse Herald-Journal*. He successfully challenged a mayor's authority more than once.

6. The Governmental Research Bureau is discussed briefly in Chapter IX.

7. "Report of the Onondaga Lake Purification Commission," December 1, 1952.

8. Hornbeck was a partner in the law firm of Bond, Schoeneck, and King and counsel to the Solvay Process Company. In the previous administration he had served as Corporation Counsel; since the Democratic victory of 1949, he had acted as adviser to the Republican majority in the Common Council.

9. *Syracuse Post-Standard*, January 28, 1953.

10. Notwithstanding its resistance, the feeling appears to have been general that the Village of Solvay eventually would find it expedient to join in common action, for powerful political and economic forces were at work there. The public relations director of the Syracuse Manufacturers Association, in a memorandum (dated June 16, 1953) to the members of that organization's Public Works Committee, commented on the situation in these words:

"Solvay is going through a rather tangled political situation at this time and its village government has made no commitments. However, Solvay is being included in the West Side District anyway, so that its participation in later steps can be expected, once the current confusion is ended."

V. Water for the Suburbs

1. Skaneateles Lake is approximately 19 miles from Syracuse (Map 2). Its elevation is some 400 feet above that of the city, which makes possible a high pressure gravity supply system.

2. The Water Power and Control Commission is a state agency charged with responsibility for allocating public water supply resources. No new source of water supply may be acquired, nor may an old source be expanded, without the approval of the commission.

3. Otisco Lake, located approximately ten miles from the city (Map 2), is also at sufficient elevation to make feasible a gravity flow system. The stream from its overflow is known as Nine Mile Creek. The lake was originally created for water-level control purposes on the Erie Canal.

4. The New York Water Service Corporation owned and operated water companies in the counties of Suffolk, Nassau, Queens, Westchester, Rockland, Wayne, Monroe, and Erie. Only the Onondaga company carried the same name as the parent corporation.

5. Interview with Fred F. Hoyt, Vice President of Carrier Corporation, August 22, 1960.

6. Dyer was serving his first term on the Board of Supervisors from the Town of Onondaga. One of the significant factors in his election had been a promise to obtain city water for a populated portion of the town.

7. Subsequently of R. W. Pressprich and Company, financial adviser to the Onondaga County Water Authority.

8. The creation of local authorities in New York requires special legislation, which is normally requested by local legislative bodies.

9. Quoted in the *Herald-Journal,* February 9, 1951.

10. Temporary State Commission on Coordination of State Activities, *Staff Report on Public Authority under New York State,* Legal Document (1940) No. 46 (Albany: Williams Press, Inc.).

11. The Post-War Planning Council had recommended study of the advisability of a "single unified water supply system." *The Post-War Report,* p. 91.

12. *Herald-Journal,* December 30, 1951.

13. The alternative to condemnation was outright purchase. Since the latter would be subject to regulation by the Public Service Commission (which was known to favor what the company considered a low price), whereas the former would be arranged by friendly local negotiation, the water service corporation not unnaturally favored condemnation.

14. Water Power and Control Commission, Water Supply Application No. 2381, June 4, 1953.
15. Ibid., Water Supply Application No. 2518, March 23, 1954.
16. The appeal was heard by the Supreme Court's Appellate Division, Fourth Department. Justice John C. Wheeler, in writing the opinion of the court, examined the opposing theories of evaluation which enabled the Public Service Commission to attach a value of less than $4,000,000 to properties which the appraisal commissioners found to be worth more than $9,000,000. *Onondaga County Water Authority, Respondent, v. New York Water Service Corporation and The New York Trust Company as Trustee, Respondents. Public Service Commission, Appellant.* 285 A.D. 655.
17. Quoted in *Herald-Journal*, June 27, 1960.
18. Sec. 251. The final decision on any proposal must come from the Board of Supervisors. Although the law does not require concurrence by the Common Council, it is generally understood that no action will be undertaken without city approval. Such a step, indeed, would be politically impractical.
19. Summarized or (as indicated) quoted from "Progress Report by the Onondaga County Water Agency for the Onondaga County Board of Supervisors" (July 7, 1960, 16 pages, mimeographed).
20. *Post-Standard*, June 8, 1960.

VI. Health and Welfare: Four Case Studies

1. To this day, as the Citizen's Committee for the Children's Court, many of the members continue to provide community support and leadership for the court's program. The Chairman of the Board of Supervisors and the Chairman of the board's Children's Court Committee are two of its *ex officio* members.
2. Senate Introduction 1370, March 3, 1936.
3. Chapter 683, *Laws of 1936*.
4. Robert S. Steadman, *Public Welfare Cases and Costs for Syracuse and Onondaga County* (Syracuse Research Committee, 1933, mimeographed).

The Syracuse Research Committee consisted of a number of professional men and business executives. Organized in 1931, it was dissolved in 1935 when the interests of its members began to revert to their reviving businesses. Professor Robert Steadman of Syracuse University's Department of Political Science provided staff assistance to the committee in its two major studies of welfare and education.

It is worthy of note that the Syracuse Research Committee was the only non-governmental organization to take an active interest in the welfare problem. There were community social welfare organizations, but at this time they normally held themselves aloof from contact with their governmental counterparts in the interest of avoidance of political involvement.

5. Onondaga County Department of Research and Development, *Public Health Service in Onondaga County* (Syracuse, 1956, pamphlet).

6. State Charities Aid Association, *The Organization of the Syracuse and Cattaraugus Health Demonstration* (Milbank Memorial Fund, 1925, pamphlet).

7. The story of the demonstration and of its gratifying results is told in a general history of public health activities in Syracuse. See C. E. A. Winslow, *A City Set On A Hill* (published for the Milbank Memorial Fund by Doubleday, Doran and Company, Inc., New York, 1934).

8. This unpublished study was discussed at a number of community meetings in 1932. Its recommendations were described in the *Syracuse Post-Standard*, June 12, 1932.

9. Senate Introduction 2472, Pr. 2707 enacted March 24, 1949 with 55 affirmative and no negative votes recorded. An interesting additional point of opposition to the amendment was its provision for appointment of a health officer by the Board of Supervisors and not by the part-county district's board of health. Several health organizations strongly objected to thus placing the health department under "political" influence.

10. In a letter of March 11, 1949 to Senator John Hughes, who introduced the bill, State Health Commissioner Hilleboe objected that the bill would "produce an administrative patchwork."

11. The report of the Survey was summarized in New York State Department of Health, *Public Health Service for Onondaga County* (no date, distributed in 1949).

12. Onondaga County Department of Research and Development, *Onondaga County and the Community Mental Health Services Act* (1955, pamphlet).

13. The difficulties encountered by the Mental Health Board have been analyzed with care by Catherine Covert Stepanek and Charles V. Willie, "A Community Mental Health Program: Its Rise and Fall" (Syracuse, May 1961, mimeographed), p. 14.

VII. Education: The Special District Solution

1. This process is officially known as "centralization," and that is the term employed here. In the vocabulary of the social sciences, and particularly of public administration, "consolidation" is preferred.

2. Lynton K. Caldwell, *The Government and Administration of New York* (New York: Thomas Y. Crowell Company, 1954), p. 317.

3. *Ibid.*, pp. 325, 330–333.

4. Julian E. Butterworth, "The Evolution of Rural School Organization in New York," in *Your School District: The Report of the National Commission on School District Reorganization* (Washington: Department of Rural Education, National Education Association, 1948), pp. 193–211. The effect of state policy on the organization of urban school districts is discussed at pp. 101–129 of Harold Herman, "The Impact of New York State Government Practices

NOTES 353

upon Metropolitan Integration" (unpublished doctoral dissertation, Syracuse University, 1961).

5. Luther Gulick, *Education for American Life—The Regents Inquiry* (New York: McGraw-Hill, 1938), pp. 64–65.

6. Report of the Joint Legislative Committee on the State Education System, *Master Plan for School District Reorganization, New York State* (Legislative Document No. 25, Albany, New York, 1947).

7. A more detailed account of the circumstances attending the creation of the North Syracuse district will be found in Cary Eugene Wood, "Study of the Influence of Rapid Community Growth upon Administrative Policies and Practices in a Suburban School System" (unpublished doctoral dissertation, Syracuse University, 1958).

8. Bureau of School Service, School of Education, Syracuse University, *Solvay School District Survey Report, 1954* (Syracuse, 1955).

9. The two legislators also proposed that new legislation be enacted permitting the use of voting machines, making known the result of the vote by districts, and requiring that proponents and opponents be equally represented on the Board of Canvass supervising a merger election. They also recommended that in a centralization proposal involving two districts, each with at least 35 per cent of the total votes cast, the law require that a majority in each district approve the merger.

VIII. Reorganizing County Government: Proposals for Reform, 1934–1943

1. Onondaga County Regional Planning Board, *Regional Planning for the Onondaga-Syracuse Metropolitan Area*, Report No. 1 (Syracuse: January, 1960, mimeographed), p. 9.
2. Chapter 846, *Laws of 1934*.
3. Chapter 948, *Laws of 1935*.
4. Chapter 828, *Laws of 1936*.
5. Chapter 862, *Laws of 1937*.
6. Chapter 863, *Laws of 1937*.
7. Committee of the Onondaga County Bar Association, *Report on Local Government Reform*, November 23, 1934.
8. Chapter 862, *Laws of 1937*.
9. In fact, Monroe County had adopted an option of the First Buckley Act in November 1935.
10. *Post-Standard*, October 29, 1939.
11. Quoted in *Post-Standard*, November 5, 1939.
12. Chapter 423, *Laws of 1939*.
13. Onondaga County Charter Commission, *Report and Recommendations*, filed July 13, 1940.

IX. Reorganizing County Government: The County Director Proposal

1. Among Atkins' teachers at the Maxwell School was Professor Robert S. Steadman, who also served as adviser on Atkins' Master's thesis on "The Administration and Finances of Suffolk County, Massachusetts: A Study of City-County Relations in Boston, Massachusetts."

2. Syracuse Governmental Research Bureau, "Memorandum: Application of the County Manager Form of Government to Onondaga County," August 1949.

3. See Wayne Hodges, *Company and Community: Case Studies in Industry-City Relationships* (New York: Harper and Brothers, 1958), pp. 14–15.

4. The Uniform County Laws Commission was created by the state legislature in 1944 to "study, investigate, codify, revise and make uniform . . . existing laws relating to counties." After six years of work, the commission produced a revised consolidated County Law which was approved by the 1950 legislature and signed by the Governor.

5. The law provided for two methods for bringing about a referendum on an optional form: one was by resolution of the Board of Supervisors; the other was by popular petition signed by 10 per cent of the number voting in the county in the last gubernatorial election.

6. Flattery, a member of the Melvin and Melvin law firm, had been a Syracuse resident until 1950, when he moved to Fabius. Standing firmly behind Flattery in this move was Crandall Melvin, bank president and partner in Melvin and Melvin, whose maverick tendencies in business and politics often set him at odds with his Republican banking and legal associates.

7. The impetus for this move came from the "reform" Republican County Chairman, State Senator John H. Hughes, who is also chairman of the New York State Joint Legislative Committee on Metropolitan Areas Study.

8. The Metropolitan Development Association is described briefly in Chapter XI.

X. Cooperation, Contract, or Consolidation?

1. At a public hearing held in Syracuse on November 15, 1957. Subsequently Mayor Mead extended his remarks in a document titled *Problems of the Syracuse Metropolitan Area* (Syracuse: Bureau of Municipal Research, December 1957, mimeographed).

2. Actually the use of special districts for the solution of metropolitan problems has been limited. See Chapter VII.

3. Harold Herman has analyzed the influence of state policies and programs on local metropolitan action in "The Impact of New York State Governmental Practices upon Metropolitan Integration" (unpublished doctoral dissertation, Syracuse University, 1961).

4. Chapters VIII and IX, the latter more especially, develop this theme at length.

NOTES 355

5. State Senator John H. Hughes, recently named Republican County Chairman, appears to command wide confidence among county Republicans. It is, however, much too early to appraise the lasting influence the new chairman will be able to exert on his party.

Introduction to Part 3

1. The most recent work in this tradition is that of August Lösch, *The Economics of Location* (1939), translated by William H. Woglom and Wolfgang F. Stolper (New Haven: Yale University Press, 1954).
2. For an excellent example of this approach as applied to an urbanized river basin see U. S. Department of Commerce, Office of Business Economics, *Economic Base Survey of the Delaware River Basin* (Washington, 1958).
3. See the series of articles by Richard B. Andrews in *Land Economics*: February 1954, pp. 52–60; May 1954, pp. 164–172; August 1954, pp. 260–269; and November 1954, pp. 309–319; Ralph W. Pfouts ed., *The Techniques of Urban Economic Analysis* (West Trenton: Chandler-Davis Publishing Co., 1960).
4. Edgar M. Hoover, *The Location of Economic Activity* (New York: McGraw-Hill, 1948), especially Chapter 8; Edgar M. Hoover and Raymond M. Vernon, *The Anatomy of a Metropolis* (Cambridge: Harvard University Press, 1959).
5. See Ezra Salomon and Zarko G. Bilbija, *Metropolitan Chicago* (Glencoe, Illinois: The Free Press, 1959).
6. Charles L. Leven, "Regional Income and Product Accounts: Construction and Application," paper for Conference on Regional Accounts, St. Louis, 1960.
7. Federal Reserve Bank of St. Louis, "The Eighth District Balance of Trade," *Monthly Review*, June, 1952.
8. Wassily Leontief, *The Structure of the American Economy, 1919–1939* (New York: Oxford University Press, 1951); Walter Isard, "The General Theory of Location and Space Economy," 63 *Quarterly Journal of Economics*, November 1949, pp. 476–506, and "Interregional and Regional Input-Output Analysis: A Model of Space Economy," *The Review of Economics and Statistics*, November 1951, pp. 318–328; Walter Isard and Robert Kavesh, "Economic Structural Interrelations of Metropolitan Regions," *American Journal of Sociology*, September 1954, pp. 152–162; Werner Z. Hirsch, "Interindustry Relations of a Metropolitan Area," *Review of Economics and Statistics*, November 1959, pp. 360–369.
9. "Economic Implications of Urban Growth," *Science*, June 12, 1959, p. 1587.
10. See Robert A. Dahl, "Business and Politics: A Critical Appraisal of Political Science," *Social Science Research on Business: Product and Potential* (New York: Columbia University Press, 1959), pp. 3–44; C. Wright Mills, *The Power Elite* (New York: Oxford University Press, 1956), pp. 30–46.

XI. Real Estate Development: Five Case Studies

1. Chapter II, above, treats of the governments of Onondaga County with some care. See especially Map 1.
2. This decision was upheld in Orbino Construction Corporation vs. Hilleboe, 167 NYS 2d. 787, Onondaga County, April 1956.
3. The principals in the Bayberry Corporation, further organized as Euclid Properties and Buckley Construction Corporation, were Dr. Howard E. Berman, Joseph Prisant, and C. Ellis Shiffmacher, all of Great Neck, New York.
4. The development of Industrial Park is examined in detail in Chapter XII.
5. The Metropolitan Development Association was organized in 1959 as a private group of business, professional, and industrial leaders to "initiate research and planning and generate action on matters related to the physical redevelopment of the Syracuse metropolitan area." (Statement by Kenneth G. Bartlett, President.)
6. *Herald-Journal,* October 31, 1959.

XII. Syracuse Industrial Park

1. For an examination of the history of industrial parks and their relationship to metropolitan area government, see Clyde J. Wingfield, "Planning for Industrial Development, with Emphasis on the Metropolitan Area" (unpublished doctoral dissertation, Syracuse University, 1960).
2. This story was related by Fred F. Hoyt of Carrier Corporation and Earl O'Brien of O'Brien and Gere, Inc.
3. Fred F. Hoyt of Carrier Corporation, interview, July 10, 1959.
4. "The Power of a Road," *Fortune,* October 1957, p. 285.
5. *Fortune, op. cit.*
6. O'Brien and Gere served as engineer for both Onondaga County and the Town of Dewitt.
7. *Post-Standard,* May 21, 1953.
8. The property comprised the 33-acre Midler-Court parcel and the 137-acre plot held by the Syracuse Supply Company (both mentioned earlier), together with 400 acres assembled by Eagan for industrial development.
9. Most of the factual data for this section were provided by Robert J. Barrett of Eagan Real Estate, Inc., from the files of that firm.
10. The New York Central has a very active Industrial Development Department and is always alert to possibilities for developments adjacent to its main-line routes. Its role in the Syracuse Industrial Park was not unusual from the railroad's point of view.
11. The legal device employed was the downgrading of the section of the road in question from state highway to county road. According to Saul C. Corwin, Department Counsel, New York Department of Public Works (letter to the writer dated August 11, 1959), state highways may be redesignated as county roads (1) by an act of the legislature amending the Highway Law;

and (2) by abandonment of a section of state highway no longer useful to the state system to the county or town. The strip in question was finally abandoned to the Town of Dewitt (after five submissions) on July 29, 1959, by Department of Public Works Official Order No. 208 pursuant to Section 341, Subdivision 32, of the Highway Law.

12. The organization's disapproval was voiced in an interview with the writer in Albany, New York, on August 6, 1959, by Gwynn Thomas, Executive Assistant to the President of Associated Industries of New York. At the time of the park development Thomas was Public Relations Director in charge of Governmental Affairs for the Syracuse Manufacturers Association. The same attitude was also expressed by Forrest McGuire of the association in a telephone interview on July 22, 1959.

13. The State Board of Equalization rates the Courtview District at 36 per cent of full valuation while the county gives the district a rating of 32 per cent. Calvin Hamilton, Town Supervisor, says that the county appraisal is perhaps more accurate since it is based upon more recent data and the county equalization officer tends to be a closer and more continuous observer.

14. Data provided by Donald Chamberlain, Town Tax Collector, in an interview held August 24, 1959.

15. Data provided by Calvin Hamilton in an interview on August 24, 1959.

16. Estimates of working force made here are derived from data supplied by William Lowe of the Lincoln National Bank and Robert J. Barrett of Eagan and confirmed by the Syracuse Chamber of Commerce. Public records which reflect number of employees or payrolls for specific firms do not exist.

17. Interview with Charles O. Maxwell, August 25, 1959.

18. See *Planned Industrial Districts, Their Organization and Development,* Urban Land Institute Technical Bulletin, No. 19 (Washington, 1954), for a more comprehensive treatment of planned districts.

XIII. Private Economic Development and the Metropolitan Problem

1. See Richard U. Ratcliff, *Urban Land Economics* (New York: McGraw-Hill, 1949), p. 200.

2. For a discussion of imperfections in urban land markets see Max R. Bloom, "Economic Criteria and the Use of Land in Subsidized Urban Redevelopment Areas" (unpublished doctoral dissertation, American University, 1959), pp. 102–155.

3. See *The Community Builders' Handbook* (Washington: Urban Land Institute, 1954).

4. William L. C. Wheaton, "Applications of Cost-Revenue Studies to Fringe Areas," *Journal of the American Institute of Planners,* November, 1959, p. 173.

5. William L. C. Wheaton and Morton J. Schussheim, *The Cost of Municipal Services in Residential Areas* (Washington: Housing and Home Finance Agency, 1955).

6. See Coleman Woodbury, editor, *The Future of Cities and Urban Redevelopment* (Chicago: University of Chicago Press, 1953), pp. 105–117; Richard U. Ratcliff, "Efficiency in the Location of Urban Activities" in Robert Moore Fisher, editor, *The Metropolis in Modern Life* (New York: Doubleday and Company, Inc., 1955), pp. 125–148.

7. Robert C. Wood, *1400 Governments* (Cambridge: Harvard University Press, 1961), pp. 123–144.

8. Ratcliff, *op. cit.*, p. 410.

9. Angus McCloskey, "Mutual Problems of Developers, Planners and Governments," *Urban Land*, December, 1959, p. 5.

10. Martin Meyerson and Edward C. Banfield, *Politics, Planning and the Public Interest* (Glencoe, Illinois: The Free Press, 1955), pp. 262–263.

11. See Robert C. Wood, *Suburbia* (Boston: Houghton Mifflin, 1959), especially pp. 135–255.

12. Wood, *1400 Governments, op. cit.*, pp. 110–113. See also the cases listed by Henry Fagin in "Financing Municipal Services in a Metropolitan Region," *Journal of the American Institute of Planners*, Fall 1953, pp. 214–218.

13. See George Duggar, "A Framework for an Analysis of Urban Development Policy," *Papers and Proceedings of the Regional Science Association*, 1956, pp. 210–224.

14. See Raymond Vernon, *The Economic Function of the Central City* (New York: Committee for Economic Development, 1959), especially pp. 49–55.

15. Harold Black, "Detroit: A Case Study in Industrial Problems of a Central City," *Land Economics*, August, 1958, pp. 219–226.

16. See Richard W. Cutler, "Can Local Government Handle Urban Growth?" *University of Wisconsin Law Review*, January, 1959, pp. 5–29.

17. John Rannells, *The Core of the City* (New York: Columbia University Press, 1956), p. 187.

18. Wood's observation on this point is probably too pessimistic: "There are few business leaders who are so adversely affected by the present state of affairs and so uncommitted in their personal life to the suburban ideology as to be interested in pushing for reform. Though they may grumble about rising taxes, conflicting regulations, and public programs, they generally prefer to live with the present situation by personal negotiation than to risk the unknown— the possibility of an effective, area-wide government where individual bargains may not be so easily accomplished." *Suburbia, op. cit.*, p. 299.

XIV. Community Power and Metropolitan Decision-Making

1. Wayne Hodges, *Company and Community: Case Studies in Industry-City Relationships* (New York: Harper and Brothers, 1958).

2. It is worth reiteration that the cases studied center on governmental decision-making. It is quite possible that an examination of decisions taken in the

private sector, as in private charity or cultural affairs, would provide convincing evidence of Stewart Hancock's power in those areas. Similarly, an analysis of day-to-day decision-making—action on zoning variances, the choice of government personnel, the letting of contracts, etc.—might produce different conclusions from those recorded here.

3. This conclusion corroborates the findings of another contemporary study of community leadership in Syracuse. See Linton C. Freeman and others, *Local Community Leadership* (Syracuse: University College of Syracuse University, 1960).

4. The creation in recent years of the Department of Research and Development and the Regional Planning Board suggests that the county is conscious of the need for developing sources of its own for general staff assistance.

5. A recent report states that the unused borrowing capacity of the local governments in Onondaga County (including city and county) totals $143,500,000. Metropolitan Development Association, *A Profile of Onondaga County*, pp. 16–18.

6. Wallace S. Sayre and Herbert Kaufman, *Governing New York City* (New York: Russell Sage Foundation, 1960), p. 562.

7. State of New York, Special Legislative Committee on Revision and Simplification of the Constitution, *Staff Report on Metropolitan Utica-Rome* (Report 6, May, 1958). The report specifically makes this point.

8. See Sayre and Kaufman, *op. cit.*, p. 562.

9. The author is indebted to Coleman Woodbury for suggesting this line of reasoning. The concept of ineffective problem-solving may provide a substitute for the normative framework ordinarily used to justify metropolitan reorganization, which in effect simply states that a metropolitan government would be more sensible. To the extent that the reports pleading for the creation of new metropolitan governments written within this normative framework are effective, it would seem probable that they produce their impact by changing the expectations of the population as to what government service levels should be. It seems plausible that they might be still more effective if they were aimed deliberately at that objective.

10. Jonathan B. Pollard, "The Effects of the 1950 Flood Control Project upon Utilization of the Onondaga Valley Flood Plain, New York" (unpublished M.A. Thesis, Syracuse University, July, 1960).

11. Some see hope for early and perhaps significant action in the work of the county charter commission appointed late in 1960. See Chapter IX for a brief comment on recent developments respecting county reorganization.

Index

Note: Public agencies and private associations are listed under key word of title, e.g., for Board of Education *see* Education, Board of. For state laws *see* legislation, state.

Alberts, Clarence, 95, 96, 337
Alcoholic Clinic, Syracuse Dispensary, 149, 150, 151, 153
Allen, James E., Jr., 170
Allied Chemical Corp., *see* Solvay Process Co.
American Legion, 87
American Stores Co., 253, 276
Asselstine, Earl L., 161, 162, 163, 337
Atkins, Richard A., and county government reform, 198, 199, 200, 201, 202, 203, 205, 206, 207; and sewage disposal, 89, 94
Auburn, 255, 256
Audit and Control, Department of (state), 188
Avery school district, 165, 167

Baldwinsville school district, 165
Baldwinsville, Village, 112, 245
Bar Association, Onondaga County, 178–79, 194, 314
Barnum, Judge, 132, 134

Bartlett, Kenneth, 256, 257, 258, 259
Bayberry real estate project, 241, 248–51
Blucher, Walter, 48, 55, 60, 62
Bond, Schoeneck, and King, 114, 133, 316, 341
Bristol Laboratories, and Industrial Park, 276; and school reorganization, 168; and sewage disposal, 84; and water supply, 114, 115
Brockway, John, 270, 337
Brown, Carlton, 51, 337
Brown, Don H., 169, 194, 209, 337
Brown-Lipe-Chapin (General Motors), 341; and Industrial Park, 265, 271, 276, 279; and water supply, 114, 115, 120
budget procedures, 13–14
Butternut Creek, 113, 126

Camillus school district, 165
Camillus, Town, 326; and real estate project, 255, 256; and sewage disposal, 81, 89

INDEX

Campbell, Fritz, 197, 200, 201, 202, 204, 206, 211, 335
Cappuccilli, Peter, 244–48
Carrier Corp., 341; and community power structure, 315; and Industrial Park, 264, 265, 269, 271, 276, 279; and metropolitan action, 219; and Post-War Report, 60, 63, 66; and sewage disposal, 92
case study method, 16–19
Cattaraugus County, 142
Charities Aid Association, State, 142
Charter Commission (county), 339
Charter Committee, Joint Citizens-Syracuse, 339
Cherry Road school district, 165, 166, 167
Child Guidance Center, 149–53 *passim*
Children's Court, 131–36, 149, 154, 215, 226, 311–12, 339; *see also* Child Guidance Center
Children's Court Case Study Committee, 132
Chrysler Corp., *see* New Process Gear
Cicero, Town, and school reorganization, 160, 161, 162, 164; and sewage disposal, 81; and water supply, 117
Civic Development Committee, 72, 341
Clary, F. Ware, 51, 338
Clay, Town, and real estate project, 248, 250, 251, 255, 256; and school reorganization, 160, 161, 162, 164; and sewage disposal, 81; and water supply, 116
Commerce, Chamber of, Liverpool, 85, 109
Commerce, Chamber of, Syracuse, 341; and community power structure, 309, 310, 315, 326; and county government reform, 198, 199; and Industrial Park, 273, 274; and metropolitan action, 220; and Post-War Report, 49, 51, 52, 58, 59, 61, 65; and public health, 143; and real estate project, 255, 256; and sewage disposal, 87, 89, 101, 107, 109; *see also* Governmental Research Bureau
Commerce, Empire State Association of, 203
Commerce, Junior Chamber of, Syracuse, 87
Common Council (city), 339; and community power structure, 318; and mental health, 153; and metropolitan action, 224, 225; party majorities, 43, 45; and post-war planning, 51, 64, 67, 69; powers, 33; and sewage disposal, 90–96 *passim*, 102–109 *passim*; and water supply, 126; and welfare administration, 140
Community Chest, 150, 309, 316, 341
community power structure, 3–19, 305–34
Conservation Department (state), 38, 86, 87, 109, 222
Corcoran, Thomas J., 225, 335; and sewage disposal, 90–96 *passim*, 99, 106; and water supply, 120
Costello, Frank J., 69, 70, 335, 336
County Director, Citizens' Committee for the, 207, 209
county director proposal, 197–213
County Government, Citizens' Committee for Progressive, 206, 207
county government reform, 175–213
County Laws Commission, Uniform, 200, 202, 204
Court Street Area sewer district, 270
Courtview school district, 167, 168, 276, 278
Crawford, Finla G., 49, 51, 53, 62, 338
Cregg, George, 116, 120
Crouse-Hinds Co., 341; and metropolitan action, 219; and Post-War Report, 51; and sewage disposal, 90, 92; and water supply, 115

Dahl, Robert A., 5, 6, 8, 9, 16, 308
Dappert, A. F., 93, 95, 101, 106
Defense Plant Corp., 263

Democratic Party, *see* politics
Dewey, Thomas E., 86, 203, 306
Dewitt school district, 168
DeWitt, Town, and Children's Court, 136; and Industrial Park, 263, 267, 270, 274, 275, 277, 278, 280; and real estate projects, 242, 255, 256, 258, 259; and sewage disposal, 81, 83; and water supply, 113, 114, 116, 117, 125
Dyer, Thomas H., 335; and county government reform, 211, 212; and mental health, 151, 152, 154; and metropolitan action, 228; and water supply, 117, 119
Dyke, Mrs. Harold, 182

Eagan, Edward, 267
Eagan, Leo T., 256, 257, 267, 271
Eagan Real Estate, Inc., 117, 244, 252, 341; and Industrial Park, 263, 266, 267, 268, 269, 272, 273, 279
East Syracuse school district, 160, 167–68
East Syracuse, Village, 81, 112, 114
economic analysis, of metropolitan problems, 235–39; of real estate business, 281–90; of Syracuse area, 26–30
education, 36–37, 157–74
Education, Board of (city), 33, 43; and mental health, 149; and Post-War Report, 50, 51
Education Department (state), 158–71 *passim*, 174, 251, 314
Educational System, Joint Legislative Committee on the State, 159
Eichenlaub, Marcellus, 103, 106
Elbridge school district, 159
Elbridge-Jordan school district, 160, 168–69
engineering firms, 293–94; *see also* Greeley and Hansen, O'Brien and Gere
Equalization, Board of (county), 278
Equalization and Assessment, Board of (state), 41
Estabrook, C. S., 242

Estabrook, Estabrook, Brooks, and Hancock, 242, 243
Estimate, Board of (city), 33, 339

Fabius school district, 159
Fabius, Town, 142
Farrell, J. J., 273
Fayetteville, Village, and real estate projects, 241–43, 260, 295; and water supply, 112
Fayetteville-Manlius school district, 171
Fearon, George R., 223, 336; and Children's Court, 134, 135; and water supply, 119, 121
federal government and metropolitan problems, 39–40
fire departments, 216, 217
Flattery, Alan, 208
Foery Clinic, Bishop, 149, 151, 153
Fortune magazine, 48, 49, 50, 52, 55, 56, 57, 62, 65, 70, 71
Franklin, H. H., 263
Franklin Park, 263, 265, 279

Gaus, John, 331
Geddes school district, 165
Geddes, Town, 44; and sewage disposal, 81, 89, 90, 94, 96, 98, 105; and water supply, 116, 117; and welfare administration, 139
General Electric Co., 341; and community power structure, 315; and Industrial Park, 264, 272, 273, 276, 277, 279; and metropolitan action, 219; and real estate project, 259; and school reorganization, 162; and water supply, 114, 115
General Motors Corp., *see* Brown-Lipe-Chapin
Gere, William, 268
Governmental Research Bureau, 313, 342; and community power structure, 309; and county government reform, 197, 198, 202, 204, 205, 209; and metropolitan action, 219; and sewage disposal, 89, 91, 101, 106, 109
Grange, 146

INDEX

Greeley and Hansen, 95, 97
Greene, Richard, 132, 312, 338
Greer, Guy, 48, 49, 50, 56, 61
Grimm, Sergei N., 48, 51, 52, 53, 55, 57, 58, 61, 62, 67, 69, 71, 73, 249, 312, 336
Grosso, Joseph, 103, 106, 108, 338

Haight, Alfred, 93, 100, 338
Halcomb Steel, 115
Haley, John, 91, 101
Hamilton, Calvin, 267, 276, 338
Hancock, Stewart F., 306, 307, 338; and county government reform, 199; and Post-War Report, 65
Hanson, Alvin T., 255, 256, 257
Harmon, Frank, 90
Health Association, Onondaga County, and community power structure, 309; and mental health, 150; and public health, 143, 145, 146, 148
Health Council, Metropolitan, 148, 154
Health Department (state), 38, 222, 312, 314; and mental health, 150; and public health, 142–48 passim; and real estate projects, 245, 246, 247, 291, 299; and sewage disposal, 86, 87, 109
Health Department (city), and mental health, 151; and public health, 142, 145
health, public, administrative agencies, 37–38; as metropolitan problem, 141–49
Henninger, Anthony A., 335
Herald-Journal, and community power structure, 309; and county government reform, 184, 194, 203, 208; and post-war planning, 64; and sewage disposal, 92, 96, 97, 100, 102, 103; and water supply, 120, 125
Hinsdale sewer district, 254
Holmes, Glenn, 85
Hoover, Edgar M., 236
Hornbeck, Lyle L., 94, 103, 336

Housing Administration (federal), 39, 245, 249, 294
Housing Authority, Syracuse, 48, 52, 58, 59
Hughes, John H., 119, 172, 256, 257, 258, 336, 337
Humpleby, John, 242
Hunter, Floyd, 3, 6, 10, 15

Industrial Park, 117, 122, 264–82, 320
institutional structure and decision-making, 13–16, 328–34

Jones, Alexander F., 126, 338
Jones, Victor, 15
Jordan school district, 168–69

Kaufman, Herbert, 4, 5, 6, 15, 16, 325, 328
Kennedy, Thomas E., and county government reform, 199; and Post-War Report, 49, 50, 58, 60, 61, 62, 70; and sewage disposal, 88, 89, 90, 91, 101, 107
Kies, Fred, 252, 253, 338
King, Clarence L., 318, 337; and Children's Court, 134, 135, 136; and county government reform, 178; and metropolitan action, 227, 228; and welfare administration, 137
Koplovitz, Michael, 243

labor, organized, 28; and community power structure, 309; and Post-War Report, 61; and sewage disposal, 94
Ladd, Gerald W., 152, 335
Lafayette school district, 159
Lakeland, 100; Improvement Association, 87
Lakeland school district, 165, 166, 167
Lakeside school district, 165, 166, 167
Lamson Corp., 115, 276
Lane, William T., 186, 187, 338
law enforcement, 37, 216

law firms, and community power structure, 316; and real estate development, 291–92, 301; *see also* Bond, Schoeneck, and King; Estabrook, Estabrook, Brooks and Hancock; Melvin and Melvin
legislation, state, and Children's Court, 132, 134–35; Community Mental Health Services Act, 151; on county government, 46, 177, 180, 184, 186–90, 192, 200–205, 308, 327; County Water Districts Law, 127, 129; Onondaga County Water Authority Act, 118–19; and Onondaga Public Works Commission, 84, 103–104, 222; Public Health Law, 146; Public Welfare Law, 137–38; on school organization, 158–59, 168, 171–72; Temporary Emergency Relief Act, 138
Lehman, Herbert H., 178, 188, 189
Lehmann, William C., 24
LeMoyne College, 314
Ley Creek Sanitary District, 81, 83, 84, 105, 219, 253, 258, 264, 270, 278, 279, 340
Limber, Ralph C., 27–28
Liverpool school district, 162, 163, 165, 171
Liverpool, Village, and real estate project, 250; and sewage disposal, 81, 85, 106
local governments, functions, 30–42, 240–41; and real estate development, 286–90, 297–300
Lynch, Robert, 267, 268, 272

Major, Charles T., 335; and county government reform, 178, 179, 184, 191, 192, 200, 201; and sewage disposal, 90
Maloney, William, and metropolitan action, 227; and sewage disposal, 85, 95, 100, 105
Manlius school district, 171
Manlius, Town, and Children's Court, 136; and real estate project, 242, 243
Manlius, Village, 112, 136

Manufacturers Association, 341; and community power structure, 309, 315; and Industrial Park, 274; and metropolitan action, 220; and real estate project, 255, 256; and sewage disposal, 90, 101, 107, 109; and water supply, 121, 125
Marcellus school district, 159
Marcellus, Town, 117
Marshall, William J., 267, 271
Martin, William C., 186, 336
Martino, John O., 166
Marvin, Rolland B., 33, 335, 337; and community power structure, 306, 307, 310, 317, 318; and county government reform, 181, 183, 184, 186, 187, 189, 190, 191; and metropolitan action, 220, 227, 228; and public health, 143, 144; and welfare administration, 136, 137, 140, 141
Mattydale, 162, 163, 164, 253
McElroy, Francis L., 336, 337
McGee, Cushman, 118
McNett, Charles A., 90, 337
Mead, Donald H., 214, 335, 337; and mental health, 151; and sewage disposal, 106, 107, 108
Medical College, and mental health, 150; and public health, 145
Medical Society (county), 145, 146, 147, 148, 316
Melvin, Crandall, 85; and county government reform, 178, 194, 210
Melvin, Myron, 117, 120, 271
Melvin and Melvin, 116, 120, 316, 342
mental health, 149–56, 312
Mental Health Board (county), 149, 153, 154, 155, 312
Mental Health Commission (state), 150, 151
Merchants National Bank, 249, 250, 251
Metropolitan Areas Study, Joint Legislative Committee on, 214, 223
Metropolitan Development Association, 213, 256, 259, 342

INDEX

Midcourt Builders, Inc., 266, 271, 273, 278
Midler-Court Builders, Inc., 270
Midler-Court Realty, Inc., 266, 268
Midler Land Development, Inc., 266, 268
Milbank Memorial Fund, 142
Miller, Paul A., 171
Minoa school district, 167–68
model of decision-making, 7, 311, 322, 328
Mosher, William E., 194

nationality groups, 24–26
New Process Gear real estate project, 241, 254–59, 260, 296, 317, 326, 342
newspapers, 7; and community power structure, 309, 314–15; and county government reform, 194, 208, 209; and public health, 144; see also Herald-Journal; Post-Standard
New York Central railroad, and Industrial Park, 267–72 passim, 279, 280; and water supply, 113
New York state government, and community power structure, 308, 327; and metropolitan problems, 32, 35, 221–23; and school organization, 158–60; see also legislation, state
New York Water Service Corp., 113–24 passim, 254, 342
Niagara Mohawk Power Corp., and community power structure, 315; and real estate project, 257, 258; and sewage disposal, 88, 91
Northern Lights real estate project, 241, 251–54
North Side Businessmen's Association, 94
North Syracuse school district, 160–65, 171
North Syracuse, Village, 81, 116
Nugent, Cornelius J., 180, 181, 183, 187, 190, 337

O'Brien, David, 259, 338
O'Brien, Earl, and Industrial Park, 267, 268; and sewage disposal, 85,

89, 90, 92, 93, 94, 96, 100, 105; and water supply, 116, 117
O'Brien, Harry T., 188, 189
O'Brien and Gere, 342; and community power structure, 313; and Industrial Park, 268; and real estate project, 249, 250, 254; and sewage disposal, 92, 95, 97, 99, 101, 102; and water supply, 116, 118, 120, 126, 127
Oneida Lake, 121, 126
Onondaga County, described, 20–26; economy, 26–30; government, 30–42; government reform proposals, 175–96; politics, 42–46
Onondaga County Savings Bank, 65
Onondaga County Suburban Water Co., 113, 342
Onondaga Hill school district, 167
Onondaga Lake, pollution of, 80–110 passim
Onondaga Lake Purification Commission, 91, 92, 93
Onondaga Lake Reclamation Association, 85–86, 87, 100, 109, 342
Onondaga school district, 159, 165
Onondaga, Town, 81, 125
Ontario, Lake, 126, 127
Otisco Lake, 113, 116, 121–27 passim

Parsons, George B., 186, 188, 336
Peluso, George, 243
Pitts, Nelson F., 336; and metropolitan action, 216, 217; and sewage disposal, 88, 91, 92, 95, 99, 102, 105; and water supply, 120
planning, agencies, 39; Post-War Report, 47–74
Planning Board, Regional (county), 30, 39; and county government reform, 176; and metropolitan action, 217; and Post-War Report, 52, 73
Planning Commission (city), 339; and Post-War Report, 50, 52, 53, 59, 62, 70; and real estate projects, 249, 274
Planning Council, Syracuse-Onondaga Post-War, 47–74, 85, 307, 312, 340

Planning Department (city), 39
Planning Federation of Onondaga Municipalities, 217
Poletti, Charles, 187
police departments, 37, 216
Polish Citizens Club, 94
politics, party, 34, 42–46, 337; and Children's Court, 134, 135, 136; and community power structure, 306–307, 308, 309–10, 315, 317–18, 326, 327–28, 333–34; and county government reform, 178, 180–95, 206–207, 208, 211; and mental health, 153–54, 154–55, 156; and metropolitan action, 223, 224–30; and public health, 146; and real estate project, 257, 261; and school legislation, 170, 172; and sewage disposal, 102–103; and water supply, 120; and welfare administration, 141
Pomeroy, Donald, 207
Pomeroy, Hugh, 60
Pomeroy real estate firm, 267, 269
Pompey, Town, and Children's Court, 136; and water supply, 118
population, city and county, 22–25
Porter, William, 252, 253, 254
Post-Standard, and Children's Court, 133; and community power structure, 309; and county government reform, 182, 194, 208; and Post-War Report, 66; and sewage disposal, 97, 102; and water supply, 129
Post-War Report, 47–74; and Industrial Park, 274; and public health, 144; and water supply, 115
Potter real estate firm, 267
press, *see* newspapers
Preston, Truman H., 188, 191, 335
proportional representation, 180, 182, 183
Psychiatric Clinic, Adult (county), 153
public finance, city and county, 13–14, 40–42, 91; and metropolitan action, 218–19; and Post-War Report, 62–66

Public Service Commission (state), and real estate projects, 250, 272; and water supply, 116, 119, 122, 123, 124
public works, administrative agencies, 37, 38
Public Works Commission (county), 39, 52, 312, 320, 340; and metropolitan action, 219; and real estate projects, 246, 247, 250, 251, 253, 254, 257, 293; and sewage disposal, 84, 85, 88, 92–98 *passim*, 101, 103, 104, 105, 108, 109; and water supply, 117
Public Works Department (state), 37; and Industrial Park, 271, 272; and real estate project, 246, 257
Public Works Department (city), 37, 99

Rapp, Herbert A., 159
Rapp Committee, 159
real estate development, case studies, 240–82; and metropolitan problem, 281–302
real property, value of, 29
Republican Party, *see* politics
Research and Development Department (county), 340; and county government reform, 212; and mental health, 152; and public health, 148
Research Committee, Syracuse, 139, 143
Richardson, George L., 94, 336
Roads, Bureau of Public (federal), 40
Robinson, William, 271, 272
Rockefeller, Nelson A., 169, 170, 172, 173
Rogers, Virgil M., 166
Rossi, Peter H., 10, 11, 12
Rulison, Lawrence M., 169, 336

Salina school district, 161, 162, 164
Salina, Town, and real estate project, 252, 253; and sewage disposal, 81, 83; and welfare administration, 139

INDEX

Salmon River, 126
Sayre, Wallace, 4, 5, 6, 16, 325, 328
Scace, Homer E., 203
Schoeneck, Charles A., 223, 337
Schoeneck, Edward, 114, 119, 223
School Boards Association, New York State, 171
schools, *see* education
Sears, Frederick R., 161
Seneca Knolls real estate project, 241, 244–48, 291
Seneca River, and sewage disposal, 96, 97, 100; and water supply, 126
Seneca water district, 245
sewage disposal, administrative agencies, 38–39; Metropolitan Treatment Plant, 80–110; and real estate project, 249–50
Shultz, Searles G., 119, 336
Skaneateles, Lake, 111, 112, 115, 127
Skaneateles, Village, 112, 119
Smith, Harry P., 160, 162
Smith-Corona Typewriter Corp., 51, 60
Sobel, Nathan, 187, 188, 189
Social Agencies, Council of, 341; and community power structure, 309, 316; and mental health, 150; and Post-War Report, 50, 52; and public health, 143–44, 145
Solvay Process Co., 27, 342; and metropolitan action, 219; and sewage disposal, 82, 86, 88, 89, 90, 92, 95; and water supply, 115
Solvay school district, 160, 165–67, 174
Solvay, Village, 44; and sewage disposal, 81, 89, 94, 96, 98, 105; and water supply, 116
Soule, Robert G., and county government reform, 198, 200, 201, 202; and sewage disposal, 87
special districts, in education, 157–74
Sportsmen's Clubs, Federation of, 87
Steadman, Robert S., 179, 187, 189
Stover, Floyd H., 117, 267–73 *passim*, 279
Supervisors, Board of (county), 335, 339; and Children's Court, 133, 134, 135, 136; and community power structure, 318, 326, 327; and county government reform, 179, 180, 184, 185, 186, 188, 190–206 *passim*, 211; described, 34, 37, 41; and mental health, 149–55 *passim*; and metropolitan action, 217, 218, 224, 225, 226, 228; party majorities, 43–45; and Post-War Report, 51, 64, 69, 73; and public health, 144–49 *passim*; and real estate project, 257, 258, 259; and sewage disposal, 84, 87, 91, 92, 103–109 *passim*; and water supply, 117, 119, 126, 127, 129; and welfare administration, 140, 141
Syracuse Intercepting Board, 83, 85
Syracuse Land Development Co., 263
Syracuse Supply Co., 267, 269, 276
Syracuse University, and community power structure, 314; and county government reform, 179, 194; and Post-War Report, 49, 51, 53, 61; and public health, 145; and real estate projects, 243, 264; and school reorganization, 160, 166

taxation, city and county, 40–41, 45, 91, 278
Taxation and Retrenchment, Special Joint Legislative Committee on, 177
Tax Commission, Citizens' Non-Partisan, 91
Tax Laws, Commission for the Revision of the, 177
Technology Club, 143, 145
Terrett, Barbara, 62
Thompson Road sewer district, 278
Thompson Road water district, 258
Thruway, New York State, 26, 37, 244, 251, 258, 340; and Industrial Park, 265, 266, 269, 276, 279, 280
Tolley, William P., 51, 62, 69, 339
town government, 34
Traister, George L., 335, 337; and county government reform, 200, 207; and real estate project, 257; and sewage disposal, 90

368　INDEX

Tully school district, 159
Tully, Town, 142

Utica, partisanship and metropolitan action in, 328

Van Buren, Town, 244–48
Veterans Administration (federal), 39, 245, 294
village government, 35
von Thünen, Johann Heinrich, 235
Voters for Democracy not Dictatorship, 209

Wampler, Cloud, 63
War Assets Administration, 264, 279
Water Agency, Onondaga County, 127, 128, 129, 340
Water Authority, Onondaga County, 38, 111, 120, 121, 122, 124, 130, 215, 254, 257, 258, 271, 275, 279, 294, 340
Water Commissioners, Board of (city), 112
Water Committee, Joint City-County, 126, 127, 340
water pollution, 80–110 *passim*
Water Pollution Control Board (state), 38, 93, 101, 106, 107, 222, 246, 340
Water Power and Control Commission (state), 112, 113, 115, 123, 125, 126, 223, 340
Water Power and Control Division (state), 38
water supply, 38, 111–30, 250–51
Welch, Walter, 85

welfare administration, 136–41
Welfare Department (county), 137, 141, 154–55, 211, 215
Welfare Department (city), 138, 140
West Genesee school district, 165, 167
Westhill school district, 167
Westvale school district, 167
Wiggin, Col. Thomas, 121
Will and Baumer Candle Co., 115
Williams, John A., 88, 89, 90, 91, 101, 107
Williams, John D., 256
Winkleman, D. W., 252
Women Voters, League of, 341; and Children's Court, 132; and community power structure, 309, 312, 313, 318; and county government reform, 179, 180, 182, 185, 186, 187, 194, 195, 196, 197; and metropolitan action, 226; and Post-War Report, 50, 61; and public health, 143, 145
Wood, Robert C., 289, 319
Woodard Industrial Tract, 255
Woodbury, Coleman, 237

Yackel, Edward O., 335; and county government reform, 186, 188, 191; and Post-War Report, 51
Yehle, Leo, 132, 135, 216, 339
Young, Carl A., 67
Young, John J., 185, 186, 188, 337
Youth Commission (state), 132, 149, 151

Zoning Appeals, Board of (city), 339

NORTHERN ILLINOIS UNIVERSITY

3 1211 00669042 0